Russian Lindbergh

Smithsonian History of Aviation Series

Von Hardesty, Series Editor

On December 17, 1903, on a windy beach in North Carolina, aviation became a reality. The development of aviation over the course of little more than three-quarters of a century stands as an awe-inspiring accomplishment in both a civilian and a military context. The airplane has brought whole continents closer together: at the same time it has been a lethal instrument of war.

This series of books is intended to contribute to the overall understanding of the history of aviation—its science and technology as well as the social, cultural, and political environment in which it developed and matured. Some publications help fill the many gaps that still exist in the literature of flight; others add new information and interpretation to current knowledge. While the series appeals to a broad audience of general readers and specialists in the field, its hallmark is strong scholarly content.

The series is international in scope and includes works in three major categories:

SMITHSONIAN STUDIES IN AVIATION HISTORY: *works that provide new and original knowledge.*

CLASSICS OF AVIATION HISTORY: *carefully selected out-of-print works that are considered essential scholarship.*

CONTRIBUTIONS TO AVIATION HISTORY: *previously unpublished documents, reports, symposia, and other materials.*

Russian Lindbergh

THE LIFE OF VALERY CHKALOV

Georgiy Baidukov

Translated by Peter Belov

Edited and with an Introduction by Von Hardesty

SMITHSONIAN INSTITUTION PRESS

Washington and London

Classics of Aviation History reprint. Revised and expanded edition of the English
translation published by Chkalov International in association with the Graphic
Arts Center of Portland, Oregon, in 1978. Originally published in Russian by
Molodaya gvardiya Publishers, Moscow, 1975.

Editor and Typesetter: Peter Strupp/Princeton Editorial Associates
Production Editor: Rebecca Browning
Designer: Alan Carter

Library of Congress Cataloging-in-Publication Data

Baĭdukov, G. (Georgiĭ), 1907–
    [Chkalov. English]
    Russian Lindbergh: the life of Valery Chkalov / Georgiy Baidukov;
translated by Peter Belov; edited and with an introduction by Von
Hardesty.
        p.   cm.—(Smithsonian history of aviation series. Classics of
aviation history)
    Rev. and enl. translation of: Chkalov.
    Includes bibliographical references.
    ISBN 1-56098-046-X
    1. Chkalov, Valeriĭ Pavlovich.   2. Air pilots—Soviet Union—
Biography.   I. Hardesty, Von, 1939–   . II. Title.   III. Series.
TL540.C56B2913   1991
629.13′092—dc20   91-6718
[B]
            British Library Cataloguing-in-Publication Data available

On the cover: Detail from the Transpolar Flight fiftieth anniversary poster.
Courtesy of the City of Vancouver; Maya Jones, artist.

All photos appearing in this book are courtesy of the National Air and Space
Museum, unless otherwise noted. For permission to reproduce individual
illustrations, please correspond directly with the museum or the owner of the work
listed in the caption. The Smithsonian Institution Press does not retain
reproduction rights for these illustrations individually or maintain a file of
addresses for photo sources.

Manufactured in the United States of America

95 94 93 92 91   5 4 3 2 1

∞ The paper used in this publication meets the minimum requirements of the
American National Standard for Permanence of Paper for Printed Library Materials
Z39.48-1984.

Contents

PART THREE: IN THE WORLD ARENA

PART FOUR: THE LAST EPISODE

Acknowledgments

The editor wishes to thank Peter Belov for his earlier work as a translator of the Georgiy Baidukov biography of Valery Chkalov and for his untiring efforts to broaden our appreciation of Chkalov's contribution to aviation, in both the Soviet Union and the United States. Georgiy Baidukov, the author of the biography and Chkalov's copilot on the historic transpolar flight of 1937, deserves special mention for his willingness to cooperate on a new English edition. His foreword to this edition is appreciated and reflects his lifelong interest in preserving the memory of Valery Chkalov. Finally, many individuals assisted in the preparation of this volume. They include Mary Kline, Yuri Salnikov, Gladys Waters, Anita Mason, Carolyn Russo, Tom Crouch, Donald S. Lopez, Jon Walker, Felix C. Lowe, Ruth Spiegel, and Rebecca Browning. Their efforts are greatly appreciated.

Foreword

My biography *Chkalov* was written in 1974 and first published in 1975 as part of the book series "The Lives of Famous People." The fourth edition of the biography appeared in 1986 and the fifth is currently being prepared.

The biography has up until now received its broadest circulation within the USSR, having been translated from Russian into the native languages of the Ukraine, Belorussia, Latvia, Kazakhstan, and other republics.

Other Soviet authors and aeronautical figures—including Bodrov, Vodopyanov, Kudrevatikh, Magid, and Rakhillo—have also written about Chkalov, for he remains a pivotal figure in Soviet aviation.

Valery Chkalov perished in a tragic accident more than half a century ago on December 15, 1938, cutting short a brilliant career. What did Chkalov accomplish in his short life? This biography endeavors to recount the main episodes of that life.

Chkalov's earliest years were spent on the great Volga River. He studied and worked with his father in a smithy as a hammerer. He also worked as a stoker on a steamship on the Volga.

Chkalov first became interested in aviation after he saw an airplane as a child. To realize his dream of becoming a pilot, he got a job as a mechanic at a nearby airfield at the age of 15, helping to repair combat aircraft for the pilots of the Red Air Fleet during the Civil War. After two years, he managed to enroll in the Yegorevsk Military Theoretical Flight School, from which he would graduate with distinction. The next phase of his training took place at the Borisoglebsk Military Flight School. Again, he graduated with high honors.

It was then suggested that he enroll in the Military Aviation School of Aerobatics in Moscow. Here Chkalov received another high evaluation from his instructor Zhukov, who offered Chkalov a post at Serpukhovsk, where the Red Air Fleet had established the Advanced Aviation School of Gunnery, Bombing and Aerial Combat.

At Serpukhovsk, Chkalov trained as a cadet with Mikhail M. Gromov, a flight instructor who immediately recognized the exceptional talent of his new student. Chkalov crossed the final training hurdle when he received a certificate of distinction from Gromov. He was then assigned to the fighter squadron of the Red Banner, located in Leningrad.

In 1927, on the occasion of the tenth anniversary of the Great October Revolution, the People's Commissar of Military Affairs and the Head of the Stavka (Military High Command) organized an All-Union Competition of advanced fighter pilots. The Leningrad Military Command sent the then twenty-three-year-old Chkalov to Moscow for the competition. Chkalov's performance, flying a Fokker D-11 at the Frunze Central Airfield, impressed the judges and his fellow pilots. The government and Stavka representatives found his skills to be exemplary. Following the competition, at an awards ceremony at the Bolshoi Theatre, Chkalov received the first prize for individual performance. He also received recognition for group flights with his squadron prior to the contest. (It should be noted that these flights, in fact, had not been authorized.)

Chkalov advocated "hedgehopping" and experimented with new techniques of air combat. He flew frequently, and often without authorization, exhibiting a reckless style that ultimately led to his brief imprisonment and discharge from the Air Force. However, he was pardoned for his indiscretions and then began work as a glider instructor.

In time, the High Command of the Air Force came to appreciate the fact that Chkalov was one of the Soviet Union's best pilots, but that he was not being allowed to realize his true potential. Among his many talents, Chkalov possessed an aptitude for work on air combat techniques. Finally, the High Command decided to allow him to conduct state tests on new prototype fighters, bombers, and shturmoviki (low-flying attack planes), in association with the talented designer Vasily Stepanchenok. This collaboration allowed Chkalov to experiment with a new technique to escape from a spin. Chkalov also worked with the designer and test pilot Pavel Grakhovsky, testing more inexpensive rescue parachutes to replace the expensive silk ones. In addition, he experimented with cargo parachutes designed by Grakhovsky, using them to drop small tanks, equipment, machine guns, and other supplies.

In 1933, Chkalov resigned from the Air Force for the more complicated and dangerous life of a factory test pilot. He expended much talent and energy test-flying fighter planes designed by the famous N. N. Polikarpov.

Chkalov's interest in long-distance flights took shape with my invitation in 1936 for him, to join me and Alexander Belyakov as pilot-in-command on a flight in an ANT-25 from Moscow across the Arctic Ocean to the Far East, to Petropavlovsk on the Kamchatka Peninsula. Chkalov, then thirty-two years old, completed his assignment successfully, flying an enormous distance and landing our iced-over ANT-25 on Udd island (now Chkalov Island) near the town of Nikolayevsk on the Amur River. In recognition of this feat, Chkalov received a first Order of Lenin and, along with Belyakov and me, the gold star, Hero of the Soviet Union.

In retrospect, the landing at Udd was truly a miracle. Chkalov's leadership and flying skill saved our lives, not to mention the valuable ANT-25, which survived without any serious damage. Chkalov then returned to Moscow and received a warm welcome. After celebrating his victory, he resumed his work as a test pilot with Polikarpov.

But our experience on the flight to Udd Island sparked an interest in an even bolder aerial trek—a flight over the North Pole to the United States. Finally, in 1937, Chkalov received permission from Stalin for a transpolar flight. He chose me as copilot and Alexander Belyakov as navigator. Our aircraft once more was the single-engine ANT-25. A second crew, consisting of Gromov, Andrei Yumashev, and Sergei Danilin, was also scheduled for a transpolar flight in an ANT-25. Being the first to make the attempt, we were to advise Gromov and his crew on various aspects of polar flying and navigation.

Chkalov's leadership was crucial to our ultimate success as the first crew to fly from Moscow over the North Pole to America. Our flight landed in the small town of Vancouver, on the shore of the Columbia River in Washington State, on June 20, 1937. Flying a month later, Gromov in the second ANT-25 reached the town of San Jacinto in California on July 14. By flying an extended route, Gromov set a new world record for distance.

Our flights took advantage of the fact that the shortest path from Moscow to the United States is across the North Pole. In pioneering this direct route, we brought greetings to the American people from the peoples of the USSR. Our efforts were designed to promote peace and friendship between our two countries.

After Chkalov's triumphant return to the Soviet Union, he went back to his aircraft factory and told the workers about the flight to America. He then resumed his work for Polikarpov, and played a key role in Polikarpov's successes in the 1930s.

Valery Chkalov is remembered today as a national hero. Throughout the USSR many memorials and monuments have been erected in his honor. Towns, streets, state and collective farms, large enterprises, ships, and tens of thousands of school divisions all bear the name Chkalov.

In 1975, a monument was erected in America to honor him. This monument reflects the initiative of the citizens of Vancouver, Washington, who wished to memorialize Chkalov's historic flight of 1937. For the dedication, I was invited, along with Alexander Belyakov, to fly to Vancouver in an Il-62, following the same route we had taken in 1937. The American committee responsible for the monument greeted us. We later met with the president of the committee, Norman Small, along with vice president Alan Cole and committee members Peter Belov, Fred Neth, Ken Puttkamer, Thomas Taylor, Lloyd Stromgren, Steve Small, Steve Smut, Jess Frost, Danny Grecco, and Mary Kline.

Not long after my visit to Vancouver, I had the distinct honor of flying with Alan Cole to the homeland of Valery Chkalov along the Volga River. Joining us for the flight was Igor Chkalov, his son. At Chkalovsk we visited the town where the great pilot was born, and it was my pleasure to show them the birthplace of Valery Chkalov. Next to the Chkalov house is a large stand on which is mounted the red-winged ANT-25, the very one we flew to Vancouver in 1937. Alan Cole carefully examined the historic airplane and exclaimed, "Your commander is worthy of world fame!"

Georgiy Baidukov
Moscow, 1990

Introduction

The Golden Age of Flight lingers in historical memory as a time of heroism and adventure. For two decades, roughly between 1919 and 1939, men and women took to the air to establish new records for speed, distance, and altitude. Aerial spectaculars punctuated public life, with air races and record-breaking flights attracting the enthusiastic attention of a global constituency of air-minded onlookers. The airplane became the unchallenged marvel of modern technology. Aviation even rivaled Hollywood with its cultural heroes and celebrities. Not even the political crises and economic depression of the interwar years dampened this popular mania for aviation.

Each new record-breaking flight brought fame to the individual pilot and prestige to his country. Conversely, failure might result in personal injury or death and, for certain, a sense of national embarrassment. The evolution of aeronautical technology, characterized in these years by a process of rapid refinement in design and performance, dictated that most records would be quickly broken—a fact that only accelerated the clamor for records and prizes. For each country, regardless of the degree of direct governmental patronage, there was an opportunity to showcase its technology. By implication, the airplane projected military prowess in an age that viewed air power as a potentially decisive weapon in any future war. Only the so-called Space Race a generation later would equal this technological competition, with all its perceived urgency and attendant high risks.

For Americans, the names Charles Lindbergh, Amelia Earhart, Jimmy Doolittle, Wiley Post, and Howard Hughes—to select but a

few—persist in the collective memory of this epoch. For other nations there are equally important aviators: Antoine de Saint-Exupéry
(France), Italo Balbo (Italy), Amy Johnson (Great Britain), and Ernst
Udet (Germany)—again to select only a random few from a large
company of record-setting aviators of the period. Along with the
individual heroes there is a more ephemeral memory of the Schnei-
der Cup races, the great air shows, the Thompson Trophy, and the
race to be the first to cross great natural barriers such as the Atlantic
and Pacific Oceans.

While our historical memory of this period recedes, it is interesting to speculate why, among all the participants in the competition
for world records in aviation, the Soviet Union is the least remembered. Few Soviet aviators from this era are well known in the West.
Valery P. Chkalov, for example, won international recognition for his
transpolar flight in 1937. Yet today this "Soviet Lindbergh" is largely
unknown outside his own country. Even at home, he has been
partially eclipsed by the latter-day space hero and cosmonaut Yuri
Gagarin. This relative obscurity for Chkalov in no way diminishes
his heroism or achievement; it merely suggests that fame for
aviators, especially Soviet aviators, proved to be short-lived.

In retrospect, the Soviet Union established a sequence of important aviation records during this period, some of unique character
and attained at high risk. In polar aviation the Soviets faced no real
challengers. During the years 1933–1938, for example, Soviet fliers
set some sixty-two world records, according to their official history
of civil aviation.[1] These official records put Soviet aviation at the
leading edge, allowing the Soviet Union to claim leadership in the
longest, highest, and fastest categories.

Stalin actively promoted these extraordinary aerial feats. Once in
power, he comprehended quickly how the airplane, already a powerful metaphor for technological progress in Soviet popular culture,
could make a powerful impact on the masses. The airplane, for
Stalin, became one dramatic and convenient avenue to suggest il-
lusory advances in the pursuit of the larger goals of his regime—the
emergence of the Soviet Union as a technologically advanced society, seeming parity with the West in a critical field, and enhanced
national security through air power.

When the Soviets landed the first airplane at the North Pole—no
small achievement in 1936—the aerial feat supported an already
established scientific expedition in the Arctic. Aerial links became a

lifeline to the ice-bound scientists on their floe, an effective means to overcome distance and time. Stalin's propaganda organs cleverly trumpeted this feat, one unparalleled in cold-weather flying, as an extension of the Soviet Union's rapid strides in science and technology.

Aviation records and heroic feats provided legitimacy for the Stalin regime. In 1937, the Soviets, on the eve of the twentieth anniversary of their Bolshevik Revolution, could point to dramatic strides the new revolutionary society had made in the highly competitive arena of aeronautical technology.[2] This was the same era that saw such massive public projects as the construction of the Moscow subway, the erection of the giant hydroelectric plant on the Dnieper River, and the building of heavy industry. The Bolsheviks presided over a new society, and visiting writers, clergy, and political figures from the West more often than not echoed these images of modernity.

It was in all respects an age of sacrifice and herculean achievement. Aleksei Stakhanov, for example—in an extraordinary display of proletarian zeal—mined 102 tons of coal in a single shift. Thus was born the Stakhanovite Movement as a means to mobilize workers. Soviet aviation provided a even more powerful symbol. Soviet aviators, trumpeted by the Soviet media as "Stalin's Falcons," became the object of public adulation. Their image in official propaganda was invariantly positive, as embodiments of the "New Soviet Man." The public quickly came to view them as exemplars of modernity and heroism. The heroic spirit of the Bolshevik Revolution, as well as the regime's commitment to technological progress, found expression in this elite group. Aviation was a pioneering realm, always associated with risk, in which both men and women could accomplish great feats and, by doing so, suggest that Soviet society had unleashed human potential in a unique way.

To set altitude records, to fly faster, and to establish a new benchmark for long-distance flying became formal state policy for the Soviet Union in the 1930s. The Soviet conquest of the Arctic in the mid-1930s served as an important backdrop for Chkalov and Stalin's Falcons. The initial penetration of the Arctic by air came in 1934, when the Soviet icebreaker *Chelyushkin* became trapped in ice. Rather than rescue the crew by sled across the vast expanse of tundra and ice, Stalin ordered an airlift. This bold venture succeeded, with the entire crew of the *Chelyushkin* being flown to safety.

The *Chelyushkin* incident created a national sensation. The rescue clearly demonstrated for the outside world Soviet advances in the area of cold-weather flying techniques. Stalin created a new medal for the heroic aviators, the gold star "Hero of the Soviet Union," which to this day is the highest Soviet medal for heroism.[3]

During the same period the Director of the Northern Sea Routes, Otto J. Schmidt, oversaw an ambitious program to explore the Arctic. The Soviets aimed to establish a semipermanent presence in the region, and aviation soon became an important aspect of Arctic exploration. With the success of the *Chelyushkin* rescue, Schmidt proposed broader applications of aviation. By 1937 regular flights by Soviet aircraft into the Arctic region had become commonplace, rivaling flights to Western Europe for public attention. That same year, four Soviet aircraft landed on an ice floe near the North Pole.[4] No one had ever flown to the top of the world.

Each new venture gave the Soviets an opportunity to experiment further with cold-weather flying.[5] Refinements in equipment and flying technique quickly followed, allowing the Soviets to develop their skills in all-weather flying. For example, during the *Chelyushkin* operation Soviet aircraft had landed for the first time on ice floes with skis. To permit the airplanes to land safely, Soviet designers equipped them with special shock absorbers able to function in the $-40°$ to $-50°C$ temperatures. Myriad techniques were also developed for cold-weather starting and lubrication.

Aviation experts in the West, in particular in the military, took a keen interest in the Soviet cold-weather flying experiments. At Wright field in Dayton, Ohio, for example, the U.S. Army Air Corps maintained extensive files on foreign air forces and their technical advances. Soviet cold-weather flying techniques were closely monitored through translations. This practice continued throughout the 1930s and World War II.[6]

Soviet designs of large aircraft in the 1930s made a similarly positive impression on rival air forces. These reflected the prewar Soviet flirtation with strategic aviation. Two Soviet designs, those for the two-engine TB-1 and the four-engine TB-3, represented new advances in all-metal aircraft construction and hinted at the Soviet Union's potential to build a heavy bomber. At the time there was a widespread apprehension of the bomber as the air weapon of the future.

Among all the large Soviet aircraft, the most dramatic technological marvel was the *Maxim Gorky*, an eight-engine behemoth with a wingspan of over 206 feet that weighed 117,000 pounds. Designed by Andrei N. Tupolev, the *Maxim Gorky* operated with a crew of twenty and could carry forty-eight passengers. This enormous monoplane, with its bright red wings, expressed an older Russian mania for "giantism": the desire to build a flying ship to master the vast Russian geography. The *Maxim Gorky* was in the tradition of Igor Sikorsky's earlier marvel of the air, the four-engine *Il'ya muromets*, which made an epic round-trip flight from St. Petersburg to Kiev in 1914.

During its brief history, the *Maxim Gorky* had no rival: it could boast a library with bookshelves, table, and comfortable chairs; sleeping quarters with Pullman-type bunks; a galley equipped with a refrigerator and a stove; and a laundry. The large red wings reflected the aircraft's political purpose. On board were a printing shop, to supply leaflets for aerial drops, as well as a projection booth to show propaganda films when the *Maxim Gorky* landed. Stalin ordered this unique aircraft to tour the Soviet Union and to make dramatic flights over Red Square on May Day.

The demise of the *Maxim Gorky*, as it turned out, was as dramatic as the aircraft's short-lived career on the cutting edge of Soviet aeronautical technology. When a small Soviet fighter attempted a loop over the *Maxim Gorky*, it crashed into the port wing of the giant airplane. Over forty people were killed. A six-engine version of the aircraft, designated the ANT-20, saw limited service during the mid-1930s.

∎

Against this backdrop, Valery Chkalov seemed ideally suited to join Stalin's elite fraternity of aviators. His origins were proletarian. As a pilot, he was fearless and talented, willing to accept all challenges. Chkalov represented a new generation, being a beneficiary of the new social order that prided itself on allowing men of talent from the lower classes to advance.

A secondary image conveyed in Chkalov was the model of collective effort; typically, he made record-breaking flights as the leader of a team. He was a pilot whose achievements embodied both collective action and heroism. Chkalov made his historic flight over the

North Pole in 1937 with two crewmen, Georgiy Baidukov and Alexander Belyakov. Together they shared the same risks and enjoyed the same limelight. This pattern was followed by other Soviet aviators such as Mikhail Gromov, Sigismund Levanevsky, and Vladimir Kokkinaki, who were best known as command pilots. By contrast, a Charles Lindbergh, an Amelia Earhart, or a Wiley Post made flights solo or, on occasion, with a copilot, and their reputations were understood to be built on individual accomplishment. Lindbergh, known as the "Lone Eagle," did not find a counterpart in the collectivist ethos of the Soviet Union of the 1930s.

Georgiy Baidukov, Chkalov's copilot and the author of this biography, generously acknowledges the dominant role played by his former commander and friend, seemingly at the cost of fully recording his own key role. Baidukov points consistently to Chkalov as the decisive leader, the resourceful pilot, and the logical spokesman for Soviet aviation. The narrative conveys an image of Chkalov as a pilot of the old school—one who boldly flew by sheer instinct and with undisguised joy. Chkalov is portrayed as a pilot who preferred the open cockpit and daredevil maneuvers. There is a rough simplicity to Chkalov, mirrored in his proletarian origins and his love of wood-and-fabric airplanes.

Yet even in the 1930s Chkalov was becoming an anachronism, a fact concealed behind his flamboyance and impressive skills as a flier. Chkalov appeared to avoid excessive dependence on instruments, although blind flying techniques and more sophisticated instrumentation were slowly being adopted. He also took only a casual interest in the subtleties of navigation. Indeed, both blind flying and navigation duties fell to Baidukov and Belyakov, respectively. It is noteworthy that Baidukov, not Chkalov, guided the ANT-25 to a landing at Vancouver, Washington, on that mist-shrouded day in 1937, largely because Baidukov was more proficient at instrument flying. Consequently, Chkalov emerges unwittingly in Baidukov's narrative as a capable but limited pilot.

The Soviet flights over the North Pole in 1937 were calculated risks, based confidently on the real strides made by the Soviet Union in aircraft design. Chkalov's airplane, the ANT-25, dramatically represented the evolving sophistication of Soviet designs, especially those of special-purpose aircraft. The ANT-25 emerged as a unique design with the single purpose of setting new records for distance. The airplane was the twenty-fifth design by Andrei Tupolev, then the chief designer for TsAGI (the Central Aero-Hydrodynamic Institute). Created in 1932, the ANT-25 was an all-metal, cantilever monoplane with an extraordinary wingspan of 34 meters and a fuselage barely 13.4 meters long. It was powered by a 750-horsepower Mikulin AM-34R engine. Such a configuration essentially made the ANT-25 a powered glider. The first prototype flew in July 1933, but failed to perform satisfactorily in the critical categories of speed, fuel consumption, and range.

A second ANT-25 prototype flew in September 1933, with Gromov at the controls. The second variant was powered by another AM-34 engine, but one geared down for greater efficiency and fitted with a three-blade fixed-pitch propeller. These adaptations allowed the second prototype to achieve a speed of 240 kilometers per hour (as opposed to 212 for the first prototype). It could fly just under 11,000 kilometers nonstop.

Although these improvements were encouraging, the ANT-25 still lacked the requisite range to establish a new international record for distance. A series of refinements followed: a new fairing was fitted to the partially retractable landing gear, the three-blade propeller was polished, and a new varnish-impregnated fabric covering was placed over the corrugated skin. Beginning in early 1934 the ANT flew a number of long-distance flights to test its suitability for international competition. In September 1934, Gromov made a twelve-thousand-kilometer, seventy-five hour flight, following a circular route within the Soviet Union. In August of the following year Levanevsky (with Baidukov as his copilot) attempted a flight in an ANT-25 from Moscow to San Francisco, only to abandon the effort after the airplane developed an oil leak over the Barents Sea. The pivotal test flight for the ANT-25, however, came in July 1936 when Valery Chkalov, Georgiy Baidukov, and Alexander Belyakov made a fifty-six-hour twenty-one-minute flight from Moscow to Udd Island, near the Kamchatka Peninsula on the Soviet Union's Pacific coastline. In near darkness Chkalov landed the ANT-25 across the width of Udd Island, skimming ponds and coming to a stop on a grass field in a dramatic ground loop. Despite the awkward landing, the ANT-25 had established itself as a formidable long-distance aircraft.

Stalin had committed himself to the idea of a transpolar flight early in 1937. In one sense this was to be just another record-breaking aerial feat, a logical extension of Soviet flights in the Arctic during 1935–1936. However, in another sense it represented a bold new initiative. Flying over the North Pole was different from earlier flights because of its intrinsic dangers and the extended flight path across Canada and the United States. Prior to this transpolar flight Soviet pilots had followed more conventional and established air routes, such as Gromov's flight to Western Europe, or had flown long-distance routes within the boundaries of the Soviet Union, as on Chkalov's flight to Udd Island. These earlier record-breaking flights had been relatively safe, because rescue operations were always feasible.

Flying over the North Pole, however, represented a quantum leap in danger. Any projected transpolar flight required boldness and an aircraft durable enough to withstand the rigors of the Arctic. But for Soviet planners, there was a compelling drive to set a new distance record by flying over the top of the world. Could the "Bolshevik Knights of Culture and Progress," as the Soviet media described them, pull it off?[7]

The 1937 flight of the ANT-25, named *Stalinskiy marshrut* (*Stalin Route*), is at the core of Baidukov's story. For Baidukov, this extraordinary flight of over sixty-two hours displayed Chkalov's unique aptitudes as a pilot, leader, and human being. This flight remains the most impressive legacy of Chkalov and no one is more familiar with the story than Georgiy Baidukov.

Less apparent to the reader of Baidukov's biography is the intense rivalry among Stalin's Falcons in the 1930s to be the first to make the flight over the North Pole. As the flight took shape during 1937, the opinion was widely held within the Soviet Union that Levanevsky would be given the nod by Stalin to make the first attempt. Levanevsky had made a flight over the North Pacific from Siberia to Los Angeles in 1936. There were other rivals to Levanevsky, such as Gromov, one of the more senior pilots (although he lacked the Arctic flying experience of both Levanevsky and Chkalov). Yet all of the three pilots possessed the requisite skills and courage for the long flight.

As it turned out, Stalin ordered Chkalov to make the first flight in June 1937, although each of the other men was to attempt a transpolar flight later in the year. (The Gromov and Levanevsky flights followed in July and August, respectively.) Stalin's reasons remain obscure. Did he trust Chkalov and/or his aircraft more completely? Stalin was aware of the debate among Soviet aviators about the best aircraft for the high-risk flight. Levanevsky had argued for a multiengine aircraft. His aircraft, the ANT-6 (TB-3), was a prototype bomber adapted for long-distance flying. Levanevsky believed the single-engine ANT-25 posed dangers: an engine failure meant 100 percent failure. Chkalov, as the story goes, retorted that Levanevsky's four-engine ANT-6 could mean 400 percent failure! A rumor persists from the 1930s that Levanevsky's Polish background may have been the deciding factor; Stalin wanted a Russian to make the journey first.[8]

The transpolar flights of 1937, even with the tragic loss of Levanevsky, momentarily catapulted the Soviet Union into the forefront of aviation. A mere two decades had passed since the Bolshevik Revolution—as Soviet propaganda organs reminded the world—and already the Soviet Union could boast parity with the West. Soviet technology had conquered distance and the extremes of climate. To reinforce the point, Stalin had sent fighters and bombers to Spain, at the time caught up in the first stages of a bloody civil war. The embattled Spanish Republic made effective use of the Soviet I-15 and I-16 fighters and the SB-2 bombers, and for a brief period of time these aircraft allowed the Republican air force to establish air superiority. This advantage for Republican Spain proved to be short-lived, however, once Nazi Germany and Fascist Italy quickly supplied the rival Nationalists with superior equipment.[9] Yet, for a brief interlude in 1937, Soviet aerial achievements, civil and military, appeared awesome.

Stalin's highly orchestrated aerial spectaculars in the 1930s took place against the backdrop of the Great Purges. As a counterpoint to the grim months of arrests and show trials, culminating with the purge of the armed forces, the Soviet media gave sustained coverage to the achievements of Chkalov and others. National hysteria and national pride intermingled dramatically in 1937–1938. The purge of the military became part of this human tragedy, bringing in its wake the execution of Jan Alksnis and other high-ranking air force leaders. Technological achievement, symbolized by advances in aviation and record-breaking flights, did provide an important prop of legitimacy and credibility to the Soviet regime at a critical time. The coincidence of repression and technical achievement—one running parallel to the other—is striking.[10]

Soviet press and radio coverage of the Chkalov flight portrayed the event as something more than an aerial stunt. M. V. Vodopyanov, the first Soviet pilot to land at the North Pole, saw the flight as a harbinger of regular mail and passenger service. Schmidt, the director of the Soviet Northern Sea routes, struck an even more dramatic note, seeing the possibility of a series of "amphibian tank" bases established for future transpolar flights between Moscow and the United States.[11] Such amphibians would provide a highly mobile means of moving across the icy wasteland, providing supplies to and enabling repair of aircraft landing on ice floes. Some even dreamed of a Soviet conquest of the South Pole, so the world would spin on a "Bolshevik axis." Mixed with these visionary schemes was the affirmation, often in strident tones, that "only a Socialist society can organize feats such as the conquest of the Arctic, of the North Pole and finally of transpolar communications."[12] Tupolev himself, the designer of the ANT-25, boasted that the Soviet aviation industry would in the future build aircraft capable of flying 12,500 miles, halfway around the world, without a stop or refueling.[13]

While the American public displayed considerable enthusiasm for the Soviet transpolar flights, the U.S. government, through the State and War Departments, expressed an attitude of restraint. The United States had recognized the Soviet Union only in 1933. Diplomatic recognition of the Soviet regime paved the way for expanded commercial ties in the 1930s, in particular with American aviation corporations. American hostility to communism, however, placed limitations on this tenuous rapprochement, and some Americans persisted in the belief that the Soviet Union was a pariah state. Yet despite this general context of suspicion, the State Department displayed a more positive attitude, seeking to normalize relations. The appointment of Joseph E. Davies as U.S. ambassador in 1936 gave full expression to this optimistic mentality.[14] Davies's uncritical approach to the Stalinist regime, despite its harsh program of collectivization and the purges, had been adopted earlier among literary figures such as Theodore Dreiser and *New York Times* correspondent Walter Duranty.[15] The United States thus displayed a mixture of suspicion and support for the Soviet Union.

The U.S. Army Air Corps had cooperated with the Soviet flights, but their posture was more polite than genuinely enthusiastic. No doubt this approach mirrored as well the attitude of the War Department. Both Chkalov and Gromov received the congratulations of Major General Oscar Westover, then Chief of the Air Corps. At Pearson Airfield the Air Corps provided many services for Chkalov and his crew, especially in the complex task of removing the ANT-25 for shipment back to the Soviet Union.[16] As did Chkalov, Gromov expressed his profound appreciation for the assistance extended to him in a telegram to General Westover on the day of his departure for home, August 4, 1937.[17]

As the Air Corps Chief, General Westover did not conceal his overall suspicion of the motives for the Soviet flight. Gromov and his crew had requested permission to visit the facilities of the Seversky Aircraft Corporation at Farmingdale, Long Island. In a message to the Seversky management, Westover cabled: "your request for permission for Soviet visitors to visit your plant is not favorably considered. Your plant is on the restricted list for foreign visitors until such time as confidential work for the United States Government is contained in separate building or can be effectively concealed."[18]

Earlier General Westover had recommended the Distinguished Flying Cross for Chkalov and his crew, an expression of Westover's appreciation of their bravery, but the Secretary of War declined to endorse the idea.[19] Westover's impulse to acknowledge the achievement of Chkalov mixed awkwardly with other requirements, in particular the determination of the Air Corps to learn as much as possible about the technical aspects of the ANT-25. The most impressive aspect of the flight had been the navigation techniques: the Soviet crew completed most of the flight without the use of a compass. Westover ordered Major Paul Burrows at Pearson Airfield to report "any data obtainable on instruments used by the Russians on the recent flight to the U.S. especially on navigational instruments. This [is] considered *secret.*"[20]

The disappearance of Levanevsky in August 1937 put enormous pressures on the War Department to deploy Air Corps aircraft in Alaska as part of the international effort to find the downed Soviet flier. Vilhjalmur Stefansson, the famed Arctic explorer, had pressured the Air Corps to do more, even as late as October 1937, by which time most had abandoned hope.[21] Bridadier General H. H. (Hap) Arnold, the new Acting Chief of the Air Corps, replied to Stefansson's appeal by stating that the Air Corps had already rendered significant support to the rescue effort, providing communication facilities at Point Barrow, Alaska, and participating in the flights seeking to find the wreckage of the Levanevsky aircraft. Citing budgetary constraints and the few available aircraft and crews, General Arnold informed Stefansson that the Air Corps would take no further active role in the search.[22]

It is difficult to identify clearly the precise motives and evolving attitudes of American officialdom, civil and military. The State Department displayed a consistent enthusiasm, seeing in the 1937 flights unique opportunities to improve the overall diplomatic relationship with the Soviet Union. President Franklin D. Roosevelt reflected this posture at the highest level: Roosevelt sent congratulations and met with both Chkalov and Gromov. The War Department and the Air Corps, on the other hand, greeted the Soviet transpolar flights and the accompanying pressures for technical cooperation with obvious reluctance.

There were expressions of genuine praise for the brave Soviet pilots from the broader American aeronautical community. Toward Soviet technology, in particular, there was respect, curiosity, and, on the part of the Air Corps, a desire to obtain as much technical data as possible. However, the interest of Americans, if intense in 1937, proved to be short-lived. Not until the wartime alliance against Nazi Germany would Americans again show a positive attitude toward the Soviet Union.

Valery Chkalov returned to the Soviet Union in 1937 as a national hero. His return prompted an extraordinary outpouring of public enthusiasm, not unlike Lindbergh's return to America from Paris a decade before. Chkalov emerged as the most popular Soviet aviator, and he toured the country as a spokesman for Soviet aviation. His heroic status, as Baidukov points out, also cast him into the role of a political leader, representing his native Volga region in the Soviet government. Throughout 1937 and 1938, even at the height of the purges, Chkalov remained untouched. There were times when he even challenged Stalin by appealing for the release of innocent victims of the purge.

One year after his epic transpolar flight Chkalov found himself drawn into a controversial episode with America's premier air hero, Charles Lindbergh. A visit by the American hero to the Soviet Union to observe Soviet Aviation Day (August 18) set the stage for a bitter controversy. Lindbergh flew to Moscow to attend the annual air show and the many aerial displays and events associated with this holiday. The invitation was part of a larger European trip in 1938 by Lindbergh, which also included his controversial, if more memorable, trip to Nazi Germany.

Lindbergh had praised Chkalov and Gromov for their transpolar flights in 1937. This expression of praise by Lindbergh had no doubt been genuine and freely given, the recognition by one flier of the raw courage and accomplishment of another. Lindbergh, however, had little sympathy for the communist regime and, in particular, for Stalin, who invariably appeared at such staged air shows as the presiding genius behind Soviet aviation.

Throughout the tour, at the Tushino air show and during visits to aviation plants, Lindbergh displayed a thinly veiled coolness toward his Soviet hosts. He was impatient, bored, and seemingly unimpressed. At every staged opportunity for Lindbergh to praise Soviet technology or aeronautical advances, he declined, greeting the whole spectacle of Soviet aviation with a contempt conveyed through silence. Once Lindbergh reached England, he expressed openly to friends his many criticisms of Soviet aviation, in a series of caustic comments that found their way into British newspapers. Lindbergh had concluded perceptively that Soviet aviation, even with its impressive records, was a cardboard reality, a sort of modern-day Potemkin Village of technology.

Criticism of Soviet aviation by such an important, even emblematic, figure prompted bitter verbal denunciations from the Soviet aviation establishment. Chkalov joined ten other Soviet pilots in attacking Lindbergh for stating that the Red Air Force had been weakened by the purges and that the Luftwaffe was now more powerful, perhaps equal to the combined air power of Great Britain, France, Russia, and Czechoslovakia. Chkalov echoed the established Soviet position and denounced Lindbergh for his "fascist" tendencies and for abusing the hospitality shown to him during his visit to the Soviet Union.

The controversy over the Lindbergh visit would be Chkalov's last dramatic appearance on the international stage. He would die in a tragic air crash on December 15, 1938, while flying the prototype I-180 fighter. Chkalov's funeral became a moment of national mourning. Among Stalin's Falcons, Chkalov had been the most famous and beloved. He remains today the most important hero in the Golden Age of Soviet aviation.

The circumstances of Chkalov's death, for decades shrouded in mystery, continue to arouse debate and controversy. The official version, first announced in 1938, reported that the cause of death was accidental. Only the relaxed political context of the Gorbachev years has allowed a more open discussion of Chkalov's last flight.

As Chkalov's close friend and copilot, Georgiy Baidukov remained silent and acquiesced to the official view for many decades. This biography, first published in 1975, reflected Baidukov's inability in the pre-Gorbachev era to state freely his private views. Baidukov's first opportunity to state his own theory came in December 1988, when he wrote a four-part article on the death of Chkalov in *Vozdushnyy transport*, the official organ of Aeroflot. This outspoken article pointed to the design bureau and its chief designer, N. Polikarpov, as being largely responsible for the untimely death of Chkalov.[23] According to Baidukov, the design defects of the I-180 set the stage for the accident. The ultimate responsibility, he argued, could be traced to Polikarpov, who, among other things, had failed to equip the engine properly for cold-weather flying. As a secondary factor, Baidukov pointed out that the undercarriage of the I-180 could not be retracted during the tragic flight. Thus, when the engine failed, Chkalov could not take measures to streamline the aircraft and so extend the glide path back to the field.

Baidukov's article prompted considerable debate among Soviet aircraft designers and aviation historians. Many critics of Baidukov accused him of exaggeration and of making an unfair attack on Polikarpov, who could not be judged solely responsible. The whole matter prompted a special seminar at the Red Army Museum in Moscow in 1989, at which a large number of experts, historians, and firsthand witnesses debated the issue. Many panelists saw Chkalov himself, not Polikarpov, as the primary factor in the tragedy. Chkalov, they argued, did not fly in the designated traffic pattern close to the airfield on that cold December day, but instead flew in a wide arc beyond the perimeter of the test site. Once he developed engine trouble, he was unable to descend immediately to the airfield, as was customary in case of difficulty on the first flight of a prototype aircraft. Moreover, Baidukov's critics argued that leaving the landing gear extended was the accepted routine on first test flights, a practice that allowed for a quick and safe landing.

According to Soviet aviation historian Dmitry Sobolev, responsibility may be traced to both Polikarpov and Chkalov. Sobolev sees a combination of bad judgment on the part of the design bureau and recklessness on the part of Chkalov. He points to the fact that the flight took place on the eve of Stalin's birthday. This event on the calendar may have prompted Polikarpov and the engineering cadre to rush the first flight of the I-180 in order to have it ready on this important date. Chkalov, in turn, displayed little caution when he took off in the I-180, flying a pattern outside the test range. Once trouble arose, he could not maneuver back to the field.

The death of Valery Chkalov remains a compelling and enigmatic episode. The debate has been fueled by the discovery of the "I-180" file. Baidukov first saw the file in 1973, but authorities denied him permission to use it in writing this biography. According to Baidukov, the file points to the failure of the I-180's air cooling system and the culpability of Polikarpov. More recently, Chkalov's son, Igor, entered the controversy with the allegation that his father's death may have been prearranged. Two untimely deaths in the aftermath of the crash aroused suspicion of a conspiracy: the chief engineer for the I-180 test program, Lazarev, was thrown off a train and died. Belyaikin, a department head in the People's Commissariat for the Aircraft Industry, also became a victim of the incident. He was imprisoned as a result of the accident and served five years, only to be murdered in his apartment one day after his release. In retrospect, Valery Chkalov's outspoken support of innocent victims of the purges—in particular his freely expressed opinion that Bukharin and Rykov (two major Bolshevik leaders purged in 1938) were guiltless—may have undermined his relationship with Stalin. To date, however, no concrete evidence has emerged to substantiate the theory of a plot.[24]

Chkalov in death manifested both his strengths and limitations as a pilot. He was always bold and, for some, reckless, but he garnered the respect of all for his flying skill. Chkalov made a substantial contribution to test-flying in the late 1920s and early 1930s, at a time when his skills were highly valued. In the late 1930s, however, he appeared to many as less effective because test-flying had taken on a more disciplined and systematic character.

Test pilots who survive typically combine technical knowledge with a measured approach to flying. As a test pilot for Polikarpov, Chkalov brought courage and considerable experience to the job. With his preference for the old style of flying and his natural aggressiveness, he did not necessarily fit the mold of a modern test pilot. Yet flying over the North Pole or over the vastness of Siberia required a special quality of bravery, which Chkalov possessed in full measure. Such a trait alone does not necessarily make a test pilot, but it is essential in a fighter pilot. Chkalov's untimely death in 1938 denied him the opportunity to test his skills in combat in World War II.

This Smithsonian edition of Baidukov's biography brings Chkalov's extraordinary career to a wide audience of Western readers for the first time. The book was originally published in Russian by Molodaya gvardiya Publishers of Moscow in 1975. Recognizing the tremendous importance of the work to aviation history, Peter Belov translated it into English, and Sodbuster Enterprises (now Chkalov International) published a small number of copies for distribution in North America in association with the Graphic Arts Center of Portland, Oregon. The Smithsonian Classics of Aviation History reprint series is now honored to offer Baidukov's vivid portrait of one of of the major figures in Soviet aviation to a larger public.

Readers will certainly admire the feats of Chkalov, but I have no doubt they will also come away impressed with Georgiy Baidukov. He emerges from the background of the story as a talented and resourceful pilot in his own right—one who deserves greater attention for his unique contributions to aviation. It is hardly possible to imagine the 1937 transpolar flight without the skillful presence of Baidukov in the cockpit as Chkalov's trusted copilot.

Von Hardesty, Ph.D.
Smithsonian Institution
Washington, D.C., 1990

Notes

1. See K. E. Bailes, "Technology and Legitimacy: Soviet Aviation and Stalinism in the 1930s," *Technology and Culture*, Vol. 17, No. 2 (April 1976), pp. 55–81. Bailes argues convincingly that aviation in the 1930s played a distinct and powerful role in the legitimization of the Soviet regime. The comparison to the Soviet space program a generation later is striking. Both episodes demonstrate dramatically how technological achievement became intertwined with political purposes.

2. Ibid., p. 60. Bailes quotes *Grazhdanskaya aviatsiya SSSR, 1917–1967*, Moscow: 1967, p. 108.

3. This award for heroism later also became the highest Soviet decoration for bravery in combat. During World War II two aces, Alexander Pokryshkin and Ivan Koshedub, each won the gold star three times, an achievement equaled only by war hero Marshal Zhukov.

4. One of the four aircraft was piloted by M. V. Vodopyanov, who had written a novel, *A Pilot's Dream*, about a polar landing. This novel was adapted for the stage in Moscow in 1937.

5. See *Vestnik vozdushnogo flota*, Vol. 15, No. 12 (December 1938), pp. 40–46.

6. See K. A. Moskatov, "Landing On Ice," *Translation Air Services Command*, No. 2 (June 1943) and "Starting Engines at Low Temperatures," a translation for the Royal Air force by V. P. Akinoff from *Vestnik vozdushnogo flota*, Vol. 14, No. 1 (January 1937), pp. 36–37.

7. Bailes, p. 63.

8. The ANT-6 (TB-3), designed by Tupolev, was a four-engine monoplane bomber of the 1930s. The aircraft underwent numerous modifications between 1934 and 1937 to fit it for long-distance flying. One version, the *Aviaarktika*, flew numerous flights to the Soviet polar station in 1937. Levanevsky's N-209 variant failed to complete the transpolar flight attempted in August 1937. No trace of the N-209 or its crew of six was ever found.

9. Soviet pilots and aircraft participated as well in the Khalkin-Gol skirmishes with the Japanese in the Far East in 1938. The demonstrated superiority of German aircraft and combat techniques influenced the Soviets to design a whole new generation of fighters and ground attack aircraft in 1940. None of the transpolar fliers were mobilized for these conflicts.

10. Bailes provides an insightful account of how Soviet aviation played a vital role in Soviet political life.

11. See the *New York Times*, June 25, 1937, p. 12. The same newspaper, in its *New York Times Magazine* of June 6, 1937, published an extensive illustrated article on Soviet polar exploits entitled "A New Adventure at the Top of the World," by Russell Owen. These and other newspaper accounts enabled the American public to follow Soviet flights in considerable detail. Only the simultaneous disappearance of Amelia Earhart in the summer of 1937 rivaled the coverage of Soviet aviation.

12. *New York Times*, June 25, 1937, p. 12.

13. *New York Times*, June 22, 1937.

14. See Joseph E. Davies, *Mission to Moscow*, New York: Simon and Schuster, 1941.

15. See Walter Duranty, *USSR: The Story of Soviet Russia*, New York: J. B. Lippincott, 1944.

16. National Archives, Record Group 373, Soviet Flights, Memorandum for Foreign Liaison Officers, dated August 16, 1937, in response to letter dated July 15, 1937, from Constantine A. Oumansky, the Soviet Chargé d'Affaires.

17. Ibid.

18. National Archives, Record Group 373, Soviet Flights letter dated July 14, 1937.

19. Ibid. General Westover made this recommendation to the War Department in a letter dated June 22, 1937. D. Y. Beckham, Adjutant General, replied to General Westover on July 3, 1937, stating in his letter that the request was "not a proper subject of recommendation by the War Department."

20. Ibid. Letter to Major Paul E. Burrows from chief of the Air Corps, dated June 29, 1937.

21. Ibid. Letter from Vilhjalmur Stefansson to Brigadier General H. H. Arnold, dated October 6, 1937. Stefansson also submitted a long memorandum outlining how the search for Levanevsky should be conducted.

22. Ibid. Letter from Brigadier General H. H. Arnold to Vilhjalmur Stefansson, dated October 11, 1937.

23. Georgiy Baidukov's four-part article, "Esli govorit' vsyu pravdu," appeared in *Vozdushnyy transport*, December 10–17, 1988. A "response to Baidukov" appeared in the September 28, 1989, issue of *Vozdushnyy transport*, "Pravda—v ob'yektivnom

izlozhenii faktov," submitted by V. Alekseyenko, M. Saukke, and I. Safronov, all aeronautical engineers.

24. See Sergei Taranov's "Valeri Chkalov: Did He Really Have to Die?" *Moscow News*, March 18, 1989 (reprinted in translation from an article in *Izvestiya*, February 3, 1989). For a detailed response to Baidukov, see G. Maksimovich, "Na puti k pravde," *Kryl'ya rodina*, February 1989, pp. 28–29; March 1989, pp. 24–25; May 1989, pp. 29–30; June 1989, pp. 24–25; October 1989, pp. 26–27; November 1989, pp. 26–27.

PART ONE

Getting to Know Life

1

Childhood

Like all people who have come from the heart of the working class, Valery deeply loved his native area. In his home by the mighty Volga, Valery gathered his strength and contemplated life. I remembered the stories of my friend when, two years after his death, I, along with Alexander Vasilevich Belyakov, went at the request of Chkalov's relatives and fellow countrymen to the village of Vasilevo, which had been renamed Chkalovsk while Valery Pavlovich was still alive.[1]

The closer we came to Gorky, the more disquieted I felt—my conscience bothered me, for when Valery was alive I had never been together with him in his native region despite his numerous, insistent invitations. How many times I answered my friend: "We'll still go! We'll make it!"

Valery's father, Pavel Grigorevich, at one time worked as a boilermaker at the Sormovsky factory in Gorky, that ancient Russian city lying on the Volga. He was later persuaded to move to the village of Vasilevo to work in a factory boatyard repairing river vessels.

Valery's sisters, Anna and Sofia, his older brother Aleksei, and his many friends and acquaintances lived here. Whenever he arrived in Gorky, we would always go to the embankment and, sitting down on a bench, he would look at the Volga for a long time in silence and recall his childhood.

While sailing on the ferry between Gorky and Chkalovsk, I admired the powerful river and came to understand Valery's intimate love for her wide expanses, the bass horns of the ferries, the soft sparkle of the waves, the slightly coarse drawl of the people with their rounded Os, and the sincere songs of the natives of the Volga region.

And seeing the high bank of the river and the Chkalovsk regional center, I recalled how Valery had said to his electors in November 1937:

> Every person loves his native places. I also love my captivating Volga, my dear Vasilevo. I not only love my native area and my splendid fellow countrymen, I am also proud of them. I am proud of my Gorky oblast,[2] decorated with an order, which is moving rapidly ahead together with the rest of the country.

My friend never found a better place to rest than Vasilevo and the wide-open spaces of the Volga. He went to a resort only once in his life, in 1936, and that was on the insistence of his friends, the members of the crew of the ANT-25, after the flight across the Arctic Ocean from Moscow to Kamchatka.

Valery heard from his relatives that his great-grandfather, Mikhail Chkalov, was a barge hauler his entire life and that his son, that is, Valery Pavlovich's grandfather, also hauled barges along the river. He later became a dockworker, a job that Pavel, Valery's father, was also drawn to as a youth.

His grandfather was unusually strong and courageous and there is a reason that later people in Vasilevo said: "Valery Pavlovich obtained his boldness and strength from his grandfather." When he was a child, everyone maintained: "Just like his grandfather! Just as his grandfather was fierce, so Valery will be just like him!"

Valery inherited from his father a love for work and an urge to perfect himself continually through diligence. At nine years of age, Pavel Grigorevich together with his father was hauling cargo on the docks; he then became a worker at the Sormovsky Plant and then a boilermaker in the Vasilevo boatyard.

A sullen, stern, and inordinately powerful man, Pavel Grigorevich had a large family. His pretty, affectionate, and sweet wife, Arina Ivanovna, loved her children selflessly and tenderly.

Pavel Grigorevich earned a good salary working as a craftsman in the difficult boiler business at the Vasilevo boatyard and when Arina Ivanovna had her sixth child, she and her husband decided to move away from his father and build their own home.

After making a firm decision, they brought in a raft from the river Unzha and carpenters from the village of Katunia constructed a durable home seemingly built to last forever. It had etched cornices, a porch made from oak beams, a mezzanine, and a gallery. Inside there were high-ceilinged rooms and a specially constructed stove that heated the bedroom and the dining room at the same time. Next to the house Pavel Grigorevich planted a fruit grove.

About this time there occurred an unusual event in the life of Pavel Grigorevich, which affected the lives of everyone in his family: the well-known journeyman was forced to quit his job because of a mean trick played by an engineer in the boatyard. Left without work, Pavel Grigorevich shifted around, not knowing what to do. His friends convinced him to buy the hull of the burned-out steam tug *Ruslo* from the merchant Kolchin and to renovate it.

Pavel Grigorevich initially protested: "What kind of steamboat man am I? I can't even read." His wife objected strongly. But finally the boilermaker took the advice of his friends and Arina Ivanovna had to take out of the trunk the money wrapped in paper that had been saved for a rainy day.

Merchant Kolchin, having sold the wreck, conducted his business very slyly and the "steamboat man" Pavel Grigorevich, not having much capital and by nature not being much of a businessman, started to work day and night to pay off the interest on his promissory note.

Fewer and fewer guests gathered at the hospitable Chkalov household. There was not much with which to prepare pies.

Arina Ivanovna sent out her oldest daughter Anna to learn how to sew. The fourteen-year-old girl sewed for friends and gave all her earnings to her parents.

It was in these difficult times that Arina Ivanovna, on the second of February, 1904,[3] gave birth to her tenth child.

He was christened, as was the custom, in a cold font and was named Valery. However, his father always called him Valerian or simply Averian or Valka.

The business of the unemployed artisan in the boiler trade and illiterate steamboat man went from bad to worse: he had to mortgage the house and tugboat for ten years.

The bailiff appeared at Pavel Grigorevich's house to auction off his household effects.

His friends came to the rescue—they went to the sales and bought the more or less valuable items and, when it was not possible to hide a raccoon coat, Pavel Grigorevich's friend Nikolai Ivanovich Shaposhnikov, Valery's godfather, always managed to buy it back. Thus,

the effects returned many times to their old place, even though the
owner loaned them out to his friends from time to time.

Valery grew and became the family favorite. The child had no
toys. He loved to climb everywhere, the higher the better so that he
could "bang" his head against the ceiling.

On summer days he would dive under rafts with his buddies or
jump aboard a steamer leaving the dock, crawl onto the rudder, and
from there climb onto one of the decks, where, before the eyes of
surprised and frightened passengers, he would throw himself head-
long into the Volga.

He could be found in the water for days at a time. He stopped
swimming in late autumn when his father threatened to thrash him.
However, he not once carried out this threat: his father was a kind
man at heart.

Then a calamity occurred. In the last weeks of pregnancy Arina
Ivanovna somehow stumbled, fell, and gave birth prematurely. After
ailing for a short time, she passed away.

Pavel Grigorevich was grief-stricken and became even more taci-
turn. His six-year-old son, robbed of his mother's affection, became
attached to his sisters Anna and Sofia.

Twenty-seven years later Valery would write in a book given to
Anna Pavlovna:

> My sister! How strange: sometime not so long ago a child brought up
> by you was a naughty mischief-maker and, generally, a hooligan, but
> now he is a famous man known around the world. But remember,
> Nyura, this hasn't spoiled me and it won't spoil me—I'm the same
> Valka I was before. Just more serious and somewhat of an old man. My
> dear sister, I give you this book; read it and realize the difficulties, but
> just the same we overcame them. This is in YOUR HONOR—I am your
> brother. I always miss you in my thoughts. V. Chkalov

He wrote to his other sister Sofia:

> Dear Sonechka. Remember how we used to fight. Your head would
> hurt; my ears would hurt. I give you this book in memory of our flight.
> A difficult flight. But it was the first. And we were the first to do it.
> And in this story is your pugnacious brother Valka. July 29, 1937.

After a short while, Pavel Grigorevich decided that it was difficult
for a large family to live without a wife. He brought home a new
wife, Natalia Georgievna, and, having gathered the children
together, he said to her: "Here, Natasha, these are now your children

and you will be their mother; and you, children, obey her at all times."

Natalia Georgievna was accepted by everyone as a real mother and this was clearly expressed by Valery, who needed a mother's affection. He loved his stepmother selflessly until the end of her days. Their friendship, their belief in each other, and their mutual love were so genuine that no one, looking at them, could guess that they were not related to each other by blood.

In 1912 Valery turned eight and was sent to the village school. He had a reputation as a very gifted pupil and was especially inclined toward mathematics: he was always the first to solve problems in his head. He was a bright and sharp child. He loved to play tricks while playing horses during recess, or he would start fights with his peers in order to compare strengths, for which he would sometimes earn a "D" for conduct in his daily grade book. His father and mother would get angry, but the lash, always hanging in a conspicuous place in the home in order to inspire fear in the children, was never used and was more a moral symbol of parental authority.

Outside of school the children of Vasilevo were divided into those from the bazaar and those from the hill. The Chkalovs lived on the hill and therefore were called hill folk. Factory hands, dockworkers, and former barge haulers settled here. Below, where the Vasilevo bazaar sprawled, the wealthier homes were gathered. The merchants and contractors lived in these homes and were called bazaar folk. The hill children and the bazaar children were always fighting with each other and little Valka was a permanent participant in these battles. Being similar to his father in build and in his unusual physical strength, Valery developed at an early age and became strong beyond his years. This made him the leader of the gang of fistfight experts on the hill.

By the time Valery was eight, he had already met several of these awful terrors, who would attack him at the same time. In one of these skirmishes, six youths attacked him and, at some point during the unequal battle, he fell and broke his left leg. So that his father would not be distressed because his son had been defeated, Valka did not once cry out with pain when his comrades carried their leader into the house.

After six weeks the mischief-maker and scrapper was again shouting to the bazaar boys: "Hey, come on out! Let's finish the fight!"

Valery once helped his father win a bet with the merchant Kolchin.

Kolchin, after forging some documents, went to court and demanded that Pavel Grigorevich return the tugboat *Ruslo*, maintaining that he had not received a kopeck for it for several years. The court refused Kolchin and the merchant appealed to the provincial court.

When nothing came of that, he went to the highest court, in St. Petersburg. While the court examination was going on, the steam tugboat stood at its mooring under guard. Winter came. During Shrove-tide in Vasilevo there was always sledding on troikas.[4] Everyone came out to watch the breathtaking spectacle. Pavel Grigorevich arrived with his boatyard boilermakers. Kolchin's coachman, Yashka, began to boast in front of them, bragging that no one could beat him on his raven horses. Pavel Grigorevich started to get angry and asked Yashka: "And if it's downhill? You'll beat anyone?"

At his point his maligner and enemy, the rich Old Believer[5] Kolchin, as if set on fire, said: "Any way you want it . . . downhill, so much the better!"

Precisely at this moment, Valery appeared before his father's eyes from behind a knoll on skis. Pavel Grigorevich turned to Kolchin and bet anything that Yashka on his troika could not reach the Volga before his Averian on his skis.

Kolchin grew savage and blurted out excitedly: "I bet the tugboat!"

The boilermaker invited everyone who had heard to act as the witnesses.

The signal to start was given and they set off.

Valery was going full speed, almost overturning on corners, but Yashka on his troika was moving further and further ahead of him. It was clear to the spectators that the skier would lose; there were only two turns left and the remainder of the road led straight to the Volga.

Valery also understood that to follow behind the troika was a hopeless matter. He recalled the face of his father, insulted by Kolchin, when he suddenly made a seemingly insane decision: to leave the road, race straight for the precipice, leap off, and fly like a bird through the air to the snow covering the Volga. The skis touched the surface of the Volga at high speed. Valery was unable to stay on his feet and he flew head over heels, breaking one ski. Kolchin's troika leaped out onto the ice just half a minute later.

Pavel Grigorevich was shattered when some of his children died at early ages. He and Natalia Georgievna wanted to give the remaining children a good education. The oldest son Nikolai was appointed to the Nizhegorod modern school. (He was mobilized during World War I and died on the front.) Hard-working Anna was tutored at home, so that she passed an examination to become a village school-teacher and then taught in grade school. Aleksei was sent to St. Petersburg, where he completed studies at a technological institute and worked for a long time as an engineer in the factories of Nizhny Novgorod, which later became Gorky. Sofia studied at a grammar school in Gorodets. Valery, the youngest, was sent to the trade school in Cherepovets. He was third in the competitive entrance examinations and was enrolled in the school.

His mother and father were very happy. Pavel Grigorevich often repeated: "Averian will make a good boilermaker."

But then came severe, difficult and transitional times. The October Revolution came. The river tugboat *Ruslo* was nationalized and sent with Red Army soldiers to the river Kama. It was sunk there in a battle against the White Army.

As if throwing off a long, deep depression, Pavel Grigorevich took heart, quickly went to the boatyard, and began with enthusiasm repairing holes in the bottom of the steamer *Power to the Soviets*, making boiler furnaces and riveting turbines.

Pavel Grigorevich once again played with a heavy sledgehammer and yelled at his assistant if he drove rivets "unaffectionately."

In the winter of 1918, on the way home, Pavel Grigorevich saw Valery.

"What brings you here, Averian?" his father asked.

His son described the famine and the closing of the Cherepovets school.

"Well, if your studies didn't turn out right, come work with me."

Working as a hammerer for a smith like Pavel Grigorevich was difficult for a fourteen-year-old boy, even if he was built like a Bogatyr.[6] But the young man tried with all his might. In his character one perceived the same determination to work and the same urge, without sparing his strength, to do everything better than others just as his aging father had.

Valery burned with the desire to continue studying in school. His father, who by this time had learned the alphabet and knew how to write, happily composed and personally wrote out in his large uneven handwriting a request to the school: "I request that you accept my son Valerian Chkalov as a pupil in that class which will be suitable for his level. For my part, I inform you that he studied four winters here in the village school and two more years toward a journeyman in lathe work at Cherepovets. Respectfully requested, boatyard master of the boiler shop, Pavel Chkalov." After signing his name, the boilermaker added: "If my son becomes disobedient and disrespectful toward his teachers, please inform me so that I know and can carry out the necessary reprimand."

Valery began to study and after lunch went to the boatyard to work with his father. This was very difficult and he sometimes said to Natalia Georgievna: "It's not easy to wave a sledgehammer. My hands itch all night."

The mother advised her son to find an easier job. When they announced a recruitment for river vessels at the boatyard, Valery left to stoke on the dredger *Volga 21*.

At first he went to Kostroma, then to Kazan, and finally to the river Kama. They wintered at the Kurshinsky boatyard in Simbirsk Province.

In spring the young stoker joined the crew of a streamlined passenger steamer *Bayan*. The ship was transporting Red sailors to the front. The captain grew to like the strong, diligent, but still young stoker.[7]

Valery had to leave this job when the steamer was converted from wood heating to fuel oil, a new staff was set up, and a family friend was left without a position. Valery decided to give him his position and once again appeared on the doorstep of his family home in green soldier's puttees and an old overcoat, but loaded down with gifts for his relatives. A sack of flour, a sack of potatoes, and calico jackets for his mother, Natalia Georgievna, and his sisters, Anyuta and Sofia— this was a great help in a time of hunger.

The year 1919 came. The fifteen-year-old youth started to understand something about life: he had heard from his comrades about the events in Petrograd, about the Bolsheviks, about the fact that the Soviet Republic was surrounded by hordes of interventionists and White Army soldiers and was in deadly danger. Several fellows from Vasilevo served in the Red Army. Among them was the Chkalovs' neighbor, Vladimir Alekseevich Frolishchev. He served as an aviation mechanic for the Fourth Aviation Depot, which was located in Kanavino in Nizhny Novgorod. When Frolishchev appeared in his native Vasilevo, Vasili occasionally talked with him. After the boy saw from the steamer *Bayan* the flights of the factory-repaired planes, upon hearing the sound of an engine, the young stoker would run out onto the deck and follow the steel bird with an admiring look.

Somehow Frolishchev took Valery with him to Kanavino and introduced him to the depot commander, requesting that the student metal worker be assigned to him in the brigade of airplane fitters.

The commander hesitated: wasn't he too young? But just the same, he agreed and promised to draw up the acceptance papers in a week. Valery was immensely happy and rushed to say farewell to his family.

"Where are you heading for?" asked Pavel Grigorevich.

"To work in the army with Levka Frolishchev in his brother Vladimir's brigade. And there maybe I'll become a pilot."

"Well, if you've decided, I'm not going to try to talk you out of it. You know what you want."

Valery said good-bye to his mother and sisters and went out toward the Volga. It was evening. And very quiet. It seemed to him that it was possible to hear the leaves falling from the trees. He came to the precipice and looked for a long time at the other side of the Volga where the sandy spits and mowed meadows were visible; and beyond them the blue August distance grew misty, hiding the pine and oak groves. Is there really any place in the world more beautiful than ours?

The loud call of the steamer on which the youth was departing to Nizhny Novgorod to join the Red Army pierced the silence.

He turned to the house where he had spent his youth. Natalia Georgievna, Anna, and Sofia stood on the porch. The women sadly looked at their beloved through tears. But his stern father said in a deep voice: "There's already enough water in the Volga. Don't drown the fellow in tears."

2

Earning Wings

Fifteen-year-old Valery Chkalov worked assembling airplanes in the shops of the Fourth Aviation Depot.

After the huge hulls of the steamers and their massive boilers and furnaces, the airplanes seemed at close range to be unnaturally light and delicate and as fragile as meadow butterflies. He touched them carefully and was thrilled with the thought of flying in one of them. But no one was eager to invite him to go flying and Valery patiently carried out his duties. Although the aviation depot grounds were not heated, the young metal worker-assembler stood for twelve hours every day on the cement floor. His feet ached from the cold, but nothing could be done—the front needed aircraft.

A year of working at the Red Army's Fourth Aviation Depot went by. Chkalov now had a much better idea of what an airplane was composed of and how the engine was constructed. He saw pilots coming from the front for refitted aircraft. Valery looked with a sinking feeling at their faces, their leather jackets and helmets. He followed their movements and considered himself the most unhappy and unlucky of persons because he could not be with the Red fighter pilots and beat the White Army. Several times Valery accosted the administration: "Commander, I want to be a pilot."

The commandant looked at the youth, smiled and answered: "Be patient, friend. Get some more experience."

So Valery Chkalov continued to work.

He had already earned a certain amount of trust and respect. He was once ordered along with two comrades to bring several damaged airplanes from the front-line area to be repaired.

After reaching the area and loading the destroyed airplanes onto a train, they set off for the return journey.

Along the way they decided that there was no reason why the three of them should freeze in a boxcar. It would be better if one of them accompanied the special train while the other two went to Nizhny Novgorod on faster trains. Valery could not understand how one could leave such a valuable cargo. So he volunteered to accompany the boxcars. His comrades were afraid that he would freeze along the way, but Valery assured them: "Everything will be all right!"

His friends set off for the city, but the next day they began to worry that something might have happened to the boy.

Imagine their surprise when, after returning to the boxcar, they saw Valery standing by a warm heated stove.

"Who rolled up such a cast-iron monster for you? That stove must weigh 240 pounds."

"My father was dragging around things like that when he was nine years old. So it was nothing for me. I found it at the station and dragged it here."

"A real strongman!" the oldest one said.

"That's why my name is Chkalov! Chka—that's ice that's found upriver and demolishes any barrier."

In 1921 the Fourth Aviation Depot gave out four authorizations for flight school. Valery immediately wrote in an application, but the depot commandant Khrisanfov ruled him out: Chkalov was only 17 and it was senseless to send him—they would not accept a minor.

Valery was very distressed. His friends went as a group to make the request for him and the depot commandant gave in: "Well, take your chances! Go ahead, try it! Break a leg, Valery!"

Valery set off for Yegorevsk with his comrades.

Recalling this period in his life fifteen years later in his book *Three Days in the Air*, Chkalov wrote:

> How much I wanted to fly with our pilots and battle the enemy in the sky. But at that time there was only one flight school in all of Russia. It was impossible to get into it, especially with my village education. In the years during the Civil War, I read earnestly, spoke with pilots and aircraft mechanics whom I knew and slowly prepared for the school.
>
> Finally in 1921 I was sent to flight school in Yegorevsk. We gave it a very funny name: "Therka," which stood for theoretical school. I took to my studies with great eagerness!

■

How great was the happiness of Valery Chkalov when he saw his name on the roll of the enlisted.

At this time the Yegorevsk school was the first military-theoretical flight school. Coming from front-line aviation sections, detachments, and depots, the Red Army soldiers, workers, and mechanics mastered a broad program here. Included in the program was a major general-studies course: algebra, geometry, trigonometry, physics, Russian, and German. Aerodynamics, navigation, and airplane and engine parts played a significant role in the program. Many hours were devoted to political and general military preparation.

The school was situated in a former nunnery. There were no barracks in the exact sense of the word. Students lived three to four to a room in nuns' cells. Chkalov roomed with Makarsky, Makhalov, and Kuznetsov.

It was difficult to study. There were no textbooks. Many students lacked the proper education. The course moved at an accelerated pace—in less than two years one had to pass about thirty exams!

But Chkalov studied with no great difficulty: in the twelve-point grading system, he never received a grade lower than ten in any of his subjects. Not only did his sharp mind, quick-wittedness, and excellent memory help him to study well; no less significant a role was played by his firm and unwavering purposefulness in achieving his primary aim—to quickly become a pilot.

Chkalov's summaries surprised his teachers and friends. They were very brief, but the most important aspects necessary for flight never escaped Valery. What was secondary was recognized immediately and ruthlessly eliminated.

Although Chkalov constantly kept his primary goal in mind, he did not ignore those things that normally interest a youth: he enjoyed sports, especially soccer, tennis, and gymnastics, not to mention swimming. He un-self-consciously played comic roles in dramatics club. As a result, his "cellmates" decided that he had uncommon artistic gifts. This was natural: Valery had a natural sense of humor.

The students were fed poorly in those days, but this did not at all affect the mood of the youngest student. He possessed a character full of the joy of life, and he infected his comrades with his optimism. When things were difficult, he cheered them up with a joke.

He was the instigator of amusing competitions. After the command "prepare for evening inspection," the students quickly got into bed under the covers wearing only their underwear. On the command "get up," they were given only a few seconds to get dressed and come to attention. The winner of the competition was considered to be the person who stayed under his covers longer than anyone else and, after jumping up last, managed to come to attention without receiving a demerit.

Once Valery, trying to break the record, continued to lie down while everyone stood at attention. In just a few seconds he managed to take his place dressed in shoes, an overcoat, and his service cap.

The sergeant-major suspected that Valery had thought up some sort of new method of dressing and decided to look him over. When the order was given to Chkalov to stand at ease and turn around in a circle, the bottom of his overcoat flapped open and underneath the overcoat was visible . . . his underwear. The monastery walls shook with laughter and for his unique invention Valery received several extra work details. Chkalov was not angry at the punishment, but took his spite out on himself for not calculating things carefully enough.

It was spring, 1923. The final exam was passed. . . . Valery, like all his comrades, received the rank of captain, or as it was called then, *kraskom*. The whole graduating class was sent to the Borisoglebsk flight school for practical exercises.

■

The group of forty-seven flight trainees that Chkalov joined was the first recruitment for the new flight school at Borisoglebsk, which was formed by a decree on April 15, 1923. They were not able to fly immediately—the school was still not completely built and they had not yet received their training planes. Rolling up his sleeves, Valery, along with his comrades, enthusiastically converted the cavalry riding school into a hangar, the stables into classrooms. He smiled while working with a pickaxe or crowbar—it reminded him of the sledgehammer of a smith's assistant.

Finally the long-awaited Avro-type training planes arrived.[8]

Ten people were selected from the class for aerial practice. The primary criteria for selection were the recommendations from the Yegorevsk school. Naturally, Chkalov was one of the first to be selected for this group of ten.

Practical studies began with so-called taxiing. The student sat in an airplane with stubbed wings and started a run along the ground at full speed, holding the aircraft straight and not allowing it to jump or lift its tail and stand up or completely "cowl-over," that is, turn on its head. Taxiing closely imitated the takeoff run up until the moment the craft left the ground.

Chkalov always remained composed and firm with himself and with those around him under any conditions. But at the same time, being highly emotional by nature, he would sing joyfully as he raced from one end of the school field to the other, taxiing in a hopelessly outdated Farman, which, despite all his desire and mastery, was not able to lift even half a meter off the ground.[9] The green flight trainee left the cockpit of the Farman unwillingly and immediately joined the line-up to experience once again the incomparable feeling of speed.

The immediate nearness of the ground, to both the left and the right, blurred everything into a single sheet seemingly veiled by a light mist. Up ahead, especially in the distance, the field markers and the spring grass appeared unexpectedly, and, racing along, disappeared into brightly glittering pieces in the close foreground.

Valery tried to compare these unusual sensations of speed while taxiing in an airplane with something he was familiar with and discovered that he had experienced a comparable thrill on that desperate leap when he flew off the steep bank of the Volga on his skis. . . . This was already innate in Chkalov—wherever he was, whatever he did, he recalled the Volga until the very moment of his death.

Finally the course of taxiing runs was completed and the flights began.

Valery Chkalov ended up in Instructor Ochev's group. He was a very demanding and strict pilot. This attentive and restrained man immediately noticed the nineteen-year-old trainee and noted his unusual will and desire to fly.

This is how N. F. Popov, one of the former instructors in the Borisoglebsk school, recalls the flights with Chkalov:

V. Chkalov was distinguished from the other flight trainees by his strength of character. I had the chance to fly with him. You would sometimes sit in the training plane in the instructor's seat and feel that this kid, who hadn't yet flown ten hours, made the machine submit to his desires and held sway over it. He was unusually scrupulous about the instructor's intervention in guiding the aircraft during a flight. After landing, he was eager to clear up what the cause was for this or that reprimand by the teacher.

Meanwhile, the days of summer training went by unnoticed. One warm August day, Ochev literally covered Valery with dust that the aircraft stirred up behind it on takeoff. Even the self-assured Chkalov was somewhat upset.

But after making a second flight, Ochev climbed out of the craft, held onto the wing of the "Avi-ushka" [Avro trainer] and affectionately and softly spoke into his trainee's ear: "Well, my dear Valerushka, now my son . . . alone. Only repeat everything like it was on the first flight . . . and nothing extra. . . . God be with you!"

The first solo flight is an extraordinary moment in a person's life, although Valery Chkalov had been working up to it from the moment he first saw a hydroplane landing on the Volga.

Valery confidently led his obedient "Avrushka" through the pattern[10] and only on the final, descending turn, when he had eased off the throttle, did he suddenly hear his own voice singing "Lads, unharness the horses." Concentrating all his attention, Chkalov made a magnificent landing.

On his second flight Valery discovered why he did not hear on the intercom: "A chicken can fly better." "Well, where are you going?" "Less of a bank, dammit!"

No outside suggestions and commands. It meant he had to be on guard. Chkalov landed the Avro even more precisely near his group's landing marker.

Ochev embraced the trainee and said: "Good boy!"

Graduation for the pilots of the new school was on October 9, 1923. This was written in Valery's testimonial:

> Chkalov is an example of a thoughtful and attentive pilot who during the course of the summer program was circumspect and disciplined. . . . From first flights Chkalov distinguished himself by his great progress in the flight program, the confidence of his actions, calmness during flight and his astuteness. He is quick to understand and acts with energy and decisiveness, realizing the reasons for his errors and successfully correcting them. He senses a plane and the flight speed well. I recommend that he would be best as a military pilot.

It has always seemed to me, who has spent many hours in the same craft with Valery Pavlovich, that Chkalov's graduation testimonial, written by his instructor Ochev, is unusually precise and just.

■

In October, 1923, Chkalov, again among the top ten students to finish the Borisoglebsk School, was sent to the Moscow Aerobatics School.

Here he was a student and not a trainee, and the aircraft were fighters—German Fokkers and English Martinsides, on which they would learn aerobatic figures.[11]

Valery said to his comrades: "This is where you can pour your soul out. . . . "

Alexander Ivanovich Zhukov, an instructor in the aerobatics school, was on the historic Khodinsky Field (now Central Field) near Moscow checking out an aircraft that had just been brought out of a hangar when Chkalov came up to him, saluted, and reported: "Senior Instructor First Class! Student Chkalov. I am assigned to your group for further instruction."

Zhukov was an experienced teacher and a great master of aerobatics. About this time he had graduated over three hundred pilots. The instructor observed that Chkalov was still very young, broad-shouldered, and by external appearances rather coarse-looking, although his piercing blue eyes softened the sternness of his face.

Soon Alexander Ivanovich once again began to teach his newly arrived students about the two-seater Fokker S-3 with dual controls and on November 14, 1923, he took off together with Chkalov on his first flight.

The instructor noticed how abruptly the pedals moved so that the craft maintained a straight line on takeoff and how the student attempted to counter the smallest hop of the machine on the uneven surface of the airfield. The instructor wanted to ease the pedals and to hold on to the handle. But what was going on? Chkalov's strength was incredible. Zhukov had already noticed this when they had shaken hands and now there was nothing he could do but shout into the intercom to stop pressuring the controls and showing his bear-like strength. Chkalov understood and turned around, and Zhukov saw the smiling, happy features of the student, who immediately eased up on the controls. Valery acted confidently and positively on the turn. His coordination was magnificent, since a first flight in an unfamiliar plane is difficult even for experienced pilots.

Zhukov liked the flight, but Chkalov put the plane into an excessively steep bank. Very cocky for a first time! And again the instructor told him off firmly. Chkalov turned his reddened face and smiled more bravely, mostly with his eyes, and yelled into the intercom: "Understood, I'll carry it out. . . ."

On the glide path and landing Chkalov again pressured the controls but this time the intercom was disconnected near his helmet and it was impossible for the instructor to help his student. They landed well, but missed by a little, that is, they touched ground past the landing marker.

The instructor demanded that the student not use excessive force or all the controls would be broken, and not glide in for a landing at such an excessive speed. He announced that the general grade was "good." Chkalov answered joyfully in a deep voice: "Understood, I'll correct it."

Chkalov's unquenchable thirst for aerobatic flying or, as they used to call it, aerial acrobatics, was amazing. He learned to do maneuvers: barrel rolls, the "Immelmann," the loop, steep turns, fighter turns, and others.[12] He did them with such precision that Zhukov, himself a great master at this most difficult kind of flying, observed the aerobatics of Chkalov and said to his comrades: "There, that's how you do it. Simply an artist! And he learned it all by working hard. . . . "

Zhukov gave Chkalov the following graduation recommendation: "He finished his studies with a certification of 'very good.' Very calm as a person and a pilot. Comprehends slowly but grasps things well. No breaking of discipline was noticed."

Afterwards, Valery Pavlovich transferred to instructors Lapin and Trofimov to continue his aerobatic figure course.

When he was flying in a Martinside fighter plane in order to carry out a series of aerobatic exercises, Chkalov somehow made an incredibly steep bank on the loop and, after pulling back on the stick, he lost power. The aircraft turned into a steep right spin at a relatively low altitude. Everyone froze, fearing that the student would not be able to bring the machine out of its dangerous situation.

At the most critical moment, the Martinside stopped rotating and barely managed to gain speed and right itself without striking the ground. But the pilot did not bring the plane in for a landing. He ascended again and, clearly intentionally, put the fighter into another spin, again at low altitude, but this time rotating to the left. He managed to bring the aircraft out of the spin just above the ground, righting the machine literally at hedgehopper level.

Everyone ran to where the aircraft landed to find out who this was and what kind of maneuver he had done in the Martinside.

Climbing out of the plane, Chkalov patted the craft on the fuselage and shouted to the mechanic: "Hey, you've got a good little machine!"

Later they found that the aircraft had snapped the reverse steel band that strengthened the biplane wing frame. They were struck by how the pilot could take the overstrain when the steel could not!

Chkalov completed the Moscow school in May of 1924 and received orders to go to the Advanced School of Gunnery, Bombing and Aerial Combat at Serpukhovsk.

■

The commandant of the Serpukhovsk School, Fedor Alekseyevich Astakhov, was an extremely strict man who never allowed breaking of regulations and military orders. He knew that a new group of trainees was coming to him from the Moscow school and that among them was Chkalov. Rumors were already flying about in aviation circles about what a very gifted person he was.

The school commandant, according to an institutionalized ritual, invited all the newly arrived students for an introductory session.

While studying Chkalov's personal record beforehand, Astakhov came across the words "enjoys flying." What this "enjoyment" meant was not clear to the commandant because in addition Chkalov was characterized as a restrained, calm, and purposeful pilot.

The student Chkalov answered the school commander's questions calmly and with a sense of humor, which Astakhov liked. Astakhov himself was an old flier who had fought in World War I, joined the revolution on the side of the Bolsheviks, and commanded an aerial detachment during the rout of Kolchak.[13]

The school commandant was satisfied with the official part of the discussion and switched to a more friendly tone. He tactfully touched on the theme of "enjoyment in the air," making it clear that in this school the preparation program for a fighter pilot was so complex that it was simply not expedient and not permissible for a student to engage in his own experiments. As proof the commandant gave tragic examples in which those causing the catastrophes turned out to be pilots who had disobeyed the flight plan instructions and school regulations.

"Unorganized and willful 'creativity' will produce nothing but bloodshed and destruction," Astakhov told Chkalov.

In conclusion, the commandant said that a new method of studying aerial combat had been introduced recently in the school. This complicated process broke the course down into elements, and until each of them was fully mastered, both theoretically and in flight, it was forbidden to go on to the next element. Only after the student had mastered all the elements in the air would the entire difficult flight plan employed in combat be taught.

By the end of the conversation, the commandant clearly understood that Chkalov's temperament needed to be guided along the proper channels, but that it would be possible to make a good fighter pilot out of the student. For this reason Chkalov was assigned to the group of flight instructor Gromov, an excellent pilot, a wonderful teacher, and at the same time an understanding person.[14]

After making his decision, the commandant stood up, indicating that the discussion was over, but saw that the student was somehow looking at him strangely.

"Is something unclear?"

Chkalov said in a deep voice with his Volga accent: "When I was still a boy working in Kanavino, a pilot who had come from the Kolchak front told me that you used to fly from a flatcar in the taiga in a Sopwith or Newport."

"It's all true."

"And I didn't believe it."

"Somewhere between Tomsk and Krasnoyarsk we had to carry on reconnaissance. We could not locate or quickly build an airfield in this region. So we came up with this idea: put a Sopwith on a trolley, attach a train handcar behind it, bring the contraption to the top of a slope, and release it down the incline. When the couple was released, the speed was over sixty kilometers per hour; before this my Sopwith was idling and held by low blocks, but now at full rev the plane easily lifted off the trolley."

Chkalov was enraptured: "That's like from a catapult!"

The commandant smiled and, saying good-bye to the student, affirmed: "Yes, there is a similarity, but a very distant one."

Flight instructor Gromov taught the students the techniques of aerial combat, initially as separate elements, then went to combined maneuvers and refined them to absolute perfection, to a level where the students did the exercises almost automatically.

When the instructor demonstrated aerobatics to this group, Chkalov slapped his palm on his knee and said loudly and delightedly: "There's an artist! A genuine god."

One of the comrades noted maliciously: "You're even praying to him."

"It's not even shameful to kiss the hand of a person like that," Chkalov snapped back, continually following how easily yet quickly the fighter turned right, then left, then up, then down. The maneuvers were linked by a single thought and their composition expressed a single desire—to attack the opponent with quick, unexpected, and unmistakably exact maneuvers.

Recalling these distant days, Gromov characterized Chkalov thus in his story, *Native Ore:*

> Chkalov was invariably first in all stages of studying aerial combat. He never hesitated; if it was said, it was done. He forged on, as they say, regardless of all obstacles. He carried out the most difficult decisions before there was a chance for the feeling of fear to arise. At the decisive moment he disregarded everything that interfered with reaching his goal. All the powers in his mighty nature rushed in one direction—toward victory. This man's quickness of action matched his quickness to comprehend. He acted so decisively that, essentially, there was no time for doubt. At the moment when the fighters suddenly entered a skirmish and risked a midair collision, regardless of a thousand precautions (and in those days we flew without parachutes), at such a moment all the others would get a little frightened. Chkalov just did not know the meaning of fear. He stunned his "opponent" with virtuoso maneuvers, pounced from above, from the rear and achieved victory.

In November 1924, Chkalov received the rank of fighter pilot, took leave of Serpukhovsk, and joined a line unit.

3

Fighter Pilot

The dream of a boy from the Volga village of Vasilevo had come true; his certification was in his hands—now Valery Chkalov was a fighter pilot in the Red Army Air Force.

The time during which Chkalov became a combat pilot was very important for the development of Soviet air power. After the end of the Civil War and during the restoration of the nation's destroyed economy, a great deal of attention was devoted to the strengthening of defense capabilities, to the Red Army and its technical equipment—after all, the young Soviet Republic lived surrounded by enemies.

The Tenth Party Congress proposed "devoting exclusive attention to all the specialized technical aspects" of the Red Army, including aviation. A three-year program for the restoration, re-equipping, and expanding of the aviation industry, sanctioned by the Labor and Defense Soviet in December 1922, was put into practice.

In the First Red Banner Fighter Squadron, which was formed from the detachment of the legendary pilot Nesterov,[15] Valery Chkalov was assigned to Moskvin's flight team. He had selected for initial training flights the French Newport-24-Bis, an aircraft that had been in numerous repair shops. The aircraft mechanic, Proshlyakov, diligently taking care of the old cripple, warned the novice about the limitations in flight of this machine and the team captain said to him sternly: "Just take it around in circles. Don't try any derring-do; the Newport might disintegrate."

Chkalov felt more and more oppressed by these limitations and sadly recalled flying in the Moscow and Serpukhovsk schools and the acrobatic flights of the instructors Zhukov and Gromov.

In addition, the miserable spring weather in Leningrad forced the squadron to sit for long periods of time at the commandant's aerodrome.

After one of these forced breaks, Valery, bathing in the rays of the rarely visible sun, was in an especially good mood and, scorning the limitations, he made his old French aircraft do various aerobatic figures.

Of course, this forced him to meet the squadron commander or, as they often called him in those days, the "komesk." He was Ivan Panfilovich Antoshin, a fighter pilot who as yet did not know what Chkalov represented. In response to the commander's demand to explain the reason for this dangerous action in the air, Chkalov, hanging his head, answered: "I couldn't restrain myself. . . . I don't fly often. . . . A whole month's break. . . . Commander, I'm guilty and deserve punishment. . . ."

Ivan Panfilovich liked the young man's answer. He was won over by the fact that the young man admitted that he was guilty of continually and unreservedly wanting to fly. And it must be admitted that Antoshin was very pleased with Chkalov's flying in the old Newport. Antoshin overcame his own softness of character and sentenced the offender to five days in the garrison guardhouse.

But Antoshin understood that it was dangerous to keep the hood on this hawk for very long. So he also ordered that Chkalov be assigned a Fokker D-7 fighter plane, a solid German aerobatic machine.

After returning from the guardhouse, Valery happily helped his mechanic prepare the Fokker, in which it was possible to fly without any special limitations.

And so one set of maneuvers was followed by a series of others. Many squadron pilots spoke well of the flights of their newly returned comrade and several were highly enthusiastic.

It seemed to Chkalov, however, that his team captain Moskvin was holding him back for some reason and not giving him the freedom to fly. He asked Antoshin to transfer him to Leontev's team in the third detachment, which was commanded by Pavlushov, an excellent fighter and a remarkable man.

The squadron commander granted Chkalov's request.

The time came to return to camp and the squadron flew to Duderhof. The pilots dreamed of carrying out their heart's desire here: to fly at will in summer weather.

Valery Pavlovich quickly reacquainted himself with the squadron members and made friends with several fliers.

He soon felt that his school training had been far from adequate; his aerial combat skills and especially his marksmanship were much worse than those of the older squadron pilots.

The young fighter was especially ashamed of his failures in aerial marksmanship with pilot balloons, which were sent up from the ground so that a pilot at an altitude of five or six hundred meters could spot one, and then destroy it with the fighter's machine guns on the first run, as Pavlushov and Leontev were able to do.

Valery carefully watched the actions of his commanders, listened to their instructions and advice, but still was not able to match their classic firing abilities.

He once went to Ivan Panfilovich: "May I speak to you on a personal matter?"

The squadron commander asked with surprise: "What happened?"

"I came for some advice."

"Well, explain."

"I just can't manage the gunnery."

"Oh, I thought it was something worse. Well, with gunnery. . . . Everything can't be done right away. It comes with time."

"But I do it worse than Pavlushov!"

"Comrade Chkalov," Antoshin said, smiling good-naturedly, "I seem to recall that Pavlushov is a detachment commander and you're still a young pilot. There is, after all, a difference between you two."

"Good heavens!" Valery blurted out involuntarily, "I have to overtake him just the same. I must overtake them. Why else did I ask you to assign me to them. And Pavlushov and Leontev are going to say: 'Look, laggard, you're holding the whole detachment back.'"

Antoshin burst out laughing. He admired Chkalov's competitive streak, which made him want to be first in everything. He had observed that day as the young pilot, locating the balloon in flight, gave a short burst from his machine gun, but the target, as if nothing had happened, continued to rise still higher in altitude. The fighter attacked again. Again a short burst was audible, but the black balloon still escaped the pilot. It continued this way until the supply of ammunition was exhausted. The pilot raced savagely at the accursed target and struck it with the blades of his propeller—a strategy that generally speaking was not encouraged by the squadron.

The commander ordered the pilot to draw a sketch of the location of the sights, the machine gun, and the target, after which he said: "I think that you still are not used to the limited field of the optical sights and shoot too soon, fearing that the object will suddenly disappear from your field of vision. Apparently, you should first try to shoot with an ordinary circular sight."

Valery Pavlovich was so touched by the commander's attention that he did not notice that he had called Ivan Panfilovich "Papa."

The next morning Chkalov and his mechanic Proshlyakov showed the commander how they had attached the drift sight to the Fokker.

Antoshin carefully checked over the night's work done by his subordinates and praised it, noting in jest: "Now Leontev and Pavlushov better watch out."

"Comrade commander, I'll beat them without fail!"

"But it seems that you and Pavlushov are friends. Won't you feel sorry beating a comrade?" Antoshin said in the same jesting tone.

"Now they'll take me as my own man sooner. They'll respect me."

"Well, if so, then that means you be above the firing range in half an hour. Watch carefully for the signal."

"Yes, sir, comrade squadron commander," the young pilot Chkalov answered sharply, saluting the commander.

After hearing the sound of the aircraft, Antoshin ordered that the signal "report readiness" be given. Chkalov rocked his Fokker from wing to wing. The squadron commander released the first balloon when the fighter flew overhead at an altitude of eight hundred meters.

The young fighter pilot continually rocked the plane from a left bank to a right, trying not to let the pilot balloon slip by, trying to catch sight of it as it rose just above horizontal level. And then the pilot saw the target just as it appeared behind and a little above the plane. A tight combat turn, a direct attack, a short burst, and the balloon disappeared—the casing was already falling below.

Ivan Panfilovich chuckled: "Not bad," and then released a second target, which the fighter dispatched as quickly as the first.

"Very good," Antoshin shouted loudly.

But in order to estimate the pilot's accuracy and concentration, his quickness and ability to comprehend, Antoshin, with the words "here's a surprise for him," released two balloons, one after the other.

Putting the plane into a turn, Chkalov maintained his position and waited for a new target. When he saw two of them and at almost the same altitude, he dealt with them so quickly that the squadron commander shouted "Good shot!" and ordered the signal "come in for a landing" to be given.

By the middle of summer Chkalov was inferior in aerial combat to neither his team commander Leontev nor his detachment commander and the squadron's best aerobatic flyer, Pavlushov.

He became a crack shot at pilot balloons, but only when shooting with the circular drift sight. It seemed firing with an optical sight was still not feasible for a powerful fighter plane. Chkalov could not relax and continually sketched diagrams on paper or on the ground when a thought occurred to him. He would whisper for a long time with his mechanic or the squadron armorer.

With their help he obtained a drift sight and an optical sight. He fastened them side by side on a billet, built a suitable tripod, and carefully hid all this from his comrades. He practiced in the mornings before his detachment arose and when others were flying. The squadron commander once discovered him at practice. One morning, Antoshin had gotten up especially early. He did exercises every morning and on this occasion, coming out of the barracks, he jogged along a narrow path winding around a grove. At a sharp turn in the path an expansive sunburned back suddenly arose before Antoshin. A man in his underwear was working on some sort of a device. It was clearly aimed at a plane flying by.

Stepping back, Antoshin hid behind a tree and watched the strange figure. "Chkalov! What the devil! What's he doing here?" Taking a good look, the commander noticed the home-made tripod holding the billet on which two sights had been fastened. He immediately understood and could not keep himself from laughing. He went up to Chkalov: "Why are you up so early?"

"Quiet, Papa, don't shout, the guys will hear."

"I'm asking you: why aren't you sleeping?"

Chkalov felt the stern note in the commander's voice.

"Comrade commander, it's permissible to train quietly even when the detachment is asleep. The guys will see and they'll start making fun of me."

"Well then tell me what you've achieved."

"I'm practicing. I aim at the plane through the circular sight, then I right away look through the drift sight and see how the target should look."

"That's well thought out. You should familiarize everyone with it."

A month went by and the results of this serious training became self-evident. Chkalov took first place in all types of target competition. It was difficult even for Pavlushov to compete with his stubborn subordinate.

■

"Have I mastered my assignments? Is this the limit? What if I ask Papa himself to take me on? After all, he was a fighter pilot on the front. Let him test me."

Chkalov once again appeared before the squadron commander: "Papa, I want you to baptize me in aerial combat. I want to engage you in a dogfight."

For Ivan Panfilovich such a request was completely unexpected; not one of his subordinates had ever made such a daring suggestion.

But Antoshin could not refuse the gifted young fighter pilot. He set a takeoff time for the next day. At dawn the commander gave Chkalov the exercise: "The area—Duderhof Lake. The altitude—2,500 meters. You attack first . . . closing range—50 meters."

The experienced front-line fighter pilot set off for the established zone. Visibility was adequate. The morning fog had not lifted completely and the sun swam beyond the horizon like a large blinding red balloon.

The commander thought that the enterprising Chkalov would take advantage of the situation and attempt to attack him suddenly while camouflaged by the sun. Actually, Chkalov continued to gain altitude and held an easterly course.

Expecting the attack from above and from the direction of the rising sun, Antoshin increased his revs. The aircraft gained speed and made a gentle turn.

Chkalov darted to the attack, diving at the commander's plane. Ivan Panfilovich was just able to put his fighter into a steep turn to keep the young pilot from coming at his tail. Taking advantage of the moment, Antoshin made an unexpected roll and was on Valery's tail.

One wild aerobatic maneuver followed another but the former front-liner did not allow Chkalov to gain a victory over him.

After landing, the squadron commander praised Valery for his excellent aerobatics but at the same time pointed out his serious flaws: "First, comrade Chkalov, you violated the closing range, which is forbidden in mock combat—you can kill yourself and take an innocent comrade along with you. Second, you delayed reacting to your partner's actions by a few fractions of a second."

After this flight, the squadron commander equated Valery Chkalov with his favorites: Pavlushov and Leontev.

And Valery, proud of the commander's evaluation, was ready to sail through the air for days at a time.

With each month the young pilot Chkalov became more artful and more vicious in his aerial battles with his comrades.

Even the experienced fighter pilot Pavlushov, in answering a question by the squadron commander, announced: "Chkalov has no fear and if it were not for my own cautiousness, he would cut into my machine. . . . He has become unrecognizable . . . like an animal. . . ."

Soon after this conversation between the squadron commander and the detachment commander, Chkalov dropped in on Ivan Panfilovich. Glancing at the concerned and furrowed face of the young fighter pilot, Antoshin asked in a jesting tone: "Why do you look as gloomy as the Baltic in autumn?"

Valery took a diagram out of his leather coat and put it on the commander's table. As if continuing a conversation started a long while ago, he answered: "Here's what's the matter, Papa: When an enemy is on your tail in the air, you cannot tell what he's planning to do with you. And you can't see the enemy because the field of vision of the lower quadrant is blocked by your own fuselage."

"So you don't sit and yawn. You turn around, roll into a steep bank. You don't let the enemy attack you behind your back from below!" the commander impatiently interrupted Chkalov.

"But, Papa! What if at this time you're attacking another of the enemy's planes and you have only a few seconds left to open fire?"

"Well, brother, if such a bum is sitting on your tail, turn immediately and take care of him first!"

Chkalov asked: "But isn't it possible to roll over and stare the bastard in the eyes? Maybe he will be caught off guard. Maybe I can take care of the person who's after me that way."

Ivan Panfilovich stood up, bumped his head against the barracks tent, and asked in an agitated tone: "Look, what do you want?"

"Papa, the French can already do such a figure."

"How impatient you are, Chkalov! The French don't fly in 'coffins' like we do. Just wait, we'll get our own planes and then we'll try it."

"For the life of me, Papa, I don't agree! Look at this diagram; put a pump here and I guarantee that the Fokker won't let you down."

Although the old fighter pilot was interested in the young pilot's idea, he understood that the risk was relatively great and asked Chkalov not to rush things. Chkalov's eyes, which had been burning with excitement, darkened. He left Papa gloomily.

The rainy, gray Baltic days became more frequent. Chkalov started reading books. He read with unusual fervor. When he had lived in Vasilevo, he had loved Tolstoy, Gogol, Lermontov, but he was especially emotional about Pushkin and Gorky, whom, together with Dobroliubov and Milinkov-Pechersky, he considered to be fellow countrymen from Nizhny Novgorod.

Valery could drink in books. He remembered many details for a long time and memorized passages that he especially liked.

Shakespeare, Dickens, Balzac, Walter Scott, and Victor Hugo were also on the list of his favorite writers. He was especially partial to Hugo's novel *The Toilers of the Sea*.

But as soon as he heard the command "man your aircraft," Chkalov dropped any book, any activity, without the least regret and seemingly turned into another person. His figure became erect, resilient and flexible; his worker's hands, which had labored since childhood, moved more quickly and energetically, although at the same time their movements were smooth.

He could not get one thought out of his head: "But the French fly with their wheels up. . . ."

Chkalov talked to the detachment commander and received permission to attempt to fly his Fokker upside down. Pavlushov did not officially recommend such an assignment, noting that it would not be proper to take advantage of the absence of Ivan Panfilovich, who had been called to the staff command in Leningrad. Valery was glad for this situation: he sincerely loved his Papa as a commander and as a pilot, and it would have been more difficult for him to decide to commit an infraction in front of Antoshin's eyes.

The day turned out to be clear and calm. Chkalov left the zone and, gaining speed, put the aircraft into a loop. When the fighter crossed the horizon, in order to pull into a dive soon afterwards, the pilot pushed the stick away from him with a decisive movement. This immediately stopped the machine's normal movement along a banked turn. Bouncing about, the aircraft flew for a few seconds upside down and fell off on its wings.

Chkalov straightened the aircraft again, gained altitude, and again put the plane into a loop—a maneuver originated by Peter Nesterov. But this time the aircraft stayed in the loop with its wheels up for a little longer. Descending, Chkalov flew upside down and felt the strong rush of blood to his head. He had to hold his legs firmly in the pedal straps and concentrate on the stick in order not to lose control of the aircraft while he was hanging on his shoulder harness. Soon the aircraft rolled and righted itself.

The satisfied fighter pilot brought the plane in for a landing.

When the squadron commander returned from Leningrad, the commissar informed him of the infraction that had been committed by the youngest fighter pilot.

After being summoned to Antoshin, Valery began to explain that this had happened accidentally: "I was simply hanging in a loop and, apparently, because the aircraft was flying too slowly, it started to glide upside down on its own."

Ivan Panvilovich smiled and said to Chkalov: "What the hell! Nothing like that has ever happened to me in a Fokker D-7.[16] Maybe it's true: instead of a loop it starts to fly with its pants up. I'll test it out today."

The guilty flier did not leave the airfield. When he saw that the squadron commander's plane was indeed being prepared for flight, he quickly went up to Ivan Panfilovich and said quietly in a deep voice: "Papa, swear at me, punish me, but I admit that I couldn't hold myself back and tried it out. . . . The D-7 really doesn't fly badly upside down, but it still falls off on its wings."

Antoshin grounded the rule-breaker for several days. This was the most severe of punishments for Chkalov, but he understood that Papa was always right.

The squadron commander liked the fact that Chkalov, although belatedly, told the whole truth himself.

Autumn was approaching. They were shifted to their base field. There were fewer and fewer chances to fly. A limitation also had been set: while performing aerobatics in the D-7, it was forbidden to leave the field, because while performing maneuvers the engine sometimes would quit and it was impossible to start it up, even in a dive. Because of this problem several planes had already crashed on forced landings and the pilots received serious injuries.

Valery once again walked around thoughtfully and would not go out for several evenings. This was a rare thing for him: he loved to go to the movies, to dances, and out on dates; he did not skip football and, as during his days at the Borisoglebsk School, he was an active participant in amateur activities, among which he favored the dramatics club.

Obviously, there must have been serious reasons for the young man to have even stopped reading.

The first fine day explained everything: Valery was doing seemingly inconsequential maneuvers before everyone at the field when he deliberately made his engine quit. Chkalov did not bring the plane in for a landing at the field as ordered by the First Red Banner Fighter Squadron; he put the plane into a deep dive, and, close to the ground, pulled up with a sharp turn to the side opposite to the revolving of the engine's shaft. As a result the blade started to rotate and, when the ignition was turned, the engine started and continued to function normally.

Chkalov noticed from the air that his illegal demonstration was being observed and he repeated the maneuver several times.

When Chkalov taxied up to his stand, Papa, Pavlushov, Leontev, Makarsky, Maksimov, and other pilots were waiting. They did not let Valery jump out of the aircraft onto the ground; they grabbed him and began to toss him into the air.

Finally the pilot stood on the ground and strode to the squadron commander to give his report. But Antoshin embraced him and said: "Thank you very much! Now you write the instructions. Then we'll oblige everyone by ordering them carried out without any changes."

Chkalov just gasped: "I . . . and instructions?" That's a paradox!"

"Okay, don't get witty," Ivan Panfilovich concluded and patted his favorite on the shoulder like a friend.

Time passed, winter came. And although the days were cold, many people noticed that the young pilot Chkalov became even more languid and excessively moody on the ground. The winter of 1925 was a special one in Valery Chkalov's life—he met Olga Yerazmovna Orekhova, a student at the Leningrad Pedagogical Institute.

The Institute was sponsored by the First Red Banner Squadron. Valery and Olga were in the same drama group at the club; they acted in the same play. In addition, they studied together with the Red Army soldiers: she studied Russian; he studied mathematics.

In February 1927, Olga Orekhova became Valery's wife. She was now teaching at one of the schools in Leningrad. Valery Pavlovich continued to perfect his mastery as a military pilot in the same fighter squadron, which had been transferred to Gatchina.[17]

Pavel Grigorevich Chkalov came to his son's wedding. He liked the bride and said confidently to his daughter-in-law's father: "Now my son is in good hands. I don't have to worry about him."

Olga's father, Erazm Loginovich, and Pavel Grigorevich quickly became friends. The old Volga boilermaker was taken to see the sights of the city and its surroundings. With the help of Papa, Valery was able to take his father for a plane ride. Pavel Grigorevich sat behind his son's back and he smiled while flying and stroked his mustache and full beard. Upon departing for Vasilevo he said to his son: "Now I've seen everything, Averian! Now I can die."

Valery moved in with the Orekhov family in their house on the Petrograd side on Teriaev street near Geslerovsky Prospect, which is now Chkalovsky Prospect. He was warmly loved by the Orekhovs. He could come in to Leningrad only once or twice a week and his short leaves were always joyfully awaited by everyone. How much cheer, life, and joy he brought to the large family of the railway machinist and book lover Orekhov.

However, those who claim to know the human heart and expected that Chkalov, after becoming a family man, would change drastically and quit taking risks were seriously mistaken.

It was precisely during this period that Chkalov, flying aerobatics to test the quality of the repair of some undercarriage frames, flew out of the zone and quickly made a phenomenal number of loops over Leningrad, for which he was punished by the squadron commander with ten days in the garrison guardhouse.

As before, Valery admitted his guilt: "I was stupid, but it just happened—I had made a bet with pilot Kozyrev that I would do fifty continuous loops, but I enjoyed it so much that I did over two hundred."

But how would it be possible to live for ten days without flying? Chkalov sent a note from the guardhouse to the squadron commander asking him to free him ahead of time.

Antoshin read Valery's request and hesitated, although he had been reproached several times for his leniency toward the rulebreaker. The squadron commander recalled the recent incident in which the fearless but artful pilot had come to the aid of the entire Red Banner Squadron during maneuvers with the Baltic Fleet. Papa gave the order to free the pilot from the guardhouse long before the assigned period was over.

Many people knew and remembered the young fighter pilot's actions during the maneuvers. . . . It was during autumn. The weather was gloomy and rainy The First Red Banner Squadron was participating on the side of the Reds.

On the third day of the mock war, intelligence had located the "enemy." But as if in spite, radio communication with the Red squadron's flagship was cut off. Antoshin walked about gloomily, cursing all the radio men and meteorologists.

The sea was stormy and low, leaden clouds continually poured down rain. The commander once again received the categorical command: "Make contact with the battleship *Marat* and warn them of the presence of the enemy."[18]

The planes on duty stood at the takeoff point and the pilots and mechanics sheltered from the rain under the wings.

While the commander was beating his head, not knowing what to do in these circumstances, headquarters called again and demanded more forcefully that the order of the Red commanding forces be carried out. Antoshin called for Leontev and Chkalov. He explained the situation to them.

"Is it clear, comrades? We have to find the *Marat* in the open sea and throw down a message bag onto the deck. I'm sending the two of you in order to guarantee the completion of the order. I'm warning you—the mission is dangerous and you're going to have to keep your eyes open: the weather at sea is even worse than here."

In five minutes the two planes took off and immediately were hidden in the gloom of the low clouds at an altitude of twenty meters. The squadron commander looked at his watch and unwillingly returned to his tent.

Time passed slowly; it seemed to the commander that his watch was not working correctly. He asked Pavlushov: "How much time has gone by?" The detachment commander answered: "Two hours."

The weather became even worse and Ivan Panfilovich's mood turned completely sour. Suddenly the air shook from the drone of an approaching airplane. Everyone leaped up to find out what had happened. A plane was suddenly visible from out of the foggy mist and came in for a landing.

"Why only one? Who hasn't returned?" Antoshin wondered while the pilot taxied up to the staff tent.

Soon afterwards, a flier climbed out of the plane and went up to the squadron commander.

"And where's Chkalov?"

"As soon as we were out over the sea and spread out for the search, I didn't see Chkalov any more."

"What's the weather like?"

"Over water it's terrible: fog, no visibility."

Dismissing Leontev, Antoshin glanced at his watch. He was already tormented by the thought: I haven't carried out the assignment and I've killed a man. He came out of his tent several times and listened carefully, but did not hear anything but the sound of the endless, tedious rain. The clouds crawled down even lower and covered the tops of the pines.

"Did his engine quit? Maybe he has hit the ship or the water. Have I killed a friend?" The old front-line fighter pilot blamed himself. But he was still waiting for something, although Chkalov's fuel supply time had long ago run out.

What to do? He would have to send the detachment commander out. But you just had to look at the field to see that it was impossible to take off.

The squadron commander was preparing to call for Pavlushov when the duty officer ran up to him: "You're wanted immediately on a call from Oranienbaum."

Ivan Panfilovich with a sinking feeling inside took the receiver from the telephone operator.

"Hello, hello! Oranienbaum? This is Antoshin speaking!"

"Papa, is that you? This is Chkalov speaking! Can you hear me?"

Antoshin forgot all formalities: "I hear you, I hear you. Go ahead!"

"I found the *Marat*. The weather, Papa, is worse than you can imagine. . . . Has Leontev come back?"

"Yes, he came home a long time ago. Tell me about yourself," the commander rushed Valery Pavlovich.

"What's there to report? Everything's all right, Papa. I read the inscriptions on the sides and was afraid to drop the message bag before I found the flagship. It was hard to tell the Reds from the

Blues. In this kind of weather all cats look gray, and that goes for ships, too."

Antoshin was already smiling but he hurried him on: "Well, and then what?"

"I decided to search until there was just enough in the tanks to make it to shore because I was afraid that I couldn't make it swimming and would only give the sailors a laugh."

"But why didn't you come back earlier? Where did you set down?"

"A couple of kilometers from Oranienbaum, right on the shore."

"Did you seriously smash up the plane?"

"Hey, Papa, this is no time to be kidding. Send a gas truck with a mechanic. I'll turn up tomorrow and you'll see—not a scratch."

"Excellent, Valery Pavlovich! Good-bye!" finished Antoshin, calling the young pilot for the first time by his first name and patronymic in a show of respect.

And later, whenever Chkalov broke a regulation or did not follow instructions, Antoshin always recalled these two memorable episodes: how Valery had learned to start up the engine on the D-7 when it quit during aerobatics, and how he had found the *Marat* and how, because of this, the command congratulated the Red Banner Squadron. After the hero who had made a forced landing in Oranienbaum in an undamaged plane returned, the squadron commander wrote in his notebook: "During this flight Chkalov made clear to everyone the most important qualities of a fighter pilot: willpower, stubbornness, acceptance of responsibility for the assigned mission, the ability to adapt oneself in any conditions, excellent knowledge of parts and the capacity to utilize everything the plane has to give."

At the same time Papa recalled with disappointment Chkalov's flight under a bridge, after which Valery got what he deserved.

According to the person who carried out this stunt, it happened like this.

There was a serious gap in the flying abilities of the pilots of the Red Banner Fighter Squadron: the majority of them were not able to land confidently and exactly on a designated square in an aircraft with a dead engine, as happens in practice in a forced landing when the engine quits. The pilots were not able to master the correct glide path. The squadron commander consulted with the detachment commanders and gave the following order: to place at the landing approach to the field a lightweight gate made from two thin ten-meter-high poles placed twenty meters apart and attached at the top by a gauze tape. The pilot had to pass through the gate without catching his wheels on the gauze and land on the directed spot.

The pilots enjoyed this exercise. Valery performed it especially well.

And so, when Papa was at a resort, the excessively energetic aerial experimenter Chkalov started to think:

> Of course, any pilot can approach these fragile sticks and gauze tape in a plane quite calmly because there's nothing to be afraid of—they won't hurt you even if you hook onto them with the plane.
>
> But after psychologically getting used to such a simple situation, it's difficult to say how you would act if, instead of the sticks, you had the massive stone foundations of a bridge, and metal girders replaced the gauze wire.

Recently he had sat in the guardhouse for doing aerobatics at a low altitude again. "They say: not according to the directives. But what if the directives improperly set the norms for me? I'm convinced—aerial combat must be carried on above and below, close to the ground. But for this one must prepare and prepare seriously, if he wants to win." These thoughts excited Chkalov. Yet he had forgotten them when, one day, on his way to the field, he neared his bus stop.

He heard a familiar voice: "Valka!"

"Bad weather again," said Chkalov in a greeting to a squadron co-worker with whom he often rode the bus to the field.

"To hell with the weather. Let's sit it out. If you want to fly, you'll get a few days in the slammer."

The pilots jumped on the bus. Continuing the conversation, Valery noted: "I heard that in Kiev there's a pilot named Anisimov. They say that he performs miracles. And because of this, they don't put much pressure on him."

"And ours don't want us to crack up before our time," his comrade ascertained calmly.

The bus went along Trinity Bridge. Valery unexpectedly jumped off, waved at his friend, walked to the parapet, and looked out over the beautiful Neva bridged with granite.

This icy, overflowing river always led him to thoughts of the Volga.

"Comrade Captain! You can't stand there." Valery saw a young policeman standing next to him.

"Don't get upset. I'll take a look and go." Chkalov jumped across the rail and began to look over the girder transom. He concentrated on remembering the form of the lower outline and the distance from the water to the arch of the bridge.

"You can't stand here," the policeman repeated.

Chkalov turned to him and suddenly asked: "What do you think, brother, is it possible to fly under the bridge?"

The policeman was confused by the unexpectedness of this and, forgetting his severity, blushed and did not know how to answer the strange question. Chkalov brightened and stared straight at the young fellow in the uniform: "Well, is it?"

"I don't know, comrade Captain. Steamers pass through," the policeman muttered, perplexed.

"Very good! That means you give me permission. Well, so long, hope you get off work soon!" Chkalov gave a loud and booming laugh and the good-natured young fellow watched with surprise and suspicion as the pilot jumped onto a moving bus.

Papa was resting on the Black Sea when Valery flew in his fighter above the city and carefully looked over the Neva.

"Yes, that's the bridge that the policeman gave permission to fly through," Chkalov smiled, remembering the rosy, confused face of the guardian of order. Spiraling steeply, he started to descend toward Trinity Bridge. He saw the heavy traffic of pedestrians, carts, and buses. People were watching with interest the airplane circling literally right over their heads.

Chkalov descended closer to the water and flew crosswise to the Neva: he studied the structure of the bridge from the side. "I'll make it! If I aim it precisely—it has to make it through." He made another pass and made another estimate. "Yes, there's hardly any room. But never mind, I'll hold up."

And the more he circled around the beautiful bridge, the more Valery's passion burned and the more excited he became. "I'll just have to manage to nose in right in the middle, otherwise I'll rip the wings or chassis either in the water or against the girder or the stone foundations."

The fighter circled like a swallow around its nest made on a precipice on the shore—and like a swallow angled itself until it was satisfied with its flight path into its nest. But now the plane climbed like a light up into the sky, going away from the bridge and along the course of the Neva.

The pilot was in that state of concentration and intensity in which danger slips somewhere beyond the boundaries of will and consciousness. The impossible becomes real. An hour ago Chkalov would not have been able to say that it was possible to fly under the bridge, but now it was clear that he would do it. Certainty filled all the pilot's movements.

Valery turned his minuscule fighter toward the bridge. The thousands of tiny parts of cold steel that made up the fighter seemed to be filled with the pilot's blood and every beat of his heart was transmitted to the obedient aircraft.

After making several arcs, he crossed the bridge from one shore to the other; his shadow drowned in the river. The plane came lower; the wheels almost touched the funnel of a frightened tug, which cried out with a sharp, squeaky toot. But Chkalov did not hear the sound and lowered the aircraft even more. The small waves on the surface of the river sparkled in his eyes.

"Just a bit lower. That's it, good." The plane flew right above the water; his eyes continually followed the distance to the surface of the river. "A bit lower—into the water; a bit higher—into the girder." The bridge came on with amazing speed. "Right in the middle?" The brain hesitated. "A little to the left," answered a lightning glance. Quick, careful movements of the feet followed immediately. "That's it! I'll make it!"

The narrow crack between the girder and the water flew at the plane with fantastic unexpectedness and at the same moment the roar of the repeated echo and noise of the engine and propeller was heard. Some sort of darkness stunned the eyes and once again the pilot saw the sparkling surface of the rushing river.

A pain in the ears and fatigue. Chkalov slowly gained altitude. The field, an excellent landing, the hangar. The engine was turned off. Taking off his restraining harness, Valery stood up on the seat and shouted to the mechanic: "Just the same, brother, I flew through it!"

He jumped onto the ground, reached for a cigarette, and offered his cigarette case to the mechanic, who, not understanding, asked: "What did you fly through?"

"'Where? Where?' you're cackling at me. Slipped right under the Trinity Bridge," answered the pilot, laughing.

"What's the matter with you? You're very pale."

"What do you want? Have you ever flown under a bridge? Well, try it; fly through and I'll watch how you look."

Rumors about the flight under the bridge traveled all through Leningrad and the entire aviation garrison with the speed of sound.

Some witnesses maintained that during the fly-through under the bridge a girder was almost ripped off its supports. Others believed that the pilot hit a girder with his wing and that the wood piece floated in the Neva for a long time. A third group proved that both pilot and machine, after flying under the bridge, crashed into the cold waters of the river and a fire launch was just barely able to drag them to the shore.

In discussing the flight, people were attracted by the stunt itself, which was remarkable for its innovativeness and audacity. Only the command and the party organization sections asked the most important question: what made Chkalov take such a dangerous and unprecedented risk?

A gloomy Chkalov, admitting his own guilt, stood in the office of the squadron commander. Antoshin paced back and forth in agitation and occasionally stopped in front of his subordinate, attentively looking him in the face: "It's clear to me: you're too big for your hat. You don't enjoy the part where you have to fly in formation according to instructions. But imagine that our pilots are going to try exactly the same thing tomorrow. What do you think will happen?"

"They'll crack up," Chkalov said pensively, not raising his lowered head.

"That's it! They'll crack up! So we don't have the right to encourage you, can't give the slightest hint that your actions are worthy of being repeated. No way! I know that you did it easily, that you didn't strain yourself, but not everyone can do it. Far from it! I'm ready to admit to you that even Pavlushov cannot yet master some of your moves. Obviously, nature has given you much. And your imitators are forced to exert themselves."

"People have to be taught," Chkalov answered firmly, sharply at attention before the squadron commander.

"Yes, on this point I agree with you. And it seems to me that a lot of people will learn from you. But only one condition is demanded: a gradual movement from the easy to the difficult, excluding all stunts which break discipline."

"But, comrade squadron commander, it's boring for me to practice what I've already mastered a long time ago. I understand that my action cannot be justified in any way, but it was done not to show off but to test my own powers—will, courage, and preciseness of calculation. I wanted to compare it with our sticks and gauze tapes. I deserve punishment and I will endure it without complaining, but I don't know how I'll be in the future."

"Oh, Chkalov! Chkalov! What am I going to do with you? Okay, I'll consult with the Air Force administration. But you'll serve the full term of your punishment!"

Chkalov turned up once again in the garrison guardhouse.

■

Around that time an important event in the life of the Soviet Union was approaching—the tenth anniversary of the Great October Socialist Revolution.

There was a great deal of talk about the possibility of a large military parade in Moscow. There were rumors that the First Red Banner Squadron would be invited to Moscow.

But at the last moment it was announced that Leningraders would be represented in the aviation parade in Moscow by Senior Pilot Chkalov and his friend Maksimov.

The position of the Air Force command turned out to be a very ticklish one. On the one hand, here was an almost unequalled master of aerobatics, the best aerial gunner and the foremost fighter pilot in aerial combat. Chkalov had saved the life of more than one pilot in the squadron by discovering a way to start the D-7 plane in the air when the motor had stopped while hovering in aerobatic maneuvers. It was the same Valery who had come to the aid of his squadron during the last maneuvers, proving himself to be selfsacrificing and fearless in finding the battleship *Marat* in the foggy Baltic. On the other hand, no other pilot had spent so much time in the guardhouse for breaking set procedures and flight regulations: for flying at extremely low altitudes, for flying under a bridge, for turning 250 loops in a row, and for many other things.

To some of his superiors and commanders, Valery Chkalov was like a coin accidentally found on the side of the road on which a very handsome drawing is visible on one side, and on the other side is an unrecognizable symbol that apparently determines the value of the discovery.

But one thing was clear to everyone: it would be very difficult for the Air Force command not to send Chkalov to the parade in Moscow, since he possessed such magnificent aerobatic artistry and a unique combination of fearlessness, will, and magical flying talent.

And so Chkalov was at the Central Field in Moscow. On November 8, 1927, Senior Pilot Chkalov took off from Khodynsky Field to display aerobatic figures to the Revolutionary Military Soviet of the young republic. He had no limitations. He was given free flight. . . .

Pleased and inspired by the attention, Valery Pavlovich, at a height of a few dozen meters, performed aerobatic maneuvers that were joined together into a single acrobatic composition.

Kliment Efremovich Voroshilov,[19] surrounded by Red Army commanders who had gained fame in the Civil War, watched with rapture the amazing flight of the Leningrad fighter.

The pilot, diving from high altitude, would first flirt with the ground, almost striking it with a wing in double or quadruple rolls that were instantaneous but flexible and precise, and then would spiral upwards, hold at a peak, and complete the climb with an impressive Immelmann or a surprisingly unexpected and unusual inverted flight. In its sharp joyfulness and purity, Chkalov's flight was reminiscent of that of a swift during the summer.

The head of the Red Army Air Force, Peter Ionovich Baranov, and his deputy, Yakov Ivanovich Alksnis, were pleased with the rare sight and were glad that everyone enjoyed the Leningrader's flight.[20]

Chkalov described this event to his wife:

> Lelik, you can't imagine what I did in my flight today. The entire field applauded my maneuvers. I was allowed to perform any maneuver at any altitude. That which earned me the guardhouse was recognized here with a special decree that said: "Present a monetary reward to Senior Pilot Chkalov for especially outstanding aerobatic figures." This was read at the Bolshoi Theater during a gala celebration.

■

On January 1, 1928, the Chkalovs had a son whom they named Igor. Valery Pavlovich glowed with happiness.

But rarely does happiness exist without sorrow. A month and a half later, Chkalov received a promotion, left his beloved First Red Banner Fighter Squadron, and arrived in Bryansk as a team commander. Prior to that, his favorite, stern but fair Papa, with whom

Valery Pavlovich would remain friends until his death, left for Odessa to a new assignment.

Far from his family, Valery relived the impressions of the last days in Leningrad. Living conditions in Bryansk were terrible and he was afraid to take his wife away from her work, hoping that he himself would not be kept here for long.

Valery was unhappy without his family and wrote to his wife:

> From the first I was with you and Igor in my thoughts. I thought only about you and I saw your image clearly. I sensed your pain and sorrow. I recalled your face on that day when I visited you in the ward after the birth. Your face spoke of what you had gone through. And at the same time on your face was written an inexplicable, lovely feeling, a feeling of motherhood, a feeling that you had given the world one more new live creature. And how glad, happy I was on that day. I wanted to shout, sing and carry you in my arms. You gave me that by which I now live and my life has become a good and dear thing. You and my son—this is my life, my air, and my light. Our son is the link in our lives.
>
> You are a friend, a comrade who will not desert me at a difficult moment and next to whom I rest both morally and physically.

Valery Pavlovich often requested his wife to write about how their son was growing:

> Lelik, why does our son still not have any teeth? Pay attention. It's bad if his teeth come out all at once later. The proper order: 2 bottom teeth, then 2 upper teeth and 4 lowers and so on.
>
> Is he sitting up by himself yet or not? Is he behaving well or not? How's his chicken pox, his teeth—has he cut them yet or not? You don't write all these details about our son. How much has he grown? What does he weigh? Take him right now and weigh him! You know how I want to know everything! Well, this is all that I can write. I can't expose my pained and burdened soul on paper, but you understand it anyway.

In the summer his section flew to a camp near Gomel. Valery went to Leningrad in order to bring his wife to his family on the Volga and to show his mother and father his firstborn.

In order to give his wife an impression of the Mother Volga, he put her and their son on a steamer at Rybinsk and showed off the beauty of his native river all the way to Vasilevo.

He stayed in Vasilevo for a few days and then returned to Gomel. Soon afterwards he had an accident. This is how the guilty one himself evaluated the misfortune in a letter to his wife, Olga:

Yesterday I smashed an aircraft. It was extremely unpleasant, although I didn't break anything important, but just the same. . . . I had no accidents for six years and then it happens here. I explain it by my bad mood. . . .

A little later, evaluating his situation as a whole, Valery in a letter from Gomel characterized the conditions thus:

I fly rarely and don't want to. Some sort of apathy. The aircraft are very poorly made and it is necessary to fly with caution. So you don't get any kind of satisfaction, but only become upset. . . . Enough, I want to write about the work and the aircraft in which it is impossible to fly. It smells of counter-revolution here.

Chkalov was always open and direct to the point of sharpness, a trait that not infrequently led to confrontations with headquarters. This was holding back his promotion in his job.

In this regard Olga Erazmovna advised him to be more flexible and diplomatic in dealing with people. This is how Valery Pavlovich reacted to this advice:

You write that I am guilty for not receiving promotions in my work. You're right, but this is not the result of the fact that I cannot work but because I cannot do something which will be impossible to use later on. In a way my flying abilities get in the way of my promotion. If I were like everyone else, I wouldn't fly like I now fly. And if I flew like everyone else, I wouldn't be "undisciplined." But since my flying is different from that of others, this has to be taken into account somehow. And so it's taken into account as "aerial hooliganism." As a fighter pilot I have been right and in the future I'll continue to be right. I should always be prepared for future battles, so that I will beat the enemy and not be beaten. For this one must be completely trained and forge in himself a certainty that he will be the victor. The victor will be only that person who goes to battle with confidence. I consider a warrior to be a warrior only if he, regardless of certain death, will sacrifice his life to save other people. And if the Soviet Union needs it, I will do this at any moment. . . .

Soon afterwards a more serious misfortune befell Valery. Flying from Gomel to Bryansk and leading behind him a team of fighters, on his own initiative he descended to a low altitude and attempted to train his subordinates to carry out an important tactical move— hedgehopping. Everything was going well. A telegraph line crossing the flight route was visible up ahead. Chkalov judged from the insulators on the poles that the wires must be high above the ground; however, he did not notice their inevitable sag and the planes struck the wires accidentally. Happily, there were no casualties, but the patience of the Bryansk command was exhausted—it decided to cut short Chkalov's unauthorized exercise in the most merciless manner.

At this time the situation regarding accidents in the Red Army Air Force was truly tragic: hundreds of people from the battle units perished from either inexperience, reliance on worn-out old techniques, or the low quality of the first Soviet aircraft. But the largest number of catastrophes and accidents could be explained by the lack of discipline of the flight personnel and the low level of leadership at the fields and in flight.

For this reason the Bryansk aviation section command decided to show its own personnel that breaking of set norms and orders would not be allowed for anyone, including Chkalov.

Studying Chkalov's personal case, the Bryansk command unfavorably commented on the First Red Banner Squadron commander, who had helped create this "aviation monster" who was not limited by any boundaries. It was strange to them that many people in aviation spoke of Chkalov as a rare, remarkable flier.

Valery Pavlovich's growing popularity among the flight personnel upset some of the commanders. They were surprised that at the jubilee aviation parade in Moscow before the Revolutionary Military Soviet, the Leningrad fliers had been represented by Chkalov, even though he had received high marks for artistry in aerobatics, which had exceeded all established norms.

It was decided in Bryansk for the sake of strengthening discipline and as a warning to make an example of the accused and put him on trial.

I think that if Chkalov had been in the First Red Banner Squadron commanded by Papa, he would not have been put in prison even for such dangerous willfulness.

But the Bryansk aviation leaders should not be blamed—strictness and severe demands existed then and should always remain for all levels of aviation leadership, otherwise many independent-minded pilots will perish senselessly.

However, it follows that the other extreme, which did not take Chkalov's unusual talents into account, should also be condemned; he was convicted by being held to the same standard as everyone else.

And so Chkalov was sentenced. On January 2, 1929, he was put in the Bryansk prison to serve a one-year sentence. The days in cell number 12 passed monotonously He thought about his family and his flying friends.

From the very first day he started to keep a notebook: "The cell is small but warm. As soon as I arrived, I started writing. At night it's hard to sleep. Thoughts about Leliuska [my dear Olga] and Igor give me no peace. How are they in Leningrad? . . . I am an unlucky person in life. If it weren't for Leliuska and Igor, I wouldn't be alive. That's faint-hearted, but that's the way it is."

He reread all the books that were allowed to prisoners. He continued his notes: "The boredom is terrifying and oppressive; the ennui is depressing. I slept in the morning. Woke up. They brought me lunch. I sat, lay down, paced; I'm sick of it all. I wrote Leliuska a first letter. Tomorrow it will go in the mail. Leliuska will read it and cry. Good night, my dear wife, our lives are still ahead of us."

Just the same it would be a mistake to suggest that Chkalov was all alone. Many sympathized with his misery and some, like his former detachment commander Pavlushov and team commander Leontov, came from Leningrad to visit Valery and to keep up his morale. There were also quite a few sympathizers in the Bryansk aviation section.

Even the hearts of the prison administration were touched by how hard the pilot was taking what had happened and they let forbidden messages from him pass to the outside. With their silent acquiescence Olga carried out a clemency request written to the Central Executive Committee of the USSR. Mikhail Ivanovich Kalinin, without delay and long before his term was over, freed Chkalov from prison.[21]

■

Thus, Chkalov spent nineteen days in prison. He then was demobilized from the Army and went to Leningrad to his family.

For a while he could not find work, became moody and reserved, and stopped speaking with even his close friends.

Of course he suffered greatly and sometimes said to his wife: "I'm going to quit flying. I'll study. I'll apply to a university."

Olga supported this idea of going to college. But after the first rumors reached him from his comrades in Moscow that he was forgiven for his past sins, all these thoughts of studying disappeared.

He was hired to work at Leningrad Special Air command—he flew passengers in a Junkers S-13 (J-13).[22]

Of course for a talented fighter pilot, flying passengers was not an ideal occupation, and naturally he continued to yearn for military aviation.

While Valery Pavlovich is flying the Special Air Command J-13, let us return to the accident and evaluate the measure of punishment meted out to the pilot.

It is hard for me, as a close friend of the victim, to remain objective in this matter. Therefore, I will provide the opinion of the well-known aviation authority and prominent pilot and aviation Colonel-General M. M. Gromov, under whom, the reader will recall, Valery studied at the Serpukhovsk School of Gunnery, Bombing, and Aerial Combat.

Two or three years after I first met Chkalov, I once again heard about him. It was said that he did maneuvers in the air in which his life was hanging on a thread. Most important, he did them out of no special necessity, just from an excess of energy.

I recognized in these tales the very same pilot whom I met in school. Yes, even then he did not like quiet, everyday work—for him being in the air was his everyday work. His urge to fly was graphic and unusual; one sensed in him Russia's boldness and courage.

It was necessary to give this person a problem, to set a goal which would enable him to utilize fully all his extraordinary abilities.

Unfortunately, at times there were people around him who were incapable of genuinely appreciating his qualities. Others measured Chkalov by their own yardsticks, but he was way above their heads.

Not being able to provide Chkalov with genuine work, they came down on him for his lack of discipline and foolhardiness. He received punishments, sat in the guardhouse; they vexed him with petty carping and finally in 1929 he was demobilized from the Air Force.

When Yumashev and I learned about this, we were upset. A person like Chkalov was unique! It was unthinkable to isolate him from a job in which he was more talented than many others!

It was necessary not to remove him from aviation but to help him find himself. He himself did not know where to direct his energies so that they were not wasted on dangerous and unnecessary maneuvers.

We tried to convince those individuals upon whom Chkalov's fate depended: He has to return. It is a crime to throw away such people.

For a long time these persons turned a deaf ear on our urgings. One of them answered literally the following: "There are a lot of people in aviation these days. And we can afford not to value an individual undisciplined person."

It was pointless to continue the conversation. . . .

But in a short while Chkalov was once again in the ranks. I do not know whether Valery Pavlovich knew that Yumashev and I, people who did not know him very well at the time, were so concerned about him. But it was easy to understand our concern at that time. Having seen Chkalov in the air several times, we could not help but enjoy his remarkable talents. This made us turn to comrade Alksnis, who decided to return Chkalov to aviation.

It seems to me that this characterization of Chkalov and his tragic situation explains completely how unfairly he was treated.

Of course, Valery Pavlovich sometimes carried out unjustifiable actions, but he himself was able to evaluate them objectively and was not offended by reprimands:

> The most grievous breaking of discipline was my stunt performed in Leningrad. I flew under the Trinity Bridge in an ordinary fixed gear aircraft, almost touching the water with the wheels. Another time, seeing two trees the distance between which was less than my wingspan, I sideslipped the aircraft and made it through the trees. I enjoyed aerial acrobatics. I thought that there was indeed a risk, but only much later, when I had mastered the art of test-flying new craft, did I understand that a genuine sober risk has nothing in common with this foolhardiness.

While continuing to work for Special Air Command, Valery Pavlovich was drawn to the youth who were attracted to aviation. It is therefore not surprising that he soon became a permanent member of the Leningrad Air Club, which was located next to St. Isaac's Cathedral in the building of the former military ministry of Imperial Russia.

Liking children, the fellow from the Volga often told the young builders and glider pilots about aviation and fliers. At the glider station near Duderhof, Valery would fly in the plywood craft of the young aviation enthusiasts.

He would usually fasten the noisily squeaking glider onto his shoulders and, surrounded by youths, would go to the starting point and before the worshipful eyes of his admirers would be the first to fly around in their new creation.

He often "baptized" the Special Air Command functionaries in his J-13. Oleg Antonov, the well-known general aircraft builder and the creator of the current Anteev, recalling his younger days, tells of when he had the honor of climbing into the cabin of the J-13 and sitting in the copilot's seat next to Valery Chkalov, who, after reaching altitude, asked where the field was and, after receiving the correct answer, gave the plane's controls to the youth: "I took the controls with a sinking heart and with careful motions tried to keep the plane on its prescribed course. I could feel that the plane was drifting to the left and that I had to guide it more positively out of a bank, but I somehow did not have enough confidence the first time to exert enough effort to control this relatively small aircraft."

When the bank became noticeable, Valery Pavlovich good-naturedly put his hands on the controls and said: "What are you gawking at? The plane is drifting off course and you're not reacting. This is how it should be done!" And with a decisive motion he leveled the plane and corrected the course.

But just the same, Chkalov longed for fighter flying. Once, after returning home after a flight in the J-13, he took a photograph of himself and wrote on the back: "It's boring to look at you, Valery Pavlovich. What you need is a fast machine like a fighter. But what can you do, keep on carrying passengers and even cargo!"

This inscription gives a complete impression of how Valery Chkalov lived.

In August of 1930 he set off for his native Vasilevo. He stopped on the way in Moscow, spoke with some friends, and as a result of their advice submitted a report to the Air Force with the request to be returned to military aviation.

Two months went by. Valery Pavlovich and Olga Erazmovna lived anxiously, both understanding very well that their future lives would be happy and their hearts and souls fulfilled only if Chkalov was serving in military aviation.

However difficult it was for Valery, he endured the misfortune that had befallen him much better at home on the Volga.

In November his report was accepted and by order number 274 of the Air Force Scientific Research Institute dated November 11, 1930, V. P. Chkalov was enrolled in the Test Pilot Institute.

PART TWO

In the World of Creation

4

Test Pilot for the Air Force Scientific Research Institute

Thus, Valery Chkalov was once again in the Red Army Air Force. His assignment to the Scientific Research Institute underscored his great flying mastery, since only the most gifted military fliers in the country were selected for the Institute. Such famous pilots as Gromov, the former instructor at the Serpukhov School, and Yumashev, who together with Gromov had succeeded in returning Valery Pavlovich to the Army, worked here as test pilots. Here he met the pilot and airplane builder V. A. Stepanchenok, the Kiev fighter pilot A. F. Anisimov, I. F. Kozlov, and A. I. Zalevsky.

The Air Force Scientific Research Institute had been in existence for only four years and was organized on the base of a scientific-experimental field.

The Institute, like a mirror, always reflects the development of military aviation technology. Here Valery Pavlovich saw convincingly with his own eyes how the Party of the Bolsheviks, the Soviet Government, and the whole nation were intensifying their strength and seeking the means to leave behind quickly and with decisive measures the backwardness left over from Imperial Russia.

The First Five Year Plan for economic development, which had as one of its primary goals the guarantee of a quickening in the pace of the nation's industrialization through the construction of heavy industry plants, foresaw the creation of a series of spin-off industries that had not existed in our country before, including airplane, instrument, and engine construction.

Chkalov was especially struck by the fact that in 1921 the Council of Labor and Defense (STO) upon the initiative of Vladimir Ilich Lenin, created a Commission for a Ten Year Aircraft Construction Program, which had as its goat the development of a maximal program for the rehabilitation of aviation enterprises.

The Soviet Government gave a great deal of significance to the role of fighter aviation, announcing in 1921 a competition to create a domestic fighter. As a result the first Soviet fighter planes were planned and constructed: the I-1 designed by D. P. Grigorovich and N. N. Polikarpov, and the MK-21 designed by M. M. Shishmarev and V. L. Korovin.[23]

Chkalov was told that subsequently a designer's bureau was to be organized at GAZ-1 [State Aircraft Factory 1] and headed by Polikarpov. His first work was the I-400 fighter, with a 400-horsepower engine and a projected speed of up to 264 kilometers per hour, which at the time significantly exceeded the accomplishments of other nations. This machine, after a series of modifications including an M-5 engine and increased armament, went into serial production in 1925 under the name I-1.

Grigorovich's design bureau simultaneously prepared the I-2 fighter, which also went into serial production.

In 1928 Polikarpov produced a new fighter, a biplane with a water-cooled engine, and it was given a designation of I-3.

The famous student of N. E. Zhukovsky, A. N. Tupolev, rolled out onto a field in June 1927 his all-metal I-4 fighter with an air-cooled engine.[24]

All these fighters were subjected to testing at the Air Force's Scientific Research Institute. Tactical devices for the military application of these planes were also worked out there.

In the spring of 1930, a highly maneuverable I-5 fighter armed with four PV-1 machine guns and capable of speeds of up to three hundred kilometers per hour was produced by Polikarpov and Grigorovich.

As he listened to the stories of the head of the aircraft division of the Scientific Research Institute, his old cohort, the engineer and experienced fighter pilot I. F. Petrov, Chkalov never thought that in two years his fate would come to be linked with that of the talented designer Polikarpov until the end of his life.

The Scientific Research Institute based its flying section in Moscow at the Central Field, on which were also situated a multitude of aviation organizations, military and civilian agencies. Surrounded by factory buildings, the tall buildings along the capital's Leningrad Highway, and the radio transmitters on October Field, the Central Field soon became too crowded for the Institute, so the Air Force command started to build a large complex of laboratory and airport facilities and a large flying field for the Institute near a small town not far from Moscow.

But while construction was going on, the experimenters at the Research Institute at the Central Field carried out investigations and tests of aviation technology.

Chkalov threw himself into a completely new line of work. He came to life again.

Olga Erazmovna was not able to move to Moscow right away because Valery Pavlovich did not have an apartment. He himself was staying with friends.

In Moscow, Chkalov quickly renewed friendship with the master of aerobatics—test pilot Alexander Frolovich Anisimov, with whom he had studied ten years before at the Yegorevsk Theoretical Aviation School.

Anisimov was seven years older than Chkalov. A former Red Guard soldier and a participant in the battle to overthrow the Provisional Bourgeois Government, he had fought during the October days against the cadets of the counter-revolutionary Vladimir School. Anisimov had volunteered as a motor mechanic in the Fifth Red Army Socialist Aviation Detachment, which fought battles on many fields against interventionist and internal counter-revolutionaries. On May 10, 1920, he had become a member of the Communist Party of the Soviet Union (CPSU).

After completing the Yegorevsk Theoretical School, Anisimov had gone to the First Sevastopol School while Chkalov enrolled in the Borisoglebsk Flying School. For a short time they had studied together at the Serpukhovsk School, and now they were together once again at the Research Institute.

Before being assigned to the Institute, Anisimov had been a team commander in the Third Kiev Fighter Squadron, where he developed into one of the best pilots in Soviet aviation and an unsurpassed master of aerial combat. He was a tall, broad-shouldered, snub-nosed brute with a smiling rosy face. When Chkalov arrived at the Research Institute, Anisimov already had two years' experience as a test pilot.

Chkalov was attracted not only by Anisimov's love of life and the romantic nature of the former Red Guard solider, but more importantly, by his wholehearted love for the art of aerial acrobatics and the search for new ways to perform.

This meeting between two talented fighter pilots, equals in bravery, resourcefulness, and flying mastery, quickly led to friendship, devotion, and a mutual respect that lasted until death.

A. A. Turzhansky, who was at that time a formation commander at the Research Institute, recalled these two friends in his memoirs thus:

> Once two of the formation's pilots, Anisimov and Chkalov, received instructions simultaneously to each test a plane. The first the I-4 fighter designed by A. N. Tupolev; the second—the I-5 fighter. Each had his own zone for carrying out the assignment. They finished their flights at the same time and both were gliding into the aerodrome for a landing. Standing at the takeoff point, I observed them with pleasure. Suddenly Chkalov's plane sharply changed his glide pattern, steeply climbed at full throttle and from there made a dive at Anisimov; but the latter, obviously having observed Chkalov carefully, moved out of striking range with a quick maneuver and decisively began to attack. An aerial "battle" began at an altitude of 200 meters. The planes darted straight up into the sky, then swooped down, and it seemed like they were going to smash up on the field. But literally right above the ground they "rolled vertically" into the sky with steep turns and up there continued their insane carousel. Coming in for a landing, the planes dashed off sideways and made another circle.
>
> The field commandant Raivicher cried in fear: "Now they're going to collide! Now they'll perish!"
>
> The "battle" continued for six or seven minutes, after which the two fighters lined up next to each other and made an excellent landing in tandem. Seeing me at the takeoff point, the pilots straightened out their leather jackets, tightened their belts, and came up to me and briefly reported that the assignment was completed. But I could see guilty expressions on their faces. I had to decide how to react to this severe violation of flying discipline. Imprison both of them for ten days? But they would expect that and it would hardly be an instructive measure to take. I decided to fight fire with fire.
>
> "I observed your 'battle,'" I said calmly to the both of them. "It was weak! No real spirit, energy; very little initiative. After refueling, repeat the 'battle' but conduct it in an exemplary manner, as if it were war. I won't limit the altitude, but I must warn you—be more careful, don't disturb other planes, but in everything else, I give you complete freedom! Carry on!"

"Yes, sir!" they both answered and glanced at each other: an expression of confusion was written on their faces. After meeting with each other, they went to their machines.

Their planes went to separate sides and met at the center of the field at an altitude of 1,000 meters. The "battle" began. There was much art, beauty and fearlessness in it, but it lacked that persistent energy of the first flight. Both attempted to restrain themselves in the allotted zone. . . .

I praised both of them and said that if one of them wanted to make a flight that went beyond the set limitations, then I hoped that he would warn me ahead of time. I would not interfere and would permit them to exceed the set altitude if it were necessary for the test.

The experiment worked.

The institute command obliged the test pilots to be able to fly all the types of machines that were being tested. As a result, Valery Pavlovich had to study a variety of different types and makes of planes, engines, and their special equipment and armament in order to be able to fly them knowledgeably. Chkalov understood that for this a higher level of knowledge was required than he had needed in the military ranks. It was essential not only to know the complete construction of the components, but also to know the fields of aerodynamics, fuel, and thermodynamics, and especially stability, guidance, and gyroscope theories.

Valery Pavlovich regretted that he had not been able to complete the Cherepovetsk Technical School, understanding very well that it does not hurt a good test pilot to have a higher technical education. Yet Chkalov's natural abilities allowed him to master quickly the complex program created by the command of the flight testing formation.

Chkalov became familiar with the first institution for scientific aviation research, the famous Central Aerohydrodynamic Institute (TsAGI), which had been founded in 1918 by a decree from Lenin at the suggestion of Zhukovsky. Chkalov was struck by the immensity of the place.

In 1931 TsAGI, led after Zhukovsky's death by the academician S. A. Chaplygin, had the world's largest wind tunnel, consisting of an eight-faceted channel almost fifty meters long and three to six meters in diameter and a two-hundred-meter-long experimental tank.

At TsAGI Chkalov learned of the prominent Russian scientists and aviation designers who had worked there from the moment of its inception, especially V. P. Vetchinkin, B. S. Stechkin, G. M. Musinants, K. A. Ushakov, N. S. Nekrasov, A. N. Tupolev, and A. A. Arkhangelsky.

Valery Pavlovich attended a lecture given by the creator of the world's first scientifically based theory of spin—military aviation engineer V. S. Pyshnov.

The value of this work was especially apparent to Chkalov, who knew very well that the spin was a complex and very dangerous phenomenon that had caused the majority of aviation catastrophes at that time.

In a short time Valery Pavlovich had mastered the majority of the aircraft found at the Research Institute. The U-2; the R-5 designed by Polikarpov; the BB-l, and R-3, R-6, and TSh-2 of the Central Design Bureau; the I-5 designed by Grigorovich and Polikarpov; the Italian ChR; the German Heinkel (I-6) fighter—this is an incomplete list of the aircraft that the novice was able to try out in the air as he carried out flying exercises testing planes, engines, armament, and instruments.

In the process of his testing work, the pilot had dealings not only with his own leading engineers, the heads of the institute's departments and laboratories, and aircraft designers, but also with creators of engines, cannons, and machine guns, and aerobatic and navigational instruments.

He met engine designers A. D. Shvetsov, V. Ya. Klimov; armorers V. A. Degtyarev, L. V. Kurchevsky, and B. G. Shpitalin; and navigators B. V. Sterligov, G. S. Frenkel, N. A. Karbansky, I. T. Spirin, S. A. Danilin, and L. P. Sergeev.

■

In the summer, Chkalov received an assignment to fly in a TB-1 to Crimea to test new bombs.[25]

Besides the crew, the commander of the airship brought along munitions men headed by an experienced chief engineer.

They reached their prescribed base point on the same day. In view of the dangerous nature of the tests, a level section of the steppe had been chosen for the flights and the experimental bombs had been brought beforehand and fitted out.

The next day had been set for bombing runs. The morning sun was already fairly hot when a slightly lazy voice with a Nizhny

Novgorod accent was heard near the twin-engined bomber: "Hurry up, you death-dealers!"

"We're finishing up right now, comrade Chkalov," answered the young ordnance specialist, turning the tail section of a bomb that had just been suspended in the clasp of the bomb-holder.

Chkalov stood under the wing of the twin-engined bomber, first looking at the steppe sprawling out to the horizon, then taking a look at the bomb, which resembled a pike hitched up high by the hand of an able fisherman.

Soon, the chief munitions engineer reported that everything was ready and the ship's captain, giving the formation command, ordered: "Start up your engines! Keep your eyes open—bomb only on a dime!"

Chkalov sat in the left seat; the flight engineer and armorer were located in the rear compartments. The chief munitions engineer crawled through last to the forward navigator-bombardier's cabin. When he came in sight of the plane's captain, Valery Pavlovich asked him: "Tell me, are your toys going to explode under the aircraft on takeoff?"

"I don't think so! They shouldn't, captain," answered the engineer-bombardier evasively.

"Tell me straight—who the hell knows what we're flying to test?"

The armorer grew silent and hid behind the door on his deck. The flight engineer announced that they were ready for takeoff. Chkalov gave both engines gas carefully. Overloaded with explosives, the plane raced along the steppe, leaving behind a wall of dust.

Everything was going well, if you did not count the wild turbulence, which threw the overweight aircraft around like a toy, first upwards, then downwards.

The sea became visible. Valery turned left and the plane flew along the coast without shaking, as if through butter. The route then led once more away from the sea and as it headed inland the machine started to toss around again.

There appeared woods, green plowed fields, fruit orchards, and whitish villages and settlements.

Suddenly, there was a sharp bang on the left. The plane was thrown on its side. The thought raced through Chkalov's head: "Did a bomb really go off?" With the strength of his steel muscles, he leveled the aircraft and at this point noticed the shaking on the port side. After a few seconds, he turned off the port engine.

Soon afterwards, the flight engineer reported that the connecting rod on the port engine had apparently broken.

With only one engine and overloaded with bombs and fuel, the TB-1 flew at minimum speed and with a slight loss of altitude. Chkalov's face was calm, although his eyes quickly glanced over the terrain. The steep, deep ravines made it impossible to find a suitable place for landing the damaged aircraft.

The engineer-bombardier sensed this especially keenly. He could clearly imagine the forced landing in a ravine and blanched when he pictured the explosion of several hundred kilograms of bombs hanging under the machine's fuselage. The bombardier, without hesitating, opened the hatch in the bomb compartment and was ready to free the aircraft of the dangerous cargo when suddenly he heard a knock on the duralumin trim of the ship. He glanced back and saw the sizeable fist of the captain in the glass bay of the navigator's cabin.

From the behavior of the craft, Chkalov had quickly sensed the hurried preparations of the bombardier in the forward cabin, and his face became so dark and malicious that the bombardier turned pale when he stood before the captain.

"Why did you open the bomb bay?" Chkalov shouted with all his might.

"To get rid of the bombs . . . otherwise on a forced landing we'll be blown sky-high. . . ," the agitated man answered, tightly buttoned up in a leather overcoat.

"You idiot! You could have hit a village!"

Chkalov turned around for a second to check on the craft's flight, then unbuttoned his holster, took out the pistol, and placed it on his knees.

"Lie down and don't move from your place until we set down," Chkalov said in a calm voice.

The bombardier lay down in the passageway between the seats of the left- and right-hand pilots.

At the same time, the aircraft descended to three hundred meters, flying toward the sea, near which Chkalov hoped to find an acceptable place for a landing.

Turning away from the populated areas in their path, the captain carefully examined every clump of even ground while the engine, working at full power, overheated and started to smoke like a boiling samovar.

The altitude was two hundred meters. The deep blue sea appeared, dotted with light-colored running stripes of whitecaps on the tops of the waves.

"It's good that a storm has come up," flashed through Chkalov's head, and he looked hopefully at the last engine, which was throwing out uneven black puffs, resulting in the aircraft's shivering as if in a fever.

Chkalov reluctantly turned off the ignition of the last engine. It suddenly became silent and only the alarming whistle and rustle of the air flowing around the machine broke the silence reigning in the ship.

The craft quickly slid down with its dangerous cargo. Every second brought the machine ten meters closer to the ground, and with every second, anxiety grew in the armorer, who had turned as white as snow.

"Everyone aft!" Chkalov barked out.

The bombardier jumped up and hid himself in an instant in the near compartment. The flight engineer hesitated, thinking: should I go to a safer place or remain here next to the captain in case he needs me? He moved toward Chkalov carefully.

"Aft, you son of a bitch!" screamed the ship's commander even more severely, not taking his eyes from the spot he had by now chosen for the forced landing.

The flight engineer moved to the back, thinking "He is concerned about others, but does not think about himself."

When there were only one hundred meters to the ground, the craft was over the very precipice of the shore of the Black Sea. The pilot turned the machine steeply to the left. The wing of the TB-1 almost touched the ground. Chkalov banked the plane emphatically and directed the leveled machine along a shoreline strip of sun-bleached ground. The pilot calmly landed his craft on three points just as at a field.

In a few seconds, the bomber stood next to the precipice, swaying slightly from the gusts of wind flying in from the sea.

Valery climbed out of the pilot's cockpit and, unbuttoning his overalls, breathed in deeply the clean sea air.

Waves crashed fiercely against the cliffs. The sky was obscured by clouds. In the distance, burning threads of lightning flashed.

"There it is, our sea," said Chkalov. The flight engineer stood nearby, looking into the face of his captain. He was struck by the calmness that filled the powerful figure of Valery Pavlovich.

"Captain, did we almost bury ourselves?" the engineer decided to ask.

"'Almost' doesn't count in aviation," Chkalov answered jokingly. "But you tell me, what the hell kind of an aircraft is this?"

"The engines are old, but it still flies. . . ."

"Well, buddy! Have you heard what they've thought up for the Five Year Plan? We will be flying with our own engines, and ours, brother, are more reliable. Hey, the golden age is only beginning."

Valery sat down, lowering his legs over the precipice, and watched the sea. Smiling, he followed the rush of the waves.

The flight engineer crawled to the damaged engine and the munitions engineer came up to Chkalov and started to circle uncomfortably around him, afraid to start up a conversation.

"Captain, what are we going to do with the bombs?"

"We are going to stun the fish in the Black Sea. What are you worrying about them for?" said Chkalov ironically, looking at the engineer.

"But Captain, these are valuable experimental bombs."

"But you wanted to throw them wherever they landed, and maybe into a village."

"Yes, but according to regulations we can't land with bombs."

"Hey you, engineer, you have loads of education but your head needs to be set straight. What if you dropped them onto a house? How many people would you have destroyed, as if that were nothing? Well? How would you look into the eyes of a mother, knowing that we had taken the life of her children? Think about it, and don't worry about your bombs. You and I will still be able to test them as they should be tested."

Valery unexpectedly rushed from the cliff down to the very edge of the water. Then, jumping across stone to stone, he stopped by the cliff, which was shaking from the crashing of the storm waves.

A few days went by at the emergency landing site before they sent a new engine to replace the old one. They took the bombs to one of the field strips of the Odessa Flying School, to which Valery Pavlovich ferried his TB-1 after it was repaired. Here he found out that none other than his favorite Papa, the former Commander of the First Red Banner Fighter Squadron, Ivan Panfilovich Antoshin, had recently been appointed head of the institution.

The meeting between old friends was joyful and warm. Antoshin already knew about all the unpleasantries that had been endured by his favorite during the years of their absence, and was upset by the vulgar disregard of Chkalov's great flying artistry and his innovative search for new techniques in aerobatics.

After finding out that Antoshin was still flying a fighter, Valery asked Ivan Panfilovich to give him his aircraft. Papa could not refuse Valery's request, and he himself was filled by curiosity.

Valery Pavlovich tried out the engine, took off, and made some amazing maneuvers right above the ground. In reality this whole flight was just one extended maneuver. Here Antoshin saw a fighter's genuine upside-down flight.

Papa was convinced that before him now was not the young flier who had served him four years ago, but a grown man who had gained wisdom from flying experience.

They attended the Odessa Opera together and also dropped by the grave of Lt. Shmidt.[26] During his time off from test flying, Antoshin allowed the native of the Volga region to fish to his heart's content, and to swim in the sea. Frequently he himself accompanied him in the early mornings.

Valery had the rare ability to become acquainted quickly with people and to become friends with them. He had already established himself among the fishermen, and on his days off, often sailed with them to sea.

After this month, the friendship between Valery and Papa grew even stronger.

■

While Chkalov was testing new bombs, the author of this book continued to serve as a senior pilot in the Twentieth Division of the Aviation Detachment, which was commanded by Nikolai Alexandrovich Andreyev, a former Czarist officer, a participant in World War I, and a flier and commander of an aerial subunit in the Civil War.

After Krasilnikov and Popov, the commander of my team became Vasili Nikolaiovich Zhdanov. (Zhdanov had just returned from an assignment in Afghanistan; he was also a former officer in the war, a music hall artist, an amazing flier and an inexhaustibly happy person.)

In a short while we exchanged the remaining German U-21 craft for Russian-made R-1 and R-3[27] planes. The U-21 distinguished itself with the perfidious habit of catching on fire aloft and without warning, turning the body and soul of aviation enthusiasts into dust in its devilish flames.

At the end of 1931, an Air Force inspection team unexpectedly came to our detachment with the assignment of painstakingly testing the piloting techniques of our flight staff. Brigade Commander A. A. Turzhansky—whom we heard from our hangar neighbors, the fliers of the Scientific Research Institute, was a stern but honest person—invited me to fly the R-1.

My detachment commander was very worried and asked me to be extremely careful in carrying out the ordered assignments. (During World War II he had been in charge of long-range aviation for the Air Force, and held the rank of Colonel-General of Aviation.)

I tried not to let Nikolai Alexandrovich down and did not worry about myself at all. Apparently because of this, the wry, intelligent, good-looking Brigadier Commander with the dark brown eyes smiled at me and thanked me for an excellent flight.

N. A. Andreyev was pleased with the results of the inspection and because of this, even days later, very rarely gave our comrades a reprimand, even when we deserved one.

But, as is known, no inspection is insignificant. For me, it turned out to be a turning point in my life.

Two months after the flights with Brigadier Commander Turzhansky, I was called to Andreyev's office. In the presence of Team Commander Zhdanov, an order was read from the Head of the Air Force, concerning my being assigned as a test pilot to the Scientific Research Institute of the Air Force, where I was required to report immediately.

I had never dreamed that such an honor could befall me, to work as a test pilot for the Scientific Research Institute. Therefore, I sincerely requested permission from the detachment commander to be allowed to stay here as a pilot.

Andreyev made several attempts, but the Air Force command firmly demanded that its order be carried out.

Not knowing anything about the Air Force's Scientific Research Institute, I was glad when I was ordered to immediately report for a night flight. It seemed to me that a pilot best becomes familiar both with his work and with others at an airfield or in flight.

Our group, consisting of four novices, gathered together near a large hangar of the Institute's flight section while the summer evening was slowly and quietly being extinguished.

The red neon obstruction lights flashed on the hangars and night irrevocably claimed its rights.

The airport landing lights snatched away long, white strips from the darkness. In the cones of light, a myriad of tiny dust particles, midges, and moths bathed in the light.

We set off for the starting point where the aircraft stood, and around which the mechanics were busy.

Not far from us, next to the craft stood two men whose faces were lit up by the flashes of cigarettes and matches.

Someone in our group whispered: "These are the ace test pilots, Anisimov and Chkalov."

Soon afterwards a commanding voice was heard, "To your positions."

The experienced field personnel, regardless of the darkness, quickly formed two lines. The section commander, calling the pilots in order, gave the instructions for carrying out that evening's flights.

"Comrade Chkalov, you have the duty this evening of conducting a flight with these pilots who have been newly assigned to the Institute and have arrived from the ranks. Check out how they fly at night, and if necessary, train them. And then release them on their own."

"Yes, sir, Comrade Commander. I will test them out and release whomever necessary."

"Get to work. Here is your group." The Commander pointed to a group of four young fliers, in which I stood on the flank (a little bit nervously) listening to every word of the Commander's.

Chkalov came up to us, and in a low, almost hoarse voice, asked, looking at me: "What is your name?"

"Baidukov," I answered.

"How many years have you been flying?"

"Five."

"What aircraft are you flying?"

"Reconnaissance craft."

"I didn't ask you that. Have you flown the R-1?"

"Yes, sir." I answered, slightly struck by the vulgar tone and also by the fact that he was addressing me in familiar terms, as well as noticing his distinctive accent.

"Well, that's what I would have said, that I fly the R-1 instead of saying 'reconnaissance craft.'"

Silent for a while, he added: "Get in the aircraft, I'll see you shortly." Chkalov disappeared without saying where the airplane was parked or what its number was. We stood there in confusion.

"An angry fellow," said my friend.

I rushed to the aircraft in order to look for, or more exactly, to guess at, the machine in which I was supposed to set off on my examination flight.

The field was noisy. In the darkness, intermittent communication signal lights blinked. At times large, fiery circles of an exhaust of some kind of fighter flashed. The evening air trembled from the noise of the propellers and engines, mercilessly cutting the darkness.

Running along a row of aircraft, I tried to catch sight of the wide-shouldered figure of Chkalov in order to find out where our craft was located.

I would walk up to a group and ask an instructor, but he would answer me, "What, don't you see that Chkalov isn't here?" in such a tone that I felt uncomfortable (although I could have explained that I didn't know Chkalov by his face since the darkness prevented me from seeing properly).

Just the same, I continued to rush between the aircraft, and, not missing a single silhouette, would run up to him and shout loudly in his ear: "Chkalov to the Commander."

I had thought up this phrase, hoping that with such an authoritative announcement I would be able to attract my instructor by voice.

Soon I stumbled into two pilots, and, repeating my announcement, suddenly I heard the voice in its Volga accent: "What are you yelling about? To what Commander?"

This was Chkalov. I grew silent, trying to think of how to get out of the silly position in which I had found myself.

"To what Commander?"

The instructor repeated the question, came up to me, and lit a match. My face was illuminated by the lighted match. He burst out laughing: "Baidukov, well, why were you silent?"

The stern features and sharp wrinkles of his face softened for a moment, but the match went out, and in the darkness I could see only a silhouette, that of a short and wide-shouldered man.

"Have a cigarette and we'll board the aircraft right now."

And he, either forgetting that I had managed to lie to him about the call to the Commander, or guessing about what I had done, calmly continued his conversation.

"I'm going to take the young ones out tonight."

"Look, you, they think they're going to make a teacher out of you?"

As this conversation continued, I recalled a multitude of stories about the fighter pilot Chkalov.

"Well, Shurka, I'm going, the guys have been standing around too long."

And, turning to me, he nodded and said: "Let's go, Baidukov."

It was noisy from the whistle of air being cut, and in the sky blue, red, and white aircraft lights appeared. The dust from the aircraft taking off formed a blanket, making the dark of the night look even darker, hurting the eyes. Soon we neared a two-seater biplane. I let out a sigh of relief. This type of machine was familiar to me from my service flying experience.

"What are you sighing about?" asked the instructor. "And why are you being tested today?"

"By an order, Commander." I answered, not understanding the essence of the question.

"We're all doing it by order, but everyone does it for different reasons. Have you flown at night for long?"

"Counting the fall flights, it will be half a year," I answered, thinking that this sparrow would not be caught in the chaff.

"Well, let's go into the cockpit. The assignment will be a simple, circular flight."

"Yes, sir, Commander." I called to the flight mechanic and together we turned on the lights and carefully looked over the undercarriage and the empennage.

Chkalov climbed into the aircraft and, ducking his head to the side of the rear cabin, was whistling something.

We had already completed the inspection when the mechanic started to say into my ear: "Look, don't make a mess of it; Chkalov doesn't like it when you fly too quietly. He'll grind you into the dust. He can't stand timid pilots."

I climbed into the cockpit of the aircraft thinking of the advice given to me by the mechanic. I started the engine. Long lines of bluish flames from the exhaust glittered softly against the side of the fuselage. I took the intercom: "Commander, I'm ready."

"Well, carefully taxi and take off."

I requested takeoff clearance. Tower gave a light signal, which signified permission to take off. I looked out along both sides, and, not seeing any kind of danger, gave full throttle to the engine and commenced takeoff. Within a few seconds we were already above the roofs of the hangars. The red reflection of the obstruction lights made the wings transparent for an instant. The contours of the wing spar and ribs were darkly outlined against the canvas. Was it the reflection of the calmly expectant eyes of the instructor that I noticed in the front-view mirror, or had the advice of the mechanic affected me? Slightly pressing the machine to gain speed, I put it into a sharp bank with a steep climb. The plane, absorbed by the darkness, turned to the left in a remarkable zig-zag and I carefully and slyly looked into the mirror, from which I expected the approval or judgment of my actions. Completely unexpectedly, the hand of the instructor, with the index finger lifted up, was in front of my nose. After the landing, Chkalov climbed out of the rear cabin and, leaning over across the side toward me, said:

"Very good, what can I say? Fly the pattern and train by yourself if you feel the need. There is no reason for me to lead you around."

"Yes, sir, Commander."

"Well, you've really taken to this Commander bit. Call me simply Chkalov since you, too, are a Commander, an instructor, and a test pilot."

"Very well, Chkalov," I answered smiling.

"What is your name?"

"Georgy."

"Well, that means Egor, and we in the Volga call people Egorushka. Well, go do something, Egor, but don't fly too far. I still have to occupy myself with the others."

In the glow of the cockpit lights, the eagle-hooked nose gave Chkalov a certain predatory look, although his bluish eyes looked at you softly and tenderly.

The next morning I found out that Valery Pavlovich had not released any other pilots in our foursome to fly independently.

So the flight that the instructor liked on that dark, summer night above a Moscow field made me familiar with this human bird about whom there were so many legends. But not one of us could foresee, at that time, that in the future, destiny would bring us closer and closer with every passing year and that our lives would become completely dependent upon each other.

Recalling this introduction into the test flight ranks, I always think of Valery Pavlovich, not only as an experienced instructor able to determine on a single flight the flying capabilities of the person being tested, but also as a completely trustworthy person.

I became convinced of Chkalov's unusual ability to judge people quickly, especially flyers, due to an incident that occurred involving a pilot, Pyotor Mikailovich Stefanovsky, who had been assigned to the Scientific Research Institute at almost the same time as I had been, the beginning of 1932. He had to retrain in order to fly heavy aircraft.

This is how Pyotor Mikailovich recalls this incident in his memoir *300 Unknowns:*

I became familiar with a typical representative of an all-around test pilot before my first flight on the TB-1 [an M-17 with two engines].

We met at the field. A stocky man in a flight suit with a fur collar, he listened to my report of arriving under his command with a good-hearted smile on his large, windblown face and waved his hand to one side.

"Let's forget the formalities," he said.

This was Valery Pavlovich Chkalov. Not yet, of course, that Chkalov whose name would soon be known to the entire country and the world. In flight circles, in those days, he was known as an extremely innovative and excellent pilot, a bosom buddy, and an extraordinary friend. I somehow trusted him right away; he was my first instructor in heavy craft aviation.

Such a person gives all that he knows, won't blow up at insignificant things, won't report you to command if you goof something up. But what kind of error was it possible to make in this aircraft? Set the route, determine the speed, follow the course, and correct the drift.

We sat in our seats in the cockpit; Chkalov asked, as if an afterthought: "Fighter pilot?"

"Fighter pilot."

"Well, then, let's go."

On takeoff, Valery Pavlovich smoothly turned up the revs on both engines and the heavy aircraft lightly lifted up into the air without any pressure. Chkalov sat quietly at the controls as if he were drinking tea.

"It's understandable," I thought. "What is there to worry about? The bomber is stable in the air, it doesn't yaw around, it doesn't roll like a fighter."

Completely unexpectedly, the aircraft went into a steep bank. There were only 300 meters to the ground—no more.

Irreproachably completing several maneuvers, Chkalov sharply turned the nose of the plane up, smoothly throttled back, and turned the craft into a steep dive. "What is he doing, dammit?" The ground was closing in quickly I looked at my instructor anxiously. After all, we were not in a fighter, and he's "drinking tea."

Now there were no more than 50 meters to the ground.

Rising rapidly, the wooden homes leaped before our eyes. A few-seconds and. . . .

Letting out a roar from its engines, the craft pulled up, turned easily, and adjusted to horizontal flight.

There was ringing in my head. A bomber in such a maneuver. I looked at Chkalov in amazement.

"Understood?" he asked, smiling broadly.

I nodded my head in agreement.

"Try it yourself."

"Right away?"

But the instructor had already completely freed himself from the controls.

"Well?"

The altitude was 300 meters. I made a no less steep bank, then, lifting the nose of the aircraft, smoothly throttled back and, just as positively as Chkalov, threw the machine into a dive. It seemed that the craft wasn't being carried down, but that the earth itself was rushing up to meet us. I felt neither the massive dimensions nor the heaviness of the ship. The altitude was already 150–100 meters. It was time. The aircraft broke off its dive with a spring and shot up.

"Very good," approved Valery Pavlovich in his Volga accent. "You understood. Go in for a landing."

After the second landing, Chkalov surrendered the controls and his face again broke out into a smile.

"Fly it yourself," he said. "There is nothing for me to do."

So, this is the way I started flying in heavy aircraft.

The flight with V. P. Chkalov opened a new road for me in heavy aircraft flight, and drastically changed my flying career. I became, once and for all, a military test pilot.

The exactness of Stefanovsky's evaluation of Chkalov and his belief in him have been justified by his successful life as a test pilot.

∎

Flying with uniform precision in all types of aircraft—fighters, reconnaissance planes, bombers, cargo and sports planes—Valery Chkalov, test pilot of the Scientific Research Institute, completed the most varied assignments. He determined the reasons for the instability of the I-5 fighter on its run after a landing, as a result of which, in many sections of the Air Force, there had been several serious accidents. He also flew in pitch blackness to test night sights, attacking targets on the Kuznetsky Target Range.[28]

Valery Pavlovich was an undoubted expert in the testing of the maneuvering capacities of new fighters in aerial combat.

In this case, Chkalov and Anisimov, two inseparable friends on the ground and two rivals in the air, would usually be assigned two fighters of different types.

When an amazing battle between these expert fighter pilots was conducted in the air, everything stopped at the Central Field. It grew quiet, the people bewitched by the battle between these talented pilots.

Afterwards, the friends would exchange aircraft and conduct a second round of uniquely complex, daring, and incomprehensibly exact mutual attacks, which would be recorded by on-board camera guns and control devices from the ground. After such flights as these, it was unmistakably clear to the chief engineer what the limits were of any given fighter.

After concluding a flight, Chkalov, when he was left on his own, would grow sad. He had still been unable as yet to get even a small room in one of the Moscow hotels and bring his wife and son from Leningrad. Without them, life after flying was boring.

At this time, there came disturbing rumors and letters from Vasilevo. His father had become ill. Like any person who had never been sick in his whole life, Pavel Gregorivich was struck unexpectedly.

Valery Pavlovich reported this sad news to his wife. Olga Erasmovna, taking her son, set off to her father-in-law.

Valery sent his father packages and cheered him up with all kinds of news in his letters. In the spring of 1931, Pavel Gregorivich died. He was buried in a traditional gentleman's burial mound.

Chkalov was greatly affected by the death of his father, but one summer day, as he climbed into an aircraft, it was as if a hurricane blew away all the sadness and grief that had been tormenting the soft soul of this brave person.

Somehow, completely unexpectedly, complaints started coming in regarding the metal undercarriage of the R-1 reconaissance aircraft. While coming in for a landing, they would, at the last moment, suddenly pull to the left or right. This always led to a wing striking the ground, after which a fire or explosion would add to the catastrophe.

One of these deformed aircraft, which had luckily remained intact, was received at the Scientific Research Institute on a railroad car. After a final assembly and survey of the defective aircraft, it was decided that they should fly it, determine the reason for the problem, and make recommendations to the fliers of various Air Force stations and also to the manufacturers.

On the surface, this was everyday work. But there was much insidiousness and deadly danger in it, since without preliminary flights it was impossible to give a simple diagnosis for the machine's defect, much less determine a course of treatment.

This is why, along with such young, fledgling pilots as I, they also assigned first-class test pilots Chkalov and Anisimov—these doctors of the art of flying—to study the defects of the R-1.

True, at this time, I had already managed to master the difficulties in testing the flat spin of an airplane in which a very experienced crew had crashed before my arrival at the Research Institute. In addition, I had been able to conduct the testing of an aircraft with a slotted wing and had familiarized myself in detail with the fine points of its aerodynamics in flight at extremely high attack angles. And finally, in the last few months of my work at the Institute, I had managed some limited flight in fighters and heavy bombers, which had significantly expanded my flying experience.

However, all that I have enumerated, all that had been recently achieved, in no way was able to place me even on the extreme left flank of the column of test pilots who were the chief aces of the Air Force's Scientific Research Institute.

This is why Chkalov was the first to go over the unresponsive, ailing R-1. Valery Pavlovich, while making a takeoff run, would not allow the craft to become airborne prematurely and held it for some time in a ground run, very near the ground, before letting the aircraft gain altitude.

After reaching a thousand meters, the test pilot started to glide toward a cumulus cloud to "set" the aircraft on it. It was evident that at a certain moment the R-1 turned sharply on its wing and started to spin. Subsequently, the aircraft again gained in altitude, climbing at an extreme angle of attack. Chkalov once again started a glide toward the very same cloud; it was only on the fourth attempt that the craft, while it was being leveled, pulled up and didn't turn on its wing.

Finally, Chkalov made the defective machine complete a series of loops, wingovers, combat turns, banks, and glides.

"Hey, that rascal Chkalov; did you see how quickly he figured it out?" said Anisimov to me with pride, carefully watching the movements of his friend in the pattern. During this time, Alexander

Frolovich did not manage to finish smoking a single cigarette. After the R-1 came in for a classic three-point landing, Chkalov taxied the plane up to us.

Anisimov waved his hands, letting his friend know that he should not turn his engine off.

Now Valery Pavlovich looked carefully at Sasha Anisimov, while at the same time telling me how and at what moment it was necessary to use the rudder and aileron in order to prevent the unexpected collapse of the plane on its wing at the moment of landing.

In the meantime, Alexander Frolovich finished his testing of the defective machine with a series of even more complex maneuvers— including those that were categorically forbidden for the R-1 plane because of its low tensile strength.

"Is it really possible to do an Immelmann in this craft?" I asked Chkalov with bewilderment.

Valery Pavlovich looked at me slyly with his soft, light blue eyes in a way that made me very uncomfortable.

"What's with you, Baiduk? Sashka can do things that even Chaplygin[29] and Tupolev would not be able to figure out how they could have been done and, in addition, how they could be done successfully," answered Chkalov, continuing to laugh.

Anisimov landed the plane in a completely different way. When he was leveling it out, he lowered it to the ground, and, with the empennage lifted up high, touched down, pushing the control handles away from himself, not letting the craft touch down with its tail skid. Although he didn't do everything according to instructions, but in fact rather contrary to them, the aircraft completed an irreproachable landing and didn't bounce about one centimeter in its landing run.

Valery said joyfully: "See how, acting contrary to flight technique instructions, it is sometimes possible *not* to destroy yourself, even when everything points to disaster?"

The Command understood that adherence to standard instructions in that case would have resulted once again in the howl of the soul-wrenching airport siren, notifying everyone of another catastrophe. For this reason, no one said anything to Anisimov, even concerning the dangerous Immelmann maneuver with the R-1.

However, the chief engineer was ordered to halt further flights immediately, place the aircraft into a hangar, and carefully examine its modifications.

After consulting with Valery Pavlovich and Alexander Frolovich, two days later I made a flight pattern in the very same craft and was convinced how exactly they had determined the peculiarities of the aircraft and how effectively they had recommended a method of preventing further problems.

After many flights during the day and then later at night, which attracted many of the Scientific Research Institute's test pilots, instructions were drawn up for the pilots, warning them of the possible problems during the landing of the R-1.

When the report was delivered, the chief engineer, N. A. Zhem-chuzhin, who had been a pilot, said to me: "You know, these tests could have been begun only by Chkalov and Anisimov. Only people with the creativity and the initiative they have, with an incomprehensible intuition, would be able to determine the optimum methods for controlling a craft that was in a disastrous situation. They are giants of the art of aviation."

In the future, I came to be convinced many times of the accuracy of this evaluation.

■

Time went by. Regardless of the very diligent selection of flight staff, the sound of the alarms of the Central Field and then the Moscow Field often notified us of a disaster that had just occurred.

Soon I was included in the group that was headed by Anisimov. It tested fighter planes according to the assignment of the department, which was headed by flight engineer Ivan Fyodorovich Petrov, who had been an active participant in the October Revolution and the Civil War. Chkalov was also in this group.

Among Anisimov's experienced fighter group, I seemed a mere fledgling.

Of course, I had studied advanced flight techniques previously, but here it was primarily aerial acrobatics and furthermore, everything was carried out at an altitude of not one thousand or even six hundred meters, but right above the ground, no higher than one hundred or two hundred meters, where not only a mistake, but even the smallest inexactness, would lead to disaster.

A tiny fighter appeared above the hangars at Central Field and, twisting in a horizontal spin in the air, made double loops and barrels, one after the other, almost hitting the roofs of the hangars with its wings. Anisimov, hitting me on the arm, said shortly: "Valka is signing his name."

I understood this as an instruction: "This is how you should fly."

"I cannot fly like that," I answered loudly at the commander's thoughts.

Anisimov gave me an assignment to go into a pattern and fly at low altitude so that my craft wasn't visible from the field.

Chkalov had already landed. He stood on the side watching my preparation for takeoff. Obviously he noticed my indecisive actions and, coming up to me, said: "Shurka has given you complete freedom. Take advantage of the situation. Do your maneuvers at one hundred meters."

I didn't respond to the advice of my friend, put on my parachute carefully, climbed into the I-4, buckled myself in tightly, and started the engine.

As I was taxiing by Chkalov, I saw his approving smile and his hand uplifted in a greeting.

I recalled the night flight with Chkalov and my desperate turn, which had so greatly pleased Valery Pavlovich, and I began to feel better. On taking off, I lost all my fears, revved the engine after takeoff, and pulled back on the stick while simultaneously putting the craft into a continual spiral. I could see how Anisimov was shaking his fist gently in my direction, while Chkalov lifted his hand high up in the air showing his index finger.

Coming out of the pattern at an altitude of five hundred meters, I made several double turns and an Immelmann. Then I completed several turns of a spin.

Feeling that everything was going normally, I made a barrel at two hundred meters, repeated it one more time, and understood that it was necessary to rev the engine at a higher speed in order to begin a double roll of adequate speed without losing power, which was dangerous at such a low altitude.

Everything was checked. I made a dive and at two hundred meters had sufficient speed that my metal fighter did not lose power after this complicated maneuver.

I grew bold and at an altitude of one hundred meters I began an Immelmann. I had observed the ground from this altitude many times, but now the height, for some reason, seemed especially low, and, flying just above the factory stacks, I turned away from the towers of radio station transmitters.

Making up my mind finally, I revved the craft at full speed and, still at an altitude of one hundred meters, began to do an Immelmann. It was successful. I was now losing altitude on the roll and, diving one more time, gave the engine full revs and brought the machine once again up to one hundred meters and did a double roll. There was a loss of power, but it was acceptable. I repeated these maneuvers again and again until I was completely tired. This took no more than fifteen minutes. Yes, this exercise was serious and not at all simple. But I enjoyed it very much. I flew toward the field and from above I saw how Anisimov in his favorite I-5 was gliding in for a landing upside down and was passing very low above the hangars.

"That means," I thought, "Anisimov has been following me in the air as I was carrying out the aerobatics."

But Anisimov acted like he had not observed me and knew nothing and for this reason did not make any remarks.

"Of course," I thought, "in such situations it is dangerous to praise the flier. He himself should know his limits. For that reason, our aerial chapaev is silent."

But I, as was customary, went up to Anisimov, who was standing next to Chkalov, and gave my report on the completion of the exercises and described everything I had done. Chkalov laughed and, betraying his friend, said: "Don't brag. Shurka was watching you. And you, like a dummy, saw nothing and heard nothing."

Anisimov, with a smile on his face, asked: "Very tired?"

"Very tired," I admitted.

"Well, take a rest and repeat everything in the same pattern with the I-5. It's more fun in that. You'll see."

In about six months I began to enjoy myself, and it was only necessary to be careful not to overstep the fatal boundaries.

Apparently I had actually managed to accomplish something in aerobatics near the ground, since once Valery volunteered to show me an aerial battle with frontal attacks. This was very flattering to me.

We took off in different types of fighters. After reaching altitude, I turned toward Chkalov and noticed that the engine of his plane was smoking slightly. This meant that he was revving the fighter. At this point, I gave full throttle and squinted into the optical sights, from time to time pressing the trigger of the camera gun. The crafts came closer and closer together. The distance between us became smaller with each second.

Judging by the range meter of the optical sights, there were only about five hundred meters to Chkalov's fighter. It was necessary to decide what to do from here, because in a few seconds we would go into what was called no-man's land where it was impossible to avoid a collision and where aerobatic maneuvers for turning away did not apply.

I glanced to the left, put the craft into a steep-angled climb, and made an Immelmann. After losing sight of Chkalov, I quickly made a landing at the field.

Those who had observed from the ground said that our airplanes, as they were coming up toward each other, head to head, had simultaneously climbed straight up, going vertically with the wheels coming very close to each other. It seemed to everyone that the airplanes were shaking each other's paws, but afterwards, after having completed the Immelmann, the planes flew apart in separate directions.

Chkalov landed after me. After taxiing up, he climbed out of the aircraft and, coming up to me, said: "You idiot, you're going to kill yourself."

"Seems to me that you're not the smartest person in the world, looking for trouble like that; you should have rolled into a bank," I answered quick-temperedly.

Instead of answering, he gave me the finger and, stepping back two steps, barked out: "You have a character just as stubborn as mine. You and I are obviously going to crash into each other. It would be better if you, Baiduk, would turn first or else, out of stupidity, we're going to destroy each other."

I understood that, in a real battle, Chkalov would never turn away from a frontal attack first because that would necessarily mean that the enemy would jump on his tail and he would be beaten.

■

In the meantime, the autumn of 1931 had begun. There was a great deal of talk about the "shelf" aircraft designed by Vladimir Sergeevich Vakhmistrov and engineered in our Institute.

We saw the twin-engined bomber, the TB-1, at the Central Field. "Two-tiered shelf" was a very apt nickname. On its wings towered two I-4 fighters.

The world had never seen anything like this: bombers that carried fighters on their wings. They would fly with them to the rear lines, feeding them fuel from their own tanks until the time came for aerial combat with the enemy.[30]

The tactical idea was enticing, but how could it be realized technically? Was it risky? How would the TB-1 act with this unusual cargo? How would the coupling and uncoupling mechanisms work in the air? What would happen if one of the fighters would not be able to come off the wing when the first plane had already uncoupled? What would happen if the engine of one of the fighters quit on takeoff?

Dozens of possibilities could lead to disaster.

The risk was very great, but the goal, for which all this was undertaken, was grandiose.

Taking into account the importance of the goal and the extreme complexity of testing, Command decided that only the most nerveless, gifted fliers—men who were totally fearless and, at the same time, very close to each other and who believed in each other—would be able to man these fighters.

It was clear that there was only one choice: Chkalov and Anisimov. You couldn't find better candidates.

They filled all the requirements. The two most experienced test pilots, Adam Iosovich Zalevsky and Ivan Frovovich Kozlov, who had been assigned to pilot the mother ship and to direct the experiment in flight, were in complete agreement with the choice.

At that time, we didn't truly judge the significance of the testing of the world's first stacked aircraft unit. Yet, this was a genuinely heroic deed for Chkalov, Anisimov, Zalevsky, and Kozlov.

When the TB-1 aircraft with the two I-4's taxied up to the starting point for the first flight, Chkalov was in the fighter fastened to the left wing and Anisimov in the fighter fastened to the right wing of the mother ship.

Zalevsky was the pilot of the TB-1 and Kozlov the copilot.

This occurred on December 31, 1931. The four propellers revolving on two stories gave the unit a fantastic but, at the same time, light and delicate look.

The takeoff, with the assistance of all four engines of the "flying shelf," occurred with lightning speed and yet, at the same time, gracefully; the aircraft immediately starting climbing.

The entire personal staff of the Frunze Field stopped their work and spread along the perimeter of the flying field, observing this highly complex and very dangerous experiment, which was the first of its kind in world aviation history.

The mother ship began to level off at an altitude of one thousand meters, then slowly turned back and took a course in the direction of the center of the field. Everything was going very well.

And then the long-awaited moment. First Chkalov's fighter slipped off above the wing of the TB-1, and after him, the fighter of Anisimov.

In a few seconds they had fixed bearings, each next to the wing of the mother ship. They escorted her during the approach; all three planes landed in close formation, simultaneously.

Thousands of people rushed onto the field where the machines had stopped. The test pilots embraced each other then went off to hug the embarrassed designer, Vakhmistrov.

After the first flight, the designer, at the suggestion of the crew, made a series of modifications and, beginning in 1932, the "flying shelf" began to fly more frequently on a test program.

During one of these programmed flights, Vakhmistrov was seated on the flight deck of the TB-1. The commander of the Scientific Research Institute aviation unit, Zalevsky, sat in the pilot's seat as commander of the ship. The copilot was Andrei Radionovich Sharopov, the squadron commander.

On the wings of the TB-1 stood the two I-4 planes and, as before, Chkalov piloted the left craft and Anisimov the right. Takeoff was successful; they reached the assigned altitude. Sharopov was given the signal to release the fighters.

During this crucial operation, the copilot of the mother ship committed a serious mistake. Before releasing the lock holding the empennage of Chkalov's I-4, Andrei Radionovich prematurely released the forward couples that held the undercarriage of the fighter to the mother ship. Valery's craft began to lift its nose too quickly. In an instant, Chkalov's plane would roll over onto its back and destroy itself, the carrier plane with its crew, and the fighter of Anisimov, who was watching this horrifying scene.

But Chkalov remained an unsurpassed test pilot and a man with iron nerves. In an instant he had evaluated the danger and, with a positive, quick movement of the pitch control devices, made his craft press its undercarriage onto the surface of the carrier ship's wing and then, after releasing the rear lock, he freed the empennage, easily lifted the I-4 from the TB-1, and gained altitude.

After the completion of the experiment, a crushed duralumin fragment was found where the fighter's undercarriage had been pressed down by the efforts of Chkalov, who maintained his composure throughout this dangerous moment.

Zalevsky, Sharopov, Vakhmistrov, and Anisimov—their lives had been saved, thanks to the fearless, instantaneous, faultless reaction of young test pilot Chkalov. The crew celebrated its "birthday" in the Dynamo Restaurant.

In future flights Vakhmistrov put three fighters on the TB-1.

This aerial ship with its fledglings flew south to test the tactics for military application of this new aerial concept.

The fighters would leave the aerial carrier ship in order to lift off at a high speed toward a target and to attack it with bombs in a vertical dive.

Chkalov enjoyed these flights. The feeling of increased speed in a vertical dive gave him much enjoyment and, after ejecting his load, it was possible to whirl about in the fighter at will, completing various aerobatic figures.

In particular, Valery Pavlovich sharpened to the point of perfection the slow hesitation roll.

Initially, without going too rapidly, he would smoothly turn the machine on its wing, then roll it over onto its back, holding it for a short time upside down, and then finally, and just as smoothly, turn the plane back to its original position.

If, in the beginning, speed was excessive, the hesitation roll was completed at a steep angle as if the aircraft were shooting upwards in a spin. Sometimes after a left roll of the craft, Chkalov would roll in the opposite direction.

After the hesitation roll, Valery Pavlovich would more often turn to perfecting inverted flight, hoping to attain a way to pull out of a dive and then gain altitude, or even go into the last part of a Nesterov loop, in a position where the centrifugal force doesn't press down on the pilot but throws him away from the craft, that is, in an inverted position.

The necessity of controlling a fighter this way was dictated not only by the caprice of this talented flier, but by life itself. While he was serving as a test pilot for the Institute, Chkalov was, from time to time, recommended by the Air Force Command for testing the regular flying staff of the ranks. Here he noticed that sometimes fliers would perish while carrying out aerobatic figures in mock aerial combat for completely inexplicable reasons. The Accident Review Board several times affirmed that a flier, in the moment of a spin, would somehow end up in an inverted position. No one had any idea how to get out of such an unusual condition.

Attempting to solve this new mystery, Chkalov continued to complicate his experiments with inverted flight.

Of course, he did not leave Anisimov out of it. They attained such perfection in this unusual flight method that they often would start to glide in for a landing holding their fighter planes upside down to a very low altitude, which seemed to be inevitably disastrous.

Watching from the side, it was difficult to determine the moment when the craft would roll on its wings just over the ground. Making a half roll, it would settle down lower, going into a landing angle, after which the machine would just as positively, smoothly, and precisely touch down on the field's landing markers. Such flights disturbed the Command no end, and Chkalov especially would get into difficulties for these unassigned flights.

But his enthusiasm for test flights could not extinguish in the soul of the pilot the sadness that was brought forth by his family uncertainties and his long separation from his wife and son.

It was only in the autumn of 1932 that Valery managed to get a room in the International Hotel. Olga Erazmovna and Igor arrived from Leningrad. They lived as a threesome in a small room for more than a year and a half. It was very difficult to organize the meals for the family. The cost of eating in the hotel's cafeteria was too high for Valery Pavlovich, but it was forbidden to prepare food in the hotel rooms.

But the Chkalovs quickly got used to these conditions. They bought a kerosene stove and prepared on it simple dishes in those hours when the likelihood of being observed was minimal. They often had to carry out such forbidden but necessary tasks late in the evening or even in the middle of the night.

Like a good family man, Valery Pavlovich spent all his free time with his four-year-old son and wife. Despite the crowded conditions of their room and the difficulties with food, Valery Pavlovich and Olga graciously opened the doors of their temporary living quarters and continued the Volga tradition of Chkalov family hospitality.

They were visited by people from Vasilevo and Nizhny Novgorod, and his former comrades in arms from Leningrad, Gatchina, and Bryansk would come by, including friends from the flying and technical staffs of the Research Institute.

Chkalov continued to carry out the most difficult, complex, and significant aviation technology tests, which, toward the end of the First Five Year Plan, occurred rather frequently at the Scientific Research Institute.

Given impetus by the nation of Soviets, the aviation industry in the early years of the First Five Year Plan had created a strong designer's bureau headed by such talented engineers and scientists as Tupolev, Polikarpov, S. V. Illyushin, S. A. Lavochkin, and A. S. Yakovlev.

The following aircraft were manufactured: the U-2, R-3, I-1, I-4, I-5, R-5, TB-1, R-6, TB-3, ANT-6, ANT-9, Ilyushin's gliders, and Yakovlev's specialties, along with dozens of aviation engines, aviation cannons, machine guns, hundreds of pilot's navigational instruments, and also bombing and gunnery sights.

Soviet aircraft were displayed at international shows and completed significant flights overseas. The U-2 (which in 1944 was renamed the PO-2), designed by Polikarpov, was displayed in 1928 at the Berlin Exposition.

Chkalov attentively followed the daily progress of aviation in his country, as it became a power in world aviation. He was very satisfied by this activity.

The Air Force's Scientific Research Institute had by now been transformed into a city.

The lively young fliers, engineers, and mechanics who served and worked at the Institute would fill up the suburban train in the early morning. They would travel to work singing happy songs and exchanging jokes.

In the compartment where Chkalov and Anisimov sat together, there was always an especially large group of people and it would literally shake from the continual bursts of laughter.

■

In the beginning of 1933, Chkalov was demobilized from the Air Force a second time. He had previously been sent for training as a commander (at that time there were no officers' ranks in the Soviet Army) to a place where conditions were set up much like those for beginning students with mandatory barracks life.

It was natural that such a popular, gifted, talented flier as Chkalov was watched by aircraft manufacturers. Socialist industries in these years had begun to develop much aviation technology and factories needed experienced flyers to test new aircraft. The nucleus of test pilots at these factories could be filled only at the expense of military fliers and primarily at the expense of the Air Force's Scientific Research Institute.

Thus Chkalov became a test pilot at the Menzhinsky Factory.

I recall how painfully Chkalov accepted his demobilization.

He loved the army and understood that he still had much to contribute to it. After all, he had conducted the most complex and dangerous tests of new craft and their armaments. I myself, to this very day, cannot really explain why it was necessary to take such unnecessary actions against him. Today, some people think that demobilization was good for Chkalov since it made him once again think about his actions and his relationship with discipline. It seems to me that such a point of view is very dubious and demands evidence. One way or another, everyone admits that Chkalov was a pioneer in the development of a series of difficult tactical maneuvers for fighter craft to use in a future war, and together with the other foremost Soviet flyers, he demonstrated the growing ability of fighter craft. Why then was Valery Pavlovich demobilized?

Chkalov asserted that aerial combat would be carried on, not only at high altitudes where it was possible to attain high speeds, but also at low levels, where bomber craft would commence action against small objectives on a field of battle or at nearby rear locations. As a result of this, Chkalov reasoned, there followed at least two very important practical problems:

> The aircraft had to be able to fly undetected at hedgehopping level using all the camouflaging characteristics of the terrain.
>
> As long as enemy craft would attack at low altitudes, our fighters had to be able to carry on aerial combat, both with bombers and with fighter craft that were protecting them, utilizing in this situation maneuvers not only of a horizontal character, but, more importantly, in the vertical plane, regardless of the proximity to the ground.

Of course, Chkalov asserted, such flights demand much: a reshaping of the Command's and flying staffs tactics and also, importantly, very serious training—both individual and in formation for the working out of flight techniques at hedgehopping levels and aerobatics at low altitudes.

At that time, the majority of commanders rejected such a theory, and those who accepted it understood very well that it was necessary to change the battle preparation of the fighters from the very roots because the existing instructions for flight in those days did not take anything comparable into consideration.

Who was right? Aerial combat in Republican Spain, China, Mongolia, and against the White Finns—had passed into history and war with Nazi Germany was threatening.

Today, at a greater distance from the past, it is possible to judge more objectively the thoughts and actions of Chkalov.

The experience of such commanders and fighter pilots of the Air Force as Anisimov, Stepanchenok, Smirnov, Yakushin, Serov, Suprun, Lakeev, Stefanovsky, Yevseev, Cherniavsky, Kraftchencko, Zimin, Pokryshkin, Kozhedub, Kronik, and Korzinchikov completely support the theories and practice of aerial combat that Chkalov, from 1924 to 1933, had created and attempted to defend. The views of Valery Pavlovich were also defended by a group of designers and especially by Yakovlev, who wrote:

> The tactical doctrine at the end of the thirties was based on the fact that aerial combat would occur at high altitudes. In all nations of the world, there was an attempt to lift the ceiling for flying combat craft. The MIG-3 was one of the more clear-cut examples of the appearance of this tactic. It possessed a serious advantage over the German Messerschmitt, not only in altitude and speed but also in armament. There were five firing points instead of the three for the Messerschmitt.[31]
>
> But in the first months of the war, it became apparent that German flyers in Messerschmitt fighters, having less of an altitude capacity that the MIG-3, did not wish to carry out combat at those altitudes where they were weaker than the MIG. Quite the contrary, they attempted to force the action to low altitudes, where the heavier MIG would lose in combat maneuvers.
>
> In the beginning, armed assault craft were received coldly by many combat experts. They considered that these craft had insufficient speed and altitude capabilities, so that they would be an easy target for the enemy, and as a result, would not be practical for combat. This opinion rose from the premise that war would be carried on at high altitudes and that what was most important for aircraft was altitude and speed. Even after the IL-2 had been tested on bombing grounds, and had proved all the hopes of Ilyushin, this aircraft was almost rejected. But, during the war, the attitude toward assault craft changed drastically.

The experts on the mastery of our aces in aerial combat, three time heroes of the Soviet Union, A. I. Pokryshkin and I. N. Kozhedub, came to the opinion that Chkalov had anticipated the character of future war in the skies when he worked out the problems of aerobatics at low altitude.[32]

Colonel Denisov, who had studied the wartime career of Pokryshkin, says:

Many of Chkalov's ideas regarding aerial combat were noted in A. E. Pokryshkin's notebook. Pokryshkin was one of the first Soviet fighter pilots who decisively put into practice—and in combat—Chkalov's ideas that it was time for these pilots to reject combat carried on only on a horizontal plane, that it was necessary to move more decisively in maneuvering in a vertical plane and to be able to combine both these activities.

Without a doubt, Chkalov's role in the development of tactics and techniques of aerial combat was a large one. And he was right, when, from the very beginning of his service he attempted to convince everyone of the necessity of being able to fly and engage in battle not only at high and middle altitudes, but also right above the ground. These beliefs led to his hedgehopping flights, and his fierce, vertical aerial battles right above the ground, which, in the beginning of the thirties, were considered by many to be the usual aerial foolhardiness and hooliganism, and violations of the set procedure and directions.

Ten years after the death of Chkalov, Marshall of the Air Force K. A. Vershinin wrote in the newspaper *Komsomolskaya Pravda:*

Chkalov's service to aviation was a great one. He was not only an unsurpassed pilot, a master of his trade, but also the creator of an aerobatic school and a school for testing new craft, an author of fighter craft aviation, and the creator of the most advanced aerobatic figures.

Continuing the work of the great Russian pilot Lt. Nesterov, who was the first to do the loop and to introduce collision tactics in aerial combat, Chkalov himself developed and utilized fifteen aerobatic figures: the vertical spiral, inverted flight, and many other maneuvers. He showed the necessity of flying at critically low altitudes. To Chkalov belongs the honor of creating a school of aerobatics which had absorbed all the best and most valuable knowledge created by such outstanding Russian pilots as Nesterov.

Thus history proved Chkalov to be right.

5

The Factory Test Pilot

The First Five Year Plan was completed and the Second Five Year Plan began. Socialist industry was developing rapidly. During the First Five Year Plan, aviation industry was established in the country. During the Second Five Year Plan, it continued to grow at a brisk pace.[33]

TsAGI turned into a powerful industrial center.

The newspaper *Berlin Tageblatt* in 1928, in an article titled "Aviation Research Work in the Soviet Union," wrote: "At the present time, the Central Aviation Hydrodynamic Institute is possibly the largest and best organized research institute in the world."

The Military Aviation Academy named after N. E. Zhukovsky, which had been founded in 1920, began annual graduation of highly qualified commanders and engineers. Dozens of flying and technical schools guaranteed the manning of new Air Force stations. A considerable number of civilian aviation institutes and technical schools were opened.

The first achievements of Soviet aviation were put on record.

In 1927, on the eve of the first year of the First Five Year Plan, an ANT-3 aircraft under the control of pilot S. A. Shostokov completed the first round trip from Moscow to Tokyo. In 153 flying hours, the crew completed a journey of 22,000 kilometers.

In July 1929, under the direction of the test pilot M. M. Gromov in an ANT-9 craft, a round trip from Moscow via Berlin, Paris, London, and Warsaw was demonstrated. In fifty-three flying hours, the three-engined passenger plane completed a distance of 9,037 kilometers.

In August 1929, the crew of the ANT-4 *Nation of the Soviets*, under the command of S. A. Shestakov, completed a long-distance flight from Moscow to New York covering 21,250 kilometers in one month.

Soviet aviation, in the First Five Year Plan, achieved significant results after demonstrating the high maximal speeds and altitude capabilities of the new aircraft.

Valery Pavlovich Chkalov was well informed concerning those milestones. Now he was interested in the concrete achievements of the Menzhinsky Factory and the problems facing his section during the Second Five Year Plan. After all, he himself had become a member of this section.

Above all, Chkalov wanted to become more familiar with the creator of those fighters on which he had previously flown and those that he would be the first to fly. Chief Designer Nikolai Nikolaievich Polikarpov was twelve years older than Chkalov. He came from a village priest's family, from Orlovschino. He was a very talented engineer and designer, a good teacher, a devotee of literature and music, and a great lover of sports and fishing.

Alexander Ivanovich Zhukov was the same flight instructor of the Moscow School of Aeronautics with whom, in 1923, Chkalov had flown in order to learn aerobatic maneuvers. He told Chkalov much about Polikarpov. Zhukov had first met Polikarpov back in 1923 when he was on a commission headed by Gromov for purchasing training planes.

After completing courses at the St. Petersburg Polytechnical Institute in the beginning of 1916, Nikolai Nikolaievich received instructions to work in the Russian Baltic Factory, Russobalt. This is where the famous aircraft designer Igor Sikorsky worked. Sikorsky, during World War I, had created the four-engined bomber plane *Il'ya muromets* and had designed the S-16 fighter.[34]

The twenty-four-year-old Polikarpov was named Chief of the Production Department at the Russobalt Plant.

Sikorsky immediately became interested in him and soon afterwards invited him to take part in the work of a design group in the planning of all types of bombers and fighters. Having noticed the unusual design abilities of the young engineer, Sikorsky emphatically advised Nikolai Nikolaievich to fly and to learn how to pilot an aircraft on his own.

Then came the October Revolution and Sikorsky emigrated to the United States, becoming an opponent of the Soviet Nation. N. N. Polikarpov remained loyal to Russia. In March 1918, he began to work for the Military Aviation Fleet Administration and soon afterwards, along with the Administration, moved from St. Petersburg to Moscow.[35]

In Moscow he received a very responsible position as the Head of the Production Department of the Duks Bicycle Factory, which had become the primary aviation enterprise of Soviet Russia.

But the young republic did not have the means for such a difficult and important problem as the creation of its own aviation industry.

Polikarpov sensed this, and, beginning with a group of designers, created a fighter plane known as the IL-400. All the factory workers gladly greeted the announcement on March 8,1923, of the creation of the Volunteer Society of the Friends of the Air Fleet (ODVF). The purposes of the Society were expressed in its motto: "Working masses, build an air fleet."

ODVF turned out to be a great help to the government in the creation of a powerful aviation industry.[36]

The development of popular aviation sport had begun.

At the head of the Central Soviet of the Society stood I. V. Stalin, M. V. Frunze, F. E. Dzerzhinsky, and N. A. Morozov. K. E. Vorshilov and V. M. Molotov took active part in the work of the Society.

Chkalov discovered Polikarpov in the Constructors and Designers Bureau.

After an official introduction, Nikolai Nikolaievich showed the pilot the general blueprints for the I-15 fighter plane (TsKB-3).

"You know quite well, Valery Pavlovich, the predecessor to this machine, the I-5 craft. On several occasions, I had the pleasure of seeing how you 'fought' in it in flight, with your friend Anisimov. You know, I'll be honest about it: it was frightening but I was glad to be able to see your corps de ballet in the air."

"Enough, Nikolai Nikolaievich. You have at your plant a remarkable aerobatics expert whom you couldn't possibly find anywhere else."

"You have Alexander Ivanovich in mind?" asked Polikarpov of Chkalov, smiling.

"Of course! Ignore that he is small in physical stature, stern, and modest. He's able to whip anyone in aerial combat."

"Well, both you and Comrade Zhukov are going to be able to test our TsKB-3. We expect much from this craft, both in speed and altitude capabilities and also in its maneuverability."

Nikolai Nikolaievich unconsciously became excited as he showed this newly created craft to Chkalov, of whom he had heard so much.

The designer and pilot spent the rest of their time poring over the blueprints and schematic diagrams of the other craft, the I-16 (TsKB-12). This was a monoplane fighter, unusually blunt-nosed, with low-set wings of small geometric dimensions. It was only about six meters long and the wingspan was not over nine meters. Initially, it weighed only 1,354 kilograms.

Polikarpov hoped to create several modifications on this machine in order to use it in the capacity of a fighter, attack craft, dive bomber, and training plane.

An armored rear plate was placed in this craft, which protected the pilot from an attack from behind.

On this new creation by Polikarpov, there were also many other innovations: retractable undercarriage, flaps, and dropped ailerons, which made it possible to obtain both the highest maximal speed during combat and the minimal speed during a landing of the craft. It was maintained that the I-16 could develop speeds of up to 450–500 kilometers per hour.

Chkalov, a completely spontaneous person with an open heart and soul, could not hide his enthusiasm: "This, Nikolai Nikolaievich, is what we need. It's remarkably conceived, and I warn you that I will fight for this aircraft even with you if you start to derail it."

Nikolai Nikolaievich first was dumbfounded by such a direct and even vulgar expression on short acquaintance, but then he saw the fiery sparks in Chkalov's eyes, which the chief designer valued in the man more than anything else.

He shook the hand of the chief pilot firmly: "Before a year goes by we must put this beauty up into the sky. You, Valery Pavlovich, will have the chance to teach it to fly in your own way."

Valery Pavlovich answered simply: "Don't worry about that, Nikolai Nikolaievich."

Neither one of these two men, talking to each other, knew at that time that this fighter would live a very long life and would take part in many battles.

Here Polikarpov introduced Valery Pavlovich to the chief engineer of the I-16, Z. 1. Zhurbina, who commenced research with the new test pilot and the factory's chief pilot.

From this time on, Chkalov and Polikarpov met very often in the departments of the Design Bureau, beside drafting boards, by the mock-ups of future craft, and on the field next to the fighter craft.

Valery Pavlovich learned to love the plant. He was proud of the fact that he was accepted into an enormous department, whose hands were creating experimental aircraft, and subsequently were outfitting thousands of them for the arming of military outfits in the Air Force.

The flying field of the aviation plant was located on the southwest corner of the Frunze Central Field, together with the enormous hangar of the Flight Research and Development Department of TsAGI.

Chkalov would arrive at the plant very early every morning. If there were flight assignments on the TsKB, then he would lift off into the sky in the experimental craft and conduct the tests. During some of his spare time, he would assist other pilots with the delivery of these aircraft, testing two or three of them in one day.

When there were no flights, Valery would go to the experimental shop, climb into an aircraft or a mock-up being constructed, and, sitting in the cockpit for hours, would study the tiniest details of this new plant production. Sometimes he would argue with the designers, who always listened attentively to the remarks and demands of the chief test pilot.

From the experimental shop, the chief pilot would go to the assembly line and enjoy, as if it were music, the many-voiced hum of labor.

Young people were attracted to Chkalov. Valery often said to the designers: "You have to climb into our skins and build the kind of aircraft that are needed by Soviet pilots."

He volunteered to start up a small flight section in the aviation club of the plant for the factory workers, and managed to obtain a U-2 plane for flight purposes.

His first students were designers. First of all, Polikarpov, then Dubrovin, Tairov, Buksakov, and others; eleven people in all.

They flew either before work, at 6 A.M., or after completion of work, before sunset. Valery Pavlovich's energies were not wasted on this activity. All his students passed the exams at the Central Aero-Club and received the right to make solo flights.

Valery Pavlovich was made the chairman of the Mock-Up Commission for planning the I-15 fighter. The assignment to build the mock-up was given to Alexander Mikailovich Polyakov, a designer.

When everything was ready, Chkalov came to see what this I-15 looked like. He very much liked the external appearance of the aircraft. The chief pilot looked the machine over from several angles, then crawled into the cockpit, at which point something confusing happened. A crackle of plywood was heard and Chkalov almost fell through.

Looking very sternly at Polyakov, Valery Pavlovich called him over: "Bad luck. Come here, take a look."

The good-looking young designer paled, and walked over to the pilot, who rapped out sharply: "What, did you want to kill me? Look, I'm a living person. Next time, my dear sir, take into account that you should choose a little thicker plywood."

Looking over the rest of the aircraft, Valery Pavlovich, in saying good-bye, said: "Don't stew about it. But think about how you can improve it, so that in the future, my friend, you won't make a mistake."

The designer thought that Polikarpov would punish him and take him off the job, but it became clear that Chkalov never said a single word to the chief about this unfortunate episode. Nikolai Nikolaievich eventually found this out from the other members of the Mock-Up Commission and of course firmly reprimanded Polyakov.

It was the autumn of 1933. September was very gray and foggy and it was necessary to wait out the weather in order to get an opportunity for a test flight.

On September 5, the nation suffered a great misfortune. There was a serious aviation disaster not far from Moscow. Among the victims was a talented organizer and Soviet aviation enthusiast, Peter Iyonovich Baranov, who in the course of the last two years had headed the Chief Aviation Industry Administration in the People's Heavy Industry Committee. A man of great sincerity, and one who understood both aircraft and pilots very well, he more than once had rescued Chkalov in difficult moments of his life. It was he who had freed him from the Bryansk Prison and had obtained employment for him in the aviation industry.

Polikarpov and Chkalov frequently discussed the experimental version of the I-15, the construction of which was nearing completion. The chief designer regarded the opinions of Valery Pavlovich very highly, and was always pleased with his recommendations on the design of the aircraft.

One October day in 1933, a new single-seater I-15 fighter, with an M-22 air-cooled engine, was rolled out of the hangar. On this day it would lift off on its first flight.[37]

Valery Pavlovich, in the preflight moments, maintained calmness and self-assuredness. He knew all the details of the planning and construction of the new machine, and he was familiar with practically everyone who had worked on the aircraft.

But he also understood very well that all the calculations, all the preflight research on the ground and tests, still did not give a solid guarantee of the stability of the new aircraft in flight. For this reason, the chief designer and his aides were quite concerned. Consequently, great demands were placed on the pilot.

Thousands of people waited for an answer to the question "Well, how's the plane?" from the pilot. The expectations and hopes of an enormous department were entrusted to him. He, the test pilot, was one of the links in a complex chain of organized labor. He did not have the right to expose the results of the general efforts to unnecessary risks.

"This will need courage and the greatest care," the calm and collected chief pilot thought to himself.

Finally everything was prepared. Polikarpov and Chkalov exchanged good wishes. The pilot was in the cockpit.

The aircraft made several runs along Central Field and then barely lifted off from the ground. Everything was going smoothly.

It was now possible to taxi to the very far edge of the field, and from there begin a takeoff against the wind. The craft separated softly from the ground and quickly gained in altitude, now flying high above the field. The plant engineers and service people held their breath as they followed the first flight of the I-15 by Chkalov.

After its perfect landing, the excited and overly anxious Polikarpov rushed to the taxiing aircraft. Chkalov fell into the embraces of the creator of the machine. Nikolai Nikolaievich hugged the apparently stern looking pilot who said loudly, so that everyone could hear: "Beautiful, congratulations on your victory, Nikolai Nikolaievich! You are all wonderful!"

The chief engineer and the pilot discussed this short flight at length.

Later began the laborious work, with its triumphs and errors, finishing and perfecting the new machine. From flight to flight, the testing program became more complicated and the pilot had to be alert at all times for the worst.

When Chkalov began the first experimental flights in the I-15, his best friend Anisimov, had already been flying at the same Central Field for several days.

Anisimov was demonstrating in the I-5, at extreme proximity to the ground, aerobatic maneuvers that had been adapted for aerial combat. These flights were being filmed in order to prepare an orientation film for fighter pilots.

Valery Pavlovich knew that Anisimov, on this day, October 11, 1933, had to complete his work with the filmmakers, and he rushed to meet his friend at his aircraft. Then the two of them would decide what they would do during the second half of the day.

The October morning was quiet and sunny Valery walked over to the rows of parked military aircraft. He noticed that the I-5 was already prepared for flight. Anisimov stood not far from the craft with the cameraman. They had set up a movie camera on the flying field.

Valery greeted his comrade: "Ah, greetings to the people's flight artist and movie star Anisimov."

"My regards to the trainer of new fighter craft," answered Anisimov, smiling.

The cameraman went to the starting point. The pilots walked further away from the I-5 on the flight field. Chkalov took out some luxurious Herezgovinia Flora cigarettes, and, offering them to his comrade, said: "Well, Shurka, today we're going to the Hippodrome." Then he made for the factory hangars.

He had already started to think about his own imminent flight on the I-15 when he heard the roar of an engine. Valery turned around and saw Anisimov's craft, after engine testing, begin to taxi toward the starting point. In a few more minutes, the I-5 lifted off above Chkalov, and on takeoff performed a forbidden double roll, first to the left, then to the right.

Chkalov walking up to rows of factory aircraft when he noticed Anisimov, for the third time, making a dive right for the movie camera, and then, from a height of about fifty meters, lifting the nose up and finished his maneuver with an Immelmann.

Chkalov started to return inside the hangar, but once again he heard the roar of the propellers and the engine of the aircraft in a dive. He turned his head back and froze for a second, and suddenly shouted out in despair and frenzy: "What is he doing?"

He ran as fast as he could toward the center of the field.

Valery Pavlovich could see that Anisimov had flawlessly brought the aircraft out of a dive and was beginning to make a half-loop in order to roll the aircraft at the upper point out of its inverted position into a normal one, and then finish the maneuver with an Immelmann. But Anisimov, coming out of the upper point, mushed in an upside-down position, and, not changing it, began to sharply fall downwards.

Chkalov ran, not seeing anything but the I-5 falling upside-down.

"Pull out! Pull out! Use your rudders, hard rudder!" Breathing hard, Valery shouted, beside himself.

But the aircraft didn't even turn onto its wing. It crashed into the landing markers in an inverted position.

The Accident Review Board concluded that the mishap resulted from the fact that the rudder pedals had broken. Without them, at a low altitude it was impossible to turn the I-5 into a normal position.

After this accident, Chkalov started to act somewhat more coldly toward Polikarpov, thinking that he and the designer Grigorovich, who had worked with him, had somewhere committed an error in the construction of the I-5.

He recalled the flier Artseuslov, lying with a broken leg under the debris of Polikarpov's first fighter, the I-400; he remembered how Gromov had parachuted from another I-400 as it was falling in a spin.

Valery was also a witness to the destruction of Polikarpov's two-seater fighter, the 21-NI, on its ninth flight, during high-speed testing, when the test pilot Filippov along with his timekeeper perished.

And now those rudder pedals, and Anisimov.

■

It was now winter. A snow cover hid the flying field. The undercarriage of the I-15 was replaced with skis.

Once on a flight at maximal speed, the reinforcement assembly on the front shock absorbers of the left ski suddenly ripped off and the nose section was jerked downwards. With the aircraft in this condition, it would have been possible, upon landing, to hook the ground with the vertical ski and, at a great speed, flip the aircraft over frontwards and land it on its back, or as the pilots say, to "cowl over."

Chkalov didn't even think of abandoning the aircraft and jumping with his parachute. In order to reduce the landing speed sharply, Chkalov brought the aircraft toward the ground in a steep attack angle, the engine at full revs; vibrating and rattling, the craft, with its downward-pointing nose, slowly glided in and started to set itself down. Not more than a meter above the ground, Chkalov turned off the engine, and the plane plowed onto the snowy landing strip and then immediately turned over. But this was not at the speed of a "cowl-over." Chkalov, hanging upside down, waited for help to free himself from his seat belt.

The pilot crawled out from under the craft, and, ignoring Polikarpov, the plant director, and the doctor, walked around the machine, lying with its belly up, and noticed a mechanic who was fidgeting about near the craft. Patting the mechanic on his shoulder, Chkalov laughingly said: "Well, yours is a good machine. It turned over and it's still in one piece."

Then he went up to Polikarpov and, as if nothing serious had happened, quietly said to the chief designer: "Don't be sad, Nikolai Nikolaievich, it's not so easy to bring up children. You'd better think about how to turn it back onto its feet now without breaking it."

Polikarpov couldn't restrain himself. Embracing Valery, he said, with a quiver in his voice: "Thank you so much, Valery Pavlovich."

Chkalov muttered good-naturedly as he climbed into the ambulance, "Forget it, old buddy. Let's just fix it up quickly, since you and I have a lot more flying to do together."

People appeared from all sides and applauded Chkalov, throwing their hats up into the air.

Chkalov's decision to save the craft above all else had a great significance to the plant and for the defense of the nation.

Polikarpov, in a short period of time, corrected the defect of the undercarriage and Chkalov quickly completed all the tests on the I-15. It was their introduction to mass production. Soon afterwards, Nikolai Nikolaievich produced the same type of craft with a more powerful engine. The fighter was designated as the I-5 bis. This aircraft had a maximal speed of 370 kilometers an hour, a ceiling of around 10 kilometers, a range of 800 kilometers. It was armed with four 7.6-mm machine guns.

Four years later, this aircraft was completely modernized, and was designated the Chaika (I-153). This was a fighter with retractable gear. It could reach a speed of 443 kilometers an hour. It was put into mass production and proved very popular among our pilots in combat against the Japanese Air Force at Khalkhin-Gol and in the war with the White Finns. At that time it was the best of all biplane fighters being produced.

If Chkalov had jumped out of the experimental machine with its defective ski, the nation would hardly have been likely to have received such an effective weapon as the I-15 turned out to be.

■

While continuing to test the I-15, Chkalov carefully followed the development and the subsequent assembly of the new I-16 fighter.

In December 1933, the new craft was brought out to the field. But just the same, things were not going well. The I-16 was prepared for flight only on the eve of the New Year.

Valery Pavlovich carried out the first flight magnificently.

Subsequently, the testing program likewise continued without any special difficulties. True, in one of the flights, Chkalov was not able to retract the landing gear due to stress fatigue on the handle of the lifting mechanism. The pilot had a similar difficulty in trying to control the flaps.

After Chkalov's recommendations, Polikarpov redesigned the entire control mechanisms of the landing gear and the flaps, and replaced manual control mechanisms with pneumatic systems.

After such alterations, test flights on the I-16 continued generally successfully. But once, as he was coming in for a landing, Valery Pavlovich was completely unable to lower the left landing gear. From the ground, they could see that something wasn't going well in flight, but they were completely helpless to assist the test pilot.

The pilot looked for a way to correct the in-flight problem.

The cable of the winch mechanism that controlled the undercarriage had stretched out, weakened, and curled into a loop. This is what blocked the lowering of the left landing gear unit into place.

Gaining higher altitude and abandoning the controls, the test pilot attempted to reach the loop with his hands. At this time the aircraft went into such a drawn-out dive that the pilot barely managed to pull it out and make the craft regain altitude, causing a brief blackout even in such a powerhouse as Chkalov.

In order to force the left landing gear into the down position, Valery Pavlovich used all the expertise he had learned in flight, including those things that ran against instructions. He completed one maneuver after another, using them to change the value of the center of gravity and pressure of the craft. These were steep, drawn-out dives, with full power of the engine, after which the pilot forced the I-16 to climb steeply upwards, first in a left spiral, then in a right spiral. He also performed rolls. He made Nesterov loops, Immelmanns, and many other aerobatic maneuvers.

The test pilot was now on the brink of exhaustion because he had been doing aerobatic maneuvers for more than thirty minutes. Also, there was very little fuel left in the tanks.

Chkalov once again gained altitude and again threw his defective craft into a dive, with such an abrupt pull-out that for a short period of time he lost consciousness. Yet when he came to, he could see by the signal lights that everything was in order. The undercarriage had released and was locked down in a normal manner.

Thus Valery saved the experimental I-16 and gave this type of fighter a ticket for an unusually long military life. The aircraft outlived the test pilot by many years.

The Designers' Bureau and the thousands of people in the aviation plant were thrilled by Chkalov's triumph.

Rumors concerning this feat reached the Heavy Industry Committee and Sergo Ordzhonikidze, who soon afterwards invited the designer and chief pilot to work with him. After a discussion with the Committee, Nikolai Nikolaievich changed the landing gear assembly drastically on the new fighter.

In the following test flights, excellent results were obtained: a maximum speed of 454 kilometers an hour, a ceiling of 9.2 kilometers, a range of 820 kilometers, and a rate of ascent of 5 kilometers in 6.2 minutes. This led the Chief of Administration of the Aviation Industry to accept a suggestion by Polikarpov, to design and construct a series of modified I-16 aircraft.[38]

However, the Red Army Air Force administration opposed this, considering that the I-16 first of all was very complicated to fly and also was extremely difficult to extricate from a spin. (The theories of spin existing in those years stated that an aircraft with a wide profile like the I-16 should not be put into a spin, because if it went into one, it would not be able to come out.)

Valery Pavlovich discussed this theory with the Air Force Command. In this he demonstrated his uncompromising and insistent character, and his unusual flying talents.

As a proof of the superior flight characteristics of the aircraft being tested, Chkalov, after completing each testing assignment, would begin systematically to carry out aerobatic maneuvers. Everyone admired and was amazed by the I-16, but many said: "What do you want? This is Chkalov flying; he could do the same thing with a stick."

Then, as a result of Valery Pavlovich's suggestions, the decision to subject the I-16 to review by a commission of experts was accepted by the Heavy Industry Committee. Two factory test pilots and two from the Air Force Scientific Research Institute were invited into the experts' group. The conclusions of the experts were generally positive. But they recommended that the aircraft controls be simplified. The Industry did not oppose such a suggestion because Polikarpov himself had already promised Chkalov to do something of this nature. The discussion concerning the spin was more heated. The Commission, headed by Professor Zhuravchenko of the Zhukovsky Air Force Academy, based on his calculations, came to the conclusion that the I-16 could not recover from a spin and for this reason had no future as a fighter craft, and that further testing was senseless until appropriate measures had been taken.

The arguments brought in the plant director, who called a meeting and, listening to the negative conclusions of the aerodynamic specialists, turned to the plant's chief pilot, Chkalov. "And what is your opinion of this, Valery Pavlovich?"

The pilot stood up, looked at everyone, and, turning to Professor Zhuravchenko, said: "Concerning the small vertical stabilizer and the prominent horizontal one, my opinion is that this is not a defect. I have been performing all the aerobatic maneuvers on the I-16 and know certainly that a spin, even a flat one, is no obstacle for the craft. I will demonstrate this not with words, or on a piece of paper, but in flight."

For a long time the directors were unwilling to allow Valery to test-fly the I-16 in a spin, although the chief designer did not doubt that the pilot would be successful.

Chkalov argued with the factory administration, traveled several times to the Heavy Industry Committee, and finally obtained permission to test the I-16 in a spin.

On his own volition, the chief pilot accepted the risk in order to vindicate the entire plant department of which he considered himself a member, not only according to regulations, but also in his own mind. He was not defending the honor of his uniform, he was fighting for a good craft that was necessary to the Army.

It was a Sunday, a sunny day, but with the thick smoke, especially around Moscow, that often creates a shroud that sharply decreases visibility.

Chkalov carefully checked out his newly packed parachute and diligently adjusted it. He rarely did this himself, usually trusting the parachute riggers and packers.

Before this flight, the test pilot was especially intent. Not speaking with anyone, he slowly walked up to the craft, climbed into the cockpit, adjusted his harness slowly, and, putting his flying goggles on his helmet, finally gave the mechanic a signal to start the engine.

The craft took off and immediately became hidden in the shroud of smoke. Minutes went by. Polikarpov was so nervous that he began to tremble. And there was reason for such extraordinary excitement. After twenty minutes, the aircraft appeared above the Central Field and descended in an inverted position. Then, above the hangars, the fighter rolled over and assumed its normal attitude, then assumed a steep climb. Everyone followed Chkalov's movements. From an altitude of two thousand meters he suddenly put the I-16 into a left spin. After several spirals, he stopped the revolution of the craft and again gained altitude. Then the fighter turned into a right spin and after the third spiral returned to a normal diving position in order to complete a combat turn, which put him at an altitude half his initial one. From one thousand meters, the I-16 spiraled first to the left, then to the right. After completing his planned demonstration of the spinning characteristics of the fighter craft, Valery Pavlovich decided to show off the machine in its full splendor right above the ground.

This was inexpressively beautiful, but, at the same time, it was frightening. Nikolai Nikolaievich never would have thought that a person could fly so magnificently, so close to the ground, with no fear of death. Forgetting why the test pilot was doing the flight, the chief instructor shouted out in despair: "My God, why is he taking such risks?"

Finally the aircraft landed. People ran from all sides to meet the I-16, which was taxiing up to its stand. Afraid of hitting someone with his revolving propellers, Chkalov was forced to turn off his engine ahead of time.

Polikarpov, as if just having woken up, ran toward the airplane. Not allowing Valery to jump out of the aircraft cockpit, the chief designer embraced and hugged the laughing pilot.

Thus science was "rectified," by Valery Pavlovich's experiment, as a result of which the I-16 was soon qualified for armament and was released to series production with several modifications. It was Chkalov who gave life to this aircraft. The number 4, 6, and 10 types each had two "ShKAS" machine guns in the center of the plane. The I-16 type 17 with an M-25 engine had two "ShVAK" 20-mm cannons and two "ShKAS" machine guns and could take up to two-hundred-kilogram bombs in the externally suspended bomb racks.

Here it is appropriate to note that, in the process of almost a ten-year military development of the I-16 plane, Air Force fighter pilots never complained, either about the complexity of the controls or about the plane's spinning characteristics.

In 1939, type 24 of the I-16 was released. With an M-62 engine, it developed a speed of 525 kilometers an hour.

Test pilot Chkalov, defending the I-16 and introducing it to its long life of military service, without a doubt achieved a major accomplishment. It is unfortunate that the history of our aviation up until the present time has not recognized it and that no author has used it as the basis for an outstanding work.

In the meantime, the I-16 fighter showed its excellent fighting capabilities even in 1936. Such gifted Soviet fighter pilots as Boris Smirnov, Mikhail Yakushin, and Anatoly Serov in their I-16's beat the best German aces who fought in Spain, in their Me-109's—a new design fighter.

In 1937 and 1938, our volunteer pilots fought in their I-16 planes, helping the Chinese people gain their independence from the encroachments of the Japanese military. The Japanese pilots especially felt the power of the modernized I-16's in 1939 when their armies encroached on the boundaries of the Mongolian People's Republic.

Carrying out their international duty, the Soviet pilots in the I-16's armed with cannons and in the Chaika-type fighter aircraft destroyed 204 Japanese planes in combat between August 20 and 30,

1939. During the war with the White Finns, regardless of the extremely cold conditions, frosts, snowstorms, and fog (frosts up to 40° below zero), Soviet fighter pilots in their I-16 aircraft were successful in aerial combat.

Finally, the I-16 showed its colors in the initial years of World War II. The First Air Fighter Division, which had fought magnificently against German craft in their I-16's, received a designation as the First Fighter Group.

In March of 1943, the 728th Group was one of the last to stop using the I-16 when it received a new fighter of a more contemporary design.

Valery Pavlovich felt that in his arguments with the scientists, designers, and engineers he did not have sufficient knowledge and that it was necessary to continually attempt to improve it. More often, he began to carry on discussions in the Design Bureau with Polikarpov and his talented scientists, designers, and chief engineers.

Chkalov was always interested in how designers discovered the most successful relationship between durability and speed, between durability and maneuverability, and between maneuverability and stability and by what methods they could prevent vibrations in the aircraft.

Valery discussed these subjects with N. M. Bakhrakh, A. G. Rotenberg, D. N. Kurguzov, L. F. Bodrova, V. B. Shavrov, A. N. Polyakov, Z. I. Zhurbina, and many other specialists.

Now Chkalov had to field-test the precision and correctness of all these theoretical calculations and computations. No one at the plant ever said to him: "This you can do, that you cannot, a certain paragraph states such and such. . . ." No one ever made decisions for him, and no one could ever do this, no matter how hard they tried. This was a result of Valery's character.

Despite incredible difficulties, we always managed to succeed. Naturally, the designer was the test pilot's continual adviser, although only a test pilot could test a new aircraft in flight and this was such a complicated and difficult matter.

■

The aviation industry increased the tempo of development in the Volga region, Siberia, the Ukraine, and Uzbekhistan, and huge aircraft engine and instrument plants began to emerge.

The design bureaus of well-known designers strengthened and widened their bases. The young designers upgraded the creative level.

Andrei Nikolaievich Tupolev produced the six-engined ANT-16 craft and the ANT-22 after producing the four-engined TB-3 (ANT-6) bomber. Later, the gigantic ANT-20 (*Maxim Gorky*) was flown.[39] Then testing began of an aircraft especially created to set long-distance records under the designation RD (ANT-25). Civil Aviation obtained the ANT-35.

The first aircraft of designer S. V. Ilyushin appeared. The young designer A. S. Yaklovev, together with a large number of great sports and training-type craft, began to build military machines.

The former students of A. N. Tupolev, A. A. Arkhangelsky and V. N. Petlyakov, set out on their own independent road to designing.

A four-engined bomber of original design was constructed by the talented V. F. Bolkhovitinov, A. I. Mikoyan, and M. I. Gurevich. S. A. Lavochkin and V. G. Yermolayev organized new design departments.[40]

The plant in which Chkalov worked produced, besides the fighter designs of Polikarpov, PI-1 and PI-2 fighters with cannon armaments created by the old designer D. P. Grigorovich.

The well-known design engineer of the "Flying-Shelf," V. S. Vakhmistrov, had previously produced a multiengined fighter, the TB-3, and was working out a project to utilize the I-16, which would be suspended under the carrier plane in the capacity of a dive bomber.

A large series of aircraft engines were produced by design organizations that were headed by the chief designers, V. Ya. Kilmov, A. A. Mikulin, and A. D. Shevtsov. A. A. Bessonov, B. A. Dobrynin, and A. P Ostrovsky also contributed much to this project.

Naturally these practical achievements in science and technology were quickly reflected in the victories of Soviet pilots.

Chkalov considered as one of the epic, magnificent victories of soviet aviation the rescue of the passengers and crew of the steamer *Chelyushkin* in 1934. Heading for the island of Wrangell, to relieve a crew wintering there after sailing the entire Northern Sea route, which was very close to its goal in the Bering Straits, the ship became icebound. After drifting for many months it was broken up by the ice in the frozen Chukotsky Sea.

One hundred and four people, including two children, ended up on the arctic ice under open skies, in frosts that were 30° below freezing, in a merciless and penetrating wind.

Many Soviet flyers offered their services to the government committee to save the crew of the *Chelyushkin*, which was created and headed by V. V. Kuibyshev. Valery Pavlovich was one of the volunteers but the plant director and the head of the Chief Administration of the Aviation Industry quite reasonably said: "Very well, you fly off and who is going to test the I-15 and I-16 in your place?"

Chkalov could not contain himself in those April days, and he was extremely glad when Soviet pilots in their TB-1, R-5, and Fleister craft, regardless of the hostility of the Arctic climate, showed themselves to be fearless and self-sacrificing and, using great flying skills, rescued all the people who were in that unfortunate situation.

Valery's fears were finally set to rest when he read in the newspapers that all those who had been saved had been transported to rescue ships. Seven of the pilots—Lyapildevsky, Levanevsky, Vodopyanov, Kamanin, Molokov, Slepnev, and Doronin, the rescuers of the *Chelyushkin* crew—were the first to receive from the state a newly established honor, "Hero of the Soviet Union."

In the summer of 1934, I joined a number of military pilots for a flight to Western Europe. After our return, Valery interrogated me incessantly regarding the French aerobatics school in Etampe. When I told him about a group of five flying inverted inclose formation and firing at targets on the ground from this position, Chkalov remarked: "These French are wonderful. But here not all the heads understand the value of such flights. They only know how to restrain."

"Well, and who forbids you?" I responded.

"But, Egor, is it just I alone who represents fighter aviation? Here I'm talking about everyone in the Air Force. Don't worry about me now; I'm a free Cossack."

But Valery was even more excited by the victory of the Soviet test pilots M. M. Gromov and A. I. Filin and navigator I. T. Spirin, who, in the autumn of 1934, flew a closed-circuit route of 12,411 kilometers in seventy-two hours in an ANT-25 and set a new world's record in this distance class.

Chkalov was extremely pleased with his former instructor at the Serpukhov School. Gromov received the designation Hero of the Soviet Union, and his fellow travelers, the Order of Lenin for this flight achievement.

Finally, the Chkalovs received an apartment in a new house, No. 76 on the Leningrad Highway, across from the Central Field. It was a rare evening when it was quiet at the Chkalovs. After the loss of Anisimov, Chkalov began to stay at home more often. Meeting and greeting his Vasilevo relatives and acquaintances, pilots, engineers, mechanics, co-workers at the Air Force Research Institute, and many of his plant comrades, Chkalov loved to entertain people at home to the point of self-forgetfulness. Olga Erazmovna slowly became accustomed to her husband's hospitality and assisted him.

By order of Sergo Ordzhonikidze of the People's Commissariat for Heavy Industry, Chkalov was rewarded for superior test flight work with a passenger car produced at the Gorky automobile plant. Valery loved to take his wife and son and also many of his friends and acquaintances for rides in it.

Continuing to test the I-15 and I-16, Valery Pavlovich, after completion of his flights, would sit for long periods of time in the Designers' Bureau, taking part in the creation of a new I-17 fighter, which, like the I-16, was designed as a monoplane with low-set wings. The new fighter had a water-cooled engine of the M-100 type.

■

It was the spring of 1935 and by established custom there was a parade on the first day of May in Moscow's Red Square in which a large number of heavy and medium bombers, reconnaissance craft, and fighter aircraft took part.

Chkalov flew across Red Square in a red-winged I-16.

And on May 2, the entire air corps and several hundred aircraft were parked in formation on the tarmac at the Frunze Central Field. In front of the aircraft were ranks of pilots, navigators, aerial gunners and mechanics.

Walking past the military crews standing at attention, Valery looked at them with a certain amount of envy and realized that he was still longing to be in the Air Force, from which he had been separated for two and a half years, through no fault of his own.

The sun rose higher in the sky and warmed the people gathered at the parade.

Chkalov, in his flight jacket, helmet, and flight suit, stood before a small fighter craft similar to a swallow with red wings. An order was heard. The field grew silent.

Stalin, Voroshilov, and Ordzhonikidze walked past the ranks of the participants on the parade grounds. Chkalov came to attention and in a military fashion put his hand to his flying helmet. Stalin stopped next to Chkalov. Voroshilov introduced him to Josef Vissarionovich, who asked a few questions of the pilot. Chkalov answered briefly and clearly. Stalin looked at the face of the pilot. Then he drew a little closer to the red-winged craft and once again asked some questions of the test pilot. Apparently, Voroshilov and Ordzhonikidze had already passed a few stories regarding the fearlessness of the pilot to Stalin and he warmly and attentively looked at Chkalov.

"And why don't you use a parachute?" asked Stalin.

Chkalov, thinking for a short while, answered: "I fly experimental craft. They are very valuable and it would be a shame to destroy them. Generally, one tries to save the aircraft."

Stalin smiled.

"Your life is more precious to us than any aircraft," said Stalin, saying good-bye.

"Am I really more precious than any machine? More valuable than this beauty with red wings?" thought the pilot.

"Man your aircraft!"—a new command was heard.

Chkalov put all his talents as a birdman and his many years of experienced flying into this flight.

This day, May 2, 1935, he always recalled as a high point in his life. It led to a new life and to happiness of great victories.

When the glowing Valery appeared at home together with his friends, who had flown to the parade from various aviation garrisons in the country, his wife hugged him and kissed him in silence.

"Did you really see me?" he asked nervously.

"We both watched from the balcony as you were doing somersaults," little Igor answered for his mother.

Chkalov carefully accompanied his wife into the living room and said: "Now you have nothing to worry about."

Three days later, test pilot V. P. Chkalov and chief designer N. N. Polikarpov, on the recommendations of Sergo Ordzhonikidze of the People's Commissariat of Heavy Industry, by order of the Central Executive Committee of the USSR, were awarded the Order of Lenin. On the recommendation was written:

> The designer of an aviation plant, comrade N. N. Polikarpov, is one of the most gifted workers in our industry. He designed the I-15 and the I-16. Both planes, as is known, have been accepted as front-line fighters.

Pilot V. P. Chkalov conducts testing of these new fighters and is considered one of the best pilots.

I request that designer N. N. Polikarpov and pilot V. P. Chkalov be awarded the Order of Lenin. S. Ordzhonikidze.

Five days after this, there was another event in Chkalov's life. On May 10, Olga Erazmovna gave birth to a daughter. She was named Valerya in honor of her father.

Valery Pavlovich's happiness knew no bounds.

■

But Chkalov's work as a test pilot increased more and more. The newest creation of Polikarpov, the fighter aircraft I-17, was rolled out onto the field. However, flights on the I-15 and I-16 were not halted. The aircraft continued to be modified.

But what is a test pilot in the mind of a test pilot himself?

This is what Chkalov wrote on the subject in the newspaper *Izvestia*, May 15, 1935:

A pilot who tests new aircraft, in the minds of those people who have nothing directly to do with aviation, is a person who takes risks. However, such an impression is not a true one. A test pilot, above all, is a person who is burdened by the concerns of a paternal responsibility. Prior to flying in any experimental machine, he participates in its birth.

The work of a test pilot begins long before flight. He follows all the stages of development of the new craft. He becomes familiar with its peculiarities, even during the design period.

Finally, the craft is constructed. A small wooden mock-up is subjected to scrupulous examination, and in the evaluation of this aircraft that is being created, the test pilot actively takes part. At the plant, during the construction of the craft, the test pilot, along with the engineers, spends days in the shop. He follows the preparation of all details and checks the function of the separate, completed mechanisms. The test pilot by this time is familiar with the craft down to the smallest detail, for this is the plane that he will test in flight. He is immersed in it completely, down to the last propeller blade, but he has no right to trust it. In the initial stages, he taxis it around the field and lifts off about a meter and a half from the ground before being completely airborne.

During the first flight, the pilot only makes one or two circles above the field. Later, the aircraft is diligently examined, and any small defects which had appeared during the flight are isolated. Then training flights begin. For four or five of such flights, test pilots must become accustomed to the new aircraft.

The craft then enters a phase of factory testing. Here the pilot no longer remains cautious. He subjects it to heavy pressure and loads. He tests it for climb, maneuverability, control, stability, and speed. He tests it for aerobatic ability, service ceiling, and finally tests it for spin capabilities. The test pilot carefully monitors the engine and the numerous instruments and takes down all his observations.

Often toward the end of factory testing, the plane undergoes a series of alterations.

Sometimes in the testing process, the pilot observes some kind of major defect in the new craft. The plane is then removed from factory testing, and is then sent to the shop for modifications. Later, the testing is renewed and continued until the craft no longer has unpredictable characteristics.

The test pilot must submit the aircraft to those kinds of pressures that might not ever be borne in the future. The testing of contemporary high-speed aircraft demands extremely good health of the pilot. It is possible to sense an aircraft quite well, but in order to test it at speeds above maximum capabilities, in order to squeeze everything out of the craft up until its upper limits, one must also possess great physical strength.

Test pilots are cautious people, and this is natural. If one incorrect movement is made, the craft is destroyed. To destroy an experimental aircraft is to destroy many months of work by an entire department.

The discovery of the spinning characteristics of the aircraft is the final and most responsible stage of testing. The final stages of testing aerobatic capabilities and spin characteristics are carried out for this reason with maximal care, in which every movement is thought out in advance.

Testing for spin characteristics is usually performed at high altitudes so that, in case the craft cannot be pulled out of a spin, it is possible to parachute from the craft. The plane is put into a spin from all positions, including those that could occur during loss of speed for an aircraft when it is flown by an insufficiently experienced pilot. In each isolated case, the craft is put into a spin in a different way; consequently, it is necessary to study all the characteristics.

The designer anticipates a correct diagnosis from the test pilot. The test pilot should be able to orient himself very quickly to all the characteristics of the aircraft and its many instruments. The ability of the test pilot to observe isolated inadequacies quickly in the machine and, most importantly, to correctly determine the reasons for them, is a very significant factor.

The work of the test pilot is extremely complicated. Here it isn't enough to rely on "feeling." It is necessary to have knowledge concerning the laws of mechanics, strength of materials, and many, many other things.

It was the second half of 1935. During this new Five Year Plan, the design bureau of N. N. Polikarpov and the experimental plant increased the production of new types of fighters.

Early on a September morning, Valery Pavlovich taxied around the flying field of the Central Field in a very striking I-17 aircraft (TsKB-15). After several runs, Chkalov lifted the craft slightly off the ground and immediately landed it. He liked the feel of the new fighter; the craft conducted itself very well during taxiing and on takeoff runs was seemingly stable and obedient to aileron and turn and pitch controls.

Nikolai Nikolaievich had often brought Valery Pavlovich to the design bureau to admire the general view of this proposed fighter with four machine guns and bomb racks for one hundred bombs.

The aircraft was reminiscent of its predecessor, the I-16. It was the same type of classical monoplane with low-set wings, but it didn't seem snub-nosed because it had a water-cooled M-100-type engine, which allowed the designer to arrange the cowl section more proportionately and in a more streamlined fashion.

During the first flight the craft conducted itself normally and for this reason Chkalov, after a week, was able to go on to the carrying out of a testing program.

As a result of a whole series of complicated flights, the pilot determined that the I-17 was capable of developing a speed of five hundred kilometers per hour and having a ceiling of more than 9,500 meters. This was a magnificent achievement.

Once, as had happened in the previous year during a flight in a new fighter, the right unit of the landing gear did not release. All attempts to place it in position were unsuccessful. There was very little fuel left. From the hellish strains, Chkalov's whole body ached and he was dizzy.

Chkalov contemplated whether to bail out of the aircraft or to attempt a landing and save the craft.

The pilot realized the mortal danger of landing the I-17 on one wheel. There was every chance that the fighter would race along for a short while, then list to the right onto the side where the wheel was unretracted, and then, at high speed, hook the ground with the cantilevered wing, turning over instantly and crashing with tremendous force into the empennage and the pilot's cockpit. In distinction from the I-16, the engine compartment of the I-17 was much lower than the upper part of the cowling under which was located the head of the pilot. This meant that, in an inverted situation, the pilot would be crushed.

Chkalov looked once again at the fuel gauge. There was only a few minutes' worth of fuel left.

"Calm down, Chkalov, calm down," Valery said to himself, concentrating on what else he could do. Having made a decision, he took his one-wheeled I-17 up. At 1,000 meters he gave the engine full revs and turned the nose of the fighter upward. The I-17 went into a secondary climb, while the pilot worked with the ailerons and watched the air speed indicator. Chkalov noticed that at stalling speed, when the craft was already nodding its nose, the aircraft was still very obedient to aileron and rudder controls. Valery renewed his hopes for saving the new, experimental fighter. He put the aircraft into a descending position.

At the field, they watched in horror at what was happening, understanding what could result from this decision.

The pilot noticed that on the ground, instead of a landing marker, they had placed a cross, which seemed to be advising Chkalov to abandon the aircraft and use his parachute; but the test pilot knew that now he was all on his own and only he could decide correctly what to do with the craft.

The pilot leveled the craft out from its gliding angle and, descending to just above the ground, turned off the engine. The aircraft softly touched the grassy cover with its wheel and raced up toward the field, gradually listing to the right side.

There were a few seconds of mortal danger. Everyone was extremely tense. The right wing tilted closer and closer to the ground, but Chkalov was smiling. The speed of the landing run for the fighter was being reduced, and now it was clear that he, as a test pilot, had risked himself intelligently and, as a result of that, saved the craft.

In a moment, the I-17 softly struck the grass with its cantilevered right wing and, almost turning over, stopped abruptly.

Valery Pavlovich moved back the cockpit cowling and, opening the seat belts holding him to the seat, went slowly out onto the wing, jumped onto the ground, and took off his helmet. His light brown hair fell down and sweat poured from his face, while in his light blue eyes shone the mischievous flame of a victor.

A pale Polikarpov hugged Chkalov and said: "Now why did you go and do that, Valery Pavlovich?"

■

In the middle of summer, Olga Erazmovna took her children and left for Leningrad to visit her relatives. Valery Pavlovich flew to Gorky to test the I-17. The main administration of the aviation industry placed much significance on this type of craft. Therefore, the testing of the craft was assigned to Chkalov.

After arriving at the factory and giving orders for preparation of the aircraft for flight, Valery Pavlovich left for his native Vasilevo. After visiting his mother, as Valery called his stepmother, Natalia Georgievna, he returned to Gorky in two days and began his testing program. The program was carried out exactly and completely. The day arrived when the modified I-16 had to be flown the kilometric base to determine its maximal speed while flying just above the ground.[41]

According to the methodologies set up, the altitude during such a flight was not to exceed fifty to one hundred meters.

Chkalov took off early one morning while the sun had not yet warmed up the air and the ground and thus had not created the upward flows that distort the true capabilities of the aircraft, including its speed characteristics.

Flying toward the measuring base, Valery noticed that the surrounding area was completely unsuitable: a large area of cut-down trees with endless stumps and small shrubs, completely surrounded by deep woods.

Noting the timekeeper's signal, "Everything is ready, you may begin your pass," the test pilot set the maximum speed and concentrated all his attention on holding the craft exactly horizontal, not losing, not gaining a meter of altitude. He maintained an exactly identical attitude on his return flight along the base.

Later the speed was increased, and the craft again made a pass in both directions.

Now the engine was roaring at full throttle, showing its maximal possible revolutions, and the little "donkey," as Valery jokingly called his I-16, shook and strained from the tremendous aerodynamic load. The craft passed above the ground at high speed, approaching the starting measuring line.

Suddenly, the pilot felt a kind of slight bump, after which the engine for an instant changed its usual even, rumbling roar. Something was rattling, and the craft began shaking as if in a fever.

"The engine has blown," Chkalov realized immediately. He could not let the craft be destroyed by these vibrations, and he turned off the ignition and sharply pulled up the nose of the aircraft, gaining altitude so that he could glide farther away from those damned stumps.

From the nose section of the plane, behind the cowling, oil was leaking. Caught in the airstream, it was flowing back and spurting on the front canopy of the pilot's cockpit. Chkalov then opened the canopy, which now allowed him to look to the side and front. The altitude was three hundred meters when the craft reached its minimal speed.

The test pilot put the craft into a glide, choosing the most appropriate course that would enable it to be airborne as long as possible. The whistle and rustle of the air flowing around the fighter was very audible.

Valery knew the capabilities and the characteristics of the I-16 very well and he utilized its maximum capabilities in this dangerous situation. After sticking his head out one more time, he decided that he was winning this encounter with death once again. He would have to land in the forest, but this was much better than landing on the stumps. Now the pilot was bothered more than anything else by the smoke and flames pouring out from underneath the engine cowling. Would the aircraft catch on fire? Now there were only about fifty meters to the tops of the trees. Chkalov noticed a clump of pine trees on the left and, without further thought, turned toward this dark green spot.

He concentrated all his efforts in order not to miss that moment when it would be necessary to pull the fighter out of a gliding angle and put the craft on its end just before hitting the tops of the pine trees.

His calculations were exact. The aircraft, cutting into the flexible crowns of the trees, smashed branches and lost speed. Near the ground, the craft unexpectedly turned over, and Chkalov felt a strong blow to his head.

Two farm workers, a husband and wife who had been working not far from the area of the emergency landing, found him hanging upside down.

They dragged Valery Pavlovich out of the cockpit of the wrecked craft and placed him on the ground. Chkalov finally came to. The woman wrapped his head, while her husband ran for a stretcher, on which they carried the pilot to the road. Soon afterwards, an ambulance raced up to them, and Chkalov was driven away to the plant.

The Accident Review Board established that the engine had failed due to damage caused to one of the pistons by some kind of tiny metallic piece, which it would have been possible to introduce into the cylinder only through an open valve. It was very similar to sabotage committed by some very experienced individual. In Moscow, Valery Pavlovich appeared with his head wrapped in a bandage and brought with him a picture showing him in such a sad state.

His wife and children were still in Leningrad, and Valery hung this photograph, with the white bandage on his head, above his bed.

Olga Erazmovna didn't know anything about the accident involving her husband, and only after seeing the photograph did she understand that something again had befallen him. In his letters and on the telephone he didn't say anything to her about it. She became upset with her husband, removed his photograph from the wall, and hid it in a writing table. When Valery returned from work, Olga Erazmovna upbraided her husband for his secrecy:

"But I didn't want to upset you with such news, Lelik. After all, you're the breadwinner," said Chkalov to his wife, smiling.

PART THREE

In the World Arena

6

The First Flight across the Arctic Ocean

One evening in late autumn of 1935, 1 dropped by Valery Pavlovich's house. At that time he lived on the Leningrad Highway.

Valery shook my hand for a long time. I glanced into his face. Chkalov's eyes had become more lively; the wrinkles had somehow softened. On the lapel of his leather jacket glittered the Order of Lenin.

"Well, Baiduk, we meet again."

He then escorted me into another room in order to show me his daughter, who easily fit into her father's wide palms.

"I live like a god," said Chkalov, showing his simple housekeeping. "And how are you?"

"All right, Valerian." I called him "Valerian" from old times.

"And so?"

"I want to talk to you."

"OK, go ahead. Why didn't you tell me earlier?"

"Not here. There are too many people."

"Listen, brother, I always have a lot of people. I love company."

"You know that the aircraft in which Levanevsky and I attempted to cross the North Pole is now being altered."

"Well? So what? That is your craft."

I was a little taken aback, not knowing how to approach Chkalov.

Olga Erazmovna very carefully listened to our conversation. She didn't like this subject. She vaguely felt danger. Catching her reproachful look, I grew silent. Valery, still not understanding everything hidden in my words, waited for an explanation.

I winked at him and nodded my head in the direction of the mistress of the house.

He understood.

"Well, all right, let's go outside."

He glanced into the dining room, excused himself, and quickly put on a coat. We came out to the alley of Petrovsky Park.

"In front of wives, it's difficult to carry on such conversations. They'll begin to worry about nothing," I noted.

"I understand. Well, go on."

■

Gromov had set the record for flying in a closed circuit in the ANT-25 craft, a distance of 12,411 kilometers.

Later at one of the receptions in the Kremlin in the beginning of 1935, the hero of the *Chelyushkin* epic, Sigismund Alexandrovich Levanevsky, asked Stalin's agreement for planning a nonstop flight from Moscow to the United States—to San Francisco over the North Pole.

The flight project was evaluated and approved. It was set into motion by a resolution of the Labor and Defense Ministry, which selected the flight crew for the ANT-25: commander of the craft, Hero of the Soviet Union S. A. Levanevsky; copilot, an auditor of the engineering faculty of the Zhukovsky Air Force Academy, G. F. Baidukov; navigator, V. I. Levchenko of the Black Sea Fleet; back-up pilot, commander of ground support squadron, V. M. Gurevich; reserve navigator and the person responsible for navigational preparation of the crew, head of the navigational faculty of the Zhukovsky Air Force Academy, Professor A. V. Belyakov.

The Long Distance Flight Committee was organized as a result of the resolution of the Labor and Defense Ministry; the heads were Sergo Ordzhonikidze of the People's Commissariat of Heavy Industry and designer A. N. Tupolev.

In the middle of the spring of 1935, I was called to the director of the Academy, A. I. Todorsky. He took from a safe a piece of paper and, passing it to me, said: "Study this very carefully and then carry it out immediately."

I read the resolution notice of the Labor and Defense Ministry assigning me to Levanevsky's crew for a flight in the ANT-25 across the North Pole to America.

Not comprehending it right away, I read the text twice. It was apparent that written on my face was some kind of confusion because Todorsky asked: "What's the matter, comrade Baidukov? Is it unclear?"

I was silent and my superior asked again: "Do you know Levanevsky?"

"That's just what's the matter. I don't know Levanevsky. The North Pole I remember only vaguely from stories about Fridtjof Nansen that I read as a child."

"Just the same, it isn't right to fulfill an assignment of Soviet Government with such a sour outlook. Enthusiasm is needed in such matters, my dear friend," the academy head concluded. Saying good-bye to me, he added, "I wish you luck. This matter is extremely important."

But in no way was I able to become accustomed to the thought that, for the sake of some sort of pole, I would have to abandon my studies, which I had dreamed of for so long.

Several days later, a packet was handed to me from S. A. Levanevsky. A member of the Central Executive Committee of the USSR, Sigismund Alexandrovich requested that I come to his apartment at 6 P.M. I arrived at the stipulated address exactly on time. I was met by a man a little over average height with blue eyes and a large head. I guessed right away that this was my commander, Levanevsky. The first minutes of conversation demonstrated the great experience of this naval pilot in flying in the north.

Around 10 P.M., his navigator, Victor Ivanovich Levchenko, showed up. He was a tall, robust sailor.

Members of Levanevsky's crew had to carry out an extensive program of flight training exercises in the course of the three months before the start of that flight.

Much had to be remodified and completed on the ANT-25 in order to prepare it for flight across the entire Arctic region of the world.

At first glance it seemed obvious that it would be simpler and more reliable to create an aerial link between the two great nations of the world, the USSR and the USA, across Western Europe and the Atlantic Ocean. However, the simplest measuring of the distances of aerial routes showed that the shortest distance between the USSR and the USA indeed passed over the Arctic. In fact, from Moscow to San Francisco, across the Pacific Ocean, it was a trip of about 18,000 kilometers. Across the Atlantic Ocean, it was about 14,000 kilometers. But across the North Pole, it was only 9,605 kilometers.

In the first days of August 1935, by early morning light, the overloaded ANT-25 made its run perfectly and Sigismund Alexandrovich successfully lifted off the concrete landing strip at Schelkovo field. A course was taken toward the North Pole and North America.

The weather was magnificent and the engine worked faultlessly.

But how quickly human hopes can be dashed. After a few hours of flying, near the approach to the Kola Peninsula, Levanevsky called me and shouted into my ear: "Take a look. What is this thin stream of oil pouring out on the left wing?"

Indeed, one could see a relatively powerful flow of oil, similar to a continuously uncoiling gigantic worm. Inside the aircraft, there was oil also dripping from somewhere.

By our computations, the flow exceeded by many times the permissible oil loss for the nine-hundred-horsepower AM-34 engine. At the same time, the reserve supply of oil should have been enough to reach the shores of the Canadian tundra, where it would be possible to land near a settlement, and so complete the most important task of the flight, to conquer the air space above the central section of the Arctic and the North Pole.

The flight headquarters sent an order by radio to immediately abort the flight, and to land at a field at Krechevetsky, which was between Moscow and Leningrad. You can imagine our complicated situation when the time to land at Krechevetsky approached.

It was dangerous to lose your head at such a moment. In order to bring the weight of the aircraft down to that needed for landing we had to expel, in flight, a tremendous amount of fuel.

We descended to two hundred meters and with explosives opened the lower underbody hatches of the fuel system's overflow devices.

Inside the craft, the concentration of fuel fumes grew with each moment and from a most insignificant spark, the aircraft could explode like gunpowder. Consequently, we immediately turned off the radio transmitter—which could have caused a disaster.

Opening the side hatches of the cockpit completely in order to air out the interior of the craft and lower the concentration of gas fumes, I asked the Commander to lower the landing gears and prepare for a night landing.

The craft made a long landing run on the hard packed surface of the field.

After turning off the engine, I immediately opened the upper hatches of the cockpit. Levanevsky was already on the ground. He had climbed out of the craft through the rear hatches. After leaving the navigational lights and the internal cockpit lights on, I rushed to the captain, who was shining a light on to the fuselage of the aircraft, which was covered in oil.

We observed that the oil was coming out of a drainage tube from the working oil sump. The sickly, sweet smell of gasoline, which had saturated the percale coverings of the metal wings, was still very strong.

The navigator was in the cockpit continuing to collect and pack the flight maps, navigational notations, and radio communications. I shouted to him not to forget the $9000 in the cockpit, which had been handed to us by Klement Evremovich with the words, "This is for when you land; be sure you have a good time." Then at the instant Victor Ivanovich turned off the on-board navigational lights there was a deafening roar from the port wing. The craft was covered with a bright flame. The percale covers of the wings were burning! Two flares, to be used in the case of a forced landing, for some incomprehensible reason were burning inside the wing. With a temperature of over 2,000°, wing spars caught on fire and fell to the ground under the left console. With a terrible hissing, the entire aircraft, which was saturated with gasoline, ignited.

Levanevsky and I, as if in a dream, threw off our flight coats, jumped up on the wings, and started to beat the flames with our coats, attempting to save the aircraft. Levchenko jumped out through the front cockpit and began assisting us in dousing the flames.

It isn't clear how our desperate attempt to save the ANT-25 from the fire would have ended but for an incredible phenomenon. Two trucks, with large tarp covers and some very knowledgeable Red Army soldiers, rushed up to the craft and began quietly and in a very businesslike manner to cover the wings with the tarps, which quickly extinguished the flames.

At night, a Government Commission arrived at Krechevetsky. Shortly, the crew was called before the Politburo. Stalin asked: "What are we going to do from here on in? What do you think, Comrade Levanevsky?"

Levanevsky was gloomy but calm. He announced that aircraft deficiency was to blame. Stalin suggested to the crew that they travel to the United States and see what they could purchase there for a proposed flight across the pole.

I asked for permission to speak and stated that the Americans had nothing similar to the ANT-25, that the trip to the U.S. would be fruitless, and asked for permission to stay home. Only one question was bothering me at that point: Would I now be able to throw off this Arctic epic and return to my studies?

But I was unable to return to the academic world. The head of the Air Force, Ya. I. Alksnis, at a meeting, stated that our lack of success with the aircraft had put not only the Air Force, but the aviation industry and the Soviet Union in an embarrassing position; he added that it would be good to remove this sensitive point. As a result, I was assigned as a test pilot to an aviation plant and my dream to become an engineer popped like a soap bubble.

In my spare time, I frequently researched the ANT-25 in order to attempt to produce the exact same flow of oil that forced the crew to abandon the flight. Moving the drainage of the oil sump to another area removed that defect.

Questions relating to the condition of the ANT-25 were discussed by us many times, including A. V. Belyakov, who returned to complete his basic duties as the Head of the Navigational Faculty of the Zhukovsky Academy. Naturally in our conversations, the question arose: "Well, all right. We bring the craft to peak condition, and then what?"

Alexander Vasilyevich stated to me several times that the selection of pilots would be up to me since I was more familiar with them.

After that I looked over hundreds of well-known and little-known pilots but most often ended up settling on Chkalov.

"But why me? I'm just a typical fighter pilot," Valery said impatiently.

"My dear friend, I have come to you, as an unannounced guest, because we need the most able, courageous, most authoritative flier in the country."

"Egor, you love to pick on your friends. Why do you call me, a soldier in a guardhouse, and make a god out of me? I don't know instrument flying; I don't know astro or radio navigation, nor do I know radio-telegraphy."

"If you're able to get permission for the flight, to lift that over-loaded ANT-25 off the concrete strip, then consider that 50 percent of this important government matter is already fulfilled. As far as flying through the clouds, that's my business. All the rest, Sasha and I will take care of. Don't worry about it."

"Well, if that's the way, then I won't refuse to come with you as crew, but to boss over people, that I can't do."

I understood that to insist further would not make any sense. It was necessary to give my friend time to think.

■

I didn't bother Valery Pavlovich for about two weeks, then I invited him to take a look at the ANT-25 and to fly it.

At that time, there was a healthy snow failing and it was necessary to put skis on the plane. Precisely at this moment, Clikalov arrived at the hangar of the TsAGI.

During the first half of the day, he became familiar with the specifications of the ANT-25 which had a record-length wing. He studied charts that would enable them to achieve these long-distance flights.

After dinner, a blizzard began, snow fell heavily, and there were low clouds scudding over Central Field. There were no other flights that day, and it was relatively easy for us to get permission to make a flight around the field.

I was glad that my old friend was relating to the ANT-25 with great curiosity. Sitting behind him, I attentively watched him during his first flight. One sensed a great flight master.

"Wonderful, what can you say? The people who work for Tupolev are wonderful." Valery lifted up his index finger in a sign of approval.

It was the spring of 1936; our crew had not as yet been officially selected by Government decree, but we were all set to jump across the North Pole; not only technically, but more importantly, psychologically. We composed a letter to the Politburo with a request for their permission for us to fly. Finally, we decided to send the letter off and from then on our anxieties began.

For a long time, there was no response. In answer to Chkalov's questions, Sergo Ordzhonikidze would just smile with his magnificent mustache.

In the beginning of June 1936, the Central Committee of the All-Union Communist Party (Bolsheviks) gathered together the representatives of the aviation industry—pilots, including test pilots, navigators, engineers, and mechanics—in order to speak frankly regarding the reasons for the large number of accidents in the Air Force, which had led to the unjustifiable loss of life.

During a break we spoke to Sergo Ordzhonikidze and asked him about the fate of our note to the Politburo concerning our project for a long-distance flight across the pole.

"There won't be enough room for you," Sergo laughed. "Everyone wants to fly. The craft has to be tested very well."

We answered excitedly that the craft in which we were scheduled to fly was already tested and we were ready to fly at any time.

"Very well," said Sergo, noting our impatience. "I'll bring you together with Comrade Stalin."

"Why is it necessary to fly over the North Pole? It seems that pilots are not afraid of anything. They've become used to taking risks," Stalin said.

Chkalov answered, with real conviction: "But the craft is a good one, the engine is excellent, and there is very little risk."

"This is your itinerary for the flight: Moscow to Petropavlovsk-on-Kamchatka."

This was so unexpected that we didn't know how to answer.

The next morning, Chkalov, Belyakov, and I gathered at the TsAGI. We accepted the suggested itinerary as an order of the Homeland.

On the same evening, we finally determined the distribution of duties among us for the flight and, without losing any time, began to prepare for our future trip,

How many sleepless nights were spent working on the flight charts! How many people were drawn into our preparation!

After a month and a half of intensified training and testing, we were prepared to make the final test flight.

Loading our gear into the cockpit of the ANT-25, we took on board an engineer and a radio operator and lifted off into the air. We were covered by the exhaust fumes of the yellow-lacquered smoke that was pouring out of the stacks of the Schelkovo factories. I turned the tumbler switch to retract the landing gears; suddenly, somewhere below, a crashing sound was heard. Everyone was startled. I looked across Valery's shoulder, and verified that the signal lights showing the mode of the landing gear were not on. The axle of the winch that retracted the landing gear was not turning, even though the switch of the motor had been turned on.

Chkalov was sitting behind the controls and steadily gaining altitude. Belyakov and the radio operator were tuning the radio; I sat on the reserve oil supply tank and thought.

"Something's wrong with the landing gear," I said to the chief engineer, Yevgeny Karlovich Stoman, who was nearby.

"I don't understand how this could have happened," the engineer answered, and began to check the elevators and cables of the landing gear.

Shortly, he returned with bad news.

"It's not good. The lift and release cables of the landing gear have been severed."

With the aid of navigational sights, Yevgeny Pavlovich and I confirmed that the left and right landing gears of the aircraft were in a tucked-in position.

I made my way up to Chkalov and told him what had happened. His eyes, for just a fraction of a second, reflected disappointment and surprise, but not a single muscle on his face twitched.

Meanwhile the ANT-25 continued to fly at an altitude of approximately one thousand meters.

The sun was still high in the sky and there was still a good four hours before darkness. There was enough fuel for two days of continuous flying.

In order to more easily determine the reasons for the failure and the scope of damage to the landing gear winch, I drew a sketch. After replacing Chkalov, I began to fly the aircraft from the rear flight control panel.

The commander climbed down from the front seat and, reaching the navigator's area, ordered Alexander Vasilyevich to report to Flight Command by radio and to request that the flight controller at Schelkovo field warn all other aircraft in the vicinity not to fly close to the ANT-25, because its crew would not have time to observe the surrounding air space.

Chkalov, together with Stoman, dismantled the front section of the pilot's seat and saw that the winch was seriously damaged.

Valery took off his leather jacket. Wearing a white silk shirt with his ruffled light brown hair, he resembled a wrestler awaiting his opponent. Before him stood the very thin, hunchbacked figure of the elderly Stoman. He was a remarkable engineer and test pilot for the TsAGI, a former pilot, and a holder of the St. George's Cross and Order of the Red Banner.

Valery ripped open the only parachute, which had accidentally turned up on board, fastened its straps to the release cable of the landing gear, and began to pull on it with all his strength.

Even his strength turned out be insufficient. The extended cable moved the left unit of the landing gear forward only a few centimeters and then returned to its original position.

Because the landing gear on the ANT-25, as it's being lowered during landing, must move forward against the airstream of the plane, I reduced the revs on the engine and flew the craft at minimal speed.

Chkalov, Stoman, and Belyakov grabbed the strap. My assistance turned out to be ineffectual. They used up all their strength, sweat was pouring off of their foreheads, but the landing gear did not budge.

We added the labors of radio operator Kovalevsky, a young, very powerful individual, a former sailor, but even his strength was to no avail. The fruitlessness of our efforts was becoming apparent.

The pale, panting Stoman lay down on the deck of the fuselage; his head was spinning.

Chkalov came up to me. I suggested that we fly as long as there was fuel left, even if that was two days; however, we had to think of something fast.

"Well, my dear Egorushka; we are flying to Kamchatka. What a disgrace," Valery said to me, with distress in his voice.

"Now you sit in the pilot's seat." I said this to the Commander because an idea was forming in my head that I wanted to share with the chief engineer.

"Yevgeny Karlovich," I shouted loudly to the engineer. "Let's try this. Sasha, Kovalevsky, and I will tug in jerks at the cable, and you can prop it up with some kind of sharp, metal object. Maybe we will be able to move the left unit and put it in the extreme forward position; then we'll try the other one."

The chief engineer smiled. "I have a little hammer with me. I'll crawl inside the left wing, and from there I can reach the landing gear support."

Chkalov descended to an altitude of five hundred meters so that it would be easier for the crew to breathe during their emergency efforts.

The hellish work continued for several hours. The sun had already gone down. It was necessary to turn on the lights in the cockpit. Oblivious to pain in our backs and our hands, and sparks flying into our eyes, with incredible effort, we fought centimeter by centimeter for some movement in the cable.

Then Valery gave out a whistle, followed by a joyful shout: "Everything's all right!"

After resting for a while, we began to work on the other landing gear unit, but the right support did not move a single millimeter.

After a four-hour, superhuman battle for the life of the craft, the fate of the flight began to depend on Valery's composure and mastery. Would he be able to save the ANT-25 while landing it on only the left landing gear unit?

Through the portholes we could see that in the evening twilight people at the field were holding their breath in expectation of a miracle. Having prepared for any possible accident that we might have had, the ambulances and the fire engines were on the alert.

In the half-darkness, Valery evened the aircraft out and turned off the engine. Only the rustle of the wind rushing by the craft could be heard. I gave the command for my friends to move into the tail section of the aircraft. I crawled up forward to the commander in order to be there if he needed my assistance in any way.

The left wheel touched down smoothly. Chkalov slowly turned the controls to the left, not allowing the craft to tip toward its right wing.

The blows on the landing gear supports became fewer and fewer. The commander turned the controls all the way to the left and sharply moved the rudder pedal in the same direction in order to effect a left turn. But the ANT-25 had already lost speed, and thus was not responsive to the controls. In an instant, it dropped on its right wing, turned to the right, and became still.

This was 2115 hours, July 10. The aircraft remained intact. This allowed us to prepare for a flight on the evening of July 19. At 1800 hours, Chkalov, returning to Schelkovo, announced to us:

"Well, Sasha and Egor, let's go flying."

■

For days we selected fittings, equipment, provisions, and instruments that had been prepared for us, and loaded them onto the aircraft. There were radios, skis, astronomical equipment, maps, sleeping bags, a rubber raft, forty pounds of salt personally ordered by Valery

Pavlovich, and many other things that would be necessary for the flight and for survival on ice in case of a forced landing. All this was very carefully packed away in the wings and the enormous fuselage of the ANT-25 monoplane, which was placed on scales in a hangar.

On the night of July 20, the mechanics and power plant mechanics, under the direction of the chief engineer, began to fill the fuel tanks. Powerful floodlights lit up the gigantic craft with its brightly polished, bright red wings.

All the innovations of our aviation technology were incorporated in the ANT-25. It was the first craft in which the landing gear would retract in flight, and which had hydraulic shock absorbers, as well as an electric lifter.

The engine is the heart of the craft. If it functions insufficiently or sputters, this could bring disaster to the fliers. On the other hand, pilots used to jokingly say: "With a good engine you can fly on a stick."

It was clear that on a long flight, the reliability of the engine took on a special significance, even more so because the ANT-25 had only one engine.

The AM-34R engine that had been placed in the ANT-25 was designed at the Central Aviation Institute of Engine Construction, under the direction of the talented designer A. A. Mikulin, and prepared at a Moscow factory. In 1936, this engine was designed for multiseries production and had been used for more than a year in intermediate and long-distance bombers and reconnaissance planes.

The blue morning sky was shining above the field. The red-winged giant, completely filled with cargo and fuel, was pulled off the scales and a tractor delivered it to a cement landing strip. The starting point was located on a slight incline on the field.

A whole procession of guests who had arrived in Schelkovo from Moscow, to see us off on our long journey, followed behind the airplane. Everyone was there, except friends and relatives. The flight surgeon and the flight commander had requested this. The crew was in agreement. The aircraft was placed on a slight mound, from which, with its nose lifted in the air, it proudly looked over the light-gray markings of the takeoff strip. From this location, the ANT-25 had to lurch forward and make a ground run in order to take off.

Photo correspondents and cameramen filmed our activities and also those who were in the area of the takeoff.

The commander of the ship sat behind the controls of the ANT-25. I took my place on the oil tank directly behind him in order to retract the landing gears after takeoff. Belyakov was sitting at the navigator's table.

It was calm at the airport. The temperature of the ambient air was 15°. The conditions for takeoff were completely favorable.

Chkalov tested the engine. The aircraft shook from the powerful rumble of the propellers and exhaust from the engine. Valery Pavlovich throttled back and gave the signal to remove the blocks from beneath the wheels.

The roar of the engine was deafening. The aircraft slowly bounced from the slight incline and began its ground run. It was gaining speed rapidly.

And so the flight began.

Chkalov gained altitude meter by meter. The ANT-25, which was loaded to its limit, passed below the smoking factory stacks of Schelkovo, even though the engine was working at full capacity. After retracting the landing gear, I announced to the commander that I was going on duty as the navigator and radio operator.

For the first twelve hours, Chkalov flew the aircraft. Immediately after takeoff, Belyakov was to sleep and rest for six hours, after which he would replace me as the navigator and radio operator.

At 1425 hours, the plane flew over Kharlovka on the Kola Peninsula, which was the last point on the European continent.

The ANT-25 came out onto the Barents Sea and approached Victoria Island.

After ten hours of uninterrupted engine work at maximal speed, the commander throttled back and the cockpit of the aircraft became a bit quieter.

At 2210 hours, according to our calculations, we were located in the region of Victoria Island. Belyakov sent a note to the pilot to change to a new course in an easterly direction, leading toward Franz-Josef Land Archipelago.

When I relayed the navigator's data to Chkalov, he couldn't contain himself.

"We're heading right toward the pole. You can shake hands with it," Valery Pavlovich shouted into my ear.

"There are babblers in the ranks," I blurted out in jest. As an answer Chkalov, smiling, poked me in the side with his fist.

The first 2,700 kilometers of the journey had been covered.

I rested, observing the shadows inside the aircraft, which were jumping about the various objects every time the aircraft changed its position in space. Then I heard.

"Look, you can see Franz-Josef Land."

Jumping from the oil tank, I grabbed a camera from a suitcase and pressed against the side portholes of the front canopy to take a series of photographs of the Arctic landscape.

At 2310, on July 20, 1936, a radiogram was sent from on board the ANT-25: "Everything is fine. We are passing over Franz-Josef Land. We can see the islands. Greetings to those wintering at Bukhta-Tikhaya from the crew. Chkalov, Baidukov, Belyakov."

It was midnight according to the clock. But the sun was still high in the sky. A fantastic panorama of the islands of the archipelago opened before our eyes.

It was now July 21, 1936. After Franz-Josef Land we saw only open seas and ahead only an endless, blinding, icy field.

Soon the ice was covered with a thick fog and from above there appeared a many-tiered cloud layer. In another half an hour the plane was flying in clouds. I began to gain altitude, but the ANT-25, still quite heavily loaded with fuel, could not make it toward the sun. A dilemma arose: either fly into the cloud layer—and into the cyclone that had been precisely predicted before takeoff by the meteorologists—or go around it in order not to subject the aircraft to icing conditions and overloading in the cumulus cloud layer.

Here we were quite convinced how inaccurate were the suppositions of scientists and meteorologists; they had maintained that in the central regions of the Arctic the upper edge of the cloud layer, even in summer, never exceeds three to four kilometers in altitude.

In the meantime, the intensity of icing conditions increased. The aircraft trembled as if in a fever.

Chkalov helped me turn on the anti-icing device for the propellers. The commander and navigator decided to alter the flight course and find a less thick layer of clouds in order to more quickly climb upward.

In searching for a better way, Chkalov and Belyakov gave me numerous possible courses. As I was flying the craft, I counted more than twelve sharp turns in our route when suddenly, through a break in the clouds, I spotted a dangerously threatening vertical cliff shooting straight up among the limitless Arctic Ocean of ice and snow.

The commander and navigator, holding maps in their hands, quickly determined that this was North Land Island. But again clouds covered the scene like a curtain being dropped on a stage.

At 2000 hours, Belyakov radioed: "Everything is in order. We are at North Land Island."

The cyclone continued, but now it was impossible to turn away from our primary course. We decided to attempt flight above the cloud layer. We came out into the sun at an altitude of four thousand meters and went on a direct course to the Bay of Tiksi. Shortly, some very high cloud layers stood in the path of the ANT-25 and again we flew by instruments and the icing conditions concerned the crew. The commander, tired and concerned, grabbed me from behind by the shoulders and shouted into my ear: "Descend, descend. The empennage is shaking about dangerously. Look, the stabilizing bars will rip off. Go, take a look."

Easing off on the engine revs, I lowered the aircraft sharply and we could soon see the mosaic colors displayed on the icy shores of Khatangsky Gulf.

Belyakov had worked the navigator's post without any relief for nineteen hours. The cyclone had knocked us off course. Chkalov replaced me behind the wheel of the aircraft and I relieved Belyakov in navigational duties.

Valery climbed to an altitude of forty-three hundred meters.

The exhausted Belyakov stretched out and fell immediately asleep on the bottom of the aircraft.

After giving Alexander Vasilyevich two hours to rest, I woke him up so that he could return to his duties.

At 1010 he radioed: "Everything is all right. We are above the shoreline to the east of Nordvik."

And at 1410, Belyakov sent out over the airwaves: "Everything is all right. Altitude 4,000 meters. Position is 72° 20' north latitude; 123° 40' east longitude near the Bay of Tiksi."

We slowly started to get back to the schedule of our duty roster.

Around 1500 hours, I once again sat in the navigator's chair, letting Belyakov sleep.

The long flight above altitudes of four thousand meters began to affect everyone in the crew. We should have been breathing oxygen but, after consulting with the crew, the commander decided that the six-hour supply of oxygen would be used at the end of the flight until after Kamchatka when we would cross the Sea of Okhotsk and head toward Khabarovsk. There it was possible that we would have to climb to an altitude of six thousand meters, and that it would be very difficult for a tired crew to carry on such a flight without oxygen.

It was now the third day, July 22, 1936.

The crew was tired, due especially to the lack of oxygen, which made everyone lose their appetite. We had some chocolate, but mainly tea and water.

I relieved the commander at the pilot's seat.

He liked to sit near Belyakov and watch how precisely the professor measured the drift angle or took measures of heavenly bodies, then quickly calculated the true course.

On the right rose Koryaksky Peak, surrounded by thick, curly caps of clouds. Further on, as far as the eye could see, the whole of Kamchatka and the Sea of Okhotsk was covered with a thick shroud of clouds.

The ANT-25 flew at an altitude of forty-two hundred meters. The Pacific Ocean became visible and below us was Petropavlovsk-on-Kamchatka. After throwing out a message container and making a circle around the city, we set course for Sakhalin, across the most stormy sea on earth.

In fifty hours of continual flight battling against the elements, we came to know well the ANT-25 with its AM-34R engine, which never stopped functioning, not even for a second.

Now came the difficult part: the final hours of the flight.

The enormous cyclone, which brought along with it thick cloud layers, rain, and fog, greeted us above the Sea of Okhotsk.

Again we flew on instruments.

The weather in the region of Sakhalin and the seacoast was very unfavorable. Just clouds, rain, and fog.

At 0638, Chkalov relieved me. Together with Belyakov, I began to evaluate the situation.

We suggested to the commander to approach Sakhalin, then descend below the clouds in order to enter the mouth of the Amur River before nightfall, and then fly at night along the river to Khabarovsk.

Chkalov agreed with our suggestions and began a steep descent.

We came out of the cloud layer at an altitude of fifty meters above the stormy Sea of Okhotsk. The wings and empennage of the aircraft shook and vibrated helplessly from the gusts of wind.

Valery P. Chkalov at his parents' home in August 1937, shortly after the completion of his historic transpolar flight from Moscow to Vancouver, Washington.

The *Maxim Gorky* (ANT-20), escorted by two I-4 fighters, flies over Red Square on May Day 1935.

Soviet ANT-6's, equipped with skiis, land at the North Pole in spring 1937. Soviet flights to the Arctic allowed a scientific team to maintain a research station on an ice floe for several months. The Soviet conquest of the Arctic received considerable press coverage in the West.

Sigismund Levanevsky (right) in Los Angeles with V. I. Levchenko in 1936 after their successful flight from Siberia across the North Pacific.

Women pilots played a prominent role in the program of the Soviet Union to establish new aviation records in the 1930s. Valentina S. Grizodubova, Polina D. Osipenko, and Marina M. Raskova completed a record-breaking direct flight across the Soviet Union (6,450 km) on September 24–25, 1938, flying an ANT-37, *Rodina* (*Motherland*).

The ANT-25 *Stalinskiy marshrut* (*Stalin Route*) in flight.

The 1936 flight of the ANT-25 *Stalinskiy marshrut* from Moscow to Udd Island near Kamchatka was the dress rehearsal for Chkalov's transpolar flight to America. Left to right: Alexander Belyakov, Valery Chkalov, Georgiy Baidukov.

Valery Chkalov receives a warm welcome at Khabarovsk in Siberia after his 1936 flight to Udd Island.

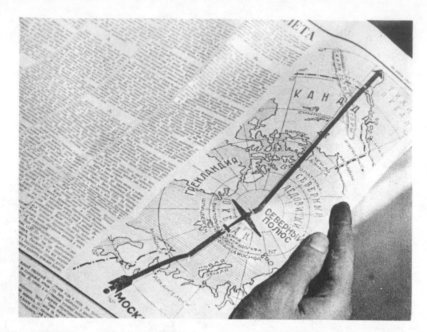

The June 19, 1937, edition of *Izvestia* gave extensive coverage of Chkalov's three-day transpolar flight, then in progress. The map shows the scheduled flight path over the North Pole.

Winner in Pole Vault Event

Portland's *Oregonian* newspaper printed Quincy Scott's cartoon of Chkalov's successful transpolar flight on June 22, 1937. American newspapers gave extensive coverage to Chkalov's flight. Courtesy of Lev Richards and the *Oregonian*, Portland, Oregon.

A rare view of the ANT-25 *Stalinskiy marshrut* at the Pearson Airfield in June 1937. Courtesy of Charles Alexander.

Aerial view (circa 1929) of Pearson Army Air Corps base at Vancouver, Washington. This is the same approach to the airfield made by Chkalov and his crew after his sixty-two-hour flight over the North Pole. Courtesy of the Clark County Historical Muscum, Vancouvcr, Washington.

Alexander Belyakov (left) and Valery Chkalov (right) after landing at Vancouver, Washington, on June 20, 1937.

Alexander Belyakov greets the press from the navigator's hatch of the ANT-25, shortly after their landing at Pearson Airfield.

Valery Chkalov formally hands over the barograph from the ANT-25 for inspection. This device authenticated his nonstop transpolar flight.

Chkalov and his crew in America on June 21, 1937. New suits were purchased for the Soviet transpolar fliers for their meeting with Soviet Ambassador Alexander Troyanovsky and General George C. Marshall, commander of the Vancouver Army Air Corps base. Left to right: Alexander Belyakov, Alexander Troyanovsky, General Marshall, Valery Chkalov, and Georgiy Baidukov. Courtesy of the Clark County Historical Museum, Vancouver, Washington.

Valery Chkalov, Georgiy Baidukov, and Alexander Belyakov at Oakland, California, in June 1937. The Soviet airmen made an extensive tour of the United States after their transpolar flight.

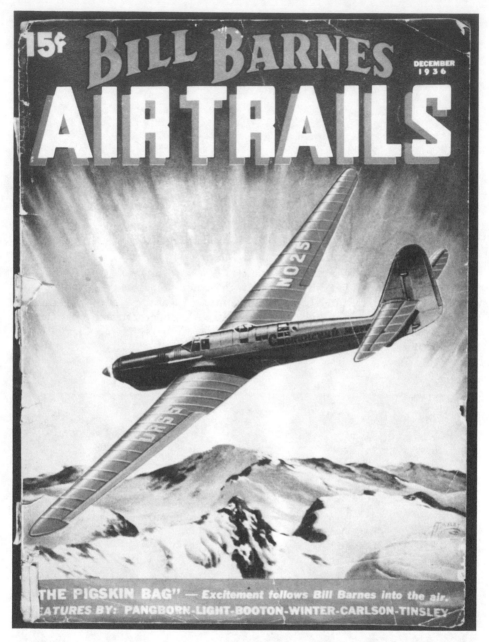

The Chkalov flight made a powerful impact on the aviation press, as illustrated on the cover of the December 1937 issue of *Air Trails*.

Chkalov made a triumphal return to the Soviet Union in August 1937. He is pictured here in a motorcade in Moscow with his wife and son.

The return of Chkalov, Baidukov, and Belyakov to Moscow in August 1937 provided an occasion for a large parade. Pictured is a large poster of the transpolar fliers.

The ANT-25 *Stalinskiy marshrut* at the International Air Fair, Paris, in 1937.

Mikhail Gromov's ANT-25 at San Jacinto, California, near San Diego, in July 1937 after his successful transpolar flight.

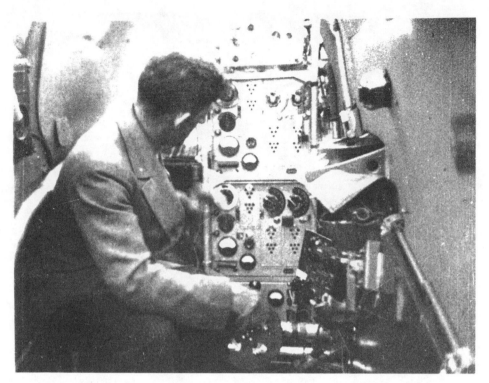

Interior of the ANT-25 aircraft showing radio equipment.

Sigismund Levanevsky with a crew of six flew this modified ANT-6 on his ill-fated transpolar flight of August 1937. Levanevsky and his crew disappeared without a trace.

Mikhail Gromov (middle) with Sergei Danilin and Andrei Yumashev in a motorcade in Washington, D.C., in July 1937. The crews of both transpolar flights of 1937 made tours of the United States and met with President Franklin D. Roosevelt.

Soviet transpolar fliers (left to right) Sergei Danilin, Mikhail Gromov, and Andrei Yumashev at the Soviet Embassy, Washington, D.C., 1937.

Funeral of Valery Chkalov, December 1937. This rare photograph shows Stalin as a pallbearer (middle). To Stalin's left is Molotov and behind Stalin is Georgiy Baidukov. Courtesy of Yuri Salnikov.

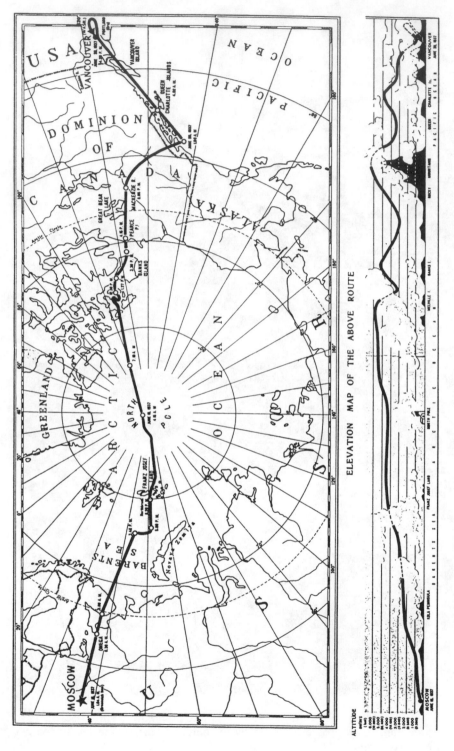

ELEVATION MAP OF THE ABOVE ROUTE

Route taken by Chkalov, Baidukov, and Belyakov on their flight from Moscow to the USA over the North Pole.

There was no way that I could raise Nikolaevsk-on-Amur by radio.

The rain became so strong that it was very difficult to determine the distance to the water. Here was a moment when it was appropriate to attempt the kind of hedgehopping flight that was very much in Chkalov's style, although not always approved of. We were just above the ocean waves.

Valery was literally glued to the controls, looking intently into the foggy gloom.

The eastern shoreline of Sakhalin glittered before us. We had come out at the exact point specified on the itinerary calculated in Moscow.

But the terrain helped the commander for only a short time in guiding the huge aircraft on its hedgehopping flight. The island was passed and we could again see the wild, gray-mantled breakers.

We had been flying for fifty-five hours.

The weather above the sea had become even worse. It was extremely difficult to determine the distance above the water. Suddenly, an enormous dark mass loomed on the left. Evidently this was a mountain on Mechnikov Cape.

We understood that under these conditions we would crash into the volcano's shoreline before we could reach the mouth of the Amur River.

Chkalov instantly made an absolutely correct decision: climb! He gained altitude, turning the ANT-25 to the east. Clouds were covering everything; air temperature decreased sharply.

At fifteen hundred meters there was an endless thick, milky fog and of course, icing became very intense. The stabilizer and the steel braces that supported it were very quickly covered with ice.

Several very tense seconds went by. The aircraft was at an altitude of twenty-five hundred meters, but icing continued.

I sat at the transmitter calling Nikolaevsk, when suddenly I felt some sharp blows and powerful vibrations in the aircraft. This was very dangerous, for the aircraft could be destroyed.

I radioed Khabarovsk and Nikolaevsk regarding the serious icing problems on the ANT-25.

Chkalov quickly throttled back on the engine and the iced-over giant started to descend. The blows became fewer and less frequent.

We came out of the cloud layer at an altitude of approximately fifteen meters above the stormy sea, which was covered by a thick layer of rain and fog.

Visibility decreased; the day was nearing an end and darkness was falling.

■

Together with Belyakov, we once again attempted to make contact with Khabarovsk. Then we heard these repeating words: "I order you to abort the flight. Land at the first possible place. Ordzhonikidze."

We arrived over the cliff-strewn island of Lange; but there was no place to land.

In the evening twilight and the foggy gloom, we spotted an island completely covered by lakes and ravines, with a few houses scattered here and there.

"We're going to land; landing gear," Valery yelled to me and decisively began to descend.

I turned on the motor and shortly the ANT-25 lowered its two-wheeled landing gear.

"You look to the right side and I'll look to the left," Chkalov said loudly when the engine had been reduced to minimum revs.

I pushed my head to the right side of the canopy and, through a small crack in the side window, made my observations.

The final tousled waves passed by followed by sand and pebbles.

The aircraft was almost touching the ground. Chkalov brought it into a final approach, then I shouted, "Go around—there's a ravine!"

Valery noticed this imminent danger and quickly revved up the engine. As usual, the responsive AM-34R engine growled and the aircraft was jerked upwards.

The commander again lowered the revs to minimum and again the ground was visible below us. At our quick pace, the pebbles and sand turned into a continuous surface, rushing up to meet us.

The speed was decreased and now there was no more than a meter to the ground.

"Aft, you guys!" shouted the commander, afraid that on landing the ANT-25 could turn over.

Belyakov and I grabbed onto the radio, staying in this position in case of a crash landing.

But the first touchdown was quite smooth. The aircraft made a three-point landing.

How useful was Chkalov's ability to land an aircraft in such a difficult situation!

The plane decreased its speed. Then the sound of a blow was heard—below and to the left.

The ANT-25 had stopped after fifty-six hours of flight as if it were rooted to the ground.

After several seconds we opened the hatches and crawled out of the aircraft extremely tired. It seemed that it was impossible to have landed here; we were surrounded by deep, dish-shaped ravines filled with water and large boulders, one of which had wedged itself between the wheels of the left landing gear and had ripped one of them out. It had flown off and hit the left wing. A small, harmless dent was visible. Not far from the aircraft, the wheel was lying together with the damaged remains of the half-axle, an outer tire, and an inner tube, which had not been punctured.

Chkalov gave us a rather guilty smile.

"Well, only Chkalov could have done something like this," I said to Belyakov.

We didn't notice the thick fog. We quickly set up the emergency radio in order to send a message about our successful landing on Udd Island, located in the Gulf of Happiness.

We must have appeared a suspicious-looking bunch to the people of the area, in our fur-lined boots and jackets, with our red-winged plane on which was written "0-25" and "USSR."

Despite the storm, two of them immediately jumped into a motor launch and left for the neighboring island of Lange, where soldiers of the Far Eastern Border Patrol, NKVD, were stationed.

Among the gathered people, we noticed men with long curls. These were the Nivkhi and the Gilyaki, who spoke in their own language. Shortly, we heard Russian being spoken.

Chkalov finished helping us set up the main radio, walked over to the cautious-looking inhabitants of the island, and as usual was able to communicate very quickly. Soon, we heard laughter and joking. The people who had met us came over to the aircraft and started examining it.

Belyakov and I, after extending the antenna, tuned in on frequency and gave the following message: "To everyone: the crew of the

ANT-25 has completed a successful landing near Nikolaevsk on Udd Island. Everything is fine."

■

With the inhabitants of the island, Chkalov organized a mooring for the ANT-25. The commander was tired and moved slowly to the wing. He rested against it several times with closed eyes.

After securing the aircraft and closing down the emergency radio and the cockpit of the ANT-25, we left with our hosts for their homes. The fishermen and collective farm workers stayed behind with the ANT-25 and set up guard duty to protect it.

We came to a home and a woman who had accompanied us from the aircraft invited us inside.

"Come in, be my guests."

"Who lives here?" Belyakov asked.

"My name is Fetinya Andreevna. My surname is Smirnova."

"So, you mistook us for Japanese?" Valery Pavlovich asked.

"I just looked up and got scared. The aircraft had strange letters written on it, though I myself cannot read."

While we got undressed, extremely tired after so many days, our hostess busied herself around the stove and continued her conversation with us.

"Of course, I got everyone excited. The aircraft was still circling while the fishermen had already set off for Lange."

"But why did you want to shoot us, Fetinyushka? You ran up to us with a gun," Chkalov added jokingly, yet in exasperation.

"This is not a gun. This is a Winchester rifle," she replied to Valery.

"But you aimed the rifle, not at me or Baidukov, but at the best-looking one—Belyakov."

"Oh you!" she blushed, red-cheeked with embarrassment.

"Very well, Fetinya Adreevna; I'm joking. You did the right thing, you do live near the border. Unexpected things do happen," Chkalov calmed her.

As the tea was boiling, we removed all sorts of things from the rucksacks and placed them on the table. There appeared a bottle of cognac, which our dear doctor, Tromfimuk, had secretly put in the bottom of the produce bag.

Fetinya Andreevna invited us to use her bed, but we refused to inconvenience her and announced that we would be very comfortable sleeping on her spotless floor.

Shortly she left, which gave us a chance to prepare for bed.

"These are such nice people," Valery said, thinking aloud. "They are both cautious and hospitable."

The morning of July 23, 1936, on the island appeared to be a gloomy one; the fog had lifted slightly, hovering in anticipation of the stormy winds coming from the Sea of Okhotsk.

The border patrol guards who had received our radio message yesterday did not hesitate in making use of this calm in the weather.

Chkalov was the first to wake up. He looked at his sleeping friends and thought: "Have we really let Stalin down? After all, Stalin suggested to us that, if we achieved our goal and made a landing, he would promise to construct a field near the Pacific Ocean. We did fulfill his assignment completely: reached Petropavlovsk-on-Kamchatka, threw down a message with a pennant, and even photographed this distant city. But we announced to the Politburo that, after reaching the destination, we would continue across the Sea of Okhotsk to Khabarovsk and perhaps land somewhere further to the west, closer to our homes and Moscow. However, we were forced to land on Udd Island, next to Nikolaevsk on the Amur. It seems that we're just braggarts, or better yet, a bunch of bums."

With these gloomy thoughts, the commander of the ANT-25 rose and woke up the rest of us.

Neither Belyakov nor I was able to calm our friend. We too began to doubt whether we had really done everything possible to honor the Soviet people who had created this wonderful aircraft and who had entrusted their hopes with us.

We began to discuss a plan of action directed at searching for a suitable place to take off, when a man in a flight suit came into the hut together with Fetinya Andreevna.

This was the wing commander of the border patrol, Shestov, who had flown to us in an Sh-2 hydroplane. He was so glad to see us that he hugged us over and over again. Valery, once again filled with lively humor, said to his guest: "It would be better if you would embrace our hostess Fetya. We haven't earned such a welcome."

"No, Valery Pavlovich. I will ask Fetinya Andreevna to kiss you for what you have done."

Chkalov became a little bit more wary, looking at this stranger who was reaching for a telegram from his attache case.

Valery read it out loud:

Nikolaevsk-on-the-Amur. To the crew of the ANT-25, Chkalov, Baidukov, Belyakov. Accept our brotherly greetings and hearty congratulations for the successful completion of an amazing flight.

We are proud of your bravery, courage, endurance, composure, stubbornness, and mastery.

A petition has been sent into the Central Executive Committee of the Soviet Union, to bestow upon you the title of "Hero of the Soviet Union" and to grant you a monetary award: to the captain of the aircraft, Chkalov, the sum of 30,000 rubles; to copilot Baidukov and navigator Belyakov, each 20,000 rubles. We salute you.

(Signed) Stalin, Molotov, Ordzhonikidze, Voroshilov, and Zhdanov.

We were touched to the point of tears. We never dreamed that we would have earned such high praise from our country.

On July 24, 1936, the President of the Central Executive Committee of the USSR, M. Kalinin, and General Secretary of the Central Executive Committee of the Soviet Union, I. Unshlikht, signed a decree awarding the crew members of the ANT-25 the titles of Hero of the Soviet Union, and the Order of Lenin including the awarding of a monetary prize.

During the day, a border patrol coast guard cutter, *Dzerzhinsky*, sailed up to meet us. The sailors took responsibility for guarding the aircraft.

Chkalov felt that everyone who flew in or sailed to meet us had to be met and that it was necessary to speak with all of them and to describe the flight, what our later plans were, and the type of assistance we would require.

Therefore, we decided on the following: I would take the hunting rifle and set off in search of a flat surface suitable for takeoff in the ANT-25. Belyakov would put all the flight documents in order so that they could be presented to the flight administration, and the commander would organize meetings with the people who were in the process of arriving.

I walked around the island for a long time, but didn't find a suitable takeoff strip and was only more surprised that Chkalov was able to land the ANT-25 on this island.

After bagging about a dozen sandpipers, I came out on the shore to listen to the sea sounds, when suddenly I noticed that parallel to the water was a strip suitable for takeoff. After I measured off more than a thousand paces in length, I ran off to report this find to my friends.

Chkalov excused himself before his guests, and, calling Belyakov, set off with me to take a look at the strip that I had found.

Valery and Sasha liked the area. It was decided then and there that we would taxi or drag the plane to this new location.

The entire population of the island, even the children, came to move the ANT-25. A long, thick rope was fastened to the undercarriage and then the Russians, the Nivkhi and the Gilyaki men, women, old people, and young people, all under Valery's command, began to tow the aircraft behind them. However, the wheels often got stuck in the ground and large stones obstructed the movement of the machine.

It became clear that it was necessary to think seriously of constructing a takeoff strip.

During this time, elements from the political administration of the Special Red Banner Far Eastern Army arrived to see us. Somewhat later, the Secretary of the Provincial Communist Party also arrived.

Chkalov convinced them quickly of the necessity of building a wooden takeoff strip, about five hundred meters in length and thirty-five to fifty meters in width.

They agreed with the suggestion of the commander.

We were asked if we would visit Nikolaevsk-on-the-Amur the following day and speak before the city workers and garrison of soldiers at a meeting in honor of our flight. We gave our approval to such a speaking engagement.

After this the regional administrators left, taking Alexander Vasilyevich with them.

On that very day, a jolly and gifted engineer from TsAGI, Max Arkadievich Taits, arrived on the island. He calculated and prepared a flight plan for the ANT-25 to achieve maximal distance. The dimpled, dark-eyed engineer hugged each of us and then asked about how we were getting along.

After a good snack and preliminary discussions, Chkalov, Taits, and I set off for the aircraft.

Max, checking what remained of the fuel and oil, said to us, happily: "You obviously have enough fuel to reach Moscow. There's more than a ton left."

Max Arkadievich listened to the engine, which Chkalov had started up. He shook his head, parted his hands, and shouted out: "What can I say? You guys are just wonderful."

Toward evening, a representative of the Giliaki Collective Farm "Pomi" (Dolphin) came to visit us. His name was Comrade Mavdin and he asked Chkalov to speak to the collective farm workers and the workers of the fish factory concerning all the details of our flight.

The administration of the Khabarovsk area, the Special Far Eastern Army, and the Nikolaevsk region did everything possible to ensure that on July 26, a landing party of seabees arrived on the island to build a wooden takeoff strip.

For several days, Chkalov supervised the work of the crew from early morning to late evening.

On July 28, the strip was completed and the ANT-25 was parked on one end of it, ready for takeoff. The weather en route to Khabarovsk continued to be poor and the flight was postponed from one day to the next.

■

We knew how highly Chkalov valued his former instructor in the school for aerial combat, M. M. Gromov, who, completing the testing of the ANT-25, had set the distance record in a closed circuit two years before our flight.

We saw in the newspaper *Pravda* an article by Gromov regarding our flight, and we slipped it to Chkalov, along with the hundreds of telegrams and letters.

At the same time, I placed on the table an article, "Chkalov," by the chief designer, Polikarpov, which was in the newspaper *Industrialization* dated July 23. Chkalov even stopped eating dinner when he saw the articles by Gromov and Polikarpov.

Gromov wrote:

There has been nothing in the world to equal this flight.

I have known Valery Pavlovich Chkalov a long time. In 1923, Chkalov was one of my students in the Serpukhov school. He always distinguished himself with courage and the positive qualities of his character.

Generally, one must say that selection of the crew of the ANT-25 was very good. They are familiar with each other and rely on their individual capabilities.

Besides an efficient crew, success of the flight was guaranteed by excellent preparation of the aircraft. The craft was flown and adapted for the north.

Of course the aircraft is not that simple. Every craft that is heavily loaded (which this one was) does not function well in bad weather. When the machine is heavily loaded, its controls in bad weather are very complex. In this regard, Chkalov's itinerary was unique.

Chkalov's itinerary is interesting because it passed over unexplored areas, unsettled and desolate places. En route, there was an enormous expanse of water and ice. From Arkhangelsk until the return to the mainland, they could not land their craft anywhere.

I assume that a flight across the North Pole would not be more complicated than Chkalov's flight. This flight confirms that a flight across the North Pole is completely possible in this aircraft.

In comparison with all other long-distance flights, this one is significantly more complicated than any of the others.

With all my heart, I congratulate Chkalov, Baidukov, and Belyakov. They have written a new page into the heroic book of our countryland.

"Egor, Sasha," Valery called to us, having read his teacher's article. "Look how slyly he writes about the fact that they should allow us to fly across the Pole."

Shortly, Moscow newspapers dated July 24 arrived on the island. In *Pravda*, there were articles written by our wives and even a message to his father from Chkalov's eight-year-old son, Igor. This letter especially touched him.

On the thirteenth of July, TASS sent telegrams and testimonials that had come from overseas:

An announcement by Charles Logsden

The 25th of July, Washington (TASS). Commenting on the nonstop flight of the Soviet pilots Chkalov, Baidukov and Belyakov, Charles Logsden, the President of the National Aeronautic Association of America, announced:

"This is indeed one of the most important flights in the history of aviation. It demonstrates the possibility of long-distance, nonstop flight and serves to improve aircraft construction in many countries, with the goal of initiating the production of aircraft which have sufficient power and fuel capabilities for completing similar flights."

Valery Pavlovich's attention was riveted by an announcement from New York:

New York, 24th of July, U.S.A. (TASS). The polar explorer Stefansson[42] revealed in a conversation with a correspondent from TASS that people who were concerned with aviation and with polar exploration were expressing the greatest amazement at the flight of Chkalov, Baidukov, and Belyakov.

The flight demonstrates that Soviet aircraft have the capability of flying across the Arctic between the Soviet Union and the United States.

Especially interesting was the flight evaluation by the Moscow correspondent from an American newspaper, the *New York Times*, W. Duranty, who wrote in our publication *Industrialization: Victory of Soviet Aviation*[43]:

The fact that the editors of the publication *Industrialization* requested that I express my opinion in regard to the record flight of the ANT-25 is an especially enjoyable duty, because, in my opinion, the industrial factor turned out to have a decisive influence on the achievement of this great victory. Stating this, I'm not for a minute diminishing the abilities and the courage of the ANT-25 crew, whose reports the whole world followed with special interest.

Just a few hours ago, I received a telegram that my paper, the *New York Times*, has this morning printed an article regarding the flight in its front page. Soviet fliers have given us so much evidence of their artistry and courage that further proof is not really necessary, beginning with the saving of the *Nobile* and the crew of the airship *Italia* by Chukhnovsky and his colleagues, and ending with the heroic drama of the *Chelyushkin*. Not to mention the exploits of Vladimir Kokkinaki[44] or an earlier rescue of the American flier, Mattern, by Levanevsky. Hundreds of times, Soviet pilots have revealed the amazing qualities of their persistence, courage, and experience. I am not one to underestimate the role of pilots or mechanics in guaranteeing the success of any flight. Without responsible people, the best technical apparatus has only a secondary value. Furthermore, I shall repeat that in my opinion, the industrial factor has a primary significance in the present flight.

This flight informs the world that Soviet aviation is indeed capable of catching up with and overtaking the Western nations; that the Soviet Union not only has excellent pilots and designers; but that Soviet plants have the technology to construct first-class aircraft. It is impossible to exaggerate the importance of this factor, not only from an economical and industrial point of view, but also from the point of international relations.

■

The day finally came on August 2, when the sun shone on the island.

True, it later was hidden by clouds, but its first rays were ones of hope for Chkalov's crew.

At 0500, the ANT-25 commander met with us and we decided to prepare for a flight to Khabarovsk. Chkalov showed us the text of a letter written to the inhabitants of the Far East by him, thanking them for the warm greetings to the crew of the ANT-25 on their island. Their assistance was very much appreciated. We all signed it.

Belyakov received an assignment to check the weather along the itinerary and also in Khabarovsk. My duty was to check the aircraft and to check out its engine.

When I started the engine, the ensuing roar brought out many inhabitants to the takeoff spot.

Many people lined up on both sides of the takeoff strip made of planks. The workers of the fishing industry, collective farm workers, builders of the strip, and our friends of the border patrol were among the crowd. Chkalov said good-bye to all of them, even attempting to joke in the language of the Nivkhi.

The weather became almost calm. The fog had lifted to about one hundred meters and was now hanging motionlessly above the enormous expanse of water. We couldn't have gotten better weather. The engine roared into life and the aircraft raced down the makeshift runway. The ANT-25, under control of the experienced commander, traveled no more than three hundred meters and lifted up into the air. I retracted the landing gear and noted the time: 0815.

Valery made a low circle above the island, saying good-bye for the last time, and then took a course toward Nikolaevsk. The waves of the Okhotsk Sea were visible below the aircraft. Soon we were following the marker beacons.

Udd Island (which in a short time would be renamed Chkalov Island) was hidden from view.

Lange Island was situated below our wing and behind it were the high volcanoes, which seemed to be protecting the mouth of an enormous river.

The aircraft flew along the middle of the river, following its curves. It was dangerous to approach the shores due to the fog accumulation, which was swirling down from the volcano peaks guarding the Amur.

Shortly, the weather forced Valery to fly above the river at an altitude of ten to fifteen meters.

But the commander quickly realized that it would be dangerous to dodge around the currents since it would be easy to crash onto the shore. He brought the aircraft up, coming out of a cloud layer at an altitude of one thousand meters.

Another hour of flight went by. The weather became clear again. The pilot saw a city ahead, and, waving the craft from wing to wing, called me and Belyakov.

"Komsomolsk. Look, this is our youngest city," Valery shouted to us, showing what was down below. "This is where the real heroes live; people with an iron will and endurance. We should say hello to them."

Komsomolsk, which was only several years old, was not similar to any other city of the Far East. It was very well planned; the streets were straight and even.

Here we could see a large city with smokestacks, radio transmitters, and many-storied houses.

The escort craft were flying toward us. Chkalov, greeting his professional cohorts in flight, rocked the ANT-25 from one wing to another, reduced the speed to a minimum, and shouted to us: "Khabarovsk. Our first stop."

Soon, we saw a field with thousands of people gathered around. In a few minutes the aircraft was landing on the runway.

When Valery turned off the engine, we heard a loud "Hurrah!" Chkalov, after opening the upper canopy of the pilot's cockpit, stood up on the seat and shouted loudly: "Greetings to the Special Banner of the Far Eastern Army. Greetings to the Marshal!"

At this time they placed a stepladder against the aircraft and Blyukher, Aronshtam, Lavrentev, and Krutov came forward.

Blyukher hugged Chkalov and greeted him warmly.

Adults and children rushed up to us holding enormous bouquets of flowers.

After the meeting, Blyukher seated us in his car and took us to his dacha, where he had set up a wonderful reception.[45]

■

At five in the morning of August 5, 1936, Blyukher escorted us home. On the way to Moscow, we still had to make stops in Chita, Krasnoyarsk, and Omsk because the residents of these cities had requested us to do so.

Above Khabarovsk field, rain clouds were quickly moving. They completely covered the high mountain ranges of Fhinghan.

With Chkalov's approval our old friend and correspondent from *Pravda*, Lev Borisovich Khvat, "the king of reporters" as he was known at that time, flew with us as an additional passenger. We put Levushka on the aft pilot's seat, after removing a rubber raft from that spot.

The front canopy of the pilot's cockpit was being pelted by rain. The altimeter arrow was showing a slight increase in altitude, at five thousand meters. The clouds were still covering the dangerous mountain range. It was necessary to gain more altitude, but at this instant our navigator passed me a note: "The correspondent is without oxygen."

It became clear to me right away. Our passenger could pass out from oxygen starvation.

I reported this to Chkalov. He shook his head and shouted: "We will suffocate that guy. He won't be able to make it at six kilometers." Saying this, the commander looked back and saw the ashen face of the correspondent.

"He isn't letting on," I shouted to Chkalov. "But he's sucking in air like a fish."

Then Chkalov answered me: "Let's return. This is not on the itinerary, but we must not risk a life."

Soon we obtained a return heading from the navigator and the aircraft turned back toward the east.

Due to the skill and navigational capabilities of Belyakov and the precise piloting of the aircraft, we broke through the cloud layer and successfully came out above the ground at an altitude of one hundred meters.

When we crawled out of the cockpit of the aircraft at Khabarovsk Airport, it was raining heavily.

We were somewhat annoyed by the fact that we would have to be delayed. We realized that all our friends had gone home some time ago. The airport's administration personnel looked at us in confusion.

And Khvat, not comprehending what was going on, asked: "What happened? Why have we returned?"

"Because of you, dammit," Chkalov answered good-naturedly to the correspondent. "Hell, you were without any oxygen. We could have gone on, but then we remembered that correspondents also breathe air."

Khvat realized very well what kind of danger he had been subjected to, but continued to be convinced that he was able to fly with us without oxygen, even at an altitude of ten kilometers, if only he could continue with us to Moscow.

Chkalov in turn understood this feisty journalist. Khvat was afraid that we would leave him behind to return by train to Moscow, precluding an opportunity for a scoop for *Pravda*.

But Chkalov did not want to offend his good acquaintance, and decided to wait another day so that a flight at an appropriate altitude could be made.

On August 6, the weather above the spires of the Khingansky chain improved greatly and, after eleven hours of flight, we successfully jumped from Khabarovsk to Chita, accompanied by the journalist, who was continuously writing articles for his paper.

At the Chita airport, the crew of the ANT-25 was met by representatives of the Party and Soviet organizations, Zabaikal Military Commission, and workers of industrial plants.

On the morning of August 7, the ANT-25 took off for Krasnoyarsk.

Now there were five people flying in the plane. In Chita the inexhaustible Yevgeny Karlovich Stoman joined us.

Despite a considerable distance between the field and the city, we were met by thousands of Krasonyarsk residents.

People rushed toward the plane throwing flowers. Chkalov shook hands with a smile and later observed how some skilled craftsmen had marked on the empennage of the craft the route just completed, Chita to Krasnoyarsk.

The next day we spent in Omsk and then, the following morning, we started for Moscow.

■

There were only approximately two hours of flight time to Moscow. Flight headquarters radioed: "Can you arrive at Schelkovo at exactly 1700 hours?"

After the three members of the crew discussed this briefly, the commander requested me to send the following message via radio: "We will be there exactly at 1700 hours. Request permission for flight over Moscow."

I received an immediate reply: "Affirmative." Valery, sitting behind the controls, asked me: "Why exactly at 1700 hours? Do you know?"

"Apparently because they want people to observe our return."

No one in the crew could ever imagine that Moscow and its suburbs, since the morning of August 10, had taken on a festive air. Streets, squares, factories, plants, and houses were dotted with red and blue flags. There were portraits of national leaders, Chkalov, and members of the crew. Starting at 1500 hours, tens of thousands of residents of the city began lining the wide road that linked Schelkovo field with Moscow. By 1600 hours, many more thousands of capital workers from the Moscow region had gathered at the field.

Young pioneers of Leningrad, Kiev, and Bauman region arrived in buses. Among them were young delegates of the TsAGI pioneer detachment, the children of the builders of the gigantic ANT-25.

We did not suspect that our wives had arrived at the Schelkovo airport and impatiently awaited our arrival, having arrived early.

Valery flew the aircraft above the tops of houses in the capital and it became clear to us that the city was preparing a special greeting for the crew of the ANT-25. Even though August 10 was a Monday and a working day.

Surrounded by an aerial escort of twelve aircraft, the ANT-25 made a smooth circle over the Kremlin, and we set course for Schelkovo field.

After landing we noticed that we were being met by state leaders, at the head of whom was Stalin.

A meeting with an impassioned speech by Ordzhenikidze, excited words about Chkalov, a trip to Moscow through the lines of joyful Moscovites, who threw flowers at our open automobile.

Later, a reception at the Kremlin, the awarding of the Order of Lenin and the title of Hero of the Soviet Union to the crew of the ANT-25, significant financial prizes, the endless meetings with the workers, scientists, collective farm workers, writers, pioneers, and Komsomol members—all this touched Chkalov. But he was especially shaken by the decision of the Central Committee of the All-Union Communist Party regarding his acceptance and the acceptance of the crew members into the Party. This occurred several days after our return.

Chkalov confided to us, "Now I owe an unpayable debt to the Soviet People and the Party."

For some time we continued to request the government to allow a flight across the pole in 1937. However, our requests were not

answered. Quite unexpectedly we received an assignment to fly the
ANT-25 to Paris for the World Aviation Exhibition.

■

Once again, Chkalov was carrying out a Government assignment.
But this time it was of an international flavor.

On November 4, 1936, Chkalov, together with his crew, landed at
France's main airport, Le Bourget.

Soviet aviation engineers and artists who had arrived in Paris
worked incessantly to make the external appearance of the Soviet
exhibit correspond to its rich content.

French specialists and workers assisted our decorators. Chkalov very carefully followed the progress of our exhibit. Sometimes,
for days at a time, he would not leave the Grand Palais, where the
exhibition was located. With the help of translators, he consulted
with the French on ways to make the Soviet section of the International Exhibit more effective. The decorators at the Soviet Exhibit listened to Valery Pavlovich's opinion in a most attentive
manner.

One day, Chkalov met a very interesting person in the exhibition
hall, the former Count Ignatiyev, who was a general in the army and,
being a military attaché at the Russian Consulate in France during
the fall of the regime of Nicolas II, began to sympathize with Soviet
Russia, and put at the disposal of the Soviet Government many
millions in valuables.

Ignatiyev wanted this new Russia, the Russia of the Bolsheviks, to
make a favorable impression in this international arena. For this
reason, Chkalov and Ignatiyev, whose backgrounds and views were
entirely different, worked together to discuss ways of promoting
Soviet aviation achievements.

Belyakov, who spoke French well, was a big help in conversing
with the French people.

The Fifteenth International Aviation Exhibition opened in Paris at
10 A.M. on November 13, 1936. The first visitors were the President
of the Republic, Lebrain, the Minister of Aviation, Pierre Cot, and
the entire diplomatic corps in Paris.

The Soviet delegation at the Paris show was an especially impressive group of forty-five people. Included in the delegation were
Tupolev; Eideman; Bazhenov; Heroes of the Soviet Union Slepnev,

Gromov, Chkalov, Belyakov, and Molokov; and other pilots and flight engineers.

Chkalov liked the fact that the ANT-25, which had so magnificently endured the merciless flight across the Arctic, was exhibited at the central platform of the exhibition hall.

Without a doubt, the other Soviet aircraft, the ANT-35, designed by A. A. Arkhangelsky and adapted from a suggestion by A. A. Tupolev, also attracted the interest of knowledgeable people.[46] The new ten-seater, two-engine Soviet passenger aircraft distinguished itself not only by an excellent cruising speed, but also by the fact that it could continue normal flight on one engine, which greatly reduced the danger of flying the aircraft.

President Lebrain and Minister of Aviation Pierre Cot paid special attention to the comfort features of the ANT-35—features such as the passenger section being heated and ventilated (as well as the crew section), with fresh air being piped to each passenger. Every seat was equipped with individual lights and hot food was served to all passengers. The French were surprised that such a relatively large aircraft developed a speed of 432 kilometers per hour and a landing speed of only 90 kilometers per hour.

Visitors paid much attention to a third craft, the I-17, the brainchild of Polikarpov and Chkalov. It was Chkalov who taught the aircraft to fly and who prevented any disasters from occurring in this high-speed fighter.

Besides these three aircraft, which were shown in full scale, the Soviet display tastefully demonstrated some models of original designs. Very noticeable were models of the Stal-7 craft, the Stal-11, and the ARK-3.

The monoplane Stal-7, a design by engineer Bartini, was a fast ten-passenger craft. It had two M-100 engines and retractable landing gear. The Stal-11 aircraft, designed by engineer Putilov, was a mail and passenger speedster with a maximum speed of 407 kilometers per hour.[47] There were numerous innovations in this craft, including a stainless steel frame with a veneer cover shielded by a protective layer of Bakelite. Flaps were utilized to decrease the landing speed of the aircraft and allowed for shortening of the ground run required for takeoff.

Everyone was very interested in the model of the two-engine ARK-3 hydroplane designed by engineer I. Chetverikov. It was designed to ferry fourteen people to work in Arctic regions. Its two air-cooled M-25 engines allowed a speed of 320 kilometers per hour, a short takeoff run, good climbing capability, as well as the capability of flying in poor weather conditions. For safety, while working on ice, the aircraft had hermetically sealed compartments in the float section of the fuselage.

The development of glider technology was also shown at the exhibit. There was a display of a series of models of special gliders, designed by engineer Antonov. This was designed for various levels of studying aviation sport, from glider flights to aerobatic maneuvers.

There were also models of several record gliders engaged in long-distance and altitude flights within storm fronts. Everyone was amazed by a model of a sky train, which consisted of six gliders and a tow aircraft.

The glider exhibit was highlighted by a single glide craft presented in its original form. It sat on an enormous rug. "Stakhanov," the name of a worker who had founded the great labor movement, gleamed on the fuselage of the glider.[48] This craft was constructed by Emelianov for night flight under any meteorological conditions.

This glider had an unusually high tensile strength, equal to ten units, which many aircraft did not have at that time.

Looking very intently at Emelianov's glider, Valery said to me: "Damn it, everything should be known about what our aviation industry and aviation clubs are doing. But in order to obtain information on it, you have to fly several thousand kilometers from home in order to find out how rapidly the wings of our country are growing."

Special attention was given to a notice board providing data on the development of Soviet commercial aviation: fifty-five thousand kilometers of cross-country airways; twenty-eight thousand kilometers of trunk and feeder lines; 650,000 hectares reclaimed; 2.7 million hectares of swamp area swept clean of malaria mosquitoes, carrier of a terrible disease; more than 25 million hectares of forest surveyed and kept under observation against fires. These figures amazed A. Tolstoy and Ignatiyev.

"This is big!" Tolstoy exclaimed loudly.

"Fantastic!" Ignatiyev affirmed.

"Just wait a while and see what else develops." Chkalov answered, smiling.

Professor A. N. Tupolev and I. D. Eideman, heading the Soviet aviation delegation, became familiar with the innovations of aircraft construction that were shown at the exhibition. They studied the works of the best aviation plants in France, looked in at the Reims air base, visited a testing center at Ville Couble, and met with workers in the aviation industry and also French flyers. Chkalov revealed a great interest in everything that concerned the creation of new planes.

Looking over the French exhibition, Chkalov asked the navigator: "Ask if it's possible to see an aircraft that has been built for flight around the world."

The attendant led us to a Cadron-Reneau craft, designated "Typhoon." This was a two-engine aircraft that had enormous fuel tanks spread along the entire fuselage, behind which was located the pilot and radio operator's cockpit. The streamlined features and the retractable landing gear should allow the craft to cover a distance of approximately five thousand kilometers without landing, coupled with a speed of 320 to 360 kilometers per hour.

"Well?" asked Chkalov of me.

"It looks very attractive," I answered.

At this time, a group of Frenchmen came near us and began talking in loud voices. Belyakov listened to them and said: "Valery, this Frenchman here, the pilot, Delmot, is testing the plane that we're looking at right now."

Chkalov bowed ceremoniously and shook the hand of his fellow pilot Delmot, who stated that the pilot Rossi was preparing to fly this craft around the world in 1937.

Valery was impressed by this interesting aircraft, its pilot Delmot, and the familiar flier, Rossi.

"Belyakov, give him my wishes for success in spinning around the globe."

Belyakov then translated the commander's words and the French applauded Chkalov and thanked him for his courtesy.

France, the USSR, England, Czechoslovakia, and the United States were exhibiting sixty-three aviation engines. Special interest was given to our AM-34 engine and the French star-shaped, water-cooled, lightweight engine, the Hispano-Suiza, with a rating of 1,150 horsepower and weight of 640 kilograms.

Chkalov looked over the in-line engine with its inverted cylinders at length.

Valery's attention was also caught by the French autogyro, the Loire-Olivier, which was powered by two Gnome-Rhone engines (with a rating of 350 horsepower for each engine). The other countries had not exhibited a single autogyro.

At the end of November, the Soviet delegation returned home.

On December 3, the dismantling of the ANT-25 began, and it was then transported to Le Bourget field near Paris. It took five days to finish this task so that the aircraft could be assembled again at the airport.

While the craft was being prepared, we visited the house on Marie-Rose Street where, in 1910 and 1911, Vladimir Ilyich Lenin and Nazhesda Konstantinovna Krupskaya lived. Ignatiyev showed us the Louvre and the Pantheon and we even attended the opera twice.

Toward the end of our stay in Paris, it became quite apparent that Chkalov was going through some unusual changes. He suddenly became gloomy and uncommunicative. He lost all interest in traveling in France; specifically he refused to fly to Marseille, where we had been invited by one of the aviation companies.

Belyakov and I had to complete this interesting journey as a twosome. The reason for such a change in Chkalov's mood was explained to us by an aviation attaché in France, division commander Vasilchenko.

It turned out that Chkalov had posed a question to the Soviet Consulate several times, requesting a trip for us to Spain where Valery Pavlovich had only one wish—to enter combat against the Fascist ME-109 in an I-16. But Moscow was categorically opposed to this idea. Vasilchenko reported this to our commander, thus aggravating his mood.

On December 18, we took off from Paris for Berlin. Several days later on December 20, we took off from Templehof Airport. Finally, Chkalov taxied to the hangar of the Institute at the Frunze Central Field. The engine was turned off and everything grew still.

Valery was as happy as a child and did not try to hide his feelings from anyone, embracing welcoming persons as though he had not seen them for many years.

7

A Second Flight across the Arctic Ocean

It was 1937. Chkalov once again was back testing new aircraft designed by Polikarpov.

After completing testing of an anti-tank fighter plane, the VIT-1, Valery Pavlovich switched his attention to the VIT-2, which had additional armaments.[49]

This twin-ruddered aircraft carried liquid-cooled M-103 engines and was later modified with the M-105. This allowed the craft to attain a speed of 533 kilometers per hour.

Chief pilot Chkalov followed the progress of the design bureau as the new types of aircraft by Polikarpov—Ivanov, SBB, and I-180—were developing.

Valery was becoming involved more frequently in social circles and frequently serving as an author of articles in newspapers and journals.

A complete collection of Chkalov's articles and speeches would be impossible to put together. Most of his speeches were not recorded, even the most significant ones. It is possible to imagine the tremendous amount of social and political responsibility for a person who required disciplined activities and sufficient rest.

The collection of articles and speeches by Chkalov, *My Life Belongs to My Country*, published by DOSAAF in 1959, is just a small quantity of what Chkalov said and wrote during the last two and a half years of his life. Despite being very busy, the test pilot did not miss any opportunities to attend the opera or to enjoy the productions at the Moscow Art Theatre and the Maly Theatre in the capital.

About this time he became familiar with such great artists as Klimov, Kachalov, Tarkhanov, Moskvin, Kozlovsky, and Mihailov.

He frequented the houses of actors and writers and conducted animated discussions on creative projects and various artistic interpretations. He always had his personal opinions on every book and every production.

When the last part of *Bruskov* was published, Valery Pavlovich said to Panferov: "Of course as a critic I'm somewhat awkward, but I know a few things. You comprehend country life quite well, but in several areas, you have painted an incorrect picture of that lifestyle."

The writer agreed with many of his comments.

Valery read *Idle People* by A. P. Chapygin with great interest. Everything that was written about Nizhny Novgorod/Gorky caught the attention of Valery and he read this with great interest. In connection with this, he developed a great friendship with V. Kostylev, a writer from Gorky.

Now when our troika had settled into a house on Sadovy Circle, we often gathered late in the evening in Valery Pavlovich's study and discussed the flight to America via the North Pole.

Continuing to perfect the ANT-25 based on the experience that we had received in flying to Kamchatka, we often spent much time in the hangar of the Central Field. Together with designers, engineers, mechanics, and power plant specialists, we worked out a program for further development.

■

The polar explorers Molokov, Aleksev, Mazuruk, and Babushkin would often stop by our plant. It was here that a clear plan of attack to conquer the pole was initiated.

We attentively studied the book by M. V. Vodopyanov, *The Dream of a Pilot*, which gave an opportunity to better understand the main concepts behind the expedition of Otto Schmidt and Vodopyanov.[50]

Naturally, neither Otto Ulevich nor Mikhail Vasilevich withheld any information from Chkalov and discussed in detail what lay before them and how they planned to complete this task.

Valery began to follow every step of the expedition organization, especially when its aircraft flew to Central Field, where Chkalov was employed.

Our commander cheered up noticeably when, during a regular meeting in his office, we decided to accelerate the detail work and to carry out a series of testing and training flights using the ANT-25.

"This is what I am also thinking, my friends, Sasha and Egor. We must study more seriously all aspects of the United States—our destination—so we won't repeat our errors. On our flight last year to Udd Island, we knew very little about the area. That is embarrassing."

"What are you suggesting?" I asked Valery.

"Well, Egor, you can prepare for us a detailed political and economic summary of development in the USA. Sasha, you can study all data concerning the Arctic, especially the Canadian part."

"Very well, I agree," Belyakov said. "I suggest that we get busy and learn about the USA from novels."

"What do you have in mind?" Valery asked.

"Well, you probably will gain an impression of the United States through the writings of Theodore Dreiser."[51]

"Agreed. We are all set. By April, each of us will have to be ready with a report," Chkalov concluded.

In the meantime, the Schmidt-Vodopyanov expedition had prepared itself for the flight. On the snow-covered expanse of Central Field stood four bright orange four-engine airships and one two-engine craft. With these aircraft loaded with cargo and people they would fly from Moscow to their base camp on Rudolph Island in Franz-Josef Land Archipelago. They would be assisted by the icebreaker *Rushnov*, which would bring necessary materials, fuel, and food to sustain the expedition personnel.

From Rudolph Island, the aircraft would convey four researchers to the North Pole, where they would live and work on drifting ice caps.

The names of these courageous individuals were Papanin, Krenkel, Federov, and Shirshov, the leader of the expedition, radio operator, meteorologist, and the hydrologist, respectively.

On March 23, 1937, four multiengined and one two-engine aircraft designed by A. N. Tupolev took off from Central Field, and headed north.

Expedition progress in the early spring was slowed down by some extremely bad weather. Only on April 19 were the aircraft able to land on Rudolph Island, the starting point for the assault on the pole.

On May 3, Golovin and his crew flew to the pole in the two-engine craft, overcoming bad weather conditions in the region of the

North Pole. The pilot made notations of weather conditions and returned with great difficulty to base camp.

This was a first and significant victory, which allowed the leader of the expedition, O. I. Schmidt, the commander of the squadron, M. V. Vodopyanov, and the chief navigator of the expedition, I. P. Spirin, to make the decision to fly from Franz-Josef Land to the pole.

■

On May 21, 1937, the flag of our country was placed on the North Pole. The four-engine craft of Vodopyanov, Molokov, Alekseev, and Mazuruk unloaded the courageous explorers, Papanin, Krenkel, Federov, and Shirshov on the ice. The cargo was unloaded for a long stay at the top of the world.[52]

On May 25, Chkalov, Levanevsky, and I were unexpectedly summoned to the Kremlin. The Government gave its permission for a flight to America across the North Pole.

At first, we didn't tell anyone at home about this. However, our preparations gave a good indication. Olga Erazmovna guessed that the question of flying to the North Pole had been decided.

One evening, coming into the study where the three of us were examining a map of the Canadian Arctic, she said: "Don't hide it, we've heard that permission has been granted. Better go and visit your wives for a while because tomorrow you are going to disappear."

"Can we really hide anything from you? You are right! Tomorrow, we fly to Schelkovo. We don't have much time right now."

Everyone left for the dining room where we saw my wife, Evgenia Sergeevna, and Belyakov's wife.

"Boy, you've become very quiet," Valery joked to our wives. "If only you were always like this."

The women smiled through their tears and our host said: "This is the reason why you are not allowed to come and visit us at the field. Instead of having a good time, you are gloomy and downcast. To hell with this mood, my friends, let's drink to the success of our trip at Schelkovo Field."

■

On June 1, we ferried the ANT-25 from the Central Field aerodrome to Schelkovo Field. Chkalov, Belyakov, and I were working on the aircraft from morning to night at the TsAGI plant. We would conduct testing and training flights, or we would prepare an itinerary and select necessary equipment, instruments, and foodstuffs for the long-distance flight.

We were quartered in one of the buildings at the field. After a few days, this room was completely filled with books, maps, guides, and special information about the Arctic.

The commander of the ANT-25 understood very well that success not only depended on the ability, courage, and composure of the members of the crew, it also depended on the conscientious and capable work of hundreds of people who had prepared the aircraft itself and also its integral systems for the flight.

Knowing the significance of the work of preparing the aircraft, Valery spent much time among them during the course of every day. As in the previous year, chief engineer Stoman was responsible for the timely and precise preparation of all the parts of the aircraft, including flight-testing the craft. Berdnik, the chief mechanic, and his power plant assistants, Karaganov and Avdankin, were responsible for the preparation of the aircraft engine instruments on test flights and the actual flight itself.

Khokhanov was assigned as the electrical technician for the ANT-25 and the instrument specialist was Yaroshinsky. Engineers Minkner and Radzevich monitored the construction of the engine at the plant. They installed it in the ANT-25, then tested it on the ground and in flight. Engineer Engiboryan checked out the electrical, navigational and oxygen devices. He was assisted by several specialists, Benediktov, Kachkachian, and Broslavsky. Arshinov and Kerber were responsible for the radio equipment aboard the aircraft. Engineer Lebedev was assigned to install anti-icing devices on the aircraft.

As usual, TsAGI engineers Taits and Vedrov played a significant role. They determined the flight plan for the crew.

Vasili Ivanovich Altovsky, the chief meteorologist, was responsible for providing meteorological data to the crew.

Vasili Ivanovich Chekalov, the head of the Department of Experimental Flight Testing, was in charge of overall operations.

Valery Pavlovich was familiar with all these people. Often he would engage in conversation, then sit back and observe their work. He would not sleep when Stoman, Berdnik, Minkner, and Radzevich would adjust engine and regulate flame exhaust to a fine degree. The commander knew how important it was to tune the only engine on the aircraft in order to be certain that it would not cease functioning, not even for a second, and would turn the propellers for three days without failure.

Chkalov carefully checked out all the innovations and modifications that had been introduced according to our suggestions after the flight to Kamchatka.

The amount of compression was increased in the engine. Premium fuel, which had been specially refined for our flight, was used. This significantly increased the power and economy of the engine and increased the takeoff safety of the overloaded aircraft.

The previous flight had uncovered certain defects in the lubrication system of the engine. Although the oil was preheated, nevertheless during the flight it became so thick that it was difficult to augment it with a wobble pump. This problem was solved by increasing the insulation in the oil tanks and improving the entire feeding system. The oil tanks now looked like gigantic thermoses. A very much improved system of fighting against icing of the propeller blades was installed.

The working conditions in the cockpit, where one would have to spend from sixty to seventy flying hours, were considerably improved. Chkalov understood that it was not quite correct to raise complaints with regard to the comfort in the cockpit. We had to take so much clothing and equipment with us that crowded conditions were impossible to avoid. Every centimeter of space was significant. Chkalov nevertheless decisively requested that a bed be placed there for our use. Sleeping on the oil tank behind the pilot's seat was not an especially attractive situation.

The system for heating the cockpit was modified. The method of heating the cockpit the previous year had not passed the test in the Arctic. Our hands were cold. Fresh fruit froze, and ice cubes were floating in the drinking water tanks. Chkalov regretted that above Moscow, at altitudes of three to four kilometers, it was relatively warm and this did not allow us to properly test the effectiveness of the new heating system in the cockpit.

The old radio compass oriented the navigator and pilot only when the radio station that the aircraft was taking bearings on was lined up right on course. Now the ANT-25 was equipped with a radio compass with a revolving O-frame, which was located above the fuselage. This gave the crew an opportunity to determine the location of our aircraft based on transmission between any two radio stations, regardless of whether they were on our heading or not. It was sufficient to know only the coordinates of these stations. We also asked that we receive Canadian and American civil aviation maps, which showed the location, call signs, and particular characteristics of the majority of radio stations that would be capable of communicating with us during the flight.

This provided an opportunity for the crew to utilize this new navigational aid widely.

Last year's experience had taught us that the success of the flight depended not only on meteorological conditions but also to a significant degree on how carefully and wisely the crew used fuel. In the upcoming flight, Chkalov and I, when we flew the aircraft, would have the opportunity of selecting, with the aid of a new fuel analyzer, the optimal mixture of fuel and air so that we would not submit the engine to dangerous thermal loads.

Instead of one radio, two receivers were installed, which insured a very wide monitoring band.

The previous year, when we would leave an area that was threatening us with icing, we would climb to high altitudes, thus quickly consuming our supply of oxygen. It was discovered that four liters of oxygen compressed to 150 atmospheres was insufficient for one person. For the upcoming flight, Chkalov obtained twice as much oxygen. In addition, the air tanks were improved and furnished with devices that regulated the amount of oxygen, depending on how rarefied the air was at the altitude at which we were flying. This significantly decreased the work of the crew members.

Even the oars for the rubber life raft were manufactured out of duralumin instead of wood. This reduced the weight, a very significant factor in our upcoming flight.

While Valery prepared for takeoff, Belyakov and I were memorizing Morse code transmissions. Our radio instructor, Kovalevsky, did not give us any breaks.

On June 5, Chkalov flew the aircraft with two thousand kilograms of ball bearings sewn into small bags. After throwing these bags onto the edge of the field, Chkalov landed the ANT-25 with an allowable flight weight.

In the evening, the crew discussed various flight dates, based on the fact that the government had assigned us to be the first to demonstrate the feasibility of flight to the USA over the North Pole.

It was decided to fly no later than the end of June, so that Gromov would be able to evaluate the flight, in full detail. This period of time was completely realistic since we had achieved much data during the previous winter, sometime before the government had given permission for such a flight. Belyakov had attained proficiency as a pilot, by completing an intensive preparation course at a flight school. This allowed us to rely on Sasha Belyakov if it would become necessary for him to fly the aircraft.

However, we decided not to include him in the rotation of flight assignments, since almost half of the journey would be over water. We needed his navigational skills.

Foreseeing navigational difficulties, Belyakov ordered special tables that would sharply reduce the amount of time for mathematically calculating our position in relation to celestial bodies.

"This means we will announce that in about ten or fifteen days, we will be ready for takeoff," the commander asked, looking first at the navigator, then at me.

"The weather could seriously affect the time of takeoff," Belyakov noted.

"But the long-term forecast does not suggest anything unusual."

"Wait," objected Chkalov. "Is it really possible to rely seriously on a prognosis for such a tremendous itinerary?"

Chkalov knew that Belyakov was well versed in meteorological sciences and consequently obtained from the navigator his detailed account on the weather forecast for the second half of June.

"As I understood Vaseli Ivanovich Altovsky," the navigator reported, "at the end of June, they forecast an intrusion into Central Europe of very warm masses of air with morning temperatures being approximately 15–18° C."

"Under such temperature conditions, we would not be able to take off in the ANT-25 with a weight of eleven and a half tons," I interrupted Belyakov. Everyone grew silent, realizing that we would have to take off no later than two weeks from now and there was little time to be able to finish all the ground and flight preparations. On the other hand, to wait for a temperature drop would take perhaps two or three weeks, which would very much complicate the takeoff of Gromov's crew.

We discussed the situation until late that night. A unanimous vote decided that preparation for the flight would be completed more quickly if the final test flight was made in about ten days.

Belyakov remembered that not one of the three of us had yet managed to fulfill the assignments that we had undertaken regarding our report on America, which included the economic-political relations between the United States and the Soviet Union and to evaluate America through the readings of Theodore Dreiser.

"You're right, Belyakov, we are a month and a half late with these assignments. If everyone's ready, let's listen to Baidukov tomorrow."

At this point, we concluded our general meeting and next day, announced our decision to Tupolev, Chekalov, and Stoman.

The suggestion of quickening the tempo of preparation seemed to some very adventurous.

On May 25, we obtained permission from the government for the flight. On June 5, everyone was informed that the flight to America would be in ten or fifteen days. Of course this was exciting.

Chkalov patiently explained to everyone who had doubts that the preparation for the new flight had actually begun in August of last year when the crew of the ANT-25 flew from Udd Island to Moscow and, if one wanted to be even more exact, two years ago.

Nevertheless, the heads of the flight committee and their staff agreed with our suggestions. Rukhimovich, the People's Commissar of Defense Industry, his deputy M. Kaganovich, designers Tupolev and Sukhoi, and Chekalov and his aides, Antonov, Kharetski, and Anishchenkov, each did everything to make it possible for us to take off as soon as possible, before the intrusion of warm air masses from Asia into the Moscow region.

On June 5, the crew went through a final medical examination. Doctors of the various specializations "worked us over," as Valery Pavlovich joked, "for quite some time." The condition of everyone's health was announced to be good for a flight that no one in the world had yet made.

Next morning, Alexander Vasilevich left for Moscow. He met with the chief administrator of the northern sea routes, also the Academy of Sciences, the Shternberg Astronomical Institute, and the World Atlas Institute.

Belyakov with his usual precision noted all that would be helpful for the flight. He ordered a list of polar radio stations and the working schedules of radio beacons on Cape Zhelainye and on Rudolph Island. The navigator wrote down information concerning transmission of the new radio station UPOL on the drifting ice, from which Ernst T. Krenkel was communicating with Moscow, polar bases, and amateur radio operators all over the world.

At the World Atlas Institute, Belyakov obtained detailed maps of western Canada and the United States. He was pleased to see a map of the world's magnetic variations.

The astronomers at Krasnaya Presnya of the Shternberg Institute received an order from the navigator regarding tables of astronomical precomputations for the sun and moon in relation to geographical points that would be of interest to the crew of the ANT-25. Alexander Vasilevich promised to give them notice to begin the preparation of the tables five days prior to takeoff.

Everyone was familiar with Belyakov and fulfilled his request without much ado.

At noon, Belyakov sent the following radiogram:

North Pole, Major Spirin.
    Greetings to the navigator of the Polar Squadron.
    Please report function of the compasses including the gyromagnetic ones in the area.
    What is the range of North Pole, Rudolph Island, and frequency of the radio beacon at Rudolph.
    Reliable range of the ADF to Rudolph Island.
    The magnetic variation at the pole.

On June 7, a reply was received.

Moscow, navigator Belyakov.
    1. The aviation group of the Schmidt expedition was still located at the Pole.
    Magnetic compasses function at the Pole.
    This requires precise observations of the flight path. The magnetic gyrocompass functioned ineffectively.
    2. The gyroscopic magnetic compass functioned well to 87°. We observed significant oscillations at higher altitudes.
    3. The gyroscopic compass can be used effectively
    4. The radio beacon provides accurate bearings. I used the Onega receiver. On the flight from Rudolph Island to the pole, it was audible for some time although we were on course. The beacon functioned normally.
    5. The radio directional finder at Rudolph and Murmansk did not function.
    6. En route from Rudolph to the pole it is best to take bearings on Dixon and Murmansk.
    7. The magnetic variation in the region of the pole is minus 110.
    8. Use of celestial navigation is a reliable means of position fixing.
    Regards. Spirin.

Chkalov after reading the telegram said: "This is a paradox. On the one hand to fix a position, one must have the correct magnetic course, but in order to determine this course one has to know the exact position. This means that in the region of the pole, we will have to be above the clouds at all times in order to observe the heavenly bodies."

"Correct," the navigator affirmed. "And that's why Baidukov and I have to know celestial navigation very well."

When Belyakov left to consult with the radio operator, Valery said to me: "We have a brainy chapaevite.[53] Baidukov, he is well organized. And he doesn't lose time at all. He is always studying."

"I'm studying myself," I interrupted Chkalov.

"Yes, but how he studies. He is quietly efficient. He does make navigational data quite interesting."

On June 7, chief meteorologist Altovsky completed linking up a complex network of weather stations in the Soviet Union, Canada, and the United States. From this day on, they began to make general weather forecasts and provide a prognosis three days in advance.

Our preparation for the flight was proceeding smoothly and we had our reports on the U.S., which had been prepared a long time ago. They were interesting and informative.

A very important detail was brought out during a discussion with the navigator. Suppose we have flown over the "pole of inaccessibility": we are over Canadian territory and are approaching the Rocky Mountains when suddenly a cyclone with a continual cloud layer more than five or six kilometers in height is confronted, and at night at that. What should we do?

In the cloud layer icing could develop, and climbing to a higher altitude would not be possible since the ANT-25 could not climb higher than six thousand meters. To descend would be equally impossible, since the tops of the mountains would be at that height. After a long discussion, Chkalov agreed with a suggestion to work out an emergency alternative for our itinerary. This would mean a sharp turn away from the polar-to-San Francisco meridian to the Pacific Ocean with a crossing of the mountain range near the city of Ketchikan, Alaska.

■

Soon a ten-hour flight to test the working of the propeller units after final adjustment of the engine was scheduled. In addition, Belyakov and I had to train ourselves in the use of a new radio compass and to demonstrate our capability to carry on communications using the radio aboard the aircraft. Chkalov and engineers Stoman, Minkner, and Taits measured the fuel consumption on various flight patterns to determine a most effective operational plan.

Everyone had so much work to do that we were surprised how quickly time passed. Everything was fine. The crew did not have any problems although Yevgeny Karlovich was displeased with something and made complaints for some time after the flight, giving orders to the aircraft mechanics.

In the evening, Chkalov asked Belyakov and myself to discuss the question of food, equipment, and clothing, taking into account that a number of factories and plants had sent us so many different items that even a four-engine aircraft couldn't carry them.

M. Kalmykov, the military doctor, recommended a diet of everyday and emergency food rations.

It was suggested that during the flight, the crew would eat only fresh food. This included ham sandwiches (100 grams per day per person); butter (50 grams); beef (50 grams); veal (50 grams); caviar (30 grams); and Swiss cheese (50 grams). In addition to this, there would also be included cabbage pies and chocolate (100 grams each); cakes (50 grams); and lemons, oranges, and apples. There was hot tea laced with lemon in the thermos bottles.

A complete daily ration for the three members of the crew consisted of approximately three kilograms of various foods.

The emergency food supply also provided a kilogram of foodstuff per day for each member of the crew. It consisted primarily of various concentrated products, which weighed very little and had high calorie content.

The daily supply of emergency food for each person of the crew was packed in waxed paper and foil. Nine of these units were packed into ten rubber bags. Each bag supplied food for the crew for three days, and the entire supply would last for a month.

All the foodstuff weighed 115 kilograms, of which one-tenth was set aside for the three-day flight.

Chkalov argued animatedly with Dr. Kalmykov and deputy flight director Antonov regarding the rations.

"Why the hell do we need so much stuff? If you get rid of 100 kilograms of food, this would enable us to fly another 300 kilometers past our destination. Three hundred. Do you understand,

Antonov? Three hundred," he pointed out incessantly to the persistent but calm Antonov, who looked innocently at our commander and smiled in his short-cut little mustache.

"Without such a minimum, meaning just a month's supply, no one is going to grant permission for the flight and further conversation is completely pointless. As it is, we have reduced the amount from 350 kilograms to this measly 100."

"Look, Dimitri Ivanovich, how can I make you understand that we are not scheduling any emergency landings, and on this flight, as in last year's, we can get by with tea and chocolate bars."

"Just the same, we must abide by doctor's orders. This, of course, is a minimum."

Chkalov only shook his head and said angrily, "I didn't expect such a dirty trick from you."

Antonov continued to smile and concluded: "Very well, Valery Pavlovich, we will consider a list of foodstuffs with which the entire crew will be in agreement."

"Well damn you, brigands and bandits," Chkalov muttered smiling and, looking at Belyakov, added, "Sasha will satisfy you in everything, the scientific democrat."

After this small skirmish, we began to check into the clothing of the crew. For the flight we were given warm and comfortable clothing, leather jackets and pants with natural down. Brown for Chkalov, black for Belyakov and me. They preserved heat very well, were waterproof, and weighed approximately 4.5 kilograms as a unit. As far as shoes, Dr. Kalmykov advised us to wear high boots with fur on both sides capable of protecting the extremities from cold. In case of an emergency landing, it was recommended that we carry extra hunting boots, fur earmuffs, and wool gloves. In addition, it was suggested that thick wool sweaters, breeches, fur hoods, and silk and woolen socks be brought along.

To protect us from the polar rays of the sun, one doctor advised us to obtain special sunglasses with light filters.

In case of a landing in an uninhabited area, we were given a silk pneumatic inflatable tent with double-thickness walls and fur sleeping bags. To heat the tent and to prepare hot food, they manufactured a special windproof stove. There was also a rubber, inflatable boat, life vests, Canadian skis, Finnish knives and pen knives, revolvers, two hunting rifles with cartridges, a hatchet, a shovel, flashlights, binoculars, and eating utensils.

We checked all this equipment three times and even Chkalov did not upbraid the doctor and the deputy flight director.

The doctor was about to describe what would be placed in a first aid kit but Chkalov interrupted him immediately

"This isn't our concern. Belyakov and I don't know anything about medicine. Let Baidukov decide what to do."

"No, no," Kalmykov said in a disturbed manner. "All three of you must know how to apply first aid."

"But what is Baidukov going to do?" Chkalov asked noisily.

The doctor reported that aboard the aircraft, there would be two first aid kits, a regular and an emergency package. And then he reminded everyone of basic first aid principles.

In conclusion, the conversation turned to the use of oxygen and parachutes.

Antonov recommended the addition of three more oxygen cylinders, but Valery grew quite obstinate: "What have you guys in the flight staff thought up? Each person is going to take 1,200 liters of oxygen. This is twice the amount of last year, not just a little bit more 'in case of something.'"

"And here are the parachutes. This time we recommend seat chutes," Kalmykov said once again. "The parachutes themselves will be underneath everyone's seat and each of you will be wearing fasteners. This will allow you to move about the plane quite easily; but in case of an emergency, you can fasten the parachute to the straps in two or three seconds."

"Honestly, this is well designed and carried out," Chkalov said. "But why we need all this, I'll never understand."

Kalmykov looked with confusion first at me, then at Belyakov. Knowing Chkalov very well, Antonov smiled: "Valery Pavlovich," the deputy flight director noted, "just the same, you're going to have to take parachutes."

"Why? Tell me please, why?" Valery turned to Antonov.

"Well, at least to show the Americans that we have a parachute industry on a par with the United States."

"This means politics. Well, that is another matter. Then taking one is enough," Chkalov quickly added, "But to take three doesn't make any sense."

"Why?"

"Listen. For the first ten hours, we're going to fly at low altitude, and by the time you get around to jumping, you'll already have hit the ground. Next is the icy Barents Sea. Well, suppose you jump out and plunge into it. How long are you going to swim in it? I think that you'll turn stiff before somebody finds you. Then there is the ice of the polar basin. Say you do abandon the craft by using the parachute. What are you going to do alone without food, fire, or weapons? You're only good as snacks for some polar bear provided you're as warm and fat as we are now. Or else even the polar bear is going to ignore you. This means there is absolutely no sense in jumping into the Arctic Ocean. But say you complete two days of flight: the aircraft will weigh less and the engine function easier as a result of the lightened load. As a result, there is no reason to think of saving ourselves with parachutes. So what does this all mean? Parachutes are very practical and necessary, but not in this case."

Kalmykov, somewhat shocked, waved his arms, shook his head, and, turning to Antonov, said in agitation: "It's impossible to work out an agreement with such people. They go against basic logic with their own opinions and conclusions."

Chkalov mischievously smiled with his eyes, although he remained stern looking. "Doctor, you should be glad that we try to think for ourselves. In flight, no one is going to think for us."

Antonov left without being noticed, but returned quickly to our room, lit up a cigarette and, smiling, listened to a continuation of the conversation between the doctor and the commander of the ANT-25.

In about five minutes, the telephone operator asked Chkalov to take a long-distance call. The deputy of the People's Commissariat for Defense Industry, M. M. Kaganovich, was on the line.

Chkalov returned immediately.

"I'm not going to talk to any finks or informers," the commander of the ANT-25 yelled loudly.

Belyakov and I came up to Chkalov. Kalmykov and Antonov stood silently around him.

"Did you notice," Valery turned to us, "that we hadn't been able to finish our argument and yet everything was known to the government commission—that we didn't want to bring parachutes and extra foodstuff and unnecessary equipment?"

"If we're already talking about kilograms," the doctor said angrily, "then your own five kilos of salt should be rubbed into my wounds."

Valery laughed out loud and stopped arguing with Kalmykov and Antonov. Indeed, after having read the stories of the Arctic explorers, especially on scurvy, Chkalov had ordered more salt placed on board.

■

Stoman ordered a routine flight for the next day and, after bidding farewell to our visitors, we went to bed. That morning, after breakfast, we left Belyakov with the flight documents, while Chkalov and I drove to the field.

Our aircraft was parked near the runway, which had been especially built in 1934, when Gromov prepared for his record flight.

Our aircraft was plainly visible now, when we suddenly noticed that an I-5 fighter coming in for a landing was headed directly for our red-winged plane.

We had hardly been able to gasp a warning when the fighter hooked its landing gear on the right wing of the ANT-25 and, after making a nose-over, landed upside down on the runway.

Chkalov stopped the car and we rushed to the spot where this had occurred. Fire trucks and ambulances raced toward the mishap. We ran up to the damaged fighter and helped to lift it somewhat in order to drag the pilot out of the cockpit. A trail of blood oozed from it.

"Quicker, dammit," Chkalov yelled. "Lift it up properly. Somebody may be dying here!"

Soon a truck with mechanics arrived, the crippled fighter was lifted, and the wounded pilot was taken out of the cockpit. Ironically, this turned out to be the division commander himself, Bazhenov, the head of the Air Force's Scientific Testing Institute.

This was the very same division commander who had sent Chkalov, when he was a test pilot in the Scientific Research Institute of the Air Force, for some inexplicable reason, to be "retrained" in courses for undisciplined pilots in the so-called "Alksnis School of Corrections."

Only when they had placed the unlucky fighter pilot on a stretcher and carried him off to a hospital did Chkalov inspect the damaged aircraft. There was a gaping hole in the right wing.

Valery climbed up to the top of the broken wing where I was studying the extent of our damage.

"Well, Baidukov?" Valery asked slowly and calmly.

"Well, this means we have 'flown' over the Pole."

Chkalov sat down on the wing next to me and began to look over and feel the torn edge of the hole that had been made.

"He was lucky," said Valery, sighing.

"Yes, it's a good thing. He was lucky."

"The craft turned on its back and slammed with great force."

"The wing saved him," I noted.

"It didn't save Anisimov, but it saved him."

At this time Stoman, Berdnik, Karaganov and Avdankin came running up.

As a result of a preliminary examination, the engineer and mechanics announced that the accident was a serious one and that it would be necessary to dismantle the aircraft and return it to the plant.

After three hours, the heads of the aviation industry arrived with all the specialists. They convinced us that we would be able to flight-test the aircraft in about a week.

But the enthusiasm of Tupolev's colleagues did little to change the gloomy mood of Chkalov which had now completely overcome him. He found it hard to believe that the results of such a serious accident could be eliminated in a week. If the repairs took a longer time, then the weather with its high morning temperatures would make it impossible to take off in the ANT-25. It would be hard to guess how long one would have to wait for a suitable morning.

On June 5, Air Force meteorologists and the Central Weather Institute began to make weather forecasts based on current and existing data. The weather reports coming in regularly from the drifting station "North Pole" were very helpful in setting up these weather forecasts.

As of June 7, daily information started coming in from dozens of meteorological stations along the flight path, both Russian and American (Seattle, San Francisco, and Washington).

On June 13, all the meteorological "biggies," whose director was Altovsky, came to the conclusion that the most appropriate date for takeoff would be between June 18 and 24.

When Chkalov was told the conclusions of the weather forecasters, he became even more gloomy and extremely edgy. Chkalov incessantly cursed the slightly hurt Bazhenov for being responsible for everything that had happened.

■

Finally, the repairs to the aircraft were completed. Chkalov took heart and rushed to complete the preparations for the flight.

We visited our families and announced to them that we were setting off very soon on our distant journey.

On June 16, about twenty days after the government had given us permission for the flight, Chkalov completed our last training test flight. He was very pleased; everything worked well and his crew completed the preparation in full.

We announced to Stoman and Berdnik that we didn't require any further testing or training and that it was possible to prepare the aircraft for the flight to America.

The rest of the day was extremely intense. The aircraft was rolled into a hangar and dozens of specialists checked it over. All instruments, equipment, and devices placed aboard the craft were thoroughly tested. Stoman and Berdnik carefully monitored their activity.

We stayed up until sunrise, continuing to select equipment and foodstuff.

We fell asleep about four in the morning and were on our feet by nine since at 1000 we would leave for Moscow.

No one thought that Chkalov and his crew would have completed their preparations so quickly.

Apparently, the news media had obtained information on our preparations, most likely from personnel in the flight office. We were convinced of this upon our arrival in Moscow and reported to Chekalov, the flight director. There were a number of correspondents in his office reception room. After seeing Valery Pavlovich, they circled him in a tight ring. Everyone wanted to know the date of the takeoff.

"Well, for Christ's sake, only twenty days have gone by and you're talking about some sort of takeoff. Do we really look like adventurers? You have to realize it is not just three people who are flying, but the entire nation will be there with us."

One of the correspondents shouted: "Wonderful! Great! But just the same, when is the takeoff?"

They were all taking down Valery's words and he continued slowly: "I'm telling you that we can't fly any old way. We are carrying on the wings of the ANT-25 the honor of our country. Does that mean that we can just make some kind of iffy flight? Only adventurers could do something like that without thinking about results."

The reporters, in the meantime, continued to jot down the observations. Chkalov realized that he would have to react to them a little bit differently, and he announced: "That's enough. No more questions. Right now we're deciding the beginning of the flight."

The army of correspondents ceased their questions and allowed Chkalov to move out of the circle. They were confused by this announcement.

Chekalov and his deputy, Antonov, talked incessantly on the telephone, giving orders to the numerous representatives of factories and plants as well as the Scientific Research Institute. Staff headquarters looked like a military camp.

We were very late to this meeting with the meteorologists, but Altovsky kept his team prepared and was waiting for the arrival of Chkalov's crew.

Chkalov, Belyakov and I, together with the flight directors, checked over the mysterious forecast maps. Valery immediately became more cautious.

"There are a lot of suspicious-looking lines," he said gloomily in a deep voice. "Are these all demarcations of fronts?"

"Yes, yes. Unfortunately the weather is not too good," the chief flight meteorologist reported softly. "There are quite a few storms en route, especially in the area of the Arctic and Canada."

"What do you suggest, Vasily Ivanovich?" Chkalov asked loudly and forcefully.

"The general situation seems to be such that it is impossible to grant permission for a takeoff in the next three to five days," the meteorologist blurted out.

"It's always the same story with you, 'generally unfavorable,'" Chkalov exploded. "And when will it be better?"

"We can't guarantee anything for June 18, 19, and 20," Altovsky insisted.

In the meantime, Belyakov was looking through the forecast maps and was whispering something to the representative of long-range forecasts, Duletova.

Finally, the calm and reasonable navigator stood up and, walking up to Chkalov and Altovsky, said: "To Arkhangelsk, or to be more exact, to the Kola Peninsula, the weather for June 18 and 19 will be adequate for a flight at a low altitude with a heavy load."

The section from Franz-Josef Land to the North Pole seemed to be the most difficult section, but meteorologists themselves had difficulty in exactly determining the speed and directions of the frontal systems.

Altovsky considered the trip over the Rocky Mountains and the coastal range, where we could encounter powerful storm fronts, to be very dangerous.

Looking at all the details of this "obscure matter," as Chkalovcalled long-range forecasting, diminished these difficulties and the weather became noticeably "better" in the opinions of these forecasters. The meteorologists laughed and agreed that although the weather was not very good, there would not be any better conditions in the near future.

The three of us went into the next room to consult with each other.

"Well, what are we going to decide, Egor?" Chkalov asked.

"What is ahead of us for the next three days, it's difficult to say, but one thing is clear: the intrusion of the warm air masses is going to begin soon and then we'll be stuck at the field. It's important to have good weather for the first ten hours and then we'll see," I answered. "This means you're insisting on a departure."

"On a takeoff the day after tomorrow, no later."

"And you, Belyakov?"

"Of course the weather is poor, but why blame the weather forecasters? But just the same, we should take off on June 18 or 19."

"Agreed unanimously. We are taking off the day after tomorrow."

Chkalov announced to everyone the decision of the crew to take off on June 18.

No one as yet could believe that after the conclusions of the meteorologists it was possible to make the flight. They were not convinced, and became upset. But slowly, the meteorologists and the flight staff came to agree with the crew. Triumphant smiles began to appear on their faces. Chkalov was already joking and egging on the weather forecasters, thanking them and hugging them good-bye, saying: "The weather depends on the psychological condition of the person, my dear meteorologists. You have to take this into account. The view of weather is like that of beauty: some people like it and others do not."

We all left for a meeting with the Central Administration in order to decide the takeoff.

Since the conversation was extensive, I requested permission to leave, together with Belyakov, to return to Schelkovo in order to complete the selection of the maps of Canada, Alaska, and the northern part of United States. We also had to make exact adjustments of the solar heading indicator. In addition, we had to pick up the tables of precalculations for the computation of the line positions of the sun and moon for a period from June 18 to 25.

While Belyakov and I completed the final selection of flight documents, our commander continued to battle for the right to take off tomorrow. Rukhimovich, Tupolev, and Alksnis were quizzing Altovsky, who was still hesitant. Only the emotional and convincing speech by Chkalov shifted the scales in our favor and Rukhimovich decided to call Stalin by phone.

Josef Vissarionovich, after listening to the people's commissar, asked how the crew of the aircraft and their commander felt about the takeoff. Rukhimovich gave the phone receiver to Chkalov. Chkalov explained everything openly and extremely clearly, but apparently Stalin felt that the fliers were rushing things and decided to personally talk to the meteorological specialists.

Valery Pavlovich carefully put down the telephone receiver and looked with surprise at the members of the government commission.

"He said there was no point in getting excited about this matter," Valery Pavlovich said slowly. "He promised to give his answer a little later."

Scientists and meteorologists played an important role in convincing Stalin to allow Chkalov to take off tomorrow or at least the day after tomorrow.

At 1800 hours, the long-awaited phone call came. Stalin agreed with the decision of the crew.

By that time, a continuous stream of engineers, mostly out of breath, came rushing into our room recommending all kinds of activity. Belyakov accepted them, thanked them for their attention, and then later said to me: "Boy, they're strange. They think that their flight instructions will be taken for some kind of light reading matter."

Finally, everything was put together. It consisted of a neat stack of papers and maps. We also added a book by the American polar scientist Stefansson, *The Hospitable Arctic.*

A joyful Chkalov burst into the room and, seeing that his crew was still not asleep, was very explicit in his statements.

After noticing that this was not very effective, Chkalov recounted the circumstances surrounding the official permission.

We slept a full four hours. Our doctor insured peace and quiet for us.

I got up first at one in the morning. It was time to get up, I yelled from the top of my lungs, and this seemed to work on Chkalov and Belyakov.

They say that history does not repeat itself, but here again, it was necessary to take an enema, just like last year. The doctors were very pleased with our meek demeanor. They observed how we conducted another procedure, getting dressed: first, silk underwear; then thin, wool underwear; then socks, silk and wool; then a sweater and leather pants with goose down; and finally, high boots made from animal skin. We would put on our jackets in the aircraft.

Chekalov arrived and took us to the cafeteria, where the meteorologists were waiting for us with the current weather information.

There were many people at the field. These were, more than anything else, people who were waiting to see us off. They watched the ANT-25 rolled out of the hangar—all prepared for the flight. The aircraft was towed to its starting point on the runway.

Each of us drank a glass of hot tea and ate a sandwich with caviar and butter.

The meteorologists were gloomy. Not a smile on any of their faces.

"The weather will be a little more difficult than was forecast yesterday," Altovsky noted quietly.

Our commander, smiling, said: "There still hasn't been a single encounter on the field of battle that went according to plan as outlined by headquarters. A plan is needed for a general course of action. Then it is a matter of looking the enemy—the elements—straight in the eye."

When the navigator and I left the cafeteria, it was dawn. The field seemed silent. The large green field lay below a clear, blue sky. There was hardly any wind. It was cool. The monoplane stretched out its red wings and, standing on the runway, seemed ready for the long journey ahead.

We attempted to pass by this large group of friends, acquaintances, correspondents, and journalists, but, after hearing Chkalov's voice and friendly laughter, decided to rescue him from this mob. It turned out that the reporters were just waiting for something like this to happen.

They photographed the three of us in our flight suits, then separately, simultaneously obtaining an interview and autograph.

Shortly, Tupolev, followed by Mikulin and Gromov, came forward to see us.

Because of his deeply rooted flying habits, everything that Chkalov did in his life that was significant or important, he would call a test. And now he had to undergo a new test to justify the hopes of the country, to fly in such a way that the nation would say: there they are, people who do not fear any kind of danger or difficulty, but consciously go forward to meet them for the honor of the country.

Our excited chief engineer, Stoman, intently wiped the window of the pilot's cockpit. Berdnik, the mechanic, sitting in the pilot's seat, started up the engine; the propeller came to life. Mechanics Karaganov and Avdankin removed cylinders of compressed air from underneath the aircraft.

Khelnitsky, a colleague of Marshal Voroshilov, arrived at the field and conveyed the best wishes of the government and the administration.

After saying good-bye to all the people seeing us off, we climbed the steps and entered the aircraft through the rear hatch.

"My God, there is no room to turn around in here," the navigator noted.

We moved some things into the wing of the aircraft—parachutes and rucksacks. On the transverse tube of the wing spar, three balloons were placed, which would be used by each member of the crew. We placed the rubber life raft onto the rear seat. After this, it seemed to us that there was a little bit more room in the cockpit of the aircraft.

It was 0040 GMT.

The steps were removed; I battened down the rear hatch. Belyakov was sitting on a water barrel, used for the cooling system of the engine. The barrel also served as the navigator's seat. Sasha selected everything he would need for the first ten hours of flight.

The aircraft commander, with the peak of his cap turned up, sat in the pilot's seat. He gave the engine full revs. I seated myself behind Chkalov and observed how the engine was functioning—it was performing in a faultless manner.

Chkalov turned around and asked: "Is everything set?"
"Everything is fine. Request takeoff."

∎

Chkalov stuck his hand through the side window of the cockpit. A green flare shot up. The starter lifted a white flag. Karaganov and Avdankin simultaneously pulled away the blocks from the wheels. The engine once again roared at full power. The aircraft slowly started moving as if it didn't want to leave the spot where it had been parked. The propellers were biting into the air. The black, wide line in the middle of the runway began to disappear under the central part of the ANT-25. We were right in the middle of the runway. It was important to continue a straight run, otherwise it would be disastrous. Chkalov was surprisingly calm. In these crucial moments he even managed to stick his hand once more outside the right side windshield of the cockpit and wave in response to the farewell gestures of the hundreds of people who were standing near the assumed takeoff point of the aircraft.

Chkalov made a remarkable takeoff. With each second, the bounce of the landing gear became softer. On the right side, the last hangar passed by. The aircraft, bouncing one more time, lifted off into the air. I retracted the landing gear in an instant. The fence of the field, which had been specially removed for the flight, slipped by underneath us. It was 0405 Moscow time or 0105 GMT.

The smokestacks of the plants were being left behind us now.

I was so glad for Chkalov's takeoff mastery that I almost choked him as I hugged him while standing on my knees behind the back of the pilot's seat.

Chkalov was smiling broadly. "Well, we're off. Everything depends on us now."

Belyakov, carrying out his duty schedule, prepared to bed down.

The duties of the crew were distributed by previous experience. Chkalov was the pilot, I was the copilot and also the relief navigator and radio operator so that Belyakov could rest. We also decided not to change the working schedule: six hours on, three hours off. Under normal conditions, the flight could last sixty to seventy hours, and if everything went as expected, each of us would work forty to fifty hours. The plane gained altitude to three hundred meters.

Chkalov listened to the drone of the engine, which was working at maximum capacity, and in a pleased tone shouted to me: "It's a symphony by Alexander Mikulin." This was how the commander of the crew characterized the roar of the AM-34 engine.

We were at four hundred meters altitude. The cities of Kalyazin and Kashin were visible below our wing. Chkalov impatiently waited for Cherepovets. He scanned the skies for the escort aircraft. One of them was a contemporary high-speed bomber, the ANT-40, the other an ancient twin-engine ANT-6. Valery frequently waved at them so that they would come closer to exchange farewell greetings with them.

Soon the snow-white, speedy monoplane retracted its landing gear, overcame our slow-moving ANT, and, making a farewell bank before us, hid in the morning fog. Behind it lumbered the ANT-6.

Beneath us were the forests of the Volga region. The sun was already high in the sky and was warming Chkalov. He asked for the thermos in order to quench his thirst with a gulp of tea laced with lemon.

Then we arrived over Cherepovets. Chkalov eagerly looked down at this city that was so familiar to him, for this was the place where he had learned the boilermaking trade.

I made routine notes in the navigator's journal. The altitude was twelve hundred meters. It was warm in the cockpit so we still had not turned on the heat.

Behind Chkalov's back I unrolled a large, soft sleeping bag made from dog skin and placed it on the cot. Polar explorer Otto Schmidt considered these kinds of sleeping bags the best, and had recommended them to Valery. Now Chkalov called me over with a gesture and expressed a striking thought: "I'm thinking: why didn't anyone tell us how we would have to conduct ourselves among Americans— what to say, how to behave?"

"Who should have to teach you that? You are a communist. It is important to fly there, and then we will see. An embassy has been established there for good reason."

"We are required to make it there!" Chkalov answered angrily and shouted at me with fury. "What are you babbling about? You're supposed to be sleeping. Get to bed!"

At 0900 I was awakened and relieved Chkalov. The aircraft was flying at an altitude of two thousand meters as required by our flight schedule. The low cloud layer was so close that the windows of the cockpit were dampened, and we could feel the cold mist on our bare, gloveless hands.

Soon the white, limitless, cloudy murk covered the aircraft so thickly that the tips of the wings were no longer visible.

According to an agreement that Chkalov and I had made a long time ago, instrument flight was my responsibility. Both Chkalov and Belyakov trusted me and so were not upset that conditions changed so drastically. This time I didn't have any of this calmness because, with an outside temperature of –4°, very intensive icing had begun. I whistled sharply and called the commander. Chkalov crawled up to me, excited, his eyes bloodshot from fatigue. He immediately understood why his assistance was required. The ice had whitened the front windshield of the cockpit and had settled thickly on the leading edge of the wing. Because of this icing, the propeller blades had become unbalanced and created a buffeting condition on the aircraft. The craft was shaking as if from the blows of an unseen, but terrifying force.

The commander sharply worked the pump while I opened the valve and immediately smelled the alcohol. It was part of the fluid that was supposed to clear the propeller blades. The blows diminished. The aircraft became quieter. Intermittent buffeting continued to shake the aircraft.

The situation was extremely dangerous since it was clear to everyone that the most dangerous enemy of aviation, icing, had seized us by the jugular in a death grip. After an hour of such flight, either it would destroy the aircraft or we would crash on the ice.

"We can't fly any longer at this altitude. I have to climb above the clouds!" I shouted to the commander and added more revs to the engine.

"Better go up!" Chkalov agreed and again began to pump the anti-icing device.

The aircraft slowly gained altitude. After five hundred meters, the rays of the sun shone weakly through from the left.

"We'll get out of it soon!" Valery shouted gladly.

After about five more tense minutes, our airship left the cloud layer.

The aircraft began to free itself from these foreign growths under the effects of the sun's rays and our forward speed. It quieted down and continued to hold its steady course to the north.

We were still flying above the clouds. Occasionally, they would open up and we could see through the windshield the black waters of the Barents Sea. Some kind of ship was visible down below. Then once again the endless cloud layer, looking like a Siberian steppe covered with snow during a long winter,

It was now 1400 hours, the end of my shift at the controls. I woke up Chkalov unceremoniously, and we again squeezed through and changed places. Sleep had refreshed the commander. He was in a good mood.

"Well, do you see Schmidt's beard or any polar bears there?" Chkalov shouted to me in jest as I tried to beat my way back between the pilot and the right side of the fuselage.

"Don't rush it. Maybe you will still meet them. We haven't seen ground in seven hours, and Belyakov, as if to spite us, has lost use of his sextant. Remember what the navigator told you, that without celestial navigation, it is impossible to fly into the Arctic."

"Oh, shut up, Baiduk! Go see Belyakov. He probably dropped dead back there."

With his tired head lowered, Belyakov was trying to receive a radiogram. His bluish lips and sharply outlined wrinkles spoke of his fatigue. He was seven years older than Chkalov and ten years my senior. But his stamina was greater than ours.

During the past few hours of flight, no celestial navigation remarks had been recorded.

Consequently, I had no idea of the drift angle and the winds aloft.

Mildly rebuking the navigator, I relieved him of duty at 1426. Belyakov immediately prepared for bed, but his long legs extended beyond the cot.

I took the sextant, became convinced that the bubble in the level was extremely small, and quickly placed the unfunctioning instrument on a pipe tube of the aircraft's internal heating system.

The commander was no longer turning in my direction. Up ahead he observed a darkening sky, which meant that "Mr. Cyclone," as we used to call Altovsky, had forecast correctly: a secondary front of a low-pressure area had cast out its nets to seize our red-winged ship, which was now flying at an altitude of three thousand meters, temperature –10°, in its cloudy clutches.

Through the polyspherical canopy of the solar heading indicator, I noticed that a cyclone was waiting for us ahead. I needed to "shoot" the sun very quickly. It had been almost eight hours since the last "fix" was made. Also we should be near a main meridian, which would give us an answer concerning our true position.

I crawled toward Chkalov, almost striking Belyakov in the face with my Finnish knife. Belyakov was sleeping like a baby.

After asking the commander to hold a steady course and to maintain the aircraft in a horizontal position, I returned to the navigator's table and took the sextant, which had now warmed up, into my hands. Even Newton, after discovering the law of gravity, would not have been as happy as I was, when I observed that the bubble of the level had widened to the appropriate dimensions. It was possible to measure the height of the sun. I did this three times in a row, and at 1442, I noted this in the navigator's log. We had drifted off to the right and assumed that we were now passing over the western section of the Franz-Josef Land archipelago.

Chkalov had already climbed to an altitude of four thousand meters. The outside temperature fell to –24°. It became quite cold in the cockpit despite the fact that the heat had been turned on. At 1700 hours, the commander requested a change in shift. I understood that I would once again have to fly on instruments and woke up the navigator.

At an altitude of four thousand meters, all hunched up, it was quite difficult in these crowded conditions to crawl to the pilot's seat; nevertheless, we were able to change places quickly and easily.

"Breathe some oxygen!" I shouted to Chkalov.

Chkalov stayed next to me and began quickly to increase the pressure in the tank containing the anti-icing fluid. I selected a temperature for the carburetor heater, turned on all of the gyroscopes to power from the engine and, after turning the aircraft exactly to the north, climbed bravely into the dark cloudy murk of the cyclone while slowly gaining altitude. In deciding to fly through the cyclone, the three of us hoped that with a temperature of –24°, there was no reason to fear icing. At 1730, everything was hidden from our field of vision and, as if cut off from the world, the ANT-25, screened off by clouds, quietly continued to climb.

The first minutes of calm were quickly replaced by alarm: the aircraft began quickly to ice up and became covered in transparent ice. Soon, we could feel the buffeting begin. Chkalov was impatient to use the anti-icing device. I opened the crank all the way and the vibration of the propellers began to diminish.

"Boy, they're wonderful, those people from TsAGI! What a simple and excellent way of cleaning they invented!" Chkalov praised the creators of the device.

But the aircraft's stabilizer and antenna were icing up extremely rapidly. There was no remedy for that condition.

"It's terrible when you are forced to be a plaything of nature." Chkalov complained at the fate of pilots. "No one would understand what we pilots feel at such a moment. It's frustrating and terrifying to think that now your aircraft is turning into an ice cube and you have to submit helplessly to the elements and blind forces of nature. Gain some more altitude, my friend. Scramble along, but climb higher."

The ANT-25, which was still overloaded, was literally crawling up meter by meter even under full power. It seemed like a powerless mountain climber who suddenly would fall off from some steep incline and drop into an abyss. Our much tested aircraft flew meter by meter, higher and higher, a feverish bouncing of its empennage and the engine at full revs.

In twenty minutes, we gained 150 meters but then—oh joy!—the clouds were boiling below us. The generous rays of the sun soaked us in its warmth.

"There you go!" Chkalov shouted exultantly and hugged me.

"Congratulations, you did it."

Tension once again diminished but I felt tired. Afraid of falling asleep behind the controls, I asked Chkalov for his pipe.

Our unyielding, ever-watchful navigator did not give me any peace and requested that I guide the aircraft along the shadow of the pin, which he had placed in front of the pilot's cockpit as a very simple solar heading indicator. Since this task was connected with celestial navigation, it was easy to carry it out with renewed interest.

Valery did not go to sleep. He was thinking about something and then crawled to me on his knees and shouted in my ear: "This is when you feel it's important not to unnecessarily overload the craft. We took almost four hundred pounds of food and the poor aircraft was barely able to crawl up out of that.

"But I think," continued Valery, "that for such a flight, we need a craft that is capable of flying at around ten kilometers."

In the meantime, the aircraft, even though it had been in the sun for two full hours, could not free itself from icing conditions. The leading edge of the wings and the frame of the directional finder were covered as if they had just been painted by some fresh white paint. Ice twelve centimeters thick formed on them.

"Just think what the moisture must be in order for it to freeze up like that in twenty minutes with a temperature of –24°. That's the wonders of the Arctic for you," Chkalov growled, crawling off the tank.

After talking with the navigator, the commander crawled into his sleeping bag and went to sleep.

The oil gauge was indicating it was time to add oil to the engine from the reserve tank. I would again have to wake up Valery Pavlovich, although I sympathized with him. Chkalov got up, quickly looked around the aircraft and, noticing the fairly good weather, commenced to pump oil with a hand pump.

"Yvgeny Karlovich really knew how to build these oil thermoses," Chkalov shouted. "You pump and don't feel any resistance. The oil is still hot!"

After finishing this procedure, the commander relieved me at the controls. I reminded him to be careful in using the anti-icing fluid. There was very little of it left.

■

The ANT-25 had been in flight for eighteen hours nonstop toward the north, yet even now, it was flying without a flutter. The steady drone of the engine and the propeller calmed the crew and filled their souls with bliss and the premonition of victory. There was so much sunshine that the navigator was unable to sit in his place very long. He often stood up, and, making use of the precise delineations of the natural horizon, took measurements of the sun's angle through the astro-bubble and made complicated calculations to determine our flight progress.[54]

Belyakov had prepared navigational charts for every stage of the flight. The information they contained could be useful to the navigator. From these maps, it was possible to know where the closest radio station was located, its call signs, power, its frequency, the topography of the area, the nearest base in case of a forced landing, and the names of the more useful stars for an astronomical determination of our location.

I noticed that the navigator kept turning the radio compass waiting for some kind of a signal.

"Until I hear a signal of the radio beacon from Rudolph," said Belyakov, "we will keep the same course."

After being convinced that the last few hours of flight had brought us close to the meridian of Rudolph Island, I climbed into the cot, curled up in the sleeping bag, and tried to imagine what our wives and children were doing. It was now midnight.

It became colder in the aircraft. The temperature dropped down to –6°.

It was easier to fall asleep sitting at the controls than it was in the cot. The sun was shining day and night. But apparently, I still managed to nod off because Valery had to bring me around with a sharp whistle.

"Land! Land!" I heard the loud voice of Chkalov and rushed to crawl out of my sleeping bag.

As I was making my way to Belyakov, I saw a notation in the aircraft log: "2000 hours Greenwich, Cape Barents on Norbrook Island in the archipelago of Franz-Josef Land." The blinding snows and ice fields, from which the mysterious and silent islands of the archipelago spread out, glistened through the window of the cockpit. Valery rocked the ANT-25 from wing to wing, attracting our attention to the rare beauty of the primordial nature of the Arctic.

I crawled through to the commander and, sticking my head between the right side of the aircraft and Valery's head, admired in silence the panorama glittering in the shining sun.

"Old familiar places!" A pleased Chkalov said to me in my ear and smiled at the same time, "Hasn't changed since last year."

The aircraft quietly and majestically flew at an altitude of 4,310 meters and the magnificent panorama of the archipelago opened up before the crew.

The striking clarity and purity of the air and the solidity of direct and indirect rays of sunlight created in the Arctic an amazing opportunity for a person to view the panorama for hundreds of kilometers. Soon, Luigi Island was visible and Belyakov, after finally determining our location, hurried to give this information to flight headquarters. But, a cloud layer appeared below and we were left alone with the sun.

"Whatever you say, the north is truly wonderful!" Chkalov concluded, "Once you see it, you remember it for the rest of your life."

While we were philosophizing on the beauty of this frozen part of the planet, Belyakov determined our flight path by the radio beacon zone on Rudolph Island. He very clearly heard the signal from the beacon and smiled with satisfaction while looking toward us. Smiles and jokes during a flight—this was not the style of Belyakov; for that reason, I wanted to ask him to explain this unusual behavior.

Belyakov was proudly looking at the map of the central section of the polar basin and said, "Now we will fly toward the North Pole along a predetermined meridian. Rudolph rescued us."

"That means, we're flying to Schmidt and Papanin?" I replied.

"Yes, toward the pole."

"Did you ask the radio station at the base on Rudolph about the aerial expedition?"

"At the send-off at Schelkovo, the polar explorers there mentioned that the entire expedition, about forty-four people, with Schmidt and Shevelev directing, in the aircraft of Vodopyanov, Molotov, Alekseev, Mazuruk, and Golovin, should have flown from the pole to Rudolph Island base on June 18, that is, yesterday. They, if there were no delays, would be in Moscow, except Ilya Mazuruk—he was to stay on duty at Franz-Josef Land."

The commander interrupted our conversation with a whistle and a slight rocking of the aircraft. This meant that Chkalov was asking to be relieved, although this was not a scheduled time to change shifts.

It was 2200 hours Greenwich time. I sat at the controls while the commander headed off toward Belyakov, then crawled into a wing and opened a valve that fed fuel to the engine from the fuel tank, then curled up into his sleeping bag.

After half an hour, the weather changed drastically. There was not a cloud to be seen, neither above nor below. Above, the sun was framed by concentric circles of the spectrum. Below were the endless icy fields lined with crevices. They grew dark just like spring roads, which brought a certain liveliness to this Arctic scenery.

The rays of the sun burned and it was impossible to hide from them. It was good that our eyes were successfully protected by glasses with special light filters.

Visibility became even better than we had seen before above the archipelago. Now it seemed that you could see half the world, the entire northern hemisphere. The altitude was four thousand meters. The outside temperature was $-24°$; inside the cockpit the temperature was $-1°$.

We were headed into a region where navigation became especially difficult. As a rule, Ivan Timofeevich Spirin had told us, the compasses would begin to dance and go around in a circle from any rolling or pitching motion at the pole. Consequently, our chief navigator would remind us continually about all sorts of insignificant things, forcing us to hold a course toward the North Pole with unwavering precision by using a shadow from a pin, which was very similar to a common large nail. True, in order not to offend the vanity of a first class fighter pilot, Belyakov in such a situation would say to Chkalov: "Guide the aircraft by the solar heading indicator as precisely as you can." But the real solar heading indicator was located behind the pilot in the astro-hatch atop the fuselage.

Nevertheless, one made a genuine attempt to pilot the ANT-25 in such a way that Belyakov would not record navigational deficiencies in the log book.

Twenty minutes later, it was cloudy below and the ice was hidden from view.

It was now June 19. We had been flying for over twenty-four hours but we were so tired it seemed as though a month had gone by. Apparently, this was the influence of being at a high altitude for such a long time, which also caused an absence in appetite. We had eaten only once and then skimpily—sandwiches, chicken, ham, oranges, and so on still lay untouched in the rubber containers.

With the beginning of a new day, I gave the controls to Chkalov and left to obtain some water for myself. There is nothing better than drinking cold water when your throat has been dried up by high altitude. Having quenched my thirst, I sat by Belyakov.

"How are things with the pole? When are we going to be there?"

"There's a very strong headwind. We will be above the pole not earlier than five or six hours from now," Belyakov answered and stuck his head back in the oxygen mask.

Chkalov called to me. He asked me to pump some fresh oil into the engine's sump, but, during that time, the oil had become cold in these containers; it had thickened and it was very difficult to push it through with a hand pump. At an altitude of 4,200 meters, this physical exertion was very strenuous. My pulse became rapid. After completing this job, I immediately lay down on the bed and, putting the mask to my face, opened the valve of the oxygen line. My breathing became even, my pulse normal. I drifted off to sleep and forgot about the cold and everything on earth.

The appearance to the right of another cyclone spoiled Chkalov's mood. Contrary to all theories, they wandered about in fairly large numbers and produced above them a mane of high, feathery clouds, which were yellow under the effects of the sun's rays. They wandered like apparitions along an enormous aerial ocean, sometimes moving at extremely high speeds. They frightened us with icing conditions and often robbed us of forward speed. It was understandable why the commander of the ANT-25 did not like this cyclone which had crossed our path. Chkalov started to move away from it to the left, believing that in doing this, he would compensate slightly for the previous drift of the aircraft to the right.

Something happened to Belyakov's radio. According to all the checks, it was working properly but yet he could not receive anything.

Belyakov tinkered with the radio for a long time, but he could not manage to pick anything up. He changed the tubes; however, this had no effect. He decided to send out a few radiograms without any hope of receiving assurance of their reception.

While I, after having enjoyed oxygen, was sleeping and Belyakov was repairing the radio, Valery successfully negotiated the cyclone and did not lose a single liter of the remaining anti-icing liquid, which was to be saved for an emergency situation.

I was awakened when the commander was flying the aircraft, using the solar heading indicator, on a course to the north. The weather was sunny with a cloudy shroud that covered the ice below. This was 0325 on June 19. Chkalov requested that he be relieved.

■

After smoking a cigarette, which was dangerous to my own health but good for calming the nerves, I drank some water and resumed control of the aircraft. Valery was very tired and his leg, which had been broken in childhood, was causing pain. He immediately crawled into his sleeping bag, breathed some oxygen, and fell asleep, although he knew that the pole was very, very close.

Belyakov asked me to fly the aircraft with great accuracy and he systematically, without hurrying, shot the angle of the sun, which, being to the right of us, indicated that we had turned away from our desired course.

By carefully observing the lines of position, it was possible to determine that we were going somewhat to the left of the pole and that we would cross 90° north latitude, that is the point of the axis of the earth's rotation, at 0400. From an altitude of 4,150 meters, we looked out over a gigantic frozen wasteland that was pocked by small and large crevices and patches of ice-free water, which ran in various directions. The compasses became more and more sensitive and would crazily spin around with the slightest pitch or yaw. Only the gyroscopes were functioning as if there was no rotation to our old planet.

Looking below, Belyakov and I once more frowned at the monotonous wilderness of ice and turned thoughts to the four Soviet scientists who had contributed much to our country and world science in overcoming the North Pole. They were somewhere very close by, possibly a bit to the left of our flight path.

Belyakov attempted to make radio contact with Ernest Krenkel and send him, Papanin, Shirshov, and Fedorov our warm greetings, deepest respect, and sincere gratitude for their data transmitted from the pole, which provided the means for the three of us to fly to the United States in the ANT-25.

Good-bye, friends. Bon voyage on the polar ice cap. Farewell, North Pole, may the rotation of the earth be always as it is.

We were now entering the air space between the pole and Canada. The crew faced the journey above the "pole of inaccessibility," where the polar bears have not heard the roar of any engine and have not seen polar explorers on the ice.

Belyakov was intently working on his calculations. All the compass arrows, having sensed the proximity of the magnetic pole, were quivering like the tail of a hunting dog that has just smelled a fox's hole. Therefore, I received a very positive order from the navigator: to use only the solar heading indicator, which had now become a significant navigational instrument during the most difficult portion of our flight. This silly pin had been elevated to a cult in astronavigation! We pilots would have to endure this because "the navigator is part of an educated elite while the pilots who carry out his orders are just normal working ones." These were the words of our commander, who at this time was asleep. We had no thoughts of waking him up.

■

Why awaken a tired pilot who still has to fly above some of the
Earth's bleakest spots? In essence, it does not matter at all to a pilot
what is beneath him: ice fields or a stormy ocean, forest or mountains, even a cloud layer, he does not care about that. The concerns
of a pilot are that the engine and the aircraft function normally and
to always steer on a true course to his destination. Sleep, commander: just by achieving a wonderful takeoff in the heavy ANT-25
from Schelkovo Field, you have performed half of your assigned task.

Belyakov had a different duty. The pole provided the navigator
with a mass of things to do. Indeed, why were we going now on a
northerly course? Had we not crossed the pole and so were flying
south to America? Was something going astray? For this reason
Belyakov had to situate the solar heading indicator in such a way
that it functioned as previously, but now showed a course to the
south.

When exact time is needed, a naval chronometer is invaluable.
Together with a sextant and tables, calculations can be made so that
readjustments can be effected by the navigator.

At 0443, the solar heading indicator was reset and time changed
to the 123rd meridian. This was the way to the United States. The
aircraft was flying normally, the course was to the south. Everything
was under control.

Belyakov notified me once more that I should not use magnetic
headings; I had to respect that pin, that nail, whose shadow indicated
the path along the 123rd meridian to the United States. Valery and I
called it the SUK-4. One had to admit that the SUK-4, this simplest
of all devices, was invaluable for the flight from the Bering Sea to the
shores of Canada.

At 0510, Belyakov sent out a telegram announcing the completion of the first part of the assignment: "We have crossed the pole—a
tail wind—white ice fields with crevices and expanses of open
water—our mood is cheerful."

To the right, we noticed a new cyclone. It was good that this one
stretched out parallel to our flight path.

At 0600 I woke up Chkalov. He, as usual, immediately checked
with the navigator. Belyakov informed him regarding the pole crossing. Chkalov was happy as a child. He laughed and the many
wrinkles on his face gathered together like an accordion. He often

would look out of the side and, blinded by the glare of the rays of the sun, would squint his eyes. He would look for his sunglasses and again would look out at the expanse of two oceans, the aerial ocean and the Arctic Ocean.

Valery came up to me. "How are things going? Why didn't you wake me up, dammit?"

"I felt sorry for you. What was there to look at anyway except for snow that had been packed down by the aircraft of Vodopyanov's expedition."

"You bums!" the commander upbraided us in jest.

"Enough of your impregnable pole!"

"You rascals!" I really wanted to see the top of the world and Papanin's crew at the pole.

"It has been snowing a lot where Papanin's men are stationed and a piece of that large axis of your favorite little world is sticking out on the summit. I noticed the axis has rusted quite a bit."

"Papanin is a practical person; he'll figure out that it should be painted and oiled," the satisfied crew commander mumbled into my ear and intently looked into the distance where we could see the next swirling cyclone.

"Baidukov, we should send a telegram to Stalin about flying over the world's belly button."

"Hasn't Belyakov already sent one?"

"He scribbled some kind of quotations."

"That damned old prune."

"Well, you write the text yourself and order him to send it."

"I'll go and compose it."

Chkalov went to check with the navigator. I noticed how he grabbed a note pad and started to write quickly. He ripped off a page, crumpled it up, and then began his composition anew. When he had finished the two-page text and given it to Belyakov, the navigator took the radio log and transformed the flowing report of the ANT-25 commander into a laconic message: "Moscow, the Kremlin. To Stalin. The pole is behind us. We are now flying over the pole of inaccessibility. We will attempt to carry out your assignment. The crew is in good spirits. Regards. Chkalov, Baidukov, Belyakov."

Chkalov, relieving me at the controls complained: "Your navigator has no humor. He rejected an entire expression of the human soul. He sent twenty-nine words in all, that professor did."

"That's because he took into consideration that Stalin is a very busy man and he isn't going to want to read your rendition," I replied.

"OK. I'll get even with you later," Chkalov threatened.

"You know that we are working with a radio-telegraph only using a numerical code, so there isn't any room in it. Even Pushkin couldn't worm his way into our radio log."

But Chkalov was already weary of jokes, and the aircraft was approaching a sea of clouds. The mountain of clouds created an illusion of foamy waves that had suddenly frozen. Chkalov added revs to the engine and the ANT-25 slowly gained altitude, leaving behind strange forms of cumulus clouds.

The altimeter indicated five thousand meters. After thirty hours of flight, it was not only difficult to work at such an altitude, it even became difficult to lie in the sleeping bag. But Chkalov, putting on his oxygen mask, convinced himself: "Endure it while you still have the strength, the journey is still long and we don't know what awaits us ahead."

Belyakov, who had been working for many hours without being relieved, was fatigued and could not work without oxygen.

At 0940, I almost unwillingly crawled into the pilot's compartment to relieve Chkalov, who at such an altitude was overcome with fatigue and oxygen deprivation. His left leg pained him so much that he was unable to sit in the pilot's seat for more than three hours and forty minutes. All this meant that the working schedule of the ship had been finally scrapped and navigator Belyakov would still have to work many hours without any rest. We were now going through the most complicated part of our flight.

After sitting in the seat and taking the controls of the aircraft, I felt my heart beating very rapidly. Apparently, this reflected the physical exertion in changing seats at this high altitude. Even our "strong man," Valery, felt terrible when he tried to pump oil. He was dizzy and he pressed the oxygen mask against his face. Valery first looked at Belyakov and then at me with a guilty expression, then after feeling somewhat better, slowly put the mask away and turned the valve. At 1045, I noticed that the fuel level in the working tank was beginning to decrease. This meant that it was necessary to switch to the outer wing tanks. This work, which was very difficult at high altitude, had to be done by the commander. Contorting himself, he crawled into the wing, and turned several valves and then pumped the remaining fuel out of the main tanks into the sump tank with a hand pump.

The commander became very pale after such exertions.

"Don't be an idiot! Breathe some oxygen!" I gave him my mask.

Valery stuck his face into the mask and, after taking several deep breaths, said: "We don't know how we will do above the mountains at night, old buddy. We might need the oxygen then."

I also wanted to turn the valve, but Chkalov rumbled sternly: "This I won't allow." After fully opening the valve, he put the mask to my face. "Belyakov is holding up, but I see that he's having a tough time."

Chkalov lay down on the bed. Belyakov sent a note: "We're flying with a tail wind. Our air speed is approximately 200 kilometers an hour." This was good! Maybe we could make it through this damn cyclone more quickly.

At 1100, our ANT-25 was flying at its maximum ceiling, 5,700 meters, and even slight fluctuations affected altitude, which caused it to clip the tops of these storm clouds. At times, the aircraft would be completely surrounded by these snow white mists. The upper edge of the cloud layer became higher. I attempted to move toward the left in order to go around it, but it consumed ten to twenty minutes of time and the aircraft once again was under severe stress. Once we almost turned around, but this action did not lead to any success. Before us the cloud layer had risen to an altitude of approximately 6,500 meters.

Belyakov woke up Chkalov and the two of them, after getting as far as the reserve oil tank, leaned over across my seat—one to the left, the other to the right—and we began to discuss what to do next.

"Get going, let's not get caught in this mess," Chkalov cheered me on. Belyakov corrected the course and we cut through the dark, wavering liquid mists with a temperature of –30°. Our poor, old, suffering, often-repaired ANT-25 trembled from the strong upward and downward current of the air mass. The aircraft lost altitude.

Chkalov and Belyakov, taking turns using one oxygen mask, did not move away from me and understood that much depended on instrument flight. We were afraid of icing conditions. Although the temperature of the outside air was very low, we had to take our chances. As they say, once bitten, twice shy. We intently watched the leading edges of the wings.

The aircraft was flung about like kindling. I was barely able to control it on instrument flight. I couldn't see anything through the front windshield cockpit: a centimeter of ice hid from view the liquid level measurement device. The SUK-4 instrument was not visible.

"We can't fly like this any more!" Chkalov shouted to me with difficulty.

I could see that after an hour of flight, there was a thick layer of ice, which was changing the wing load and seriously overloading the aircraft. In addition, the anti-icing liquid was exhausted and the aircraft began to vibrate fore and aft very dangerously "Let's go down!" I quickly eased up on the throttle.

After twenty-six hours of flight, the engine, for the first time, received an unexpected rest and, since it was unused to such a condition, coughed several times quantities of undetonated fuel from the exhaust manifold.

We quickly lost altitude. At three thousand meters, it suddenly became dark below and the aircraft soon was flying between two layers of clouds.

Above us was the layer of storm clouds that had brought us all this unpleasantness. Below us was visible a scattered cloud layer and through it, it seemed that an island was visible in the distance.

Chkalov and Belyakov checked the maps and attempted to determine through the portholes what was below us and where we were located.

The outside thermometer indicated a temperature of 0°. I hoped that in this layer we would quickly lose the ice that had frozen onto the aircraft and I started to add revs to the engine in order to bring the craft into horizontal flight. At this time, something suddenly spurted from the front section of the cowling. The front windshield was still iced over. There was a smell of alcohol. I immediately understood that the almost impossible had happened—obviously the pipe that vented the exhaust away from the cooling system of the engine had frozen. This was caused by insufficient heating of the pipe by the exhaust gases, when I had reduced the engine revs. If this was the case, then the increase in pressure had, I believed, ruptured the tank and the liquid was thrown onto the canopy of the cockpit.

Shivers ran up and down my body. I yelled so that someone would give me a knife. Valery managed to hand me a sharp hunting knife. After catching sight of the indicator in a shaft of light, I paled: the level of the water, or, as we called it, "the little line," which was located above the tank of the cooling system, was hidden underneath a glass mantle; this meant that the engine cylinders heads were not being cooled by cold water and that, if I didn't turn off the ignition, in five or six minutes the engine would seize up. It would either quit and fly into pieces or the whole thing would end in a fire. I instantly lowered the revs and began to work the hand water pump madly.

But the pump was not bringing up water, and it moved easily without drawing any liquid. Was it really a disaster? Were we really coming to a situation that would lead us to a forced landing in the desolate region of the pole of inaccessibility? I shouted to Chkalov: "The pump isn't drawing any water! Water, I need water or else we're going to burn up the engine!"

This is where my friends showed themselves to be calm, courageous, and resourceful as they saved us from a terrible calamity.

In these minutes of danger, one could feel Chkalov's enormous inner strength behind his external calmness. After calmly evaluating the situation, he instantly made a correct decision while maintaining his composure. His teammates felt that if there was a way out, he would find one.

Chkalov moved quickly toward the extra tank and together with Belyakov checked it over. It was empty. Where to get water? I continued to glide. There remained only two thousand meters of altitude.

When I turned back, I could see that they were cutting into the rubber bags with the emergency water supply. But it had frozen so much that, after breaking the icy crust, my friends found only a few liters of unfrozen liquid. They quickly poured this remaining water into the tank and gave me the signal to use the pump. But, once again, the hand pump worked to no avail.

Chkalov came up to me and quickly tried to pump the fan.

"Here's the trouble. It's just not taking it in!"

"The balloons! Try to add water from them!" It suddenly occurred to me.

Chkalov hurried into the tail section, with Belyakov behind him. Soon the contents of the three balloons were poured into the tank and, oh, happiness, the pump started to force the mixture of clean water and urine, which now we would not be able to give to the doctors for analysis. The float pin suddenly came up from below and showed itself under the glass mantle.

Valery and Belyakov did not leave me. Chkalov shouted: "Let's go up and I'll work the pump! And you, Sasha, figure out more exactly what these islands are that we noticed."

Carefully warming up the engine by increasing the revs, I slowly heated the iced-over tip of the steam exhaust pipe and then started to gain altitude. In judging what had happened, the three of us came to the conclusion that, after the freezing of the tip of the steam exhaust pipe and the increasing of pressure in the line, the expansion tank of the water-cooling system for the engine did not explode as we had originally thought, but apparently worked loose the reduction valve, through which a large amount of water was expelled.

We were once again flying at an altitude of five thousand meters and soon were convinced again that we should not fly for long in cloud cover because the aircraft would begin to ice over. Once again, the commander and the navigator approached me and we decided on our plan of action.

"Let's go below," I suggested.

"But not the way you did the first time," Belyakov said.

Now I decreased the revs of the engine somewhat and descended primarily to increase the speed of our glide. At an altitude lower than three thousand meters, the cloud layer ended and before us there were enormous islands as far as the eye could see. In the straits there was endless ice, which was lit up by variously colored hues. It was like a mosaic. I rocked the aircraft and called my friends to look at the colorful panorama of rare beauty.

Chkalov stuck his head into the pilot's cockpit on the left side, and Belyakov to the right of me. I said something to them about the beauty of the Canadian Arctic.

"It's very well to engage in poetry, but these three hours of battling the cyclone have cost us a lot," Chkalov said into my left ear.

"Well, did you get scared?"

"What do you think! There's nothing here, no weather stations, no polar expeditions," Chkalov answered.

"And you?" I looked to Belyakov.

"He's a chapaevite, how could he be scared?" Valery egged on the navigator.

"It's no sin to admit that the whole matter was very unpleasant," answered a very tired Belyakov.

Taking advantage of the fact that the faces of my friends were pressed up against mine, I bussed them both on the beards that had already started to grow on their cheeks and said: "Boy, you guys are masters of getting out of things!"

"All right, I'm deeply moved," Valery good-naturedly blurted out and crawled back. Belyakov followed him.

Of course, the beauty of the Arctic after an exhausting battle with the elements leads one to think about music and poetry. In flight conditions changed as in a kaleidoscope. Doubts began to creep in. Has the devil dragged us to Greenland? What is this huge, brown-colored land covered with endless ravines and rivers? The shores of the islands were high and had many cliffs. It was very similar to the northern section of the Kola Peninsula. Maybe we had gone straight to Greenland?

Belyakov continued to employ the sextant in measuring the angle of the sun. The meridian would run through Banks Island. Valery brought out a map and together we affirmed that below us was indeed Banks Island.

Chkalov said: "Our navigator is completely worn out. How about if I sit behind the controls and you relieve him while the weather is still good."

I gave up the aircraft controls to Chkalov and opened the rubber bags with our food supply. Here was chicken, meat, oranges, apples, and chocolate. In forty hours of flight, we had eaten only once and that was thirty hours ago.

I selected a red apple. It was frozen but very juicy. I gave my friends an apple each and began to dig into mine. The oranges were completely frozen, and they thawed only after being put on the heater pipes. Chkalov demurred on the oranges. The navigator was not squeamish about eating an orange and some chicken. I did a good job of eating. Everything that was left, I finished immediately.

How good it was to fly at an altitude of 3500 meters—it was easy to breathe, my mood was excellent, all misfortunes and failures were quickly forgotten. And after I had smoked a pipe, which test pilot and airplane designer Vasya Stepanchenok had presented to Valery, I was ready to play our Siberian song, "Oh! The Lowlands!" on my balalaika. But I didn't have a balalaika and, giving up my bed to Belyakov, who had exceeded the normal work schedule for a navigator/radio operator, I sat in his chair, thinking about our adventures to this point.

I looked in the navigator's log. "Thirteen hours, twenty-seven minutes: between breaks in the clouds, Banks Island is visible." I noticed on the map that the island stretched along our route for hundreds of kilometers. At 1640, the brown earth of this gigantic island was still visible. The outside temperature was only –1°. Inside the craft, it was 9°. The altitude is the same—3500 meters. I was experiencing a relaxed feeling. Like on vacation. I picked up the flight log again, and the blissful state changed like water freezing when the temperature is lowered. At 1115, a telegram had been sent by Belyakov to Moscow and Dixon: "Everything is fine. I am transferring communications to American stations. The speed is 200 kilometers an hour. I calculated that at thirteen forty we will be above Patrick Island." Since that time, no messages had been received on board the ANT-25. What did that mean? Above all, this signified that we would be flying above foreign lands without knowing the weather conditions. The situation was not the best.

While these gloomy thoughts were upsetting me, I did not want to spoil Chkalov's mood. He was flying our ANT-25 above open water in exceptionally good weather and had just left the southern tip of Banks Island.

■

Open waters seemed strange after the endless ice of the polar region." Even now, it seemed strange because somewhat to the left or slightly to the right, there still stretched out expanses of ice instead of water. Along the shore was a solid path of ice, which stretched out into the distance.

At 1615, Cape Pierce Point, which we had talked about so much in Moscow, was visible below.

The crew had carried out the primary objective—Canada was beneath us and we now had the right to land at the first airfield that came up.

I crawled up toward Chkalov from behind without him noticing and heard him singing his favorite, "Unharness the Horses, Lads." This meant that he was thinking about the same thing that I was, and I quietly returned to the navigator's seat.

I reflected on the achievements of the flight. We had gone 6,200 kilometers. But how many kilometers had been used by the voracious Arctic winds? How much extra fuel had been wasted in steep climbs into the clouds and going around cyclones? We had flown approximately 1,500 extra kilometers, about 25 percent of the entire trip. But who would blame us if they realized that we were the trailblazers in this difficult journey, that we were the first to make this journey and that it was made quite successfully. Based on our experience, it would be possible for aircraft to fly this route with greater speed and with a more practical use of fuel.

1637. A fine anticyclone. There were hardly any clouds. Plenty of fuel in the tanks. How could we now alter our initial desire—to reach the territory of the USA? Of course, we had to fly to the United States.

We were still resting while flying at an altitude of three thousand meters. There was a light mist and it was warm.

At 1800 hours, Bear Lake became visible.

I noted on the map the precision with which we had maintained our assigned route. I compiled a report of our achievements to be sent through Canadian radio stations to the Soviet Union. I began to work the transmitter and verified a weak output from the antenna. Everything else on the radio worked quite well, so I decided to send a prepared text:

> To everyone from RT No. 35. To Stalin, Voroshilov, Rukhimovich, M. Kaganovich, and flight headquarters.
>
> I can understand how concerned you are. But please realize this—although the flight is going well, it hasn't been simple. There have been many difficult hours of flight. I am flying on VFR since the coast of Canada is clear and calm. I give you the best of wishes from our crew. We thank you for everything and ask you not to be concerned. The difficult part has been overcome and we are glad that basically, we have already carried out the assignment of our government and people. Regards. Baidukov.

■

The weather continued to make us happy. Below us enormous Bear Lake was still visible covered by thick ice. As usual, the land was lifeless, having a naked, brown color. Without any woods or shrubs, it seemed like a scorched desert; however, this was not completely true if you considered the ice on the lakes. It would soon be three hours Belyakov had been sleeping. I made it look like I was busy with navigational work. The weather was excellent, you couldn't ask for better visibility, and so it was very simple to navigate and keep on course.

It would soon be time for me to relieve Chkalov, so I should get some rest now. I didn't want to wake up Belyakov—he had used a lot of energy in the flight from the Kola Peninsula to the islands of the Canadian Arctic. I would let him sleep some more on his newly selected place—on the floor of the fuselage. Beneath his head was a pile of books, among them, *The Hospitable Arctic* by Stefansson. We were planning to visit him. The legs of the navigator were somehow stretched out beneath the seat of the secondary controls of the aircraft.

I worked my way up to Chkalov. The numerous instruments of the pilot's console showed that the heart of the ANT-25, the engine, still had a normal pulse.

The engine revolutions were decreased to 1480; this seemed quite unnatural, almost crazy: there was hardly any sound and certainly not that fervent ring that had been continuous during the course of the preceding forty-two hours of flight. It was possible to talk very easily at a distance of two to three meters in the cockpit. Taking advantage of this new comfort and good weather, Valery and I started talking, almost nonstop.

"It seems that we're on a training flight testing how the engine and the instruments are functioning," said Chkalov, smiling.

"Of course, this is a training flight. If we are planning to fly across the South Pole, then we have to consider this as a training flight."

"For the South, we need another aircraft! You understand? With a pressurized cockpit! We have to order one."

"But, this will take two or three years," I replied.

"In the meantime, we will fly around the world in this old craft."

"With landings?" I asked.

"Perhaps we'll be able to refuel in the air. I think that Tupolev will be able to invent something like that."

"You sure can dream," I said to Chkalov and changed the conversation to the business matters of the flight: "I don't understand what's the matter with the radio. There is no output from the antenna. No one is sending us a word about the weather."

"Well, what's the matter, radio operator?" Valery asked me slyly.

"I don't know the answer yet."

"That's not good. We can't arrive in the United States with a nonfunctioning radio," he concluded.

I left for the navigator's chair. With good weather and not much to do, I started to get sleepy. I put my head down on the little table and went to sleep. But I wasn't able to do that very long. Rocking the aircraft, Chkalov had me quickly back on my feet. It was exactly 1900 hours. I woke up Belyakov and handed him the flight log. I relieved the commander in the pilot's seat.

At 2000 hours, the lush, winding Mackenzie River, carrying its waters into the Arctic Ocean, was visible to the right of our aircraft. The river was freeing itself of ice, and the large overflow spoke of the recent flooding and the beginning of spring in this region. Isolated ridges of low mountains appeared below. These were the spurs of the range located in the region of the Mackenzie River. While gaining altitude, a huge formation of cumulus clouds with the most fantastic forms appeared. The aircraft started to bounce a little. I directed the craft between the cloudy ridges and slowly gained altitude since we were approaching mountain peaks that rose to three thousand meters above sea level.

Chkalov continued to rest in his sleeping bag, and Belyakov was valiantly trying to solve the mystery of the nonfunctioning transmitter.

Now, the weather began to grow worse. Somewhere in the distance to the left, a solid cyclone moved up toward us and blocked our flight path. On the right I could see a shaft of light on the horizon. Because visibility was much better along the horizon, I decided it would be better to steer over to the right and slowly gain altitude and then, when the altitude of the aircraft would be higher than the level of the cloud layer, to return to our normal course.

I didn't want to fly directly into the cloud layer because the temperature at an altitude of 4,400 meters was –15°. Recent experience had shown us that the aircraft could ice up even in lower temperatures than at the present time.

With every minute, the situation became more acute. The cyclone above the mountains, the tops of which now reached more than four thousand meters, would not allow us, in case of icing, to descend to a warmer air layer. We simply could not fly over the high layer of clouds. The anti-icing liquid supply was exhausted. Oxygen was almost gone. Night was approaching. What could we do? Continue further or turn back and land at one of the Canadian fields? Should we battle our way through to the United States? There was still a good supply of fuel, and the engine components were functioning normally. The radio, which had not worked for many hours, had been repaired by the knowledgeable hands of Belyakov. One of us, while crawling between the side of the fuselage and the radio transmitter, had brushed against the antenna wire and caused a break in contact. Now that everything was repaired, there still was no one responding to our prearranged code, which our old friend and correspondent for *Pravda*, Lev Khvat, had brought to America some time ago. Sasha would sometimes catch snatches of conversation in English, which he was unable to understand. The navigator received a communication from an amateur radio operator regarding very bad weather conditions in the Coastal Range area. Belyakov understood this telegram very well because it was transmitted in French.

I was thinking about all this as I continued to gain altitude. At 2100 hours, I brought the aircraft up to 5,500 meters. Above were high, feathery clouds that were illuminated by the sun.

Sasha put on his oxygen mask. Valery felt the altitude, woke up, and crawled to the back seat and also breathed in some oxygen. For a short time, some breaks in the cloud layer were visible below, and I noticed that there was a lower layer at the tops of the mountain ranges.

2250. Altitude six thousand meters. It grew cold. The outside temperature was −20°. Now it had become evident to us that the internal heating system of the aircraft cockpit was ineffective when the engine was working at low revs in order to economize on fuel.

Therefore, it was not at all surprising that water, or, to be more exact, a certain mixture in the reserve tank had frozen. On the other hand, increasing the engine revs for the sake of raising the temperature in the cockpit was also not a solution since there would be insufficient fuel to reach the United States.

After forty-six hours of flying at four to five thousand meters, it was no fun to fly at an altitude of six thousand meters, even for such an experienced test pilot as Chkalov.

I asked the commander to relieve me for a short time. At 2300 hours Valery gathered his remaining strength to complete a change of shifts. Valery had become very pale and blood was trickling from his nose. My head was spinning. I lay down for a long time on the tank behind the pilot. Chkalov was clinging to the oxygen mask. The blood flow from his nose had almost stopped. I barely crawled up to a free oxygen mask and, having refreshed myself, gathered some strength.

In the meantime, the cloud barrier was forcing us to turn right. Chkalov was very disturbed by this and, rocking the aircraft, he invited me to come up to the cockpit. Once again, I relieved the commander. At an altitude of six thousand meters, working the controls is so difficult physically that the pulse goes up to 140 and the heart begins to flutter slightly. Oxygen once again brought me back into a condition where I would be able to function. I checked the engine instrument panel; everything was normal. The water measuring float had lowered somewhat, the reserve mixture had frozen, and the water pump was working idly.

Belyakov announced that there was approximately an hour of oxygen left. I called the commander and the navigator to me. We discussed our plan of action, taking into consideration that it would be very dangerous to fly at an altitude of six thousand meters without oxygen, especially after two days of continuous flight.

The navigator brought the map with an alternate route that had been worked out by us before takeoff. The basic concept was to cross the Rocky Mountains horizontally and reach the Pacific Ocean before nightfall, then to descend and continue to follow the coast during the night, holding a course for Seattle and San Francisco.

"That's the way!" an exhausted and pale Valery said to me slowly.

"We have to force through to the Pacific Ocean, to the Pacific!"

"Belyakov and I will lie down so that you can use the rest of the oxygen. Understood?"

"It's understood, understood. But how will you be able to breathe without oxygen?"

"By lying down, we'll be able to make it. Don't worry about us," Belyakov assured me.

I gave the engine full revs. Our reliable ANT-25 would not be able to fly higher than six thousand meters. I maintained a course toward the Pacific Ocean. Clouds surrounded the aircraft. Instrument flight routine began. The aircraft was strongly buffeted, and it was difficult to hold an assigned course toward the Pacific. At an altitude of 6,100 meters, we came out of the clouds. At 2250, Chkalov relieved me and, scraping the tops of the cumulus clouds, we continued the flight across the Rocky Mountains. At 2355, I again took the controls over from the commander and soon flew into a gloomy, dark wall of clouds. After forty-five minutes of instrument flight, the oxygen was exhausted. Without it, it was very difficult to pilot an aircraft at this altitude, although I was a trained pilot. My dear friends huddled against each other by the radio receiver, which the navigator left on. He was stubbornly awaiting news from Canadian and American weather stations.

0048 Greenwich mean time, June 20. This means morning? No, by local time, it would soon be evening, then night.

We had been heading toward the Pacific Ocean for over three and a half hours, and by our calculations, we should have crossed the mountain range. I began to descend. At an altitude of four thousand meters, I could see water through the break in the lower cloud layer.

After two days of stress, pressure, and oxygen starvation, we finally came out into a region where icing would not be such a terrifying situation—it would be possible to descend toward the waters of the warm ocean, and here, the temperatures would be above freezing. It was important not to fly into a storm cloud layer.

Chkalov and Belyakov became more lively. The navigator gave me a new heading—108°, which would slowly bring us toward the shore. I descended to 3,500 meters so that the crew members of the long-winged craft would be able to breathe clear mountain air.

Belyakov looked tired, but still maintained his responsibilities as navigator. Another course correction was given by him. He said that Chkalov should rest because he had started to bleed through the nose again when he had crawled into the wing in order to turn the valves on the gas tanks. I looked at our chapaevite. He also had a look on his face that was not his usual expression.

"You both lie down while there is still an opportunity to fly at this comfortable altitude," I advised Belyakov.

Chkalov agreed and laid down on the cot, but Belyakov continued to fuss near me, looking for breaks in the lower cloud layers and fog that was hiding the shore. At 0120, we saw some islands on the left. They looked forbidding with cliffs completely covered in snow.

We could see that the water was calm since there were no white-caps visible from the foaming waves. The sun had been hiding behind the clouds for many hours; therefore it was impossible to determine exactly the location of the aircraft. Once again everything below was covered in clouds and fog. At 0225, Belyakov became sleepy. He lay down on the floor of the cabin.

The navigator woke up in an hour. Seeing the dim sun which was almost on the horizon, he measured its height with the sextant. A curious-looking moon somewhat in front and a bit to the right came out and, as if laughing at us, would hide in the upper layers of the clouds and then appear again. Belyakov took a measurement of the moon with his sextant.

This was perfect—astronomical calculations could give the exact fix of our location. Indeed, in twenty minutes Sasha officially announced that we were approaching the northern tip of the Queen Charlotte Islands.

At 0400 Chkalov woke up. This short rest was sufficient to enable him to again take the controls.

I gave up the controls to the pilot with pleasure and directed the commander's attention to the fact that the red line that showed the level of liquid in the water cooling system of the engine was lower than optimum, and that the mixture, or what remained of it, had frozen in the reserve tank. For some reason, the thermometer had failed and now it was very important not to overheat the engine and turn the water into steam.

There was no more oxygen left. The remaining oil had become quite thick. There was enough fuel left for ten to fifteen hours, depending on how the flight was to be maintained: altitude, speed, engine revolutions, propeller pitch, all these factors would determine the amount of fuel left in our tanks.

But all of the significant and insignificant items that I recounted to my commander did not affect his mischievous and even quick-tempered mood because he clearly understood that our calculations were being proven to be correct in the final analysis.

After wishing Chkalov and Belyakov good flight weather, I crawled into the fur sleeping bag and fell asleep instantly.

■

Just like a heart, after it misses a beat, makes a person somewhat concerned, so a most insignificant shudder of the engine would come to the immediate attention of the pilot and he, quickly checking all of the instruments, would attempt to determine the reason for this unexpected behavior.

Chkalov was calm: the compass heading was a 128°, air speed was 135 kilometers per hour, altitude 3,250 meters, outside temperature −8°. The engine had not strained itself for quite some time and was not even buzzing. In its fifty-second hour of continuous operation, it was purring like a contented cat that was being petted by a friendly hand.

Valery filled his pipe, lit up, and looked down below between the rare shafts of light in the clouds and noticed the stormy ocean waves beating against the far shore.

The commander and the navigator were concerned about the same thing—a complete uncertainty about weather conditions for the second day. This was very strange since the transmitter and the receiver has been repaired some time ago. Belyakov nevertheless sent out messages requesting information regularly. He did not receive a response from Canada or from the U.S., and we were so distant from our own stations that there was no point in waiting for their messages.

In the meantime, the lower level of the cloud layer was slowly lifting and the aircraft slowly flew into the jaws of the many-layered strato-cumulus clouds in the evening twilight. There were few breaks in the clouds down below and there was nothing visible through them because the ocean was no longer being illuminated by the sun.

The narrow jaws of the cloud layer squeezed more tightly against us and overcame the numerous resistance efforts by the ANT-25. The aircraft was shaking from wing to wing, then it would pitch upward and then plunge down.

The commander turned on the lights in the cockpit and the craft's navigational lights.

"Get up, get up!" I could feel the heavy hand of Chkalov through a light sleep. I tumbled out of bed with my head still groggy.

It was so bright in the aircraft that for some time I couldn't figure out where I was—we had been flying at night for hours. My watch said it was 0620 but it was dark around us.

After fifty-four hours of flight, we no longer had to contend with cramped quarters, which made changing shifts very difficult. Now the person who was to relieve the one that was fatigued sat behind him and, very slowly, related what he had dreamed. The person waiting to be relieved filled his friend in on everything that had happened during the last few hours of flight.

"Things are really poor with communications. Can't get in contact with anybody," Valery said to me very calmly and matter-of-factly.

In response, I uttered some kind of nonsense and related my dreams.

"I thought that after crossing the North Pole, you would have become more intelligent. Well, what are you talking about? Just think, wise guy, there hasn't been any communication for more than a day, and you are blabbering. Here, sit down! As you can see, the clouds have descended completely around us!" The commander shouted angrily as he gave me the pilot's seat.

Sitting behind the controls, I sensed how much lighter the aircraft had become and how responsive it was as it quickly reacted to the movement of the controls.

The sun had disappeared completely No matter where you looked, it was dark. The outside temperature was –7°. I turned on a light that lit up the water meter. I switched in the gyroscopes.

What a mess! Instrument flight again, at night and above the ocean. At 0630, the aircraft crawled unnoticeably into the clouds and began its IFR flight. I slowly gained altitude.

Occasionally, I would stick my bare hand outside the side windshield of the cockpit and feel the biting blows of the icy sleet. One couldn't expect things to be better.

After checking the fuel supply, I turned on the lights in the pilot's cockpit. The phosphorus dials of dozens of instruments shone with fantastic beauty. They seemed to be animated, alive. Each of them noted quickly and accurately all that was happening inside and outside the aircraft. A tense hour went by. The icy sleet flew invisibly into the open windshield of the cockpit and cooled my face and hands in a pleasant manner.

The temperature at an altitude of 4,500 meters was –20° but I was hot from the intensity of instrument flight. I unbuttoned my coat.

The commander asked me in an agitated tone: "What's the matter with you?"

"I am sweating a lot."

"It's going to freeze you!" Valery shouted in my ear. "You are going to catch a cold, you Siberian, you!"

My throat had become very dry and I very much wanted a drink.

Valery could not find any water so he suggested ice.

"Well, then, let's suck on some fruit drops."

The commander brought a second portion of ice and we enjoyed it like children.

Soon the ANT-25 entered a calm layer of the aerial ocean and flew in a stable manner not demanding great physical strength in order to control it. We were packed in a double container. One was the endless clouds with the icy sleet, the other was the night over the Pacific Ocean. Together, they created complete isolation from the world. The radio, as usual, was not informing us about the weather. It was as if mankind had died, that civilization had disappeared and we, stubbornly believing in a miracle, hoped despite all difficulties to overcome them and reach our destination.

"Do you sense how boring it is?" I asked the commander.

"Like in a prison cell."

"Go lie down," I suggested to Chkalov, noticing the dim light of the moon on the right.

At this time, the navigator came up to us and said, "Egor Fiii-povich, I have picked up the Bellingham radio beacon. Hold your bearing on it."

"And where will we come out?"

"It will lead us to San Francisco."

"This is very good," the commander concluded.

Soon the ANT-25 at an altitude of 4,500 meters clambered out of the clouds, which in the lunar light would change every minute, first into mysterious dull-colored mountains, then into sleepy cities with gothic structures, then suddenly into endless flocks of snow white sheep that had been whipped into tight sheaves under the blows of the stormy wind.

0822. The outside temperature was –20° and the temperature inside the cockpit was –9°.

Belyakov made a calculation of the amount of fuel used. If the indication of the fuel gauge could be believed, then there were 718 liters of fuel left, which guaranteed six to eight hours more flight on the condition that the pattern provided by the schedule would be strictly observed.

About 1000 hours the navigator woke up. He radioed Seattle to send a transmission so that bearings could be made from the aircraft. Soon, he passed me a note: "Watch the radio compass, and fly according to it." I understood that the Seattle radio beacon was functioning and that the zone control almost completely coincided with the compass course. It was hard to think of a better possibility: we were controlling our journey by two means—the radio and the magnetic compass.

The moon was setting toward the horizon and it became deep red. After half an hour, it had become completely scarlet. Then quickly it hid. It became darker and, as a result, a myriad of stars glittered above our heads. It was impossible to distinguish the sky from our Moscow sky and I soon located Polaris. The east was becoming more rosy and it sharply outlined the border of cloud layer. It seemed that there was an enormous tooth-shaped mountain range.

Belyakov made contact with Anchorage but could not understand the message that he had received. Apparently, they were transmitting in English, which we did not understand at all. They were supposed to communicate with us using a numerical code. Apparently, there was some sort of confusion. Offended by this, Belyakov once again lay down to sleep after having checked the accuracy of the course. Chkalov was still asleep. My shift was stretching out. I would not have guessed that my shift, which had begun at 0630, would continue until landing time. I was happier since it was now morning. With each minute, the strip on the left became brighter and broader. I could turn off all the lights inside. I left only one lower light of the fuel gauge on.

At 1100 hours, the sun jumped from behind the clouds and, as if it had overslept, it rushed to make up for lost time and watch what we had done during its five hours of absence.

Along with the sun I saw a two-layered cloud system below us. The upper one was thicker while the lower one consisted of fog that was beginning to break off. At 1200, the lights of the coastal cities glittered below. I descended to three thousand meters and could make out some kind of bay and mountains. My friends continuously looked through the portholes on the left side and joyfully verified that the shoreline of the United States was in sight. Our calculations proved to be quite precise.

■

The ANT-25 was flying to the south through a cloud layer and was being tossed around like a small pup. Belyakov calculated the ground speed. Headwinds along the shoreline were holding us back. This especially affected fuel consumption. According to the calculations of the navigator, there was enough fuel left for a maximum of five hours of flight.

I exchanged my cap for earphones and guided the craft according to the bearings from the Seattle radio beacon. Belyakov was listening to the same signals and monitored the precision of my actions. We were upset by the English communication of the radio beacon. We could not understand anything and it was quite possible that it was providing weather information along our route.

What was below? Fog? Low cloud layers? Or high cloud layers? Where would it be better? Seattle, Portland, Eugene, or San Francisco?

"We have been flying for sixty hours exactly," Chkalov shouted, lifting my right earphone.

At this time, the indicator of the radio compass turned 180°, although I held the same course to the south using the magnetic compass.

The commander turned to the navigator. Soon, I received a note.

"Monitor the radio beacon of Portland airport." Valery returned to me with a map. I could hear the call signs of Portland very well and corrected the course according to its directions.

At 1430, I brought the aircraft into a calm cloud layer, which covered our red-winged giant with rain. The outside temperature was plus 7°. I had been sitting behind the controls for eight hours. The cloud layer continued to cover us and separate us from the world.

Valery Pavlovich attempted to pump some water because the "little indicator" was so low that it had started to concern us. Regardless of the warmth that existed in the aircraft cockpit, the water pump was working idly. Chkalov did all he could to add to the liquid. He filled the water system up to a normal level and the "little line" was now out looking impishly from underneath the bell glass.

But the commander became gloomier. Belyakov informed us with a note that, according to his calculations, the fuel was being exhausted. Chkalov climbed into the wing once more and was convinced that all the main tanks were empty. This meant we should be thinking of landing.

Chkalov and Belyakov were sitting behind my seat and they looked over the map of the section between Portland and San Francisco. I also checked the map, from time to time turning my eyes away from the instruments by which I was steering the aircraft through the clouds.

The Portland beacon was attracting me. It had a beam zone along the relatively wide Columbia River, although it was quite mountainous around the banks. I relied upon the accuracy of the American radio beacons and had taught myself to hold to the center of the zone.

"While we still have some fuel," I shouted, "let's try to break through to Portland and look at the weather in order to have a hopeful alternative for making a landing."

"But wouldn't it be better in Eugene, which is between Portland and San Francisco?" Chkalov asked.

Belyakov shook his head. "Eugene is in a mountainous area. If we are going to try, we are going to have to do it now. Let's go to Portland."

"Let's go, let's try." Chkalov agreed sadly and added, "Does it have to be this way? Fly the entire route and then in the end not know where to land because there is no code communication by radio?"

I lowered the aircraft in a spiral. At an altitude of around one hundred meters, I crossed into the beacon's zone and soon the waters of the Columbia River could be seen below us. Its mountainous shores in some places were covered by clumps of clouds or fog. This entire picture was visible through a thick curtain of rain.

I looked back. Chkalov was smiling.

"Now even the devil cannot scare us!" Valery shouted to me. "Come on, let's climb and head south."

Once again, our ANT-25 cut through the rainy clouds moving toward San Francisco.

We were in our sixty-second hour in the air.

Chkalov was upset by the situation and lifted my right earphone and said: "Imagine what is happening in our country when we haven't been able to make contact with anyone for more than a day."

"There will be a surprise."

"It's bad to fly alone. The only thing that keeps you going is the knowledge that the engine is working, the moving arrows of the instruments, the shaking wings of the plane, the roar of the engine and the propellers—this is our Motherland; this is the work of our comrades and this is how they show their concern for us."

We were upset that we were unable to make two-way communication and we imagined what kind of concern this was causing our nation and our ambassador in the United States. In fact this is how our flight was reported to the government commission in Moscow according to the reports from the United States, where Ambassador Troyanovsky was waiting for the ANT-25 in San Francisco, Consul Umansky remained in Washington, Head of AMTORG[55] Rozov and Consul Borovoy were in New York, and engineer Vartanian was in Seattle. This is what their telegrams reported:

Seattle, June 19, 8:28. Beginning with 1500 hours GMT on the 18th of June until 1300 hours 45 minutes on the 19th of June, the aircraft sent

10 telegrams with information about the flight from Rudolph Island to the 84th parallel and 110th meridian and further.

At 8:16 GMT, the aircraft sent a message to radio NP27 regarding its conditions and the fact that it was attempting to make contact with the United States and suggested that it would be at Patrick Island at 1000 hours 40 minutes. This radiogram was received by stations in the U.S. and Canada.

No further communication was received from the aircraft at this time. The information from independent Canadian radios had still not been received.

All stations received an order to monitor the aircraft continuously on three frequencies. We have suggested that they report the weather and request communication. Vartanian.

Washington, 19th of June, twelve hours, thirty-seven minutes. At seventeen hours ten minutes GMT, San Francisco radio monitored the aircraft which was calling Seattle to make contact. Umansky.

New York, 19th of June, sixteen hours, fifty-eight minutes. Vartanian has reported that at twelve hours, twenty-five minutes Seattle time, Fort Smith radio received a signal from Chkalov's aircraft reporting that its position was 64° north and 124° W longitude. Rozov.

San Francisco, 19th of June, 2 hours, 12 minutes. At 12 hours 25 minutes, Pacific Time, the Royal Communications Corps in Canada intercepted our aircraft's radiogram from Fort Smith which stated— "Everything is going well. The aircraft position is 64 degrees north latitude, 124 degrees west longitude. We are located 100 miles south of Fort Norman." Troyanovsky.

Seattle, 19th of June, 8 hours, 41 minutes. A report was received here that at 3 hours, 50 minutes Greenwich time, on the 20th of June, the aircraft had crossed the Rocky Mountains and was flying along the coast line. Vartanian.

New York, 20th of June, 0 hours, 14 minutes. Between two and four hours Greenwich time, a number of stations received a radio signal from the aircraft, which broadcast that it had crossed the Rocky Mountains and was flying along the coast line. The aircraft was located in the Ketchikan area, approximately 500 kilometers north of Seattle. Rozov.

Washington, 20th of June, one hour, forty-four minutes. The U.S. Signal Corps of the Department of War announced at 3 o'clock 55 minutes GT on the 20th of June, a radio station for the Aeronautics Administration of the Department of Commerce in Seattle and Ketchikan received the following message: "I am changing course and continuing the flight. I read you fine. We are flying along the Canadian coastline."

San Francisco, 20th of June, one hour, fifty-six minutes. San Francisco has made direct radio contact with the aircraft. Troyanovsky.

Khabarovsk, 20th of June. We are transmitting the weather reports received from Seattle at 1700 hours, 20 minutes. The aircraft reported that it is guided by radio compass toward the Portland beacon. At the same time, the Coast Guard has stated that it observed an aircraft flying to the east. Vartanian.

This is how those people on the ground, who attempted to make our flight easier and to decrease the risks for the ANT-25's crew, followed the passage of our flight.

Our biggest problem in communications was our inability to receive weather reports on a regular basis.

June 20, 1500 hours. Below us, without a doubt, was U.S. territory. The red-winged Soviet craft was being washed after its long, dangerous flight as it flew through the rainy cloud layer.

We were approaching the city of Eugene. Soon it would be San Francisco. But, then an unexpected event occurred: fuel pressure began to drop quite sharply Now what? Further south? Land in Eugene? Return to Portland? Or struggle through to San Francisco?

Again, the three of us, huddling against each other, very quickly discussed a plan of action. The three of us agreed, "Let's return to Portland where we observed meteorological conditions. It's not one of the best, but we have no information on San Francisco. It could possibly be worse there."

"Turn back to Portland, Egor! And you Sasha, tune in on its beacon. We'll slowly descend," Chkalov concluded.

■

Turning toward the north at 1551, I soon heard the signal "PD" and after fifteen more minutes of flying I began descending to its radio beam zone.

We went through one layer of clouds and then another. We were flying above the scattered clumps of fog which were covering the mountains and forests, of which there were so many in this area. A little lower and directly below was a river. The altitude could not have been more than a hundred meters because a bridge above the Columbia River appeared before us in the foggy, rainy gloom and it looked like an extremely high skyscraper.

Turning to the right of the bridge, toward Portland, at an altitude of fifty meters, we began to approach the airport landing strip. I made a circle around it and saw that no flights were being made in this area. Many aircraft were parked on the field, which was covered by water puddles.

But where did the thousands of people waving their hands and hats come from? Did they really know something about us?

"Let's not land here! They will take the aircraft apart for souvenirs. Let's go to the other shore," Chkalov directed.

"Where?"

"In Vancouver, there is a military airport! There has to be!"

Chkalov pointed with his finger at the map that he was holding in front of my face.

I carefully turned around above Portland, being cautious with the high city buildings, and flew toward a bridge, which was both a railroad and an automobile bridge. Passing it, I noticed that along the right, by the river, was a green strip and tall hangars, indicating that it was the property of the U.S. Army Air Corps. There were no markers on the airfield at all. The strip was narrow and its length was relatively short for our ANT-25. (We had removed the brakes before takeoff.)

Chkalov and I looked around carefully and noticed that the field was wet from rain and, although the landing strip was not that large, it would slow down the landing roll considerably.

"Let's land, no more discussions!" Chkalov shouted.

I banked the aircraft above the treetops and once again flew along the landing strip. On the left was the Columbia River with train tracks on both sides. On the fourth side, the approach was more open.

I lined up on the open side and throttled back. Being free of five tons of fuel, the aircraft was light as a feather and it sailed above the ground like a regular glider. Then it began to settle down. The commander was sitting behind me and was also watching very carefully But this was not a landing on Udd Island! Although I understand Valery as a pilot. . . . "Throttle forward!" Chkalov shouted and I could indeed see that it was necessary to pull up a little bit or else we would pancake into a plowed section of the field.

I revved up the engine slightly and again throttled back. The aircraft, as though not wanting to land, was unwillingly settling itself down and was slowly losing altitude. I did not like the way the

ANT-25 was acting because we had previously determined, at a higher altitude, that the landing strip of this military base was very limited. Chkalov was also concerned.

"It doesn't want to set down!" Valery shouted.

In response to this, I switched off the engine in order to increase the braking factor and the aircraft came closer to the green grass. I pulled the yoke toward me and the aircraft smoothly touched down on United States soil.

As the aircraft traveled along the ground, I spotted through the cockpit windshield a guard standing near a hangar, drenched by the rain, becoming quite excited. I realized, however, that the ANT-25 was rolling smoothly along and was quickly slowing down its momentum. Now it was time to turn the engine on again while the propellers were still turning from the airstream around the aircraft. The craft unexpectedly jumped. Valery, in excitement, pushed his body from the right side of the craft toward me and, touching my head, asked, "What did you just bump over?"

"Some sort of cross walk."

The aircraft completed its landing roll. Valery said, "Well, superman, after ten hours of flying, such a landing! I'll never forget it."

"That's partial payment for the landing at Udd Island."

"All right, I'll take it into consideration," Valery answered and looking behind him noticed that Belyakov was not reacting at all to the fact that we had landed on U.S. soil, but continued to gather up his maps, flight logs, books, thermoses, rubber bags, and bits of string.

Chkalov said, "Apparently, nothing surprises this chapaevite."

The aircraft had stopped but I had no idea where to park it on this foreign, military field. I turned around and saw how my tired and jubilant friends were huddled against each other and then Valery disappeared into the tail section of the aircraft.

I opened the upper hatches of the cockpit and felt the warm air soaked in rain that had been following us continuously for many hours. Our commander had already begun to carry out his new diplomatic obligations.

Belyakov and I were now watching with a smile to see how effective Chkalov's incredible ability to make contact with people under any conditions and in various locations would be on this foreign soil. Chkalov stood beside some type of American military person twenty-five meters away from the ANT-25, which had finally

stopped after its long, continuous flight. Chkalov, with animated
gestures, "agreed" to instructions on where to park the aircraft. The
AM-34R engine, which was lazily turning the three-bladed propeller,
rumbled after its remarkable feat and did not give us an opportunity
to hear how Valery Pavlovich was requesting chocks in "English."
After lifting the chock above his head, he carried it toward the
aircraft, placed it underneath the right wheel, and gave me a sign to
start a ground maneuver. When the aircraft was next to some gates,
he crossed his arms, giving me a sign to turn off the engine. I turned
the ignition switch to the off position. Suddenly, it became surprisingly quiet after more than two and a half days of continuous flight.
Belyakov made a last notation on the flight log: "June 20th, 1937.
1620 GMT, landed in Vancouver. We had been airborne for a total of
63 hours and 16 minutes. Seven thousand nine hundred and thirty-
three liters of fuel were used, or five thousand six hundred and
fifty-eight kilograms. Seventy-seven kg. of fuel remained."

Belyakov and I were still in the aircraft. Soldiers and automobiles
rushed toward us from somewhere. Soon, Chkalov was shaking
hands with a tall, stern-looking general and, hitting his palm on the
fuselage of ANT-25, shouted, "Hey, guys! Get a move on! General
Marshall is waiting for us!"

Belyakov looked at me, "I did not anticipate anything like this,"
the navigator said, smiling.

"But I did not quite understand Valery: Is it a general or a marshal
that's meeting us?"

"I don't think there are any marshals in the United States, but
they do have generals," Alexander Vasilevich answered me.

Chkalov continued to drum persistently on the aircraft.

"Hey, come on, faster, you guys! They're waiting for us."

When we had crawled out of the ANT-25, we saw hundreds of cars
and an enormous, colorful crowd, which was being held back by
armed troops.

"Apparently, this is the result of our flying over Portland," the
navigator noted. "Look at the cars crossing the bridge."

Fellow correspondents of local newspapers had already appeared
near the aircraft, and, not paying attention to the rain, they asked us
to stand in a threesome next to the fuselage. We did not have to be
coaxed; this suggestion met perfectly with our wish to take a look at
ourselves after our long flight. Having reached our goals, we were
smiling at each other, although extremely tired and unshaven. The

photograph that showed the smiling navigator, with his wet hair and eyes closed, was especially interesting.

Valery and I, with our leather coats spread over our shoulders, our hats on our heads, were looking at Sasha laughing good-naturedly.

Attempts to conduct detailed interviews and give out autographs were halted by General Marshall, the garrison commander. He ordered that a safety zone be set up with posts and ropes. The soldiers were to guard this restricted area to keep the public away from the aircraft.

However, this did not free us from the persistent representatives of the press.

"What make is the aircraft engine?" they asked.

"At what altitude did you fly?" others queried.

"What was the weather like along the route?" still others wanted to know.

It was necessary to request that a stepladder be set up and open the engine cowling to demonstrate that our engine was not American, English, or German, but our own Soviet design built in a Moscow plant.

A middle-aged man began to translate and assisted the sergeant, George Kozmitsky, who was the first person whom Chkalov had met on the ground.

They translated the inscriptions on the factory label—a dark blue enamel emblem of the Moscow plant.

The correspondents were somewhat embarrassed and frantically photographed the engine and its emblem.

The soldiers started to cover the cockpit of the ANT-25 with a tarp while Chkalov was handing out all the reserve supplies, including the emergency rations, giving them out as souvenirs. When the Americans caught on to this, they began to take out money from their wallets. We were surprised and asked the sergeant and the person who had voluntarily become our translator to explain that we were giving these out free and we would not accept any money.

We must have been taken for very strange types, or at least "unbusinesslike" people.

Of course we had to sign quite a few autographs as we stood under the umbrellas of the curious American public. Soon, reporters from the *San Francisco Chronicle*, the *Los Angeles Times*, and the *Colorado News* came over for interviews.

They questioned us regarding our flight experience, food rations, clothing, "the pole of inaccessibility," and many other items as only enterprising members of the American press are able to do.

The chain of requests for autographs and questions finally came to an end as the gray-haired, well-built garrison commander, General Marshall, reappeared. After giving all the appropriate orders concerning the safety of our ANT-25, he placed us in his own car and took us away from the excited public and reporters, taking us directly to his own home.

8

Chkalov in America

We were driving along the streets of the small city of Vancouver at the beginning of a rainy morning. It was easy to see that many areas were inhabited by military personnel.[56]

We stopped next to a two-story private residence. The wife and daughter of the general, having been previously informed of our arrival, greeted us very warmly. Introducing us to his family, the general called Valery the chief pilot, and he designated me as the copilot and Belyakov as navigator. The hostess had already prepared breakfast. We were invited upstairs to the second floor in order to rest and relax.

From our conversations, General Marshall understood that we wanted to change out of our warm flying suits. He brought us his own civilian suits. We laughed together with the general for a long time when I was trying on "Sir" Marshall's pants and realized that I had to fasten the buttons almost up to my chin. Even Belyakov, who was the tallest of us, had to refuse the general's generous offer because the suits were too large for him.

Soon, Valery was called to the telephone. He rushed to the phone. The general was holding the receiver.

San Francisco was calling. It was Alexander Antonovich Troyanovsky, the plenipotentiary of the USSR in the U.S., as Soviet ambassadors were called, who was waiting for us. Chkalov stated in his heavy accent, "I am reporting that the government's assignment has been carried out. We were ordered to fly across the pole and to land on the American continent. Stalin said that it was sufficient to land in Canada. But we flew over Canada and landed in the United States."

After breakfast, we took baths and shaved.

However, reporters managed to photograph an unshaven Chkalov next to General Marshall.

When we were getting ready to sleep, a translator came in and asked one of us from the crew to come to the telephone. Moscow was calling.

"See how 'close' we have flown from our homes?" Chkalov said to me. "I authorize you to be our spokesman. Go ahead!"

History's first telephone conversation between Moscow and Portland took place.

Moscow: "Who is speaking?"

Portland: "Baidukov, here."

Moscow: "Members of the Government Commission of the People's Commissary of Communications, P. A. Halepsky and Deputy People's Commissar of Defense Industry M. M. Kaganovich, here. We congratulate you on your successful flight. How do you feel?"

I answered, "Everyone is fine, the landing was successful." I gave our regards to the Party, the government, Stalin, the members of the Politburo, and our country on behalf of the entire crew.

Moscow: "We embrace all of you and send you our warmest regards!"

Soon, we fell into a deep sleep.

At this time, a telegram was sent from Washington to Moscow: "June 20, at 1630 GMT or 1930 Moscow time, Chkalov has made a landing at a military field near Portland (in the State of Oregon). Umansky."

Flight headquarters prepared a text, which was signed by the members of the Government Commission in charge of organizing a nonstop flight, and passed it along to the press for publication. Here are several excerpts from it:

A statement of the government commission for organizing a nonstop flight from Moscow over the North Pole to North America. . . . The first nonstop flight in history from Moscow over the North Pole to North America has been achieved. A dream has been realized. The heroic crew of the ANT-25 aircraft, consisting of Heroes of the Soviet Union Chkalov, Baidukov, and Belyakov, after their takeoff on June 18, at 04 hours 05 minutes, Moscow time, from the Schelkovo airfield near Moscow, flew the following route: Moscow, Onega, White Sea, Kola Peninsula, Barents Sea, Franz-Josef Land, North Pole, Arctic

Ocean ("the pole of inaccessibility"), Patrick Island, Cape Pierce Point (the northern coast of Canada), crossing Canada (Fort Simpson, the provinces of Alberta and British Columbia). The crew decided to cross the Rocky Mountains at this point and arrived on the coastline of the Pacific Ocean; they flew over Tillamook Bay (State of Oregon), entered U.S. territory on June 20, and at 19 hours 30 minutes Moscow time landed at a military field near Portland (State of Oregon).

The aircraft was airborne 63 hours and 25 minutes. During this time, they covered more than 10,000 kilometers of distance and 12,000 kilometers in the air. The aircraft passed over oceans and ice for 5,900 kilometers. The flight altitude for a major portion of the journey was 4,000 meters and higher, due to cloud layers and poor weather conditions.

The amazing crew displayed exceptional mastery and courage in carrying out a truly wonderful flight and one of the greatest flights in history. They overcame the most severe and difficult part of the world in opening a new era in the taming of nature by man.

The Government Commission for Organizing the Nonstop Flight.

Apparently, due to a loss of regular radio communication between the aircraft and the radio stations in Canada and the U.S., several details in the statement of the flight of Chkalov's crew turned out to be incorrect.

However, we heard about this official statement at a much later time. Meanwhile, the three of us, headed by Chkalov, slept peacefully in the private residence of General Marshall.

During this time, the inhabitants of Vancouver, photographers, reporters, and military personnel created such a racket in front of General Marshall's house that he became very annoyed after noting film cameras with floodlights and radio announcers with microphones who had set themselves up along the walls.

Western Union messengers came running up to the house one after another with congratulatory telegrams for Chkalov. The blond and hospitable Miss Marshall, who was just as tall as her father, accepted the mail and gave interviews to numerous journalists, whom she seated at a large circular table as she served cocktails.[57] Soviet Ambassador Troyanovsky appeared out of nowhere at the general's home, having flown from San Francisco to Portland by commercial airline despite the bad weather. The general once again became excited, but the very calm and friendly tone of the Soviet ambassador relieved the tension immediately. Troyanovsky organized future activity for the crew of the ANT-25 in the vicinity of their landing.

The general announced that he had gone through his entire wardrobe but was unable to find anything to fit the Soviet pilots and consequently he had called for tailors from Portland stores with custom-made suits. The ambassador approved this and inquired "Are the pilots still sleeping?" Marshall expressed his concern. On the one hand, his guests had not slept for more than three hours, on the other hand, there were the endless phone calls from cities in the United States, Canada, and other countries.

"You have seen, Mr. Ambassador, what's going on downstairs. America wants to see Chkalov and his companions on movie screens and to hear their voices."

The general brought the ambassador over to the window and Troyanovsky observed the large crowd. The bright umbrellas fluttered against the background of the fresh greenery of firs and cedars.

"Yes, I feel sorry for the fellows," the ambassador sighed, "but we must wake them up."

Troyanovsky later related how difficult it was to wake up our crew.

They first woke up the chief pilot. He immediately recognized the ambassador.

"Comrade Troyanovsky! Thank God, we meet at last."

After seeing Chkalov coming out of the bathroom in the general's coat, the bottom of which had been tucked into the belt, our amazing rescuer Troyanovsky understood the entire comic situation. He went out together with the General and returned in about fifteen minutes accompanied by some people with boxes and suitcases. These were representatives of various firms in Portland who had brought suits and tailors to help fit the clothing according to our measurements.

"Well, my dear guests," Troyanovsky said smiling, "now we are going to get dressed up."

Less than two hours had gone by when we were completely reoutfitted in the latest American style.

Troyanovsky quickly noticed that Chkalov chose the color and cut of his suit very skillfully and expertly made his tie.

"Valery Pavlovich, you dressed yourself very tastefully," approved Troyanovsky.

"He's one of Moscow's fashion plates," I noted.

"And you should change your tie," Chkalov advised me seriously.

As we were dressing ourselves, General Marshall asked Chkalov through Troyanovsky to lend the owners of the clothing stores our flight suits, which they wanted to display in their store windows for display and public relations. Troyanovsky, looking at us with his intelligent chestnut-colored eyes, relayed the request of the American businessmen to us and advised us to respect it.

Thus, our leather coats and pants turned up in the display of fashionable clothing stores in Portland.

Dressed American-style, chief pilot Chkalov was very elegant and blended in very well with the surroundings. The "diplomatic work" of the crew of the ANT-25 had begun.

At the same time Troyanovsky took out of his briefcase some sort of material that was typewritten.

"Here, my dear friends, is the first contribution of the special correspondent for the newspaper *Pravda*, R. Johnson, regarding your flight to the United States."

New York, June 20 (Special Correspondent for *Pravda*). Chkalov, plane landed at Vancouver field. This military airport is located near Portland. . . .

. . . Because of strong headwinds, the aircraft was forced to use more fuel than had been planned. There was a threat of a forced landing in an unknown and uninhabited area. Consequently, Chkalov chose to land in Portland.

Here in the United States, a great significance is given to the fact that an aerial route had been established between the USSR and the USA over the North Pole. This is the first and primary significance of this heroic flight.

Secondly, the significance of the flight, in the opinion of numerous sources in the United States, is based on the fact that for the first time, a completely unexplored section of the Western Hemisphere has been traversed by aircraft and, in addition, for the very first time, the magnetic pole has been traversed by an aircraft.

Thirdly, they noted that the flight was conducted under extremely difficult conditions. . . . The most dangerous part was located between 84° and 50° north latitude. Flight through this section was made with a complete absence of two-way communication. The crew oriented themselves primarily with their celestial navigation devices.

Fourthly, since the flight of Lindbergh years ago, no other flight has created such literally nationwide amazement and excitement, in the USA. All American radio stations are providing very detailed accounts of the flight. Today, people are discussing this event almost everywhere. The newspapers are filled with reports of the flight. Chkalov's name is mentioned by millions of Americans. An enthusiastic reception awaits the Soviet fliers.

New York (Special Correspondent for *Pravda*). Your correspondent has just spoken with Georgiy Baidukov, who reported that he, Chkalov, and Belyakov are in a very cheerful and lively mood despite their fatigue. Baidukov has requested to send through *Pravda* the warm greetings of the entire crew to the workers of the Soviet Union.

All three of them have taken a bath and are now resting.

The landing of the aircraft was skillfully accomplished and aroused general amazement. Thousands of people have gathered at the airport. Despite heavy rain, they are coming here to view the aircraft, and if possible, the fliers themselves.

The design of the craft, its dimensions and construction have aroused great interest among American fliers and the general public.

Troyanovsky, after finishing reading the reports, asked: "Well, Valery Pavlovich?"

"If you skip the details, then generally, Johnson is apparently close to a proper evaluation."

"What don't you agree with in Johnson's observations?" the ambassador asked.

"Alexander Antonovich! You're a Russian and understand that an immediate elevation of your heroism makes you into a superman. This is very unnerving," Chkalov answered seriously.

"Well, you didn't have to fly to the United States, especially over the pole!" Troyanovsky said, smiling.

The conversation was interrupted by the appearance of the host. General Marshall invited the Soviet ambassador and the crew of the ANT-25 to the dining room, where a table had been set. Chkalov was courteous and appreciative. He smiled warmly at the hostess and her daughter. Through Troyanovsky, he gave them several compliments, thanked the Marshall family for their hospitality, and asked to be excused for the inconvenience that they had caused with their aerial intrusion.

The two ladies were pleased, but the general said frankly: "What inconvenience? You can't imagine how lucky I am: I, an old warrior, have been sitting for a long time in this hole. In the last war, I commanded a division in Europe! With your help, I have attained popularity and in America this is sometimes worth more than money."

Chkalov was photographed with the general and in conversations with the journalists always stressed the participation of the general and his family in the heartfelt reception of the "Russian fliers," as Americans now called us.

During dinner, a stack of telegrams was brought to us. General Marshall suddenly smiled and started to say something to Troyanovsky in an animated tone.

"Well, my friends," the ambassador said, "you've gone and done something unbelievable."

"Have we broken some rule?" Chkalov asked anxiously.

"You have broken an old tradition and made the President himself send you his greetings on Sunday, when the entire government life of the country usually comes to a standstill."

Troyanovsky looked through the telegrams given to him.

"Not only the President of the United States, Roosevelt, greets you and makes note of the historical significance of the flight and courage of the fliers. Even Secretary of State Hull had to break his own unwavering principles and traditions and follow the example of the President."

And, holding up the telegrams, Troyanovsky added: "He congratulates you and sends greetings!"

Ten minutes had not gone by when an excited messenger from Western Union came into the dining room and handed a packet to the ambassador. Troyanovsky became animated when he looked at the text of the telegram, which had been sent from Moscow. He stood up and read a telegram from the Politburo of the Central Committee of the Party:

> The United States of America, the State of Washington, the City of Portland. To the crew of the ANT-25.
>
> Chkalov, Baidukov, Belyakov.
>
> We heartily congratulate you on your amazing accomplishment. The successful completion of a heroic, nonstop flight from Moscow over the North Pole to the United States of America arouses the love and admiration of the workers of the entire country.
>
> We are proud of the bold Soviet fliers who know no bounds in achieving the goal assigned to them.
>
> We embrace you and shake your hands.

We did not feel like eating lunch, and, speaking of Chkalov, he was no longer concerned with the United States for the moment since this telegram from the Politburo carried all his thoughts back to the motherland that had entrusted this flight to him.

Soon, they brought a telegram from Kosarev, Secretary of the Central Committee of the All-Union Lenin Communist Youth League, and dozens of other telegrams from many parts of the United States.

■

Chkalov went to the window. It was continuing to drizzle. He saw the huge crowd covered by a wavering mosaic of umbrellas.

Troyanovsky and General Marshall invited Chkalov's crew to meet those who had gathered outside.

As soon as the chief pilot appeared on the balcony, the huge crowd came alive: hats flew into the air; applause broke out; one could hear the powerful outbursts: "Hurray, Russian fliers! Hurray!"

America's largest broadcaster, the National Broadcasting Corporation, had prepared everything for a program that, as the representative of the radio company mentioned to Troyanovsky, would have an audience of more than twelve million Americans.

The announcer first warmly greeted the Soviet fliers, followed by questions to the commander of the crew. His answers were immediately translated into English by our ambassador.

Question: "What was the object of your flight?"

Chkalov: "We set ourselves the goal of proving the feasibility of an aerial link between the USSR and the USA over the North Pole, along the shortest route."

Question: "Do you think that it is possible in the future to have regular commercial flights along this same route?"

Chkalov: "Without a doubt. I think that we will successfully accomplish a comparable project if we are provided with aircraft that have a service ceiling of approximately ten kilometers, and sufficient speed."

Question: "What was your average altitude?"

Chkalov: "From four to five, at times higher than five kilometers."

Question: "Could you have flown to Oakland, weather permitting?" (According to reports from Vancouver, visibility did not exceed two kilometers during landing in other locations on the route; farther to the south, the visibility was close to zero; clouds completely obscured the mountainous regions; it was clear only in the San Francisco area.)

Chkalov: "We could have flown further, not only to San Francisco but even to Los Angeles. However, our primary aim was to reach the territory of the United States and to make a successful landing at one of the American airports."

Question: "What were the weather conditions like during the flight?"

Chkalov: "The best conditions were above the Barents Sea in the area of Franz-Josef Land, partially above the Pole itself and farther on in the Patrick Island region."

Question: "What did you eat during the flight?"

Chkalov: "We had a three-day supply—primarily fruits, vegetables, sandwiches—and also an emergency supply in concentrated form to last a month."

Question: "How was radio communication?"

Chkalov: "Radio communication was satisfactory, excluding the area around Patrick Island." (Chkalov, characteristically for a Russian and a Soviet hero, modestly did not refer to the fact that the aircraft, along the flight route from Patrick Island until the landing in Vancouver, was unable to receive weather forecasts for a period of twenty-two hours.)

Question: "A flight of such unprecedented proportions obviously demanded long preparation. How much time did it take?"

Chkalov: "We began to prepare on May 25."

Question: "What are your present plans?"

Chkalov: "We plan to visit the United States, the cities, several plants, and to become familiar with your technological accomplishments."

The radio announcer asked Belyakov and me other questions and then Troyanovsky made a comment. General Marshall came to the microphone and announced: "I am flattered that the honor of taking these courageous gentlemen into my home has fallen to me."

The American crowd did not leave for some time and continuously hailed the Soviet fliers. They expected the chief pilot to say a few farewell words to them. So Valery gave a short, magnificent speech. He spoke of the rivers Volga and Columbia, which were located on separate continents, had different characteristics, and whose shores were surrounded by different mountains and forests, but which flowed on and in the same planet, did not interfere with each other and, in the final analysis, were elements of one and the same world ocean. And so our peoples—the people of the Soviet Union and the people of the United States of America—should live peacefully on the same planet and work together to adorn the ocean of life of mankind. He concluded his speech in this manner: "Accept from our great people the wish for happiness and prosperity to the people of the United States of America, which we have brought on the red wings of the ANT-25 after overcoming all odds and obstacles of nature."

After the radio broadcast, we bid farewell to the crowd that had gathered around the general's home, and came downstairs from the balcony, where we were immediately confronted with bright floodlights—filmmaking had begun. This footage appeared on America's movie screens next day. The filmmakers did not leave Chkalov's crew and Ambassador Troyanovsky in peace until late in the evening. Chkalov invited his host to stand next to us since this was so important for the general.

It was a busy day. Troyanovsky, who acted not only in the capacity of ambassador but also as our translator and adviser, was even more occupied.

Chkalov was patiently signing his autograph on papers, notebooks, and albums and struck the appropriate pose for the still and movie cameras and even praised Coca-Cola. The last visitors left by 10 P.M. and Chkalov, taking off his dress clothes, said:

"Well, Alexander Antonovich, how meticulous your Americans are—they created work for us that was no easier than flying over the pole."

"This is only the beginning," Troyanovsky said with a smile. "From now on all this will increase hyperbolically, since you have really surprised the Americans and they have really taken a liking to you."

"But what's it all for?" Valery was surprised.

"Well, above all, because you reached them despite the assurances of the Hearst press, which proclaimed the inability of the Soviets to bring about such an undertaking. Especially after the death of Wiley Post, who attempted in 1935 to upstage the Levanevsky flight over the pole. Levanevsky himself was forced to return from his mission."

"Well, and for what other reason?" Chkalov continued to ask.

"The average American has realized that up until now he has been deceived in a most blatant way It is no accident that the representatives of the press yesterday were amazed when they noticed that the engine of the ANT-25 was Russian-made. The Americans had been convinced that it was possible to fly in a single-engine craft only if the engine was manufactured in America or England "

During the conversation, a messenger arrived with telegrams for Valery Pavlovich from Olga Erazmovna and their son.

The next day the Soviet fliers had considerably more activity than on the preceding day.

After breakfast with General Marshall, the crew left for the field to carry out a series of formal presentations.

Several American officials negatively reacted to the crew's decision to give away everything that was not a structural part of the plane. Many sadly shook their heads, stating that the Russian fliers had clearly missed the opportunity of making a profit on the souvenirs.

General Marshall brought Chkalov's crew and the Soviet ambassador to his office, where we were presented with official honors. By order of the general, a detachment of soldiers were marched up, at the head of which, American flags fluttered. Not far from us stood some old cannons. A review was given in honor of the Soviet ambassador and the Russian fliers; Troyanovsky accepted the honor. The traditional nineteen-gun salute from the old weapons created such a screen of smoke that we could not see the parade ground, the thick grove, or even the soldiers who were taking part in the parade.

Later, we climbed into a car and, accompanied by an escort of motorcycle police, sped at a furious pace along the streets of an excited Vancouver. This trip to the City Hall building along the narrow streets, filled with people and cars, was achieved with such unsurpassed mastery that it seemed to us that we were going into a circus arena.

"Don't be surprised, friends," Troyanovsky said, "all this is being done in the true American style."

The day had become sunny and hot. Hundreds of autograph hunters and film and photo-reporters had gathered in front of the City Hall. We were greeted with friendly whistles. That is how Americans express their approval and good wishes.

We did not stay long at the mayor's office since we were soon due at the Portland Chamber of Commerce. We sped across the bridge over the Columbia accompanied by the wail of the sirens from police motorcycles. Washington State troopers saluted us at the end of the bridge since the troopers from the state of Oregon were waiting for us at the other end of the bridge. The wail of the sirens from the Portland police was even louder.

"Hell! They sure tear along!" said Chkalov, shaking his head.

The reception at the Portland Chamber of Commerce, where the governor of the state met the guests, was broadcast all over the United States. In his answering statements, the commander of the ANT-25 spoke of how American efficiency, the output of its workers, and the high quality of its technology, were respected in the Soviet Union: "We are learning this from everyone but, above all, from you. But we intend to overtake you in the development of technology. We ask you to forgive us for the fact that we, Soviet fliers, have been the first to fly over the pole to visit you."

When Troyanovsky translated this speech, the applause in the Portland Chamber of Commerce did not die down for quite some time. Then Belyakov and I spoke, followed by our ambassador. The governor of the state also gave a speech. Toward the end of Charles Martin's speech, three beauty queens appeared in the hall with wreaths made from white roses. Smiling warmly, these beauties placed the wreaths on the Soviet fliers. Valery accepted this honor without any special surprise, although he did not surmise that such a custom was borrowed by the Americans from the Hawaiians. It served as a sign of the highest honor and respect toward honored guests.

After a military salute the mayor of the city asked Chkalov's crew to walk out to the square, where an enormous, festive crowd had gathered.

Accompanied by the ambassador, the governor of the state of Oregon, the mayor of Portland, and local officials, the Soviet fliers with wreaths around their necks walked along the streets, filled with city residents.

We were greeted with shouts, whistles, exclamations of "Hurray, Russian fliers," and smiles and smiles.

A comfortable Douglas passenger aircraft of United Airlines received the crew of the ANT-25 to transport them to San Francisco, according to schedule.

Besides the Soviet ambassador and Chkalov's crew, the aircraft also had on board representatives of all three network's of the United States, and other news media, including correspondent Duranty. Naturally, during the three hours of flight, the chief pilot of the ANT-25 had to carry on a number of conversations and give many interviews. In answer to the question of what was the most important scientific result achieved by the flight across the North Pole, Chkalov answered: "In my opinion, the most significant achievement of the flight was the meteorological discoveries. We determined that the height of the arctic clouds averaged six to seven kilometers and not three, as had been assumed before."

Duranty asked Chkalov: "How serious was the problem of icing?"

"There was a period," Valery answered, "when our red-winged giant was so seriously iced over that it took fifteen hours to eliminate the ice by means of the sun and the airstream flow."

The conversation between Chkalov and the correspondent was interrupted by a friendly stewardess, who had brought coffee, tea, sandwiches, and an enormous cake with American and Soviet flags and an inscription in Russian: "Greetings to the Soviet Fliers."

Meanwhile, a telegram from the president of the New York Explorers Club addressed to Stalin and Molotov was handed to the ambassador, Troyanovsky: "On behalf of the staff and members of the New York Explorers Club, I am honored to offer our congratulations in connection with one of the greatest accomplishments in the history of aviation—combining exploration and flight. Explorers from all over the world admire your government for its active and continual support which has been given to Arctic exploration in the last few years. Vilhjalmur Stefansson."

Correspondent Duranty showed Chkalov and his crew the newspaper *The Daily Worker* with its greetings from the Central Committee of the Communist Party of the USA: "Our plenum greets you with joy and pride, our heroic comrades, on the occasion of this historic flight, which is the latest triumph of the brilliant accomplishments of Soviet science and aviation. All America and the entire world is delighted by your wonderful victory in battling against the previously unsubdued regions of the Arctic. But we know just as well as you do that such victories can take place only in a socialist nation under the control of the Bolshevik Party."

After hearing the telegram, Chkalov said to me: "This is from the other America."

The correspondent brought to our attention the greetings to the crew of the ANT-25 published in the Soviet newspapers on June 20–22. Words of praise were spoken by Aleksei Stakhanov, the founder of the great working class movement in our country, the knowledgeable steel founder Makar Mazai, the famous machinist Peter Krivonos, and the heroine of collective farm labor, tractor operator Pasha Angelina.

Paying tribute to the American fliers who were flying us to San Francisco, Chkalov through Troyanovsky asked the stewardess to give a piece of the cake presented to the Soviet fliers to the crew of the Douglas. Chkalov went to the cockpit together with the stewardess.

The American pilots were deeply touched by the attention of the "chief pilot of the Russian fliers" and almost up to the very moment of landing insisted that Valery try his hand at piloting their craft, and asked for autographs on various kinds of paper. The crew of the Douglas presented Chkalov a ball point pen with a light from a tiny battery that enabled the pilot to make notes at night without turning on other light sources.

Fifteen minutes before the landing, the weather became sunny, without a single cloud, as is to be expected in the state of California. Two large cities appeared on the horizon: San Francisco and Oakland. Forty-story skyscrapers and the famous magnificent bridge uniting the two neighboring cities were sharply outlined against the background of a bright bay opening into the ocean with ships in the harbor.

The pilots of the Douglas gently landed the aircraft on the large cement runway. Correspondent Duranty and Troyanovsky explained to us that it was from this airport that the great American pilot Wiley Post had set off some time ago; it was from here that Amelia Earhart had taken off for a flight around the world along the equator.

The ambassador and representatives of American telegraph agencies and the press asked Chkalov's crew to come out of the aircraft wearing their wreaths made from roses, which had been presented to them by the beauty queens from Washington and Oregon. Valery Pavlovich at first tried to protest, but then agreed and even presented a rose to the stewardess.

To my protest that it would not be polite to arrive in another city wearing the wreaths presented to us in Portland, our commander reacted decisively and angrily: "Don't kick up a row! If diplomatic considerations demand it, then, my dear friend, we have to conform to them."

Thousands of people filled the airport. The flags of the Soviet Union and the United States of America were brightly lit up by the sun. A banner with a gold inscription, "The Communist Party of California Greets the Heroic Fliers for Their Outstanding Socialist Accomplishments" drew special attention.

"This is the other, working America that is meeting us," noted Belyakov. Now, seeing a sea of heads, the crowd expressing its frenzied delight, he remained unflappable.

Chkalov was touched by the joyful shouts, the rollicking whistles, the rain of red roses and bouquets of carnations that were falling at our feet.

We sped across the famous thirteen-kilometer bridge stretching over the Golden Gate in a fancy automobile accompanied by a wail of sirens of the police escort. Far below, ships of the Pacific fleet, commercial passenger liners, and the federal prison of Alcatraz were visible.

Our column of cars whizzed along the streets of San Francisco, the beautiful, carefully planned city with high skyscrapers, numerous restaurants, stores, and expensive marble homes. All this sparkled in the lights of neon signs. The streets, some going steeply uphill, some going downhill, were overflowing with buses and tens of thousands of trucks and passenger cars. In the middle of colorful bustling activity, we sped along with the ringing, howling sounds of the siren.

Here was the Soviet consulate—a little corner of the motherland in a distant foreign land. The press was waiting for us. Chkalov, embracing us, posed without grumbling; he was in a good mood.

At 9:50 P.M., Moscow called us for a radiotelephone conversation. The representatives of the Soviet press had gathered at the Moscow Central Telephone switchboard.

Late at night on June 21, 1937, the meeting between Chkalov's crew and their Soviet diplomatic comrades, who, far away from their motherland, were carrying on a difficult and painstaking daily task for the sake of her development, was concluded.

During the night, Chkalov was awakened by sounds that were strange in peacetime: somewhere a large-caliber machine gun was chattering away. Valery even woke me up to hear these night sounds in California's major city.

"You're hallucinating," I answered my friend and turned on my other side.

In the morning, we heard from sensational news in the papers that late at night, one of San Francisco's banks had been robbed by bandits. Both the police and the bandits even used armored cars in this clash.

After breakfast, we received the Russians who lived in San Francisco.

The day was filled with official receptions. First the crew of the ANT-25 was received by the mayor of Oakland, then there were gala receptions for the crew of the ANT-25 in the Oakland Chamber of Commerce. Later, more receptions in the San Francisco Chamber of Commerce, where, in addition to the civic leaders, military personnel in the person of the commander of the military district, General Simons, and the head of the naval base, Admiral Smith, were also present. In honor of Chkalov's crew, General Simons ordered a nineteen-gun artillery salute.

Salutes rang out more than once in honor of Chkalov's crew in many cities, both large and small; the crew was met by crowds of many thousands of people. Everywhere there were flowers, smiles, excited exclamations, and armies of correspondents and reporters. We shook thousands of hands, left tens of thousands of autographs and gave more than one interview.

But the meetings with the workers always produced the greatest impressions on Chkalov. This is how it was along the way to Washington. In Ogden, the workers of a train depot greeted the Soviet fliers; in Chicago, a sincere welcome awaited us at the railroad depot. Among them were many Communists and emigrés from Russia. Those meeting us sang the "International" with great feeling.

■

On June 27 at 8:25 A.M., Chkalov's crew arrived in the capital of the United States. They were met by the entire Soviet colony, local authorities, the press, and, as customary, an army of photographers and correspondents.

After the coolness of the air-conditioned car, one could immediately feel the damp, stupefying humidity of the American capital.

Again flowers, smiles, and greetings. The embassy adviser Umansky reported that today the head of the U.S. Army Air Corps, General Westover, had invited us at 5:30 P.M. to a reception or, to be more accurate, for cocktails.

"Tomorrow will be a very busy day: At 11:35, Secretary of State Cordell Hull will be waiting for you; at 12:00—meeting with the President of the United States. At 1:00 P.M. a lunch in the Mayflower Hotel, where an association of journalists will ask you to answer a series of questions. At 3:30, you and I will attend a meeting with the Secretary of War."

After hearing this, Valery Pavlovich noted that appropriate equipment was needed for such official visits. As it was, Umansky had taken care of this. It cannot be denied that Chkalov had become a happier and more approachable person among his fellow countrymen. The conversations did not cease until dinner. We left for a reception given by General Westover, head of the U.S. Army Air Corps.[58] The general, a man of shorter than average height, heavyset, dressed in a white civilian suit, greeted us very warmly. In spite of the warm and humid weather, the remaining American fliers were in uniform. The reception was organized in the Officers Club at Boning Field. Among the two hundred invited guests, besides the pilots, were many prominent representatives of the U.S. Army command.

When we returned to the embassy, the Secretary of Agriculture, Henry Wallace, a well-known political activist, candidate for president, and future vice president, came to visit us. The Secretary explained the organization of weather stations in the United States and promised that, for our next flight, the forecasting would be more precise.

After the meeting with Henry Wallace, there was a reception by the Soviet colony in Washington, D.C.

The second day of our visit in the American capital was even more hectic. Important conferences were arranged.

The first visit of the crew of the ANT-25 was with Secretary of State Hull. At 11:30, Chkalov, Belyakov, Troyanovsky, and I went into the office of Mr. Hull. We were met by a tall, well-built old man who spoke in a high tenor. He courteously greeted each of us, congratulating us and our country on the great importance of our achievement in aviation. Troyanovsky easily conducted the conversation, also carrying out simultaneously his role as interpreter.

The Secretary of State was interested in the details of our flight and especially how the crew solved the problems of navigation between the pole and the Canadian shore. The Postmaster General was also present.

Mr. Hull asked Chkalov's opinion on the possibility of setting up an aviation link over the pole.

"I think that this can be realized by significantly raising the flight ceiling, let's say, to nine to ten kilometers, by having aircraft with a cruising speed of three hundred to four hundred kilometers per hour, and finally by the creation of a series of polar bases in the Canadian part of North America comparable to our bases on Rudolph Island in the Franz-Josef Land archipelago."

At 12:00, we were in the White House. Here we were brought to the President's office. Roosevelt was sitting in some sort of a special chair behind a huge desk that was crammed with models of sailing ships, planes, other items, and also books. He was sitting near an open window that looked out onto a garden and was dressed in a light white shirt with an open collar. I recall his gray head and friendly smile. When we walked up to the President to shake his hand, two persons lifted Roosevelt by the arms from his chair: his legs were paralyzed. After noticing that we were attentively looking at the paintings in his office, the President said: "You are fliers and I am a sailor. For this reason, I have all sorts of things connected with sea duty."

Valery spontaneously answered Roosevelt: "You don't have enough paintings here by our Aivazovsky."

Troyanovsky, smiling, translated these words for the President, who livened up and said: "I like Aivazovsky very, very much."

In conclusion, the President wished us the greatest success and asked us to be his guests in the United States. Chkalov thanked him for the warm hospitality and wished the President and the people of the United States happiness, prosperity, and friendship with the Soviet Union. Roosevelt liked these words very much. In saying good-bye, he shook Chkalov's hand for some time.

At the gala banquet in the Mayflower Hotel, given by the leaders of the National Press Club, more than two hundred writers, journalists, and other representatives of the literary world took part. The National Broadcasting Company transmitted the speeches all over the country and abroad.

Numerous greetings were read out to Chkalov's crew, including a telegram from Admiral Byrd—the great expert on the Arctic and the Antarctic: "I ask you to give my most heartfelt and friendly greetings and most ardent congratulations to the great Soviet fliers, who have accomplished a remarkable historical feat which will always be remembered in the annals of world aviation. The flight from the USSR to the USA was a brilliantly planned and executed flight."

The banquet was followed by a meeting with the Secretary of War.

In the evening, Ambassador Troyanovsky organized a large reception in the Soviet embassy in honor of the crew of the ANT-25.

There were more than eight hundred people at the reception. Among the invited were the members of the diplomatic corps headed by their doyen, the British Ambassador Lindsey; Secretary of Commerce Roper; Secretary of Labor Perkins; the chief of staff of the U.S. Army, General Craig; the head of the Army Air Corps (or as we would call him, the head of the air force), General Westover; about seventy members of Congress including Senators King and La Follette; Under Secretary of State Kerr; the head of the far eastern section of the State Department, Hornbeck; and the director of the Civil Aeronautics Board, Fagg. Among the guests were journalists, writers, representatives of business circles, military fliers who had flown in from other states, and representatives of major aviation plants and civilian aviation companies in the United States.

It was somewhat difficult for the crew of the ANT-25, headed by its commander, since each of us had to shake more than eight hundred hands while meeting the guests and just as many more when we bid them farewell.

Chkalov was amazing: elegantly dressed, handsome, courteous, he stood out like a dancer.

On June 29, we visited Secretary of Commerce Roper, who was in charge of civil aviation. Then a meeting of the weather service of the Department of Agriculture, where we were received by Dr. Clark. Here the conversation was interesting and businesslike. Dr. Clark, holding before him a map of North America, with our flight route drawn on it, said: "You maneuvered exceptionally well to the right in order to cross the Rocky Mountains by the shortest distance and exit into the air space of the Pacific Ocean coastline. This was a very wise decision."

The fourth visit was made to the Canadian embassy. The crew of the ANT-25 expressed to the ambassador their appreciation for the assistance rendered during the flight above the territory of his country.

The evening was devoted to a tour of Washington.

On the morning of June 30, we boarded a train for New York and in four hours we covered the four hundred kilometers separating these two cities.

■

The largest city in the United States festively greeted the crew of the ANT-25.

Vancouver, Portland, San Francisco, Chicago, and Washington, D.C., had already prepared us for meeting this gigantic city and its inhabitants. Nevertheless, Chkalov was moved by such a noisy demonstration of friendship by the Americans.

After a short speech by Chkalov, his crew sat in a convertible and, accompanied by a police escort, sped along the streets of the city to

City Hall, where Mayor LaGuardia was expecting us; he said a few words of greeting in broken Russian.

On the way between City Hall and the Soviet consulate, the police had a difficult time, although they had changed the route taken by Chkalov's crew from the route announced in the morning New York papers. We were forced to stop many times in front of crowds of people who had blocked the traffic on the street.

To the surprise of people who were familiar with the United States, the popularity of Chkalov and his crew did not wane.

Once our guide, Misha Milsky, who was driving the car, committed a traffic infraction and was stopped by a traffic officer as we were on our way to Coney Island along the crowded city streets.

The usual not very objective conversation of traffic officer and motorist began. Mikhail apologized, saying that he was hurrying to bring the three Soviet pilots who had crossed the pole to an appointment.

"Chkalov? North Pole?" the officer asked again in disbelief. He then went up to the car, opened the door, and, after seeing Chkalov, broke into a smile and, turning to Milsky, asked, in a different tone of voice, for the Soviet pilot to give his autograph on a sheet ripped off from his ticket book.

Chkalov signed and shook the hand of the chunky Irishman; the policeman saluted, climbed on his motorcycle, and escorted us at high speed with the wail of a police siren through the streets of New York.

No less surprising were the reports in the press: continually in the course of many days they spoke in positive tones concerning our flight and about the Soviet Union.

"The flight of the Soviet aviators from the Soviet Union to the United States has earned an honored place in the history of aviation. They selected the shortest route to our country over the North Pole and the summit of the world. This seemed not humanly possible, but the Russians showed that this was possible," wrote the *Philadelphia Public Ledger*. The *Cleveland Plain Dealer* noted: "Three men, whose names will be engraved in history, have flown across the top of the world from Moscow to the United States in 63 hours. New horizons for aviation have been opened up. . . ." "The feat accomplished by the Russians is a miracle of ability and endurance. The obstacles along the route were great, the risks unbelievable and natural barriers frightening. Only imagination can foresee the practical results of this flight. In the meantime this is a striking example of Russian courage and resourcefulness and a remarkable demonstration of the possibilities of long-distance flight," stated the *Detroit Free Press*.

When Troyanovsky had translated for us several articles in a row, Chkalov implored him: "Enough, my dear Alexander Antonovich! Enough! In these three days I came to realize: I have become of such historical value that I even feel as if my body were turning to stone and covered in bronze or covered by mold in the vault in which the documents of the past are stored."

Troyanovsky showed Chkalov the schedule for the rest of their stay in the United States. Chkalov rumpled his hair: "What have you thought of next? For a whole month? It's time to go home. They are waiting for us."

Consul Borovoy, holding a telegram in his hands, said: "Valery Pavlovich, the government has extended your assignment and we have planned everything based on an estimate that the trip around the United States will end about July 25."

Chkalov was dumbstruck, then blurted out with renewed strength: "We can still return here as tourists and travel around as much as we want. But now, it's enough: please plan the quickest possible return home. That's my opinion, let Sasha and Egor confirm it."

Belyakov, who was familiar with the plan to travel around the country, objected: "It seems to me, Valery, that it is completely impossible to refuse since the Americans have invited our crew as guests."

"But, Sasha, a week of this is enough," Chkalov answered.

At this moment Consul General Borovoy placed a new piece of paper in front of Troyanovsky. He quickly glanced over it and said with a smile: "All our arguments are for naught. Here are the government's orders—your crew will stay in America until Gromov arrives."

The consul confirmed that the takeoff of Gromov's crew was set for the period between July 10 and 14.

"This is something else entirely! Otherwise it would be just excursions and visiting," said Chkalov and he hurried to find out the schedule of the transatlantic liners.

Borovoy explained that according to the timetable the *Normandy* was leaving port on July 14.

"Fantastic!" said Chkalov in a deep voice, "Fantastic!" I have a feeling Gromov will take off on the 10th and will be here on the 12th. We will meet him and pass the baton in traveling across America. But we won't return to the Pacific coast—it will take too much time. Egor and Sasha can travel along the Atlantic coast."

"And where are you going to disappear?" I asked Chkalov.

"I'm going to wait for Gromov's takeoff and the liner *Normandy*."

Belyakov just waved his arm, and, sitting next to me, started to work out a plan for our travels based on our new time frame: all excursions would end around July 10 or 12.

That same evening there was a gathering of famous travelers, cartographers, military and civilian pilots, and Arctic explorers.

The celebration in honor of the Soviet fliers, which had been organized on the initiative of the Explorers Club and the Russian-American Club for Cultural Exchange, took place in an enormous hall of the Waldorf Astoria, one of the best hotels in New York. There were people here whose names were well known in the Soviet Union: Vilhjalmur Stefansson, the president of the Explorers Club, which also had as one of its few honorary members our own Otto Yolevich Schmidt; fliers Hatty and Mattern, who had flown across the USSR; Matthew Hanson, a black who had taken part in Peary's expedition to the North Pole; the flier Kenyon, who had participated in Ellsworth's expedition to the Antarctic, and many others. One of the American journalists said that this was a "gathering of celebrities" and that it would be possible to write a book about each of them.

The stately, gray-haired, and tall Stefansson joyfully greeted us and led us to the Explorers Club globe, which was standing in the foyer: the globe was intercrossed with lines going in different directions that signified the routes of journeys and expeditions. Personal autographs of the explorers stood above the lines marking the routes. Here were the autographs of Nansen, Amundsen, Stefansson, Lindbergh, Byrd, Post, Hatty, Wilkins, Clarence, Chamberlain, Amelia Earhart, and others. There was a new line stretching from Moscow to the United States on the globe.

Chkalov put his signature above the new route of this very unique globe. After Valery's name, Belyakov and I signed our names.

Opening the gala meeting, the old polar explorer Stefansson made several deeply-felt remarks and read numerous telegrams that had been received from various parts of the United States and Europe.

The daughter of Robert Peary congratulated Chkalov's crew on their accomplishment: "My father," she telegraphed, "predicted that the North Pole would be conquered by aviation and this has turned out to be true."

Admiral Byrd radioed: three Soviet fliers have completed one of the greatest flights in history. He expressed certainty that this work would be continued. Charles Lindbergh sent his greetings from England.

The gala reception at the Waldorf Astoria was broadcast on the radio.

The vice president of the Explorers Club, Lowell Thomas, proposed a toast to the North Pole, toward which numerous expeditions had strived. General Westover, the commander of the U.S. Army Air Corps, gave an impassioned speech concerning the heroism of the crew of the ANT-25 and concluded the speech with the following: "Military aviation in the United States considers this flight to be the most significant in recent time."

Gardner, the secretary of the Explorers Club, who had visited the Soviet Union in 1936, told of the popularity of sport aviation in the USSR, the skydivers, and the remarkable work of the TsAGI.

It is impossible to recount all the speeches.

Those that spoke underlined the scientific and technological significance of the flight and noted that with this achievement the USSR had added a brilliant page to the history of mankind.

The speech by the Hero of the Soviet Union, Chkalov, brought forth an outburst of noisy enthusiasm.

Valery Pavlovich said: "We carried in our hearts the hearts of 170 million people. Neither storms, nor cyclones, nor ice could hold us back because we knew that we were carrying out the will of our people."

While returning to the consulate after our next reception, we encountered a picket line of strikers on one of the central streets. The poorly dressed people were carrying signs and were shouting out something. Our consul explained: "These people are trying to boycott their boss—the owner of a large garment shop who has lowered the wages of his workers."

Our largest meeting took place on 34th Street in the enormous hall of a riding school. More than ten thousand citizens were gathered here, most of them workers from New York. The editorial staff of the magazine *Soviet Russia Today* organized the meeting with us. When we appeared in the hall, a ten-minute ovation ensued.

Finally, the storm of enthusiasm began to quiet down and the chairman, the manager of the Hayden Planetarium, Dr. Kingsbury, began his speech with reference to Chkalov's crew in Russian: "Welcome, comrades! Glory to the heroes!" He said in his speech: "Lindbergh was greeted in the Soviet Union as a friend. We greet you in the same way. We love you because you have helped us to gain more knowledge about the Soviet Union. You are not only conquerors of the Arctic expanses but also bearers of human truth."

Stefansson, the president of the Explorers Club, spoke of the enormous work of the Soviet Union in the north.

The well-known fliers Kenyon and Fowler, representatives of the mayor's office, also made their statements.

As soon as the chairman of the meeting announced that "the chief pilot of the Russian fliers," Chkalov, was going to speak next, everyone stood up and began to applaud. Greetings were carried from all corners; the riding school shook from the applause. Someone struck up our "Aviation March" in English and thousands of voices carried the song.

"The Soviet Union," Chkalov began loudly, "is moving forward from one victory to the next. Our flight belongs entirely to the working class of the whole world. We three fliers, who have come from the working class, can toil and create only for the workers. We overcame all difficulties during the Arctic flight in order to bring greetings to the American people."

Valery spoke grippingly, with emotion and perceptiveness.

"We know very well," he continued, "that time is on our side and our motherland will overtake America in all areas! Neither the urge for profit, nor vanity or glory-seeking arouses the Soviet people to heroic deeds. The people, who have destroyed exploitation and elevated socialism, are moved by feelings that are the most exalted and noble among mankind. Love for our Soviet motherland, devotion to the ideas of communism, the striving for universal human happiness—this is what makes our people invincible.

After Chkalov's speech what transpired was incredible.

On July 2 after lunch, Dr. Stefansson came to visit us. We spoke for a long time in the living room of the consulate about the problems of exploring the Arctic.

In the evening there was a meeting with the Soviet colony in New York. It took place in the AMTORG Club. Chkalov spoke of how Levanevsky dreamed of a nonstop flight; of Gromov, who had flown a long-distance aircraft and set a world record in a closed circuit; of the death of the American flier, Post, in 1935; of the return of Levanevsky's crew from its flight, Moscow to the North Pole; and of our flight from Moscow to Kamchatka over the Arctic Ocean.

"Our flight over the Pole to America had least of all a sporting character. We strove toward scientific awareness of nature in the central section of the polar basin and the regions of the inaccessible pole in order to answer the ancient question of mankind: is it possible to link Europe and Asia with America via the shortest possible routes, which cross the regions of the North Pole?"

Chkalov showed on a map possible aviation routes.

"God forbid that these short routes would be used by military instead of civilian aviation," our commander unexpectedly expressed his thoughts out loud. "Let us not make guesses, but analyze for now the results of our first Soviet flight, which has a peaceful and humane character."

■

The most important aspect for Chkalov became the anticipation of a takeoff of the ANT-25-1. He refused to accompany us on many trips so Belyakov and I often had to respond alone to the invitations of the Americans. During this time Valery Pavlovich did not cease pestering the consular and AMTORG Soviet employees, demanding information from them on the preparation of Gromov's crew and also the search for Amelia Earhart.

However, Chkalov eagerly traveled to the testing center for U.S. Army aircraft, but, with the exception of a Boeing bomber, new American aircraft did not make a very big impression on him.

We once went to a free wrestling match.

"Bite off his ear! Rip off his nose! Smash his head!" the spectators shouted in a frenzy, watching how two wrestlers of different nationalities carried on a bout in which everything was allowed: tripping, squeezing, hitting, and biting.

"Enough! Let's go! It's so disgusting," Chkalov unexpectedly protested and we left for the consulate without waiting for the outcome.

Once at midnight we were taken up the Empire State Building, the highest skyscraper in the world. Three high-speed elevators in a row carried visitors first to the 61st, then the 92nd, and finally the 101st floor, where we climbed up some stairs to the platform on the

102nd floor. Usually the upper third of the skyscraper was hidden in fog or a low cloud layer, but on this night it was clear, which made it possible to observe how the giant city, glittering in a multicolored carpet of playing lights, flowed out in various directions and how these playful lights slowly vanished into the distance.

Chkalov looked at the confusion of multicolored signs and said loudly: "Here it is, the belly of America, the place which our Gorky called 'the City of the Yellow Devil.' This devil feeds itself as it beckons the buyer into its stores."

Gromov, Yumashev, and Danilin started at 2221 on July 11 New York time, that is, on the morning of July 12 Moscow time.

Chkalov brought out our flying maps and had prepared flags on pins to follow the movement of Mikhail Mikhailovich Gromov's crew.

Chkalov advised L. B. Khvat, the special correspondent for *Pravda*, to take off immediately for San Francisco.

Meanwhile, Belyakov and I visited yet another series of aviation plants and when we returned to the consulate in New York, our commander became indignant: "Heartless devils! Look at the map: see how 'Mikh Mikh' smoothed over the Pole—twelve minutes ahead of schedule!"

"That means they're outstripping us," Belyakov said.

"That's the style of our Mikhail Mikhailovich," Chkalov answered proudly.

On July 13 I stopped by the living room at 8 A.M. Chkalov was dozing at the table with his head on the map. The last flag pin was placed on Patrick Island and near it, written in Chkalov's hand: "13.7.37.5 hours 47 minutes New York time or 10 hours 47 minutes Greenwich."

At this time Belyakov came in and, not understanding that Chkalov had fallen asleep on the map at the table, asked loudly: "Where are they now?"

Valery lifted his head, stretched himself and, sharply jumping off the chair, with his hand began to smooth down his brown hair, which had fallen over his eyes.

"Well, you've all waked up, damn you!" our commander mumbled good-naturedly and, embracing Sasha and me, he leaned down on the table, where the map lay with its chain of little flags.

"Have you seen how 'Mikh Mikh,' Andrei, and Sergei are winging along?" said the still half-asleep but satisfied Chkalov joyfully.

Soon Vartanian called from Seattle and reported that the Rocky Mountains, toward which Gromov's plane would approach at 1900 hours Greenwich time, were covered by clouds to an altitude of 4,500 meters. In addition, Artak Armenakovich reported that, because of atmospheric interference, communication with the ANT-25-1 was intermittent, although the aircraft radio was working properly.

In half an hour Belyakov called from Newark airport, where he had been invited by some Americans. The navigator warned that to the south of San Francisco, especially on the coastline strip between Los Angeles and San Diego, they were expecting night and morning fogs.

After hearing this, Chkalov quickly shaded the coastal strip south of San Francisco.

"So, what now, Baidukov? Rectify the course to the right and then head for San Francisco?" the "chief pilot" asked in an uncertain voice—and this was completely unlike him.

"I guess that for Gromov, San Francisco, in a situation where he has a reserve supply of fuel, is a completely unsuitable point because our friends can fly as far as the southern border of the United States."

"So that's the way it is," Chkalov said in his Volga accent.

At this moment the telephone rang: adviser Umansky asked for Chkalov and reported the latest radiogram from Sergei Alekseevich Danilin, who reported that at 1920 Greenwich their position was 55° north latitude and 120° west longitude. They were flying at a height of four thousand meters; there was no radio contact with group stations but everything on board was all right.

Chkalov asked Umansky to wait a minute while we work out some recommendations.

"If Gromov has brought himself up to four kilometers, that means he realizes the danger and consequently he should turn right in order to avoid the thick cumulus storm cloud layer," I said.

"Have them turn toward Seattle, to the Pacific coast!" Valery shouted to Umansky. "But keep in mind that there will be night and morning fog south of San Francisco. Therefore, tell Vartanian that he should ask Gromov about the fuel supply and report to us; we will act as godmothers here."

The special correspondent for *Pravda*, Khvat, called us from San Francisco after lunch. He shouted into the receiver: "To hell with this aviation! You can never keep up with fliers or guess their desires."

"What's the matter, you paralyzed or something?" Chkalov asked the correspondent with a laugh.

"This is some kind of mockery!" Khvat continued to complain. "Here, listen to what we've just received from your favorite Mikhail Mikhailovich signed by the navigator: 'l hour 20 minutes, July 14, 1937 Greenwich. We are going along the shore. We are located somewhere between Seattle and San Francisco. Altitude 4,000 meters. We request that the commission record our fly-by over Oakland airport. We will land in the morning, beyond San Francisco. Danilin.' I hope you now understand what kind of dirty trick your intellectual Gromov has played on me and hundreds of other correspondents? What am I supposed to do now? Where am I supposed to set out for?"

Chkalov was laughing until tears came to his eyes.

"Lev, get in your chartered Boeing, fall into formation behind the ANT-25-1, fly behind it, and don't let it out of sight."

During the final tense hours of the flight of Gromov's crew, Alexander Vasilevich familiarized Borovoy with the history of long-distance records in aviation.

This history can be outlined briefly as follows: in 1925, the first long-distance record was recorded by the French fliers Lemetre and Arrashare—in twenty-five hours they flew in a straight line 3,166 kilometers without landing. Three years later the Italians set a new record, but the French immediately regained it. Later the Americans held first place, but in 1933 the record was taken from them by the Englishmen Haywood and Nicholetts, who had flown 8,544 kilometers from England to South America. Five months went by and in the same year, 1933, the French fliers Codos and Rossi flew 9,104 kilometers nonstop from New York to Damascus and regained for their country one of the most difficult aviation records. And now Gromov had exceeded all these records, covering a distance of approximately 10,300 kilometers.

Of course we did not feel like sleeping, although it was already late at night in New York. We sat by the radio and listened to reports relating to Gromov's flight.

Finally, July 14, 1937, the day of departure for the motherland. We already had tickets for the liner Normandy. But it was as if this did not matter to Chkalov: he had not packed his things, his records with the works of Beethoven, Tchaikovsky, and Rachmaninoff performed by renowned musicians including Rachmaninoff himself. He was wrapped up in one thought: would Gromov have enough fuel to locate an airfield where the fog had already lifted?

We ate a late breakfast in a tense atmosphere and Chkalov once again went to the table where the map with the southern and final section of the route of Gromov, Yumashev, and Danilin lay. The stereotyped "everything is fine" that Sergei Alekseevich Danilin had sent seemed like some kind of mockery.

Borovoy asked us to prepare to leave for the port of New York.

"How can we talk about this if our friends haven't completed their flight?" Chkalov cut in sharply, and reminded the consul: "I request that you make contact with San Francisco and check what is known of the weather in the region of Los Angeles and San Diego!"

Fortunately, the ubiquitous, all-knowing, and perceptive special correspondent to *Pravda*, Khvat, was still active on the other side of the country. Khvat asked Valery to come to the telephone and informed him that "Gromov has pushed off from San Diego where, to tell the truth, there were already breaks in the fog. He apparently made a circle above March Field."

We searched for some time, trying to find a more detailed map with such a small town.

"Well, thank God!" Now fellows, let's go home."

When we arrived at the port, we saw thousands of well-wishers, among whom were our beloved American polar explorer Stefansson, explorers, scientists, and American pilots. Before departure, we were informed that Gromov was circling near a military airfield but had not landed yet.

"Apparently, the field is too small for him," I noted.

"Mikhail Mikhailovich will somehow select a spot and land his ANT" said Chkalov without a shadow of a doubt.

At the very last moment Chkalov made the following announcement to the newspaper and radio correspondents: "We are leaving on a very significant day. Our friends Gromov, Yumashev, and Danilin have once again proved the feasibility of establishing a transpolar route. We once again thank the government, scientific organizations, and press of the United States and also many friends in this country for their valuable assistance provided during the flight and for a very warm reception. We consider that this hospitality was accorded not only to us but also to our country and our people."

New York was sliding from view when Chkalov, Belyakov, and I were summoned to the radio room of the *Normandy* We were informed that we could talk directly with March Field, where Gromov, Yumashev, and Danilin were located.

Apparently an American communications company had arranged it so that the fliers of the two crews could exchange greetings with one another on United States soil. However, besides "Hello, *Normandy!* Hello, *Normandy!*" we were unable to make anything out because of the loud crackle created by the atmospheric interference. But even this was sufficient for Chkalov to discard all doubts and not be concerned for the safety of Gromov, Yumashev, and Danilin any more.

"It was the voice of 'Mikh Mikh.'" Chkalov convinced Belyakov and me that this was the case: the crew of ANT-25-1 were safe and sound.

The newspaper that was published on board the *Normandy* reported that Admiral Byrd, the famous polar explorer, made the following announcement to the press on July 15: "For the third time in the course of several weeks I have the honor of congratulating the Soviet Union. The establishment of a drifting station 'North Pole' and the two flights across the North Pole to the United States—these are three most difficult historical achievements. The fact that all three of these difficult undertakings ended in complete success reflects not merely coincidences but diligent, thorough planning in all aspects of these activities."

On the morning of July 19 the liner approached the docks of Southampton, an English port. The noisy voices of the crowd of newspaper correspondents, who had burst through to our berths at 5 A.M. local time, awoke us. Besieged by the enterprising representatives of the press, we quickly got up, washed ourselves, dressed, and soon were being filmed for the news and answering questions all asked almost simultaneously: how did we fly, what did we feel, was it frightening or just "nothing"?

At this time our ambassador in England, Ivan Mikhailovich Maisky, appeared with his wife, Agnya Aleksandrovna. We had become friends the previous year while vacationing in one of the resorts at Sochi. Seeing that we had already reached the irreversible stage of interviewing, Ivan Mikhailovich invited the entire press corps to come with us to the salon.

In the *Normandy*'s salon there arose a curious conversation between Valery Pavlovich and a reporter from the *Daily Herald*, who asked our commander: "Tell me what you felt during the flight above the North Pole."

"Nothing special," answered Chkalov, smiling, "routine work and even rest according to a time schedule."

"Where did you study?" the same correspondent asked a second question.

"Where all our people studied in those bygone days. Our real school was the Civil War, the Revolution, the Party of the Bolsheviks. This was the second phase of our learning. Practical learning at that, I assure you," Chkalov said cheerfully and then added: "Report that I was instructed by Mikhail Mikhailovich Gromov, the ace of Soviet fliers."

"In that case the teacher must be pleased with his student," observed a London correspondent of an American newspaper and then asked in turn: "What is the difference between your flight and the flight of Gromov's crew?"

"Well, you see, we were advance scouts on a nonexistent route. Little was known about the atmospheric conditions in the central polar basin. It was assumed that the upper layers of clouds there did not exceed three to five kilometers. Based on this, we took on board sufficient oxygen to supply the crew for only eight hours. What in fact occurred you probably read in our reports and I will not repeat it. But I will say one thing: although it was difficult, it was nothing. We flew over the Arctic Ocean and its Pole and reached the United States. Gromov took these conditions into consideration and had significantly more oxygen, which allowed him to fly, as a rule, in a straight line when clouds forced him to increase the flight altitude."

Someone in the group of unfamiliar people surrounding us in the salon asked a personal question of Chkalov: "Are you very rich, Mr. Chkalov?"

Valery, after thinking for a short while, looked over the whole group surrounding us and said seriously: "Yes, I'm very rich!"

"How many millions do you have?" the foreigner asked again.

"One hundred and seventy million!" Valery answered mischievously.

"Rubles or dollars?" the person, apparently an American, attempted to make the question more precise.

"One hundred and seventy million people!" Chkalov clarified to the surprised foreigner. "All of them work for me and I for them," Chkalov concluded cheerfully.

■

On July 19 the train, traveling at a speed of one hundred kilometers per hour, brought Chkalov's crew from Le Havre to the St. Lazare station in Paris. There was an enormous crowd of greeters. The first to welcome us was the ambassador of the USSR to France, Ya. Z. Surits. With him were the representatives of the French ministry of aviation and general staff; the vice president of the aviation commission from the chamber of deputies, Vaillant-Couturier; embassy staff, the Soviet colony, participants in the second congress of the International Writers Association, including Mikhail Koltsov, Agnya Barteau, and Louis Aragon; and many journalists and correspondents from the French and Soviet press.

Marlene Dietrich, the famous movie star, sailed with us on the *Normandy* and now arrived at the same time we did in Paris. Chkalov, feeling unwittingly guilty at having spoiled her reception, gallantly presented her with a bouquet of roses. At the train station Chkalov gave a brief but impressive speech on radio. He was excellent at unrehearsed talks.

After the five-day journey across the ocean from America to Europe, we still were wobbly on dry land and, therefore, a few hours of rest at the Soviet embassy in Paris were necessary.

On the morning of July 20 everything was suddenly turned topsy-turvy; someone was shouting, roaring, and laughing Homerically in the living room of the embassy.

"They have arrived," the ambassador said mysteriously while we were seated in his dining room eating breakfast.

The three of us quickly walked into the living room. Imagine our surprise when we saw only three people: Aleksei Tolstoy, Vsevolod Vishnevsky, and Mikhail Koltsov.

"I thought a company of soldiers had arrived and been given the command: 'At ease! Dismissed!'" Valery Pavlovich jested.

"But in reality what?" Tolstoy asked, embarrassed, and embraced Chkalov.

"But in reality only one sailor, one commander of a squadron, and one count," Chkalov roared with laughter.

"A former count!" Vsevolod Vishnevsky corrected Chkalov.

They discussed America, Spain, the second congress of the International Association of Writers, and Gromov's flight. Chkalov asked to be informed about the congress.

Vsevolod Vishnevsky began: "Our congress has gathered at a very threatening time. The danger of war has become much greater. The writers of the world, in foreseeing the events of the near future, consider this congress to be at least a preliminary preparation for mobilization. We have seen the face of a new war in Spain. Valery Pavlovich, prepare yourself so that you can endure more profound and serious tests, examine and train yourself for major combat on a grand scale. Fate may decree that all of us will have to meet again on the fronts."

After meeting with the writers, Chkalov was deep in thought: "We must create a new fighter quickly or we will not be able to stop fascism."

Our commander rushed the ambassador to board us as quickly as possible on the Moscow Express.

■

The train was speeding across our native Russian soil. Along the way, Soviet correspondents constantly asked Chkalov about the flight. I. Rakhillo, a friend of the crew and author of the novel *The Fliers*, brought fresh newspapers. Chkalov's attention was caught by what was written at the bottom of the third page by G. A. Ushakov, "The Problem of Trans-Arctic Communication," but first he read a collective letter from S. Levanevsky, M. Shevelev, M. Babushkin, P. Golovin, A. Alekseev, B. Chukhonovsky, F. Farikh, and G. Orlov, which in addressing Chkalov's crew ("You have opened a great aerial highway") confidently spoke of the reality of an aerial path that had been forged by the two ANT-25 aircraft. He then read the opinions of G. Ushakov very attentively and answered the correspondent from *Pravda:* "Here Ushakov writes 'The Problem. . . .' and indeed that's what it is, because a reciprocal desire must exist on the part of the United States. But judging from personal experience they are not ready for this yet. The Americans still haven't built an ANT-25. Do you understand?"

All the correspondents and journalists looked at Chkalov with surprise.

"It was not without an ulterior motive that Andrei Nikolaevich Tupolev was carried off the ship onto the pier in New York like a saint, and not by just anybody, but by Sikorsky, Douglas, and similar luminaries of American science and technology."

The guests wrote excitedly in their note pads.

Chkalov skimmed through a long article by Vsevolod Vishnevsky, "For the Motherland," and D. Zaslavsky's "The World Press on the Flight of the Soviet Heroes" and began to read out loud the message from Mattern[59]:

> I deeply respect the heroic fliers of the Soviet Union. . . . Their masterful control of a heavily loaded craft and their remarkable navigation ability revealed the high level of accomplishment achieved by Soviet aviation. The second flight showed the entire world that in the near future it will be possible to plan regular flights. In addition, the Soviet fliers Gromov, Yumashev, and Danilin set a long-distance record which, in my opinion, will not be broken soon. . . .
>
> I deeply value the fact that the Soviet government allowed me to fly over Soviet territory and were ready to assist me with weather reports from their radio stations.
>
> Once again, I congratulate the Soviet heroes, fliers Chkalov, Baidukov, and Belyakov.

Everyone waited to see how Chkalov would react to this message. Straightening his eternally falling lock of brown hair, looking through the window of the car, said: "There is no hint in this article that Jimmy is planning to fly our route! Refueling above Canada or Alaska is not so easy a thing to accomplish—Baidukov and I studied this matter for some time at the Air Force Research Institute six years ago."

"But why is it so complicated?" someone present asked.

"It is difficult to link up with a tanker aircraft even in the proximity of your own field. But what if the weather is bad? Then what?" Chkalov answered.

At 1613 the train smoothly came up to the depot of the Belorussky Station. A happily smiling Chkalov appeared in the doors of the car. He was excited, seeing the thousands of people crowding the platform and hearing the enthusiastic ovations.

We crossed a corridor lined with thousands of people. Some of those were the leaders of the Moscow party, along with Rossinsky, Tupolev, Schmidt, and the polar fliers Spirin, Babushkin, Alekseev, Slepnev, and Shevelev, our wives and children, relatives, and friends. We appeared before tens of thousands of Muscovites who had filled the enormous square in front of the train station. We climbed the podium with our wives and children.

The square broke into a frenzy. There were thunderous ovations and shouts of joy. Valery said to me in my ear: "Dammit, I'm as excited as if I had never been to America at all."

"It's easier in America; there you get rid of worries with a whistle."

Only the sounds of the booming orchestra amplified by the speakers, which played the "International," were able to calm down the enthusiasm of the well-wishers.

Chkalov was holding Olga Erazmovna and their son by the hand. Nine-year-old Igor, wearing a new sailor's outfit, stared continually at his father. The boy bent his father's head down to him and whispered something. Chkalov laughed infectiously and kissed his son on the cheek.

The meeting began. One orator followed another. The stormy applause often made them pause. By order of the Central Committee of the Communist Party and the Soviet People's Commissariat of the USSR, Chkalov's crew was greeted by the People's Commissar of the Defense Industry, Rukhimovich.

A short, responding speech was given by Chkalov, whom thousands of well-wishers did not allow to begin to speak for some time in greeting him with continuous, enthusiastic applause.

"Hello, my native land!" the commander of the ANT-25 began. "Hello, my native Moscow! We are very glad and proud of the fact that we had the opportunity to be first to blaze a new route over the North Pole to the United States of America."

And once again there were applause and shouts of "hurrah," which did not die down for a considerable length of time.

The meeting was adjourned. We climbed down from the podium. Each of us was seated with our family in a convertible entwined with garlands of flowers. We slowly came out onto Gorky Street, the traditional route for heroes. People stood in lines five deep from the Belorussky Station all the way to the Kremlin itself.

Pressing his wife and son to him, Chkalov said excitedly: "Lelik, Igorushka! Look around: what smiles, what good will!"

As we moved along the Gorky Street route, the blizzard of paper thrown from balconies and the windows of buildings became increasingly thicker, reminding Chkalov and his friends of those real polar cyclones and snowstorms through which the ANT-25 flew across the region of the "pole of inaccessibility."

The car in which my wife and I were riding followed just behind Chkalov's car, and I could judge by his gestures that the commander of the ANT-25 was deeply touched by the reception. The cars stopped in front of the Kremlin Palace.

A reception was given at St. George Hall. Our crew was greeted with our family, members of the household, and friends.

The reception of Chkalov's crew at the station was described in much detail in the newspapers the next day, including many articles concerning the reception at the Kremlin.

Early next morning, Valery, dressed in a nightgown and slippers, knocked on our door. he was holding *Izvestia* in his hands and asked me: "Have you read Troyanovsky's article?"

"Valerian, I've been sleeping like all decent people."

"You and Belyakov—I've told you this hundreds of times—are people with a low sensitivity for matters of the heart."

Chkalov began to read the article, "Messengers of Peace and Friendship":

> The flights of Chkalov, Baidukov, and Belyakov, and Gromov, Yumashev, and Danilin are the pride of our nation, while at the same time carrying a great international significance.
>
> Above all, these flights make it possible to understand our nation correctly and evaluate its growth and strength. They serve as a clear example, warning all adventurers who would sharpen their knives against the Soviet Union. Enormous creative powers are beginning to appear in our country and we will be able to rebuff any attempt against efforts of the workers who are building socialism. Thus, the flights of our heroes contribute to the strengthening of international peace.
>
> In connection with the flights, a strong liking for us has grown among wide sections of the population in many nations. They will also serve as a deterrent to the warmongers who would profit at the expense of others, including the Soviet Union.
>
> The solid contact which was made between many representatives of other nations and our heroic fliers has dispelled many prejudices, ended many slanderous ideas, and shown the whole world a genuine face of the Soviet Union. . . .

"Very good!" I said, interrupting Chkalov.

"Excellent!" Chkalov answered and immediately disappeared behind the door of our apartment.

On the very first morning the telephone began to tire out Chkalov as endless requests to "speak about the flight" came pouring in. My telephone also rang endlessly; the purpose of the calls was the same. The frequency of the calls became so great that I had to ask my wife to answer the phone and explain vaguely that I had just left "for some place." Of course, this was not exactly a scientific method, but by evening its effectiveness had increased significantly. My Evgenyia

Sergeevna shared this experience with Olga Erazmovna, and Valery Pavlovich immediately realized the practical benefits of family life.

However, new forms of requests and invitations were soon put into tactical use.

This was done very simply A leader of a large group of Pioneers would come to our building on Sadovaya Street. They would stand at the entrance, where "Auntie" Lusya, who was not impartial to flowers and children, would place the children in the elevator, take them up to the fifth floor, and with the friendliest of smiles would push the doorbell of apartment 102. Usually Chkalov himself opened the door and the group of children would steal his heart straight off. He would lead them into his office, flip through the pages of his calendar, sniff the flowers presented to him, mumble, then select the possible dates for visiting their school, camp, or youth meeting.

If the children did not find Chkalov at home, then according to advice given by the elevator operator, Auntie Lusya, they would ring the bell of my apartment, 101, across the way. I often became the "unwilling" victim of the children, in the absence of Chkalov. Their third alternative was to get to Belyakov, who lived in the neighboring building. While we racked our brains planning our trips, the schedule of elevator operator Auntie Lusya worked optimally and without fail.

■

On August 2, 1937, the papers reported that Chkalov was in Rybinsk; at the city square he gave a report on the flight before fifteen thousand workers of the city and nearby villages.

On August 3, I was informed that Chkalov was once again in the ranks of the air force and that he had been promoted to the rank of colonel.

I telephoned Rybinsk and had Valery located in the Party District Committee. He was preparing to appear before the city's most active party members.

"Congratulations, Valerian, on being promoted to the rank of colonel!"

"Yegorushva!" my friend said in his Volga accent with excitement and asked: "What about you and Sasha?"

"I've been made a major and the professor, a brigadier engineer."

"Well, I'm happy for you and Sasha. But wait for my return. We'll celebrate together."

Next day at 6:00 in the evening, Chkalov arrived on the steamer *Gleb Uspensky* in Yaroslavl, where he gave a talk on the flight at a meeting organized by the regional and city party organizations. More than eighty thousand people gathered on Soviet Square, the largest in the city.

Chkalov's magnificent speech was often interrupted by ovations and shouts of "hurrah!"

That same evening, Belyakov and I spoke in the Krasnopresnensky Park of Culture and Rest in Moscow, where an audience of many thousands of people had gathered.

While Chkalov was sailing down the Volga from Yaroslavl, First Lieutenant K. P. Kaitanov set a world high-altitude record for skydiving with an oxygen device. He bailed out from an altitude of 9,800 meters. Valery's friend test pilot Yulian Piontkovsky completed five hundred flights in one day while testing A. S. Yakovlev's UT-1 aircraft—an unheard-of number! Each flight, including a takeoff and a landing, lasted one minute ten seconds. Each time, after it had taken off, the aircraft would circle at an altitude of seventy-five to one hundred meters and then land, and take off again. This continued from 10 A.M. to 8 P.M. with three ten-minute breaks for refueling.

On the morning of August 9, Valery Pavlovich arrived at the Gorky docks. Despite the early hours, tens of thousands of people, headed by the Secretary of the Regional Commissariat of the All-Union Communist Party came out to meet their hero and fellow countryman. The commander of the ANT-25 reported to the citizens of Gorky in good form, describing many interesting episodes about his fantastic travels.

While Chkalov was conversing with his fellow countrymen, the following resolution was signed in the Kremlin:

In recognition for the accomplishment of a heroic, first nonstop flight from Moscow over the North Pole to the United States of America, the Central Executive Committee of the USSR resolves:

1. To bestow the Order of the Red Banner of the Soviet Union on:
   Chkalov, V. P.—commander of the crew of the ANT-25
   Baidukov, G. F.—copilot
   Belyakov, A. V.—navigator.
2. To award at the same time a monetary reward to the participants

in the flight—Chkalov, V. R., Baidukov, G. F., Belyakov, A. V.—the sum of 30 thousand rubles each.

President of the Central Executive Committee of the USSR, M. Kalinin
Secretary of the Central Executive Committee of the USSR, A. Gorkin
Moscow, Kremlin. August 9, 1937.

Belyakov and I immediately sent off a congratulatory telegram to Chkalov.

On August 9 and 10, Chkalov spoke before a collective of ten thousand at the Krasnoe Sormovo plant, then set off for an automobile factory in order to give a report to the workers there.

On August 11, Chkalov sailed from Gorky on a swift cutter *Dzerzhinets* up the Volga and in the afternoon arrived in his native village of Vasilevo.

On the Vasilevo pier and the high embankments of the Volga, thousands of fellow villagers waited for their hero—Valery Chkalov.

All the homes in Vasilevo were decorated with flags as if it were a national holiday. Banners of greetings and portraits of their fellow countryman were raised above the heads of the well-wishers.

Embracing his aged mother, Chkalov with his wife and son made their way through the crowd onto the square on the banks of the Volga, where a meeting took place.

"My dear fellow countrymen," said the famous native of Vasilevo, "allow me to report to you that the crew of the ANT-25 has honorably fulfilled the assignment of the party and of the government."

Valery spoke in detail concerning the flight, the aircraft, the people who built the machine, his friends and, of course, his stay in the United States.

The citizens of Vasilevo, proud of their fellow countryman, warmly greeted Chkalov. They asked him to visit his native Vasilevo more often and for longer periods of time.

On August 13, *Pravda* published Chkalov's letter to Stalin. Valery Pavlovich thanked the leadership of the party and the nation for awarding the members of the crew of the ANT-25 the Orders of the Red Banner. In conclusion he wrote:

I would like to express the opinions of my comrades Baidukov and Belyakov. In response to this award I give you a promise—any of your assignments, any assignments of the party and the government will be carried out. I personally will fly as long as my right hand can guide aircraft controls and my eyes can perceive the ground.

Yours, Valery Chkalov
City of Gorky

On August 12, 1937, a four-engined aircraft, the N-209, designed by the engineer V. F. Bolkhovitinov, took off from Moscow.

An announcement of the government commission stated that "the government has approved the application of the Hero of the Soviet Union, S. A. Levanevsky; pilot, N. G. Kastanaev; navigator, V. I. Levchenko, to make a nonstop flight—Moscow-North Pole-North America."

Included in the crew were also mechanics G. T. Pobeshimov and N. N. Godovikov, and N. Ya. Galkovsky—the radio operator. Returning home after seeing the N-209 depart from Schelkovo airfield, I called flight headquarters and requested to be systematically informed on Levanevsky's flight. On the day of the takeoff, ten radiograms were received from the radio operator, Galkovsky. The last one was sent out at 2353 and signed by the radio operator and the navigator: "At 23 hours 39 minutes, we passed the island of Morzhovets. Flight altitude 2,600 meters. We have been flying at night for three hours. Levanevsky and Kastanaev are piloting the aircraft on instruments. All the cockpit lights are on in the aircraft. Everything is fine. Galkovsky, Levchenko."

In the morning, P. S. Anishchenkov reported that everything was going well with Levanevsky.

After obtaining the newspapers of August 13, I glanced through the reports on yesterday's takeoff for the N-209 aircraft. There were articles on the members of the crew, the aircraft, and its engines.

Belyakov telephoned me from flight headquarters. He said: "After turning the aircraft toward the Fairbanks meridian above the Pole, Levanevsky was flying at an altitude of six thousand meters above a limitless thick cloud layer when suddenly his outside starboard engine malfunctioned."

"And what have you thought up for our crew?" Chkalov asked. "You saw them off?"

"Valery, besides the aircraft on an expedition to the North Pole, we have nothing on hand right now," I answered my friend. "As far as the ANT-25 and the ANT-25-1 are concerned, they could be here in a month at best."

"What did they take with them?" Chkalov asked again.

"Supplies for a month and a half; they have tents, sleeping bags, warm clothing, and weapons," Belyakov enumerated.

"It seems to me that the best thing to do right now is to request a flight to the United States and, after purchasing their best aircraft, search for Levanevsky's team from Alaska."

Chkalov's suggestion seemed unexpected to me, but entirely logical.

At this moment, two automobiles stopped in front of us; Rukhimovich, the People's Commissar for Defense Industry, stepped out of one and out of the other stepped Alksnis, the head of the Air Force. Chkalov decided to make use of this opportunity, and turned to them requesting permission to start a search for Levanevsky's crew.

Alksnis decisively refused our suggestion: "Your aircraft are all dismantled and God knows what kind of condition they're in and where they are. Vartanian and Mikhail Belyakov report that Crosson, the American flier, is ready to fly from Fairbanks on a search. We have already given the order to charter a Lockheed Electra."

Rukhimovich noted in a softer tone: "As I understand it, designers and their new aircraft are waiting for you and Baidukov. Also, Chkalov, I carefully read your letter to Stalin from Gorky. You completely refuse the idea of working at a desk."

"It's completely unthinkable!" Chkalov firmly answered the People's Commissar, but added: "We just wanted to come to the rescue of our friends and do it properly."

The People's Commissar calmed us: "We have decided to draw on the experienced polar explorers: Vodopyanov, Alekseev, Molokov, Golovin, Mazuruk, and others, with their multiengined aircraft, who have bases of operations on the islands of Franz-Josef Land and the ice fields of Papanin's group. We are taking all possible measures."

Winter was approaching and the polar night was beginning to rule over its realm. No one has ever solved the mystery of the tragedy that befell the crew of the N-209 on August 13, 1937. Even the heroic, long-distance flights of Wilkins and Kenyon, who reached 86° north, and the courageous, risky flights of Soviet pilots from Shevelev's and Vodopyanov's group and others did not give any hope for illuminating the latest Arctic mystery, which had captured the crew of the N-209 aircraft.[60]

It was somehow possible to confirm Amundsen's death in the Arctic by a broken float of the hydroplane *Latham*, which washed up on a shore in Norway seventy days later. People learned of the disaster of the balloon *Eagle* thirty-three years after it took off from Spitzbergen Island bound for the North Pole. But there has been no information concerning the whereabouts of the crew of the N-209 to this day.

PART FOUR

The Last Episode

9

After the Flight

While the search for the crew of the N-209 continued, Chkalov was carrying out new test flights every day. The time came for the first selection of the People's Deputies to the Supreme Soviet of the USSR. Naturally, many Soviet people nominated Chkalov among the candidates for Deputy. In reply to the numerous attempts to draft him, Chkalov answered: "The faith and confidence of the people—this is an important matter. It is necessary to justify this faith of the people by new achievements. But I will be a candidate where the Central Committee of the party dictates. I am a Bolshevik. . . but I have to confess that I would like to be chosen by my fellow countrymen."

And so on October 23, 1937, in the city of Gorky, a meeting was opened: the nomination of candidates for Deputy of the Supreme Soviet of the USSR began.

The very first speaker, a worker from the Ordzhonikidze factory, proposed to the Gorky Electoral District that their beloved fellow countryman, Hero of the Soviet Union Valery Pavlovich Chkalov, be nominated as a candidate. This proposal instantly spread through the entire Gorky Region and the Chuvash Republic. Workers of Smorvo, metalworkers of Vykusa, the railway workers of Murom, the collective farm workers of Pyshchug, and the employees of many other enterprises and organizations warmly supported the group at the Ordzhonikidze factory.[61]

On November 10, 1937, Chkalov sent a telegram to the Gorky District Commission for Election to the Soviet Nationals of the Supreme Soviet of the USSR. "I wish to express my deep thanks for the trust to all the electors who have advanced my candidacy for the Soviet Nationals of the Supreme Soviet of the USSR. The Central Committee of the All-Union Communist Party had instructed me to remove my candidacy in other regions and to become a candidate in the Gorky Electoral District, to which I give my approval. V. P. Chkalov."

In response, hundreds of telegrams from the cities and villages of the Gorky Region and Chuvash descended on Chkalov with requests to meet with the electors. Many wrote: "The electors not only want to read about you, but to see you personally, dear friend and fellow countryman." It was clear that such a sensitive person, such a patriot as Chkalov would quickly respond to the invitations.

On November 21, 1937, Chkalov arrived in Gorky.

He gave a speech that was broadcast on radio. Chkalov talked about himself, especially in detail about the flights across the Arctic Ocean to Kamchatka and the United States, the strength of our motherland. He finished his radio speech with the following words: "Comrades, electors! I will not allow myself to defame your trust in me either by my work or my behavior. I will dedicate my whole life until my last breath for the cause of socialism. Long life to our nation!"

From November 22 in the course of twenty days, Chkalov participated in more than seventy meetings with electors in the various regions of the electoral district. More than half a million people both saw and heard their hero — the candidate for Deputy.

The well-known journalist and writer, Leonid Aleksandrovich Kudrevatykh, wrote at that time: "Chkalov displayed one more exceptional ability: he turned out to be a wonderful campaigner. At conferences and meetings, he not only talked about his flights — and he had to discuss them everywhere because the electors demanded this — he also without fail discussed matters that related directly to the voters. Whether he spoke with students or teachers, with workers or collective farmers, he always found precisely the right words for them. He transmitted to the listeners his deep feelings of love for the Party and for the motherland and absorbed himself in these very same feelings of the people. He more than once said: 'What a people! The strength of Russia! Could anyone really defeat such people?'"

The appearance of Chkalov was always met with excitement; they brought flowers and presents to him. He received many notes.

These were not always questions. The great love of the people for the Party of Lenin, for their hero fliers, for Chkalov was expressed in these notes.

Kudrevatykh precisely noted Chkalov's love for the people of labor, his sincere interest in their lives, his striking resourcefulness, and his ability to find the right words in each situation.

Participating in a meeting of thirty thousand in the city of Dzerzhinsk, Chkalov noticed a gray-mustached old man in the uniform of a river transport worker standing near the podium. Jumping from the podium, Chkalov with genuine excitement and joy embraced the old man and shouted to those surrounding him: "This is comrade Barmin, my former captain on the steamer *Bayan* on which I worked as stoker as we sailed the Volga."

Chkalov traveled across the entire northern part of the Gorky region. He spent some time in Chuvash. The endless trips and speeches in the frosty air fatigued him: he became exhausted and hoarse. It was therefore decided that in the future, Chkalov would speak only in enclosed buildings. But what could be done if, after arriving in Kanashi, Valery saw twelve thousand voters on the square waiting for him, regardless of the fact that the temperature was 30° below zero!

Listening to the objections of the leaders of the Chuvash Republic who were accompanying him, Chkalov came out on the square and refused to put on a sheepskin parka. "What next?" Chkalov said sharply. "What kind of flier am I if I can't stand before the people in an overcoat!"

The meeting lasted for an hour, at the end of which Chkalov gave an impassioned speech. It was like that everywhere.

In December, the first elections of the Deputies to the Supreme Soviet of the USSR took place. Chkalov was unanimously elected in the Gorky Electoral District, which included the Gorky Region and the Chuvash Republic. On December 14, 1937, Valery left for Moscow. Valery Pavlovich received deputy's number 17, signed by the President of the Presidium of the Supreme Soviet of the USSR, M. Kalinin, and the Secretary of the Presidium, A. Gorkin. On the ticket was written: "The bearer, comrade V. P. Chkalov, has been selected as a Deputy of the Soviet of Nationalities from the Gorky Electoral District of the RSFSR."

Two and a half million voters elected Valery Chkalov and he felt that the trust that had been placed in him had to be justified constantly, diligently, and responsibly, regardless of the heavy load of flight work and important social activities.

Olga fulfilled the secretarial duties of a deputy. From January 12,1938, she recorded 288 announcements, complaints, and requests addressed to Valery Pavlovich as a Deputy of the Supreme Soviet of the USSR. Not a single message or request was left unanswered.

The conscientious manner in which Chkalov fulfilled his duties as deputy, his constant communication with his constituents, how he assisted individuals and organizations, and how he was concerned with his native Vasilevo (which was renamed during Chkalov's life as Chkalovsk). It was possible to determine by the many letters addressed to the deputy that have been preserved, and by his articles published in the newspapers.

"Chkalov was interested in all the small things in the life of his region," wrote the Secretary of the Chkalovsk Party District Committee.

> On every trip, he was anxious to know all that was going on in the factories and the collective farms. He went to the Party District Committee of the District Executive Committee and checked on the progress in carrying out the plans of the economic-political campaigns. He was in stores, barbershops, clothing stores, joiner shops, markets, collective farms, factories, hospitals, schools, reading rooms and clubs, libraries, and radio centers. And all in order to know better how his fellow countrymen were living, how they were working and creating.

A fire threatened the Chistoe peat-extracting plant. A fiery monster fifteen kilometers wide was besieging the Chistoe plant. All the plant workers were thrown into battle with the flames, but they were not successful. Chkalov was in Gorky. Discovering the danger, he arrived in Chkalovsk at the fire site in order to help organize the collected farm workers to help the plant. Thousands of collective farm workers came out to battle the flames and it was soon extinguished.

Chkalov helped us complete the construction of two clubs: at the Chistoe peat-extraction plant and for the craftsmen of Katunki. With his active help, an improvement in services was achieved in his native village. He dreamed of paving the roads and putting in a water supply system.

In Katunki, when the club that was constructed with Valery Pavlovich's aid was being opened, the people of Katunki invited him to the opening. And he accepted. The weather was cold, foul, rainy, and muddy and it was impossible to get to Katunki by car. Chkalov proposed to go eight kilometers on foot. I obtained a cutter. Because it was dangerous to sail at this time, the helmsman could not make this decision. Chkalov took the responsibility upon himself and, indeed, on the return trip at night, he himself stood behind the wheel and took the helmsman's place.

In order to get at least a small impression of Deputy Chkalov's sensitive, attentive attitude to his constituents, it's sufficient to read his article, published in the newspaper *Gorky Commune* three days prior to the death of Valery Pavlovich:

> I recently received a letter from one of my constituents—a comrade Arefyev. He works in an advisory department, is satisfied with his conditions, but he desires to be of more use to his country. Comrade Arefyev requested that I help him go to a winter camp in the Arctic or to the Far East, where there is a great need for people. I helped Arefyev realize his dreams.
>
> Voter Vorobyev complained to me: he was seriously ill and was not receiving the necessary medical aid. As a result of my letter, an aircraft was sent with a neuropathologist to Vorobyev, who lives in a distant area of the Gorky Region; a diagnosis of the ailment was made and measures were taken to have Vorobyev sent for a cure at a physiotherapy institute.
>
> Young constituents send letters to me from the collective farms and factories. They are inspired by patriotic feelings and wish to help the nation in her defense measures and wait for the day when they are called into the ranks by the Red Army Young people asked their deputy to help them enroll in flying school. They write about schools and hospitals, report the cultural growth in their villages, mention people without education but with great natural talents, and so on. I received a letter from my constituent collective farm workers from the village of Beseda in the Vasilevsky region. They wrote that oil has been discovered near their village. The people love their motherland and are deeply interested in the development of its productive strength. I, as a deputy, take a very active part in answering all these questions.

With the same pressures of test flying that Chkalov bore to the last second of his life, which demanded an uncompromising bestowing of all his spiritual and physical strength and professional talent, I must confess to this very day I remain surprised by his additional duties as deputy, his links with the world of writers and artists, his endless passionate oratorical performances, his fishing trips on the Volga, his hunting trips, his attendance at the theater, and his association with a continually growing circle of friends. I stated more than once to Chkalov that for a test pilot to live so intensely without a respite was wrong and dangerous. But to this, he always answered quite simply: "Then what is the purpose of living? To fly? To create something? No, I realize life first of all through my heart and the souls of people. After all, I'm a person."

I looked at his infectious smile, listened to his rumbling laugh, groaned in his bearlike embrace, and thought: "What a person!"

Chkalov was an inveterate fan of motor sports, and, as a very authoritative person, he was often invited to competitions in the capacity of a chief judge.

After a short "breather" from his social duties behind the controls of an experimental fighter, Valery in the autumn of 1938 prepared for a trip to Kiev to organize the All-Union Motorcycle Competition to establish a national champion. He came down on the leaders of the All-Union Physical Education Committee. "I look at you, brothers, and I'm saddened. You are brave, persistent, have a great deal of strength to set records, but you ride on foreign machines—Harleys and Indians. You should follow the example of us fliers. We turned away from foreign aircraft a long time ago and things aren't going too badly for us. In my opinion, it's time to start using our own domestic machines. Think about it very sincerely. The championship should be decided on Soviet machines."

Chkalov sent out dozens of letters to factories having a direct relationship with the production of new brands of motorcycles. Here is one of the letters, sent to a director of an auto-tractor equipment factory: "I request that you manufacture some high-quality spark plugs. The plugs needed are of the 3MG and 4MG types. Among the participants in the competition are champions and record holders in the motorcycling sport. The spark plugs should match the high-speed engines produced domestically."

Many factories answered this appeal of the chief judge of the competition.

Valery arrived early for the competition. Knowing the risks associated with reaching high speeds, Valery Pavlovich checked the entire race circuit himself and conscientiously had every turn and every bridge marked. Finally, the day of competition came. More than two hundred of the best racers from Moscow, Tashkent, Tbilisi, Arkhangelsk, Vladivostok, Novosibirsk, Leningrad, Gorky, Odessa, and Baku were lined up.

Chkalov was wearing the uniform of a brigade commander. Wide-shouldered, smiling, he once again walked around the rows of sportsmen.

"Remember," the chief judge repeated, "if a competitor has an accident, each one of you is obligated to aid him in his misfortune."

Chkalov stood on a podium on the Zhitomir Highway of Kiev. Next to him were the members of the Ukrainian government, distinguished people, sports judges, representatives of factories, and journalists. Chkalov turned to the writer Korneichuk, a deputy to the President of the Ukrainian Supreme Soviet, who was standing to his right: "So many cities, Alexander Evdokimovich! The soul is happy to see these young racers and many Soviet-made motorcycles."

Chkalov's organizational abilities were revealed in the initiation of popular competitions. Many records were set during these races yet they were never marked by a single accident.

The races continued for several days. Chief judge Chkalov characterized the achievements of the races in the newspaper *Pravda* of September 27, 1938, in the following manner:

> The All-Union Motorcycle Competitions in Kiev have ended. It is proper to state that their sporting and technical results were sufficiently high.
>
> New records were set in all categories of distances, in both classes of motorcycles made by Soviet factories and in men's and women's divisions. In a majority of cases, the old All-Union records were broken at the same time by a number of competitors.
>
> It is especially pleasant to note the success of youth. They not only turned out to be stubborn competition for the acknowledged masters, but in many cases emerged as the victors. . . .
>
> The prohibition of foreign-made motorcycles in the runoffs aroused protests for a while. There were quite a few disbelievers who maintained that the absence of foreign machines would diminish the sports accomplishments and interest in these All-Union races. The results of the competitions just completed smashed these "imported" theories. Keen competition, a high level of sport—these are the distinguishing features of recent competitions.

While he was in Kiev, Chkalov naturally spoke many times to students, Young Pioneers, workers, and scientists of the capital of the Ukraine.

Chkalov did not hide his feelings of pride that he was able to arouse in thousands of children's hearts an ardent dream for exploits, a certainty that for each of them a time would come when they would be able to perform heroic deeds.

It was interesting how he could communicate with children. He learned that one boy, demonstrating his bravery, would rakishly grab onto a moving bus. The game ultimately ended in tragedy: the boy's legs were amputated. Valery quickly submitted an article, which read in part:

I read in *Pionerskaya Pravda* the letter of Tolya Perylgin, the boy who suffered this accident. Tolya Perylgin writes about heroism. He and his friends considered themselves to be brave when they jumped onto a moving vehicle and hung on the running boards. "Risk is a noble thing," they surmised. But senseless risk has never been considered and never will be considered heroism. A genuinely courageous person will never take risks senselessly, without any purpose, without necessity.

When Vodopyanov flew to save people of the *Chelyushkin*—this was courage. Was there risk involved? Of course, there was. The aircraft could get lost in a fog, ice up, lose an engine, make a forced landing, or break up on an ice pack. This was risk—brave and noble, but also calculated and substantiated.

That individual risked his life to save the lives of others. He did not do this to amaze the world, but to carry out his responsibilities.

When youths jump from vehicle to vehicle, grabbing onto the handles, they do take quite a risk—but this is not heroism, simply stupidity. If you want to instill in yourself courage, agility, resourcefulness—this is very good. This will prove useful to you when you become grown citizens of the Soviet Union. Our motherland needs courageous people. But courage is not learned on the running board of a vehicle. There are better means of achieving this. Take up sport. Ski, skate, jump, shoot, swim. But playing on vehicle running boards is a way to become a cripple and not a hero. Traffic is very chaotic in Moscow. Because of this, our transportation system suffers. Our cars travel much slower than in other countries. One cannot develop normal speed when there is no practical traffic regulation. Furthermore, this jars the drivers' nerves unnecessarily. I, for example, have stopped driving in Moscow. In flight, no matter how difficult or dangerous, I feel calmer than I do on the streets of Moscow, where people ride the running boards, grab onto buses and trolleys, and run across the street whenever it comes into their heads.

Children in the streets can develop a quality that always goes hand in hand with courage. This is discipline. You have to teach yourself; you have to make yourself walk properly along the streets, to observe the rules of street traffic. This is not very difficult, but it is a very helpful exercise for developing discipline, a necessary attribute of every courageous person. V. Chkalov.

There were test flights, trips to his constituents, public appearances in the news media and from a speaker's podium, endless meetings with friends and acquaintances, and conferences with scientists and writers, children and soldiers, workers and composers, artists and painters. A fast pace and a varied life were normal for Chkalov.

How did Valery win people over? Above all, by his simplicity and strength, which was visible in his whole appearance; in his stocky figure, his powerful hands, his look of an eagle. Each of us upon meeting him would be happier and feel more fully the heartbeat of life.

In Tvardovsky's poem, "The Bogatyr," that which was most characteristic of Chkalov was well noted:

Of all the great heroic names
Which we know through and through,
Somehow in a special way
In their own way,
The people called out this name.

Put simply—
We loved him so much,
And for everyone he was
So much his own,
As if we were all personal friends,
And drank, ate and flew with him. . . .

During the meetings of the 18th Congress of the All-Union Communist Party, Fadeev, a writer, discussing heroism with Vodopyanov, Sholokhov, Tikhonov, and me, said: "Chkalov was the people's pride of our Soviet Land, one which we carry deep in our hearts."

10

The Last Test Flight

It was autumn and Polikarpov's new fighter was not yet fully completed. Chkalov did not take leave, waiting for the I-180 to be prepared for flight.

Valery devoted much attention to the preparation of the female crew of the *Motherland*, which was scheduled to complete a flight to the Far East.

"Train yourselves for flight with one engine," he said to Valentina Grizodubova and Polina Osipenko.[62] "Imagine that one engine has quit and you have to be able to fly on the other one. You must definitely be able to turn on one engine; learn how to cope with it."

Chkalov very actively took part in the work of carefully preparing the *Motherland*, as if he himself was planning to fly in it.

"There is no point in being diplomatic about it," Chkalov instructed Grizodobova's crew when he discovered that instrument installation in the aircraft was delayed. "You have to demand and not be soft!" And here he added: "Don't think that I always swear at people. I love you with my heart and wish you well. But understand, this is not just your own affair but that of our entire people. Once you have agreed that I'm your chief, you must listen to me."

Valery was very glad when the flight of the *Motherland* was successfully completed in September of 1938. He telegraphed the courageous women: "I warmly greet our fliers Valentina Grizodubova, Polina Osipenko, and Marina Raskova, who are returning to Moscow in victory. I wish my glorious friends new successes in the battle for aviation supremacy for our motherland. Brigade Commander V. Chkalov."

By this time, Valery Pavlovich was promoted to his latest military rank—brigade commander.

Meanwhile the dream of flying around the world had flared up to such an extent that the three friends composed a letter to Joseph Stalin:

> We remember your promise to allow us to fly in 1939 beyond the borders of the USSR. There is not much time left until 1939 and therefore we have decided to ask you in concrete terms concerning the following:
>
> 1. To build a plane with a range of 15–20 thousand kilometers, a diesel engine, and a service ceiling of 8–10 thousand meters.
>
> 2. To allow flight preparation as soon as the aircraft is completed, beginning with its testing.
>
> 3. To provide a directive to the People's Commissariat of Defense all the measures connected with the above request (construction of several models of the aircraft and diesel engines and their accelerated testing with our participation).
>
> We sincerely ask the approval of our request.
>
> The crew: Pilot V. Chkalov, pilot G. Baidukov,
> navigator A. Belyakov.

Valery carried this letter in the pocket of his jacket, planning at the first appropriate moment to give it directly to the addressee.

An early autumn snow fell and Chkalov still did not take his leave, spending his days at the plant, where construction of the new fighter was being completed. Sometimes Chkalov took to the air, flying production fighters and "cleansing his soul." For the last few months, his soul had been in a state of nervous expectation. First, the assembly of the I-180 fighter was being delayed, and our volunteer pilots, fighting in Spain against the newest aircraft of fascist Germany, and the entire fighter aviation staff of the Soviet Air Force were anticipating this aircraft; second, because it was entirely unclear how Stalin would react to our request for permission to fly around the world.

Chkalov was clearly depressed and noticeably gloomy. Only in the evenings did his steadfast heart "soften." Left alone with his children, he was transformed into a completely different person. Then the rooms shook from the rumblings of furniture, the bustle, and the laughter, so much so that the neighbors "feared" for their living quarters.

If the children were sleeping, then, after returning from the field, the pilot would drag his wife to the House of Actors or the House of

Writers or he would turn on the record player given as a gift by the government, and listen together with Olga Erazmovna to records of Shalyapin. He especially liked "Dubinushka"—no wonder his great-grandfather and grandfather were barge haulers. Valery said to his wife: "I regret that in Paris we didn't have the chance to visit the great Russian singer."

Sometimes Chkalov would go to the bathhouse straight from the field; he would steam himself heartily and many fans of this form of enjoyment would often have to set themselves down lower than Chkalov, who would zealously beat himself with the birch branches at the very top of the steam room.

It was late autumn of 1938. The snow unexpectedly melted and dark rain clouds once again stretched over the sky. Chkalov finally decided to take his leave, which meant heading along the same old route and visiting his native Chkalovsk. As usual, he invited Belyakov and me to go with him to rest on the Volga and not to hanker for the seaside resorts. He became angry when we advised him to go to Sochi and try the healing waters of Matsesta: "You're always pulling sly ones and finding excuses to get out of it. But I'm going and I'll go alone—the Volga is calling to me very strongly."

On November 17, he was in Gorky at a meeting of the city Stakhanovites. Valery visited his brother Alexie and his sister Sofya. On November 19, he dropped in on his father's old friend, Dr. Postnikov.

On November 21, 1938, Chkalov, together with his childhood friend, Pavel Volkov, the director of a Leningrad factory, stopped by to visit the editorial staff of the newspaper *Gorky Commune*, where Chkalov was always received with genuine hospitality. It was here that photo-correspondent Kapeliush took the last photograph of Chkalov in Gorky. Valery invited everyone to visit him in Vasilevo, but they corrected him—he should have said in Chkalovsk.

■

Natalia Georgievna was overjoyed to the depths of her heart by the arrival of her beloved son.

"How I've waited for you, Volenka! You write so painfully rarely. My only happiness is to look and admire your photographs!"

"Okay, Mama, I was here not long ago, true, for only one day," answered the son, kissing her. "Now I will be your guest for a whole month! You won't get tired of me? Tell me," Chkalov joked.

"You're unhappy, son, I can tell. Has something happened?"

"Autumn, Mama, makes me sad. See, the leaves have fallen from your garden and the Volga has become cold and gloomy."

"Enough of that," his mother softly interrupted. "It's good that you've come because without you the house is unhappy."

"You exaggerate, Mama!" answered Chkalov, smiling. "You always say that to me. Better feed your starving son." With these words Chkalov walked up to his mother, seized her by the arm, and whirled her around the room.

"What are you doing, Volenka, my bones are crumbling and you want to break them off."

Natalia Georgievna rushed about and busied herself around the table and Valery went out onto the terrace. Breathing in the damp and cold air, Chkalov looked at the expanse of the Volga region, which was fogging up in the autumn twilight. He surveyed Chkalovsk from a high point. Valery could not get used to the fact that Vasilevo had been renamed Chkalovsk—he felt guilty of something that had happened during his lifetime.

"Well, okay," he used to say to Belyakov and me, "they renamed the islands of Udd, Lange, and Keos in the Straits of Happiness in the Sea of Okhotsk as the islands of Chkalov, Baidukov, and Belyakov. But why change the ancient name of Vasilevo?"

Chkalov went through the empty garden, recalling that once in childhood he and his gang had picked clean the best apple tree and how Natalia Georgievna, telling her husband what had happened, said: "What a generous son. He gave the very best to his friends."

His father did not touch Valery for such mischief, but said to him: "To be nice to everyone—such a person doesn't exist even in fairy tales. There are unkind, evil, and bad people in the world, whom one must not indulge! Remember this, Valeryanka."

The rain became stronger and Valery Pavlovich returned to the house. The table was already set. Natalia Georgievna said: "I thought that my Volenka had gone to visit friends and comrades."

"No, Mother, I arrived today unnoticed by car by design so that I could sit quietly in the evening and have a chance to talk to you."

"Yes, that's right; tomorrow when they discover that you have arrived, we'll hardly have a chance to see you."

"Don't be offended, Mama! Now I am a deputy—a servant of the people. And you know how a servant must work? You obviously know this."

"It's good to do things for people, Volenka; pleasing to yourself and also a sacred duty." And his mama looked unconsciously at the icon and the lighted candle burning next to it. Valery noticed this glance of his mother and said: "Forgive me, Mother, but fliers don't believe in a deity. We haven't found him behind any clouds. By the way, we haven't met the devil either."[63]

"Maybe, son, you want me to put out the candle?" his mother asked, uneasily.

"But how can I, Mama? I am your guest and you are the hostess and my mother! You carry on as you believe."

Natalia Georgievna put out the candle just the same, and her son, as if noticing nothing, remained silent.

They went to bed early, although they fell asleep only toward morning. Their beds were in the same room and it was easy to carry on a conversation. Only the wild wind disturbed them, first flinging wet snow against the window, then wailing through the chimney of the warmly heated stove.

"Bad weather has begun," his mother said quietly.

"I love storms and foul weather," her son answered. "There's something special about them in our flights, when your heavy aircraft is tossed in the clouds like a snowflake."

"Volenka, is it true what they say, that Stalin himself offered you a good job with a large salary, but that on this job you wouldn't fly?" Natalia Georgievna asked her son with a certain timidity in her voice.

"It's true, Mama! I was offered a position as an administrator with the Party, but I told everyone, as I said last year: 'Flying, flying—that's my contribution to the Party.'"

"Yes, I know you—just like your father. He also crawled into a fire in order to repair a steam boiler on a steamer."

"And I gave a public oath that I would not abandon the controls of an aircraft as long as I am alive."

"Your craft is very dangerous, son. Why produce orphans?"

"Don't worry about me, Mama, although our business is indeed dangerous."

"That's what I'm saying."

"But who is supposed to take the risks, if not I? What am I, some kind of a braggart? I'm a working man and I know my business no worse than a lot of others. And the business of being a test pilot, Mama, believe me, can't be turned over to just anyone."

His mother was quiet for a short while, not knowing how to convince her son; then she asked: "Why did you crash into a forest last year and not land on a road? You even hurt your head."

"But how can you land on a road when a lot of cars are using it with people inside them? Why should innocent people perish?"

Again Natalia Georgievna did not know how to answer her son and only said: "You must always remember your family. Even when you are flying at high altitude or heading for the pole."

"I love Lelik, Lerochka, and Igorka more than anything in the world, and you know this very well."

"I know you love them, but the work of a man often takes everything away from him without any returns," his mother said somewhat vaguely, and added: "But how beautiful it is to fly! I'll never forget how I flew with you over our Mother Volga and above her open spaces."

"Well, and you want to deny your son all this pleasure?"

"Because, son, I also pay attention. Your craft intoxicates a person, and you know that people perish from wine. They become alcoholics, and don't know how to free themselves from this disaster."

"You're right, Mama. But it's impossible to simply abandon flying; only death or some kind of a serious disaster can separate a flier from aerial elements, which an ordinary person is not always able to understand."

His mother was quiet for a long time, worrying about the fate of her youngest.

"But they say, son, that lately you did not conduct yourself properly in front of Stalin?"

"Who's been telling you tales?"

"Olga told Sofia, and she mentioned it to me. There are rumors that you started a fight with him right in the Kremlin," Natalia Georgievna said seriously.

"They talk nonsense, and you believe it," answered her son, beginning to laugh. "What really happened? Well, I was attending a reception with our group in the Kremlin Palace, suddenly Stalin comes up to me and says: 'I want to drink, Valery Pavlovich, to your health.' I answered: 'Thank you, my health is fine. It would be better, Joseph Vissarionovich, if we drank to your health!' Stalin was holding a small glass and smiling. I guessed immediately that in his glass there was mineral water—Borzhon or Narzan, because the sides of his glass were covered with bubbles. I stood up, took Stalin's glass from his hand and placed it aside, and in place of it chose a large goblet and filled it with strong drink. I gave one goblet to Stalin and took the other myself, and said: 'Joseph Vissarionovich, let's drink to our brotherhood!'

"Stalin smiled. Our arms crossed each other. I, of course, knew that Joseph Vissarionovich did not drink vodka and saw very clearly that he only touched his lips to it, wet his mustache, and watched me with curiosity. There was nothing left for me to do but empty my goblet to the bottom, then I put my arm around his neck and embraced him."

"But how could you dare to?" his mother asked in fright.

"There were no bad intentions, but then security became upset."

"That means it won't be long before something bad happens! This is impermissible. Stalin is not Volodka to you, and you, a little drunk, might not have known your own strength."

"Oh, Mama, it's nonsense. I did it from my soul."

Chkalov smiled in the darkness, thinking that in the eyes of a mother, a child is indeed always a child.

The two of them—different, unrelated but precious to each other —talked for a long time.

Natalia Georgievna was right—in the morning many friends and acquaintances came to the house, sufficiently early to find their famous fellow countryman at home.

When Valery came out to the chamber, he saw his godfather Shaposhnikov, his grandfather Ipat, and the fisherman Schipatin, who were dressed up for the occasion, guests from Katunki and Puchezh, and many other well-wishing, smiling people. Without a doubt all his plans were changed. He had wanted to see his old friend, Volodka, then visit an old carter, to ride a troika along the fresh covering of snow with Valdaisky bells, and then to go hunting and top all this activity at the ancient Volga Savna.

But after an enjoyable breakfast with his mother and everyone else who had come to visit, Chkalov set off immediately for the boatyard, where dozens of ships scheduled at the river port were already moored. Walking around the port, several steamers, and a ship repair factory, Valery conversed for some time with sailors, workers, and plant administrators and at lunch time, he returned home, happy and jovial.

"Well, Mama, I had a good look around the boatyard. What wonderful people at the factory and on the steamers."

"All right, Volenka! You love to flatter people. Your father spoke about this more than once."

"Well, it's worse to be spiteful and untrusting."

"This is true, Volenka, but it's bad to oversalt even soup."

"Our people are unspoiled," Valery continued. "In a couple of years I'll put my Igorka on a Volga steamer to learn life, so that in the boiler room he can experience the hard work of the people."

"But is this possible?" The old woman slapped hands together. "The son of a famous pilot—in such a situation?"

"Precisely, Mama, in such a situation, so that he will be tested, forged, and become a real man for his whole life."

After lunch, Chkalov went on foot to the neighboring village of Gumnische to inspect what the team of flax grower Sasha Prozorova was doing. She had invited him as Deputy of the Supreme Soviet, saying: "Do you know how much flax my comrades and I have gathered this summer? If you stretched it out in a single thread, it would go around the whole world."

Valery relaxed in his native area, but his leave turned out to be a brief one—a telegram came from the plant: "Everyone is ready. Your presence is essential."

Chkalov left for Gorky and the next morning was in Moscow.

■

On December 3, Valery appeared at the flight station of his plant, but the I-180 was not to be found at the flight test station. Chief testing engineer Lazarev informed the pilot that things were not going well with the new aircraft at the plant; a number of defects had been discovered. A testing program had not yet been scheduled, although everyone knew that the People's Commissariat and the Chief Administration were pushing the project—the craft had to be flown as soon as possible.

"Don't frighten yourself with these defects. After all, the aircraft is being created, my friend," Chkalov calmed the young engineer.

Chkalov knew the great difficulties linked with the creation of every new aircraft. Its appearance was the result of the efforts and intense labor of many hundreds of people—both designers and builders. In the process of transforming ideas of the designer into a project blueprint and translating the blueprint into separate details and constructing the craft and, finally, assembling the aircraft, many questions arose and necessitated the solving of large and small technical problems. Chkalov knew all this very well.

He also spoke with the flight engineer and then went to see the plant director and the chief engineer. They joyfully greeted Chkalov.

"So, you've arrived?" the designer asked the pilot, as if an apparition stood before him and not Chkalov.

"If I'm called for, I come. What is there to be surprised about?" Valery answered with displeasure, and added: "I know, there are rumors about me going around now: prior to becoming a hero, before the pole, before becoming a Deputy, they said, Chkalov could fly on a stick, like a witch on a broom, but now that he's become a big shot it's different to have him perform difficult things."

"We don't listen to such talk," Polikarpov said seriously, "we know who Chkalov is. Let's get down to business."

After conversations with the chief designer and the plant director, Chkalov understood. Many people were waiting for the I-180 and were taking measures to place it into production as soon as possible.

Concerning the list of defects, these would naturally be eliminated.

A fearless person, and a talented pilot, Chkalov had limitless faith in the designers, chief engineers, and mechanics. He knew very well that in transferring the aircraft from production to the flight test station of the plant, a document would be drawn up signed by the head of the Technical Inspection Department, the head of the flight test station, the chief engineers for production and testing, and the military representative. This document would be made official only when the I-180 was ready for flight. Chkalov trusted everyone who had created and prepared the I-180 for flight.

■

Despite the beginning of winter, there were no solid freezes or snow remaining in the first half of December. This meteorological condition seemingly had no direct relationship to the creation of the I-180. However, some workers attempted to take advantage of the whims of nature. The new aircraft was not equipped with special heat carburization for low-temperature conditions. Some designers and the plant administration considered that a comparatively warm beginning of winter allowed them to hope that the first flight could be carried out without any special devices regulating the temperature of the cylinder heads.

The urge to produce quickly a new fighter that the Red Army was eagerly awaiting obviously made them take such a risk. A new fighter was indeed essential. The international situation was becoming more tense with each passing day. The fascists were openly preparing for a new major war. Hitler used Spain as a bombing range. They tested new types of armament. A new model of fighter, the Messerschmitt, appeared. The ME-109E surpassed our craft in speed and firepower.

On the evening of December 7, the I-180 was transferred from the plant to the field without any documentation concerning this transferral.

From notations in the diary of Lazarev, the chief testing engineer, it is clear that on December 8 and 9 the aircraft was hurriedly prepared for the first flight; the imperfections and defects were eliminated.

On December 11, Valery had agreed that on the next day, Sunday, December 12, he would fly to the gunnery range and would fire the cannons on the VIT experimental craft, which had been earmarked as an aerial antitank weapon. Barsky, the chief mechanic, had left for there to prepare the aircraft and the armament. Apparently, Chkalov did not suspect that toward evening the situation had changed drastically since the Central Administration of Aviation Industry was demanding clarification regarding the introduction of the I-180 into mass production by the New Year.

On the morning of Sunday, December 12, documents were signed concerning the plant transfer of the I-180 to the flight test station and concerning the readiness of the experimental craft for its first flight.

While these documents and assignments were being processed at the plant's flight station, Chkalov was at home. After looking through the morning newspapers, he started to go through the letters from constituents, departments, and individuals who had turned to him with suggestions or requests. He was still seated in his nightdress when he was telephoned from the field. At first he thought that chief engineer Barsky was speaking from the gunnery range, where the VIT plane awaited Valery to continue a program of testing Kurchevsky's cannons in an air-to-ground situation. But Chkalov was being called to Central Field for the first flight of the I-180.

"What's the weather like?" Chkalov asked the engineer and, after receiving a response, said: "Prepare the craft. I'll eat breakfast and be right over."

He went into the dining room, where his friends from Gorky were sitting—his older brother Alexei and the writer V. Kostylev.

Pouring himself some tea, the host sat at the table as if nothing was going on and asked the writer: "Well, when am I going to be able to read your *Kuzma Minin?*"[64] While Chkalov was eating breakfast, a peaceful literary discussion turned into a heated discussion on what kind of czar was Ivan the Terrible, about whom Kostylev was planning to write a novel. The driver appeared at the doorway.

"Today is Sunday, Valery Pavlovich," the writer reminded Chkalov.

"Yes, but you see, the craft is ready. I will fly for a short while. I'll return soon." Turning to the driver, he said: "While I get dressed, have some tea, Filipp Ivanovich, then we're off."

Chkalov went into the bedroom and informed his wife that he was being called in for a flight; he put on his military uniform and soon came out into the corridor, where he saw his guests dressed to leave.

"Where are you going?" Chkalov asked with surprise.

"Take us to Mayakovsky Square. We have some business," Alexei answered his brother.

After dropping his passengers off at Mayakovsky Square, Valery became silent and did not joke as usual with Utolin, his driver, a modest and not very talkative man.

Chkalov did not notice the eternal bustle of the streets in the capital. He looked upwards into the sky, covered with gray clouds. The forecast was that the weather today would be warm for December and good for flying, as the chief testing engineer had told him previously on the telephone.

At the field, the pilot noticed an unusual conglomeration of people by parked aircraft at the flight test station. These people worked not only at the plant but also in the various sections of the People's Commissariat of Defense.

"People always gather around as if in a circus or hippodrome," Chkalov thought unhappily as he headed for the I-180.

From a long-standing habit, the pilot, as he was approaching the aircraft with a smile, greeted the mechanic and the engineers.

"Well, how is it?" asked the test pilot of the chief engineer.

Lazarev said that everything was ready. The document authorizing the first flight was signed; the I-180 aircraft and its M-88 engine had been inspected and modified.

"That means, everything is all right?" the pilot asked in a friendly tone.

"Yes, you can prepare for takeoff," answered Lazarev and immediately added: "Nikolai Nikolaevich is here."

Chkalov headed for the building where the fliers' room was located. Along the way the test pilot met acquaintances and, smiling happily, he greeted each one.

Within fifteen minutes the pilot, dressed in a winter flight suit with a parachute thrown over his shoulder, was walking toward the aircraft, together with the equally broad-shouldered but taller Polikarpov, the creator of the new fighter.

It was evident that the chief designer was nervous.

"A beauty!" the pilot ascertained briefly, looking at the aircraft, clearly addressing the compliment to Polikayov.

"I wish you luck," answered the chief designer, shaking Valery's hand.

The test pilot, after putting on his parachute, slowly walked around the new aircraft, stepped onto the wing, and climbed into the cockpit. The mechanic helped him fasten his harness to the seat more snugly.

"Start the engine," Chkalov said firmly to the mechanic, ignoring all that was superfluous.

Soon the fourteen cylinders of the M-88 engine were rumbling quietly.

The test pilot listened to the engine, which was working at low revs; he attentively looked at the dials for each instrument, carefully noting the functioning of each one. The oil temperature was rising and the pilot moved forward with his hand a lever controlling the engine, which instantly increased its revolutions. The engine exhaust gases and the blades of the propellers cutting through the air totally altered the quiet environment; the air whirled by the propeller roared and rang throughout the field.

The eagle profile of the test pilot was hidden from view for a short time as Valery lowered his large head, covered by a leather helmet, in looking carefully at the instrument dials that were located on the front panel of the pilot's cockpit.

The engine was pushed to full power. It turned the propeller forcefully, throwing behind gusts of air with great force. The aircraft was vibrating and it seemed that the surroundings were trembling from the blast of the air stream.

Chkalov pulled back with his left hand the throttle controlling the power of the engine. The engine was brought down to low revs, sharply expelling exhaust gases from its cylinders.

Chkalov straightened himself up and began to turn the aircraft stick first to the left, then to the right, observing how the ailerons on the wings of the fighter first lifted up, then lowered themselves. Then he turned his head back and, moving the stick away from himself and turning toward himself, he checked the movement of the rudders on the empennage of the I-180. Finally, with positive action of his legs, he moved the rudder pedals and observed that the rudder moved to the left and the right.

The test pilot was pleased; everything seemed to be all right. He smiled, looking at the "toilers" standing by the aircraft, as the pilot loved to call the mechanics. He lifted his gloved left hand, and extended his thumb straight up. Everyone now understood; according to the instruments and the visual check by the pilot, he had not observed anything suspicious and gave the sign that he was ready to taxi away from the tarmac of the plant's flight test station.

The test pilot adjusted his flying goggles more comfortably over his eyes. The brakes were released; the aircraft moved from its position. Everyone—the plant director, the chief designer, the chief engineers, the mechanics, the representatives of the People's Commissariate of Defense—all joyfully waved to the pilot and wished him success.

What happened next?

Putting aside the legends of days long past, this is how I perceived the events that took place for the test pilot and his craft after all the well-wishers were left behind.[65]

The time was 1331, December 12, 1938. Chkalov taxied away from the flight test station.

As an experienced pilot, he had not been satisfied with the taxiing two days prior. Most important, the aircraft had still not been tested on a ground run with a liftoff from the ground, even for half a meter.

The pilot, recalling the responsibility of the chief engineer, understood that Lazarev, apparently from inexperience, had forgotten about such an elementary test as lifting off the ground, even though it was forbidden to release any new craft without a preliminary hop into the air. For this reason Chkalov decided not to rush and attempted from the very first to take steps to submit the aircraft to his will. He first decided to taxi quickly; then to make a high-speed run; then to lift off slightly from the ground and immediately set down; then finally to taxi out to the far corner of the field, near the TsAGI hangar, and from there begin a run and takeoff against the wind along the diagonal of the field. Valery increased the revs of the engine; the I-180 began to gain speed. The pilot lowered the revs of the engine and began to brake sharply. The plane quickly stopped. Again increasing the revs, the fighter began to move forward and Chkalov turned it to the right, then to the left, determining how responsive the aircraft was to the action of the brakes and the rudder; was there any tendency to yaw or uncontrollably lift its tail? Everything went well.

At the same time Chkalov frequently looked forward so as not to accidentally strike some unexpected obstacle. He also looked up into the sky above the field, although he knew that today was Sunday and that after 1 o'clock they did not anticipate the arrival of any aircraft.

Now Chkalov turned the craft to the right, deciding to give the fighter enough speed to lift the tail so that he could get an idea of aileron and rudder effectiveness. Chkalov estimated that if he eased off on the engine revs to a minimum at the main gate transverse of the field, he would succeed in decreasing the speed, lowering the tail and braking the machine long before reaching the corner hangars, the furthest point away.

The turn for the runway was made. The pilot smoothly increased the revs and suddenly a message was received to return immediately to the tarmac. Shortly, the chief engineer and mechanic came running up to him.

With their aid Chkalov turned the I-180 around and taxied toward the flight test station. Valery Pavlovich was disappointed and attempted to guess the reason for such a strange order from headquarters to cease testing. The pilot looked at those accompanying the aircraft and noticed that they were walking calmly, indicating to him that he could taxi faster. Chkalov nodded, which meant: "I understand and it will be carried out," and began to move the throttle with his left hand. But suddenly he felt that the lever started to move freely forward and the engine, instead of increasing power, diminished its revolutions, made a last gasp, and quit, refusing to function any more.

The sudden malfunction of the engine was completely unexpected, since in the confusion and haste of aircraft preparation for flight status he had decided to take the I-180 on its first flight only with a firm understanding that the M-88 engine would work without reproach.

"What kind of nonsense is this?" Chkalov shouted to the mechanic and, turning to the engineer, said: "According to the instruments everything was normal: the oil temperature, cylinder heads, temperature and pressure in the oil and gas lines. . . ."

The engineer and the mechanic ran to the flight test station stand and returned in a truck, in which many aircraft specialists and engine specialists also arrived. They quickly unloaded the stepladders, placing them around the cowling of the fighter. The engine compartment was opened.

Chkalov, gloomy and angry, continued to sit in the aircraft. He noticed everyone who was attempting to determine the reason for such an engine malfunction. It was possible to vouch for each of them as honest individuals and competent specialists.

Chkalov recalled a conversation with Anatoliy Serov, who had just returned from Spain. The "Donkeys" or "Snub Noses," as our fighter pilots loved to call the I-16 craft, in the skies above Republican Spain were in difficulty, carrying on an unequal battle against the newly designed Messerschmitt fighters, provided by Hitler to the pilots of General Franco. For this reason, the I-180 was a much needed item. But now this. . . !

The short December day was on the wane; it was beginning to get dark when Chkalov climbed out of the cockpit, jumped from the wing onto the ground, unbuttoned his parachute and, throwing it off his back, said calmly to the chief engineer: "I won't get anything more done today."

"You go, and we'll get to the bottom of it. I'll report to you," answered Lazarev.

"You'll be digging around in the dark for nothing. Tow the craft into the hangar," the pilot said decisively to the engineer and added: "Look it over carefully!"

Undressing in the pilots' quarters, Chkalov sensed its inexplicable silence. On normal working days one could often hear the jokes, stories, news, and sometimes the songs of the test and military pilots who had arrived to take delivery of aircraft.

His driver was waiting in a dark blue Packard, presented to him by the Soviet government the preceding year after his flight to the United States. Chkalov opened the front door of the car, while close by the the brakes of a car squealed and the chief designer stepped out of the automobile.

"Just a minute," Polikarpov said softly.

"Well, have you found it, Nikolai Nikolaevich?" Chkalov asked calmly.

"Yes, the cable controlling the choke valve of the carburetor came off."

There was a pause. Chkalov asked the chief designer sharply: "And you didn't find anything else?"

"What else could there be?" Polikarpov answered nervously. "What else?" he repeated with bitterness and added: "After all a reworked, reinforced cable snapped quite recently, Valery Pavlovich!"

"Well, if it's only that, then I know that you will get to work on it again and quickly think of a better design."

Polikarpov listened to Chkalov's answer carefully. He liked the confidence and limitless faith of the pilot in the power of human logic, but sensed that something was missing.

"You wanted to say something else?"

"I'm not going to wag my tail, Nikolai Nikolaevich, but I'm scared; is that enough?"

"Of course, everything isn't going as smoothly as we would want. . . ."

"Nikolai Nikolaevich, it's pointless to talk to me as if I were a child. We need an aircraft; our army and our friends need a new fighter. So don't pull a cat's tail when everyone knows what the score is," Chkalov cut in sharply.

Polikarpov was jarred slightly by the sharpness of the test pilot and he became silent. Chkalov sensed this immediately and said: "Don't be angry! I've gotten quite a few bumps, bruises, and scrapes! Most of them were in your aircraft. But remember, I must conduct our work so that everything is done correctly and without loss of time."

"As a pilot, you must have better control and consider. . . ,"
Polikarpov began, but Chkalov cut him off:

"We've talked more than once about this. I repeat, alone, I cannot
test the thousands of details and parts from which you create an
aircraft; there are engineers and mechanics involved in this activity.
An entire army of controllers. I cannot replace them," Chkalov
asserted hotly. "My business, comrade," solemnly continued the
pilot, "is to lift the aircraft into the air and conduct various tests.
This is my task! And no one is going to do this task for me, my
friend."

Polikarpov was silent. Valery was familiar with this decisive,
strong-willed, and talented engineer, who did not tolerate criticism.
The pilot, extending his hand to the designer, said: "I live by trusting in people, you, our entire collective. I am ready to fly in the I-180
at any moment. Just call me. But in the meantime, I'll fly the VIT;
we have been dragging out test-firing the cannons." After being
silent for a second, he added: "You and I are soulmates: we promise
much and then rush around like people on fire, sweating our guts
out."

"And so?" Polikarpov could not restrain himself.

"I advise you, as one of the most wise men said, 'to make haste
slowly.'"

Polikarpov understood that he would not hear anything else from
Chkalov. He extended his hand to him and responded from his heart:
"I understand, thank you for your trust, Valery Pavlovich."

Chkalov sat next to Utolin. The driver headed for the southwest
gates and soon the Packard was moving along the streets of Moscow
with a green light. Traffic controllers knew that Valery Pavlovich
was in a hurry.

The Packard owner was indeed hurrying, hurrying toward Kursky
Station, where on Sadovaya Street stood house number 14/16 and in
an apartment on the fifth floor lived his wife and children.

That is my interpretation of those several dozen minutes in the
life of Chkalov that occurred after 1330 on December 12, 1938.

I had no idea that Valery was planning to make a first takeoff in
the I-180 on Sunday. It was a surprise to me when he appeared in his
military uniform at my apartment. Usually, he crossed over to us
from the opposite door of our common stairwell in his robe, and I, at
first, thought that my friend was going off somewhere to make a
speech and wanted me to come with him. I had prepared my

refusal, but I noticed the stern wrinkles between his winged eyebrows smooth out, and Chkalov squatted down on his haunches and waved to my four-year old daughter, who was running toward him as fast as she could.

"It's amazing how children sense that you're a person and not a devil with horns," I said to Chkalov, trying to tear my daughter loose from his embraces. "You're suffocating her, damn you."

But Chkalov did not pay any attention to my protests, went off with the little girl first to the kitchen to greet the hostess, then to my office, where he saw Dmitri Lvovich Tarasov, a script writer.

"Why didn't you tell me?" Chkalov hooted, looking at me reproachfully.

I introduced Valery to my guest, explaining: "We're attempting to write a screenplay together."

"Well, Baidukov, I see that you've fallen completely in love with scribbling."

"What can you do," I answered, "the situation calls for it."

"Of course, once a member of the Union," my friend teased, playing with the child.

"And where are you going?"

"I came from the field. We have big problems. . . ."

"What the devil are you doing—you're working on a day of rest?"

"Time is driving me, Baidukov, time!" And becoming stern once again and putting the child on the floor, Chkalov added: "I was planning to take off and while taxiing the engine controls malfunctioned. . . ."

"Why are you manufacturing experimental aircraft out of junk?"

Chkalov glanced at my guest, stood up, and said calmly: "You don't understand anything," and moving his palm across his throat, he added: "That's how badly the I-16 needs to be replaced by a new fighter. That's why we are rushing it."

After opening the outside door, he said to me quietly: "Drop by, we have to talk."

When I walked into Valery's large office, he was seated at the table on which lay a map of the two hemispheres of the world.

"Take a look, Egor! Here is Australia, here's the South Pole, and this is the southern tip of South America."

"I've seen it a hundred times," I answered angrily, making Valery realize that he should not beat around the bush, but come directly to the point.

"But take a look, dammit," Chkalov insisted good-naturedly.

"Have you forgotten about our letter concerning the new aircraft?"

"The new craft will take care of itself. That's a long story. We have to consider the ANT-25 in our calculations."

"We have done that," I answered.

"Now we need exact calculations. It seems to me that Joseph Stalin will agree," Chkalov said with enthusiasm, tearing himself away from the map.

"Well, Belyakov will show up and we'll begin the calculations."

"Where is he?"

"He should arrive tomorrow."

"I would like to have Sasha and you together with our wives to travel with me to the Volga for the New Year's."

"Can't be done," I answered. "I need a week of free time for such a trip and I've already used up all my leave. Better come visit us for the holiday. Evegenya Sergeevna has sort of convinced Olga Erazmovna."

"No! Lelik and the children are coming with me to Vasilevo. I promised my mother. . . ," and with sadness he added: "I'm never going to be able to drag you devils to my homeland."

"When are you leaving?"

"I'll make the first flight in the I-180 and then I'll go home for a while."

■

On the morning of December 15, it seemed to Chkalov that he had overslept. The evening before he had again been called to Central Field. He got up and quietly opened the door into the children's room. Igor was still sleeping. "When will he get ready for school? What time is it?" Chkalov asked himself, going to the window. He noticed the snow, which had apparently fallen during the night, lit up by the street lights.

Moving on to the dining room, Valery observed through the window an occasional pedestrian rushing along the empty alley. Swirls of steam surrounded the heads of pedestrians; automobiles left whole clouds of quickly evaporating steam behind them. This meant that the freezing weather had become colder.

Valery did a few limbering-up exercises, took a shower, and, putting on his robe, quietly went to his office. A new, large pile of letters and telegrams from the most varied corners of the country lay on the desk.

"The secretary to his excellency the Deputy...," smiled Chkalov and thought about his wife, who had diligently taken care of her husband's correspondence with his constituents and helped him organize it.

He mumbled to himself the words, "his excellency," and Valery for some reason recalled how he had visited Alexi Tolstoy's dacha, where the writer had in his employ, according to an established tradition, a person who was not quite a porter, not quite a butler; he was a strong, tall, grey-mustached old man in a frock coat with sewn-in gold lace. Opening the hall door, this guardian of domestic order would announce loudly: "His Excellency the Deputy to the Supreme Soviet, Count Alexi Nikolaevich Tolstoy, requests you to enter."

This memory aroused in his soul many vivid and emotional things from his meetings with the prominent and original writer who had become his friend.

Busying himself with the mail, Chkalov did not notice that the entire household was bustling above. Olga Erazmovna was tenderly making a fuss, getting the children ready. Soon Igor ran into the office and hung on to his father's neck. After putting his son on his lap, Chkalov pressed him close to himself, kissed his cheek, and continued to read the letters.

"You see, little Igor, how much work there is."

"What are they writing, Papa?"

"One lady requests to have a House of Pioneers built."

"It's already built. We were there together."

"That's here in Moscow. But they're writing so that one may be built in a Ukrainian village, son. Here a boy writes: he requests that I help him get into flying school."

"I want to be a pilot, too." Igor said.

"You study. Become a man. Then you can become a pilot."

"A man, and then a pilot?" his son asked with surprise, attentively looking at his father's eyes, trying to understand whether his papa was joking or speaking seriously.

"Yes, son. That's the way it is. If you don't become a real man, better not enroll in flight school."

Olga Erazmovna came in with Lerochka and invited everyone to the table. Chkalov, taking his daughter by the hand, covered her with his robe and together they sat for breakfast.

Looking at the clock, Valery said to his son: "It's time for school."

In the entranceway, Valery, after kissing Igor, said his usual parting words to him: "Take care and be good."

"So as to become a man," his son smiled and looked at his father with love.

"No, Igor, not simply a man, but a real man! Then you can become whatever you want."

Igor left for school. Olga Erazmovna was preparing to go for a walk with her daughter.

"Lelik! Careful, it's freezing today. Don't let Lerochka catch cold and don't catch cold yourself."

It became unusually quiet in Chkalov's large, spacious apartment. Valery went up to the record player and put on a disk. Beethoven. Chkalov was alone with the symphony, which he had first heard in Leningrad in 1930. "Is it really only eight years that I have been enjoying the beauty of Beethoven's music? Well, I missed much in life," thought Chkalov and mentally thanked Ivan Semenovich Kozlovsky for his friendly lesson—you are never too young to appreciate the beauty of the arts.

The record player went on . . . Tchaikovsky, Wagner, Beethoven again, Glinka. . . .

Valery leafed through a photo album and looked at the faces of his friends for some time. "In reality, I've accomplished little but lived a lot. . . ." Chkalov again thought of his obligation to his people. His wife, coming home from her walk with her daughter, found him looking through the photographs. Lerochka's cheeks looked like ripe apples.

Valery turned off the record player and instantaneously shifted himself to another joyful world. Taking off his daughter's overcoat, he again covered her with his robe—only her fair-colored head looked out, like a fledgling looking out of a nest with shiny eyes.

"Utolin is waiting at the entrance," Olga Erazmovna said to her husband.

"Why didn't he come up?"

"He's afraid to freeze the car."

"To freeze it?"

"It's very cold outside."

Chkalov asked for some tea, saying: "Lelik, did I give you the lemons?"

"What lemons?"

"Oh, goodness! I bought a couple of lemons in the buffet of the Hotel Moscow with Ivan Rakhillo and forgot about them. They are in the pocket of my overcoat. Lemons are very good for you now; I read that somewhere recently. Oh, yes, Mendelevich will call; tell him that I'll be there no later than 4 P.M."

"It seems to me that it will be a fine sculpture."

"I don't like it when they make a god out of you!"

"He told me yesterday that only one session remains . . . and what about the school children?"

"Tell them that I'm leaving tomorrow and returning to Moscow in February of next year. But this evening, since I've promised, I'll be there without fail, tell them not to worry."

Several minutes later, lifting Lerochka in his arms and kissing her cheeks and nose, Valery went out into the corridor, put on his overcoat and service cap, and shouted "So long!" and slammed the door.

The dark blue Packard, driven by the experienced Fillipp Ivanovich, sped Chkalov along the wide circular highway of the capital. Many trucks and passenger cars moved along through the steam. People walked briskly along the sidewalks.

Valery loved the bustle of the capital city, considering that it objectively reflected the energy and businesslike character of the Soviet people.

He glanced with a smile at the entrances to the newly constructed underground subway stations, which were similar to fantastically resplendent halls of ancient palaces and theatres.

The neon letters "M" flickered dimly through the frozen haze of the steam, which was rising from the ground like smoke from a fire.

At Mayakovsky Square, the traffic officer quickly noticed the Packard and immediately gave it the priority to turn right. Chkalov waved a greeting to the officer wrapped up in his sheepskin coat.

Then Begovaya Street. Chkalov recalled Sasha Anisimov, with whom he often attended the hippodrome. What enthusiastic fans they were of races and sprints!

Chkalov suddenly turned to his driver with the question: "Well, have you made up your mind? Come with us on leave to Vasilevo. We'll go hunting. I'll take you to our Nizhny Novgorod sauna. We'll find a bride for you."

But the conversation was cut off because Valery noticed that a train crossing was closed with a long line of cars in front of it.

"This will take a long time! And I don't have much," Chkalov said calmly "I'm getting out and you, Filipp Ivanovich, drive to the garage. Maybe in two hours or so, we'll visit the sculptor."

Valery got out of the Packard. Straightening his hat on his head and taking the bottom of his coat in his left hand, he hunched up and clambered between the cars of the train.

Soon, the test pilot was greeting the security officer and, passing through the entrance, he appeared near the hangars. At the parking area of the flight test station, he noticed the I-180. The red color of it burned like a torch against the background of grainy, frozen snow that covered the hardened surface of the field in patches.

Rubbing his ears, Valery observed with surprise as the plant director himself rushed around the aircraft, shouting at dozens of people who were near the I-180. Valery shook his head and decided to don his flight suit quickly to halt the "witches' sabbath."

In the pilot's quarters, Chkalov saw Vladimir Konstantinovich Kokkinkaki and Yulian Ivanovich Piontkovsky. They were talking with the engineers and preparing for their scheduled tests.

"Greetings!" Valery said to his comrades loudly, shaking their hands. "Why are you missing this 'play'? The director himself is running around my fighter, out of which steam is just pouring and swirling."

"But what does he know about preparing an aircraft for takeoff?" Piontovsky answered, smiling.

"It makes you want to cry," Chkalov said gloomily.

"Yes, this is another matter," Kokkinaki said seriously and resumed his discussion with his engineer.

"Are you scheduled to fly?" Chkalov asked Vladimir Konstantinovich.

"Yes! I'll take off in a TsKB for a few hours."

"Do you really want to squeeze the juices out of it?" Chkalov continued to ask Vladimir Kokkinaki.

"Valery, we are thinking of traveling from Moscow to New York by the shortest route and you need additional fuel to make the trip."

"A familiar matter," Chkalov said good-naturedly in his Volga accent. "You should have a spare supply of fuel. And don't skimp on the oxygen like we did. Follow Gromov's example and it should be fairly easy."

"We'll take your experience into consideration, of course."

"Who are you going with? Alone or with someone else?"

"I think with Mishka Gordienko."

"The navigator from the Air Force Research Institute?"

"The same one," Kokkinaki answered in a deep, good-natured bass.

In the meantime Piontovsky had left the building for a few minutes and returned shortly.

"Polikarpov is looking for you. Damn them all, Valery! I don't like this leapfrog play!"

"Yulian Ivanovich!" Chkalov blurted out after standing up. "You yourself know that our I-16 is obsolete. Talk with the guys who have been in Spain. Willy Messerschmitt. His 109 will be a tough nut to crack! And can you guarantee me that after swallowing Austria and chewing the Czechs together with the Slovaks, tomorrow Hitler likewise won't put his fork on that fine Polish grandee Pilsudski, who besides conceit has nothing?[66] You have the fascist on our borders. Then. . . ."

"But I-180 isn't the one that is important," Piontovsky somehow unexpectedly and not very clearly began, then grew silent.

"I don't follow you," said Chkalov.

"Alexander Sergeevich [Yakovlev] began designing a fighter. . . ."

"Yulian! You know that from design to production takes quite a while. God grant, as the common folk say, that everything goes well with you and your talented Sanka Yakovlev! But it's dangerous to lose time. . . ."

"Valka's right!" Kokkinaki supported Chkalov.

Meanwhile, the chief testing engineer came into the room.

"We have completed the preparation of the aircraft and approval of the documents. I would like you to look at the schedule and the papers.

"Sit down. Let me put on my pants and boots. . . ." Chkalov answered calmly.

Chkalov as an infinitely courageous person with a fine, trusting soul, certain of his own mastery in flying, was calm; nevertheless he observed the behavior of this young engineer. He noticed that Lazarev's fingers were shaking unusually and his eyelids were slightly twitching.

"While I get dressed, you, my friend, play 'patience,' bring out the cards!" he tried to calm the chief engineer.

In the meantime, Kokkinaki completed the preparation for his assignment. Taking his oxygen mask, parachute, and map case, he headed for the exit. By the door he stopped and said: "I wish you luck, Valery!"

Soon afterwards, Piontkovsky left and also wished Valery luck. He said that he would come out to watch his flight.

Valery put on his leather pants with special goose down and praised the craftsmen who had made such a comfortably warm, light flight suit: "This is what the golden touch means! Last year, I flew for three days in these—didn't bother me at all."

The engineer, apparently very nervous, did not understand what the pilot was saying and said irrelevantly: "Now, just a minute, I'll put everything out. . . ."

Chkalov stared intently at the engineer and noted: "You're strange today! I said that for last year's flight, they made really fine suits for us and you say 'I'll lay everything out. . . .' Haven't you slept enough?"

"All these days and nights I haven't felt like sleeping."

"You're a weakling!" said Chkalov, smiling. "Take a look at the work of the chief engineer of the ANT-25, Evgeni Karlovich Stoman! Here's a holder of the St. George's Cross, the Order of the Red Banner, a former pilot in the Civil War, a man getting along in years: he prepared our craft for a long-distance flight, and he usually worked for days at a time without closing his eyes.

"When he accidentally hit his leg against something and fell to the floor of the aircraft, he fell asleep so soundly that they carried him off in a stretcher to his bed. . . ."

Going up to the table on which Lazarev had spread his papers, Chkalov whistled: "Now! There's enough here to last to New Year's."

The engineer looked with confusion at the pilot.

"First tell me how you eliminated the defect in controlling the engine."

The engineer located a document and gave the test pilot the data from December 14, in which were confirmed what type of adjustments to the engine were made and other pertinent information.

In conclusion, it was demonstrated that on December 14, a testing of controls with sharp bursts from low revs to high was repeated twenty times.

Everything was working normally.

Chkalov, putting the paper on the table, glanced at the chief. "That means twenty times? And everything is fine? "

"Yes, the controls worked normally."

"Normally?" the pilot said.

"Well!" Lazarev affirmed.

"Let's say, that it was well," Chkalov said vaguely. "Now let's look at the specs concerning the readiness of the aircraft for takeoff."

The pilot read the specs, made up on December 14 by a deputy to the chief designer, the chief engineer of the Special Designer's Bureau, the chief production engineer, the head of the Technical Inspection Department of the plant, and a series of other specialists. They confirmed that the defects appearing in the defects list from December 11 would not be an obstacle to the first flight. They stated that the aircraft was ready for its first flight without retracting the landing gear, with a limited load and speed. The list of defects was added to the specifications.

There are instances when a test pilot is obligated to fly with lowered landing gear. Such a condition is completely acceptable, but then a provision must be made regarding the necessity of retracting the landing gear in an emergency if an accident is imminent.

Chkalov was advised to fly with his landing gear lowered.

Yes, dear Valery, you, as an intelligent person and an experienced pilot, should have pounded your fists as your comrades had advised you! But you were true to your responsibilities, you were courageous without any reservations and a sincere patriot. You trusted people and now you were going to carry out this all-important first flight.

Chkalov did not know that by request of the plant director, the head of the flight test station was writing a report in his name in which it was reported that the program of ground testing of the aircraft had, in most cases, not been carried out.

Many questions were asked: should Chkalov, after observing the preparations for the first flight, have agreed to fly? One has to know Chkalov, his rare punctiliousness, honesty, and devotion to duty and discipline in order to understand: Chkalov could not refuse to carry out this assignment. He was a hero, a deputy, a world-famous pilot. He was obligated to fly. There were documents confirming the readiness of the aircraft. In addition, there was an air-worthiness certificate signed by appropriate authorities.

Chkalov, ceasing to look out of the window, cast out all doubts, read the schedule for the flight once more, and signed his name with a red pencil, which meant that he had familiarized himself with the flight procedure.

With this the formalities were completed.

"Gather up the rest of the bureaucracy," Valery said good-naturedly and got up from the table. After putting on his helmet with the goggles, Chkalov pulled out his parachute from a special bag.

"Well, shall we go?" the pilot joked in a deep voice, turning to the engineer.

They left the room. Polikarpov met them in the corridor.

"I had decided to visit you," the chief designer said, greeting him.

Outside, they were enveloped by the cold. Lazarev, understanding that he was a "third man," said: "I'm going ahead to the aircraft."

"Go ahead," Polikarpov answered dryly.

It was noticeable that, despite a biting cold, the lightly dressed designer talked for a relatively long time with Chkalov and gesticulated expressively. Probably, Polikarpov was explaining to the test pilot his aircraft assignment, reminding him of the estimated flight schedule of the I-180.

In those days, every plant and flight station had its own, often unwritten, rules for ground and flight testing based on the experience of the designers in concert with the flight and technical staff. There was no single, standardized flight testing procedure in the aviation industry.

As a rule, the most crucial schedule for the first flight was signed by the chief designer or his deputy or the head of the flight station or his deputy. For Polikarpov, this document was simply signed by the chief testing engineer. In doing so, he referred to the oral command of the chief designer, who had talked with the pilot before the flight.

Chkalov concluded his discussion with the designer. Polikarpov shook Chkalov's hand for some time. Chkalov walked away from Polikarpov and looked at the cloudless, freezing day. The bluish sky beckoned and the bitter wind froze not only the face but also the metal of the small, red-winged aircraft. The pilot began to concentrate on his responsibilities and the forthcoming test flight.

Chkalov walked around the aircraft. He liked its precise and predatory form and the neat, compact components.

Chkalov put on his parachute and, giving a command to mechanic Kurakin, who was seated in the pilot's cockpit, walked to one side. The engine started easily and soon wound up to high revs. Chkalov listened attentively to the roar of the powerful engine. There was nothing unusual or disconsonant to be found in the music of the metal. He liked the way the engine was functioning and was now waiting impatiently for the mechanic to ease off on the revs and give the ready sign.

Polikarpov went up to Chkalov one more time. Chkalov was shouting something to Polikarpov when the engine was reduced to low revs. They both smiled. Finally, the mechanic climbed out of the cockpit and reported to Polikarpov and Chkalov on the condition of the aircraft.

"The weather is so cold that the engine will cool very quickly," the mechanic noted, helping the pilot settle himself more comfortably in the cockpit.

Chkalov closed the canopy tightly and started to check out the engine. He attentively looked at the instruments and diligently felt all the levers and knobs. Chkalov was calm. The moments of nervous excitement before a first flight had already passed. How would the aircraft behave on takeoff? Would it flip hopelessly on its wing; would the pilot and the craft perish? Would some component start vibrating, as a result of which the craft would fly apart in pieces? Would the engine let him down?

Thousands of small reasons, often difficult to detect, could place the pilot in a hopeless and disastrous situation. But Chkalov was calm; many designs had gone through his hands and he had a good eye that could distinguish a poor craft from a good one. Today, he was convinced that the aircraft would not fail him.

The pilot concentrated his attention on the instruments that controlled the engine. If only the engine did not fail him, everything would work well.

The crowd of designers, engineers, mechanics, and workers who had built the aircraft, which the legendary Chkalov must now lift into the air, stood in trembling excitement.

Chkalov released the brake and the beautiful, short-winged, red bird was swiftly carried along the field powdered with snow. The pilot quickly cut back on the revs of the engine, and the pull of the propeller decreased; a sharp braking followed and the plane stopped immediately. Chkalov was testing the action of the rudders on the ground. "Everything is all right," the test pilot concluded and taxied to the starting point.

The starter waved a green flag. Valery readied the aircraft for takeoff. The frequent bumps of the wheels on the ground, which had been numbed by the cold, were transmitted to the entire craft. The strong hand of the Volga warrior firmly controlled the aircraft. The plane lifted off. The pilot carefully moved back the stick, gaining altitude. The I-180 was flying obediently above the ground. Chkalov smiled—the aircraft was all right. The test pilot smoothly pulled the stick toward himself and the red-winged bird flew upward in an instant.

Reaching five hundred meters, the pilot slowly and almost tenderly rocked the craft from wing to wing—this meant that the ailerons, which control the banking of the plane, functioned normally.

Valery decided to make a first turn. This was not one of those dashing turns that we were accustomed to observe when we knew that Chkalov was aloft. No, this was a shallow bank and slow movement along a smooth curve. After all, Chkalov the test pilot, was now piloting the aircraft, not Chkalov the virtuoso in a proven aircraft.

Wait a few days and you would see how Chkalov would fly this craft up from the ground in a dizzying Immelmann that would make a spectator's heart stop. Everything in its own time, Chkalov the test pilot reasoned, as he completed his first careful 90° turn to the left.

Everything that occurred subsequently can only be imagined, knowing Chkalov's character and the conditions of his death.

"I have to remember: rudder controls are stiff," thought the test pilot.

He observed on the left a cluster of radio transmitter antennas—he had wandered far from the field. He made the second turn more forcefully. The fighter turned 90° again and headed quietly past the Fili airfield, toward the hangars of the TsAGI. Hundreds of people were awaiting the return of Chkalov.

Those left on the ground looked up into the frozen sky and heard the even rumble of I-180, which was making a circle along the perimeter of the Central Field.

Vladimir Kokkinaki, having taken off in the TsKB, had completed his flight schedule when he saw the red-winged fighter approach him closely and rock its wings. Kokkinaki saw how Valery had lifted his gloved left hand with his thumb pointed up.

After this meeting aloft Valery Pavlovich turned the I-180 for the third time in a 90° turn and took a course similar to that on his takeoff. Carefully watching the air speed indicator, the pilot was cheerful: "This will be a good fighter." He felt that the aircraft was holding great reserves inside itself. "Apparently, we have attained the speed that we dreamed about."

But what's this? The oil temperature and the cylinder head temperature were falling for some reason. Chkalov quickly turned left, closer to the field. Something was wrong with the engine and the pilot started a careful descent.

The engine coughed out a black cloud of preignited fuel and shook several times so that the vibration was felt the entire length of the fighter. "It's quitting, dammit." The pilot's concern increased and he turned closer to the Central Field.

The engine was functioning in spurts and altitude was quickly being lost. Chkalov, in moments of fatal danger, was always composed. He had come out on a landing pattern. He had slipped to the right of a refrigerator plant. In front of him were barracks. "I'll have to make it over the living quarters or else I won't make it to the perimeter of the field." Chkalov moved the throttle controls forward with his left hand. A deafening sound rang out in the engine, after which it did not increase the revolutions at all. The aircraft descended sharply. "That means the engine has quit or the controls have malfunctioned. There's no hope for it." The pilot evaluated the situation.

"Oh, hell. Will I really not make it? Have I really fallen into a trap?" At this time the aircraft was gliding steeply toward a low-set house, next to which flashed the flowery overcoat of a child. "Children. . . ." And Chkalov sharply banked the aircraft to turn away from the structures. The aircraft was in a steep, left turn, similar to those provocative combat turns that the pilot had been making for sixteen consecutive years. The craft obediently turned away from the house and at the same time . . . from the field, which was visible right next to it.

On the left, Chkalov noticed a small strip, covered with ravines, but free of structures. "That's the place, no people there and I won't kill anyone." The pilot, using all his skills, intently led the craft, squeezing every centimeter of height. But the altitude decreased mercilessly with each second. There were only four hundred meters remaining. Up ahead, he noticed stumps and some sort of a barn blocking the path to the space that he wanted to reach. "No good," he thought and perhaps here his stalwart heart became dejected for the first time.

But he was alive and fighting to save the aircraft, turning it away from striking the barn. The wings were even with the ground.

The plane was approaching the ground at excessive speed. Many structures were already higher than the line of flight. It was necessary to avoid direct collision. Chkalov mobilized all his mastery and presence of mind.

There were only a few meters left to the ground when Valery in the last seconds of flight again had to turn away from some squat barracks, which had unexpectedly loomed before him. Behind them were high poles rising from the ground.

But the test pilot did not lose his self-control and, concentrating all his willpower, continued the attempt to save the aircraft and himself. With his left hand, he pulled against the lock handle of the canopy; it opened immediately. The whirlwind of fresh air poured over the face of a man of a stern profession who was carrying out his last battle with death.

He gulped the air in spurts and heard how the red wings of his plane and the blades of the nonfunctioning propeller whistled sharply against the oncoming flow.

Suddenly, his entire front view was filled with the roof of a large barrack building. If this were a barn, he could have smashed into its weak rafters, which would soften and lessen the blow. . . . But this was a barracks; smoke was coming out of its chimney; people were living there. Without hesitation, the pilot banked the plane instantly in a final turn, missed the building, and hit a pole straight on.

The impact with the pole was so great that the seat and the electrical accessories connected to it were ripped off their moorings and thrown as if from a catapult along with the pilot who was fastened to them.

The pilot lost consciousness from the tremendous impact and immediately struck his head against the butt end of a stack of one-inch metallic fixture rods. With this, the final, tragic flight of the fearless Volga warrior ended.

The inhabitants of the barracks, those barracks that could have still possibly saved Chkalov, rushed to the destroyed craft and immediately noticed the blood flowing from the pilot. It seemed to those that had rushed here that the pilot was still alive and they took quick measures to get him as quickly as possible to the Botkin Hospital.

■

On December 16, 1938, all the newspapers and radio stations in the country reported:

Government Announcement.

The government of the USSR announces with deep sorrow and regret the death of the great pilot of our time, Hero of the Soviet Union, comrade Valery Pavlovich Chkalov, while testing a new fighter on December 15 of this year.

The condolences of the Soviet People's Commissariat of the USSR and the Central Committee of the All-Union Communist Party.

The Central Committee expresses to the family of comrade Valery Pavlovich Chkalov its condolences in connection with the death of the Hero of the Soviet Union, comrade Chkalov.

On the same day, the government of the USSR decided to bury Valery Pavlovich Chkalov in the Kremlin Wall on Red Square and also to create a government burial commission, including friends of the pilot—Gromov, Baidukov, and Belyakov.

An obituary, "Valery Pavlovich Chkalov," signed by sixty-eight people, headed by the signature of K. E. Vorshilov, was published on the first column, front page of *Pravda* next to a lead article entitled, "The Great Pilot of Our Time." Here, an objective evaluation was given of the life and achievements of the son of a worker, a son of a victorious people, ward of the Red Army and the Party:

The death of the great pilot of our time, whose name has become synonymous with heroism and courage, Valery Chkalov, was the bravest of the brave. Among Soviet pilots, he was greatly respected as an incomparable master of his work. Among the entire Soviet people, he was universally known and loved as a people's hero. . . . The great Russian scientist and poet Mikhail Lomonosov once wrote:

The Russian Columbus, scorning sad fate,
Will open a path between the ices to the East
And our nation will reach America

Valery Chkalov was the first to realize Lomonosov's dream.

The pioneers of trans-Arctic flight Chkalov, Baidukov, and Belyakov amazed an entire world with their heroism and courage, flying above the icy roof of the world and in 63 hours 25 minutes covering a distance of more than 10,000 kilometers. . . .

Chkalov announced to his constituents,

"I pledge to concentrate all my energies so as not to besmirch the exalted title of Deputy to the Supreme Soviet of the USSR: I will never be crafty, never turn away from the path of Lenin, never forget my

dependence on the people, on my constituents . . . and I will show all
my mastery as a military fighter pilot if the fascist warmongers dare to
attack our beloved motherland.

"I vow that our enemies will be convinced that there are more
Chkalovs, Gromovs, Baidukovs, and Yumashevs in the Soviet Union
than they could ever imagine. . . ."

Chkalov unfailingly kept his solemn oath as People's Deputy until
the very end of his life. . . .

The unwavering strengthening of aviation power in the Soviet
Union—this is the best monument to the great pilot of our time,
Valery Pavlovich Chkalov.

The Soviet people, saddened by such a cruel loss, have lowered their
military banners before remains of their hero. Valery Chkalov is gone,
but his memory will live forever. The glory of his exploits will never
be tarnished: Never will the flame of his legendary name be extinguished.

The coffin with Chkalov's body was placed in the Hall of Col-
umns. Despite the freezing weather, hundreds of thousands of Soviet
people waited in line to say farewell to their favorite hero. For two
and a half days—December 16, 17, and 18—more than a million
people passed by his bier.

Early on the morning of December 18, the body of Valery Chkalov
was cremated. During the afternoon, a state funeral took place on
Red Square.

Tens of thousands of people with funeral portraits of their hero
and lowered banners with black bands filled all of Red Square.

At the end of the meeting, leaders of the party and the government came down from the podium of Lenin Mausoleum and carried
the urn to the Kremlin Wall.

While artillery salutes were fired, the urn with the remains of the
great flier was walled in a niche in the Kremlin Wall on which there
was the inscription in gold: "Valery Pavlovich Chkalov. 2/02/1904–
12/15/1938."

As stern as Joseph Stalin was, he did not consider it possible to
remove Polikarpov from his work—he was given a task: to produce a
high-speed fighter in honor of Chkalov—the type of which Valery
Pavlovich had dreamed. A decision to build three new experimental
models of the I-180 immediately followed.

However, time showed how inseparably the designer Polikarpov
and the test pilot Chkalov were linked together. The tragic end of
the pilot turned into a tragedy for the designer. In the words of the

designer A. S. Yakovlev, Polikarpov was, for many years, the only indisputable authority in the area of fighter craft: a man of indomitable will, great knowledge, and organization abilities, a uniquely talented designer always attempting to express something new. He created world-famous fighters. At the end of the 1920s and the beginning of the 1930s, it is possible to say that he was the only designer of Soviet fighter craft. His I-15 and I-16 planes stood the test of time. For many years, they were part of the armament of the Soviet Air Force. Soviet fliers in Polikarpov's fighters defeated enemies in the skies of Spain and Mongolia and destroyed the fascist aggressors on the fronts during World War II. His famous PO-2 (U-2) lived an even longer life. Polikarpov trained many wonderful designers who in the future became the heads of the new design bureaus.

As the meritorious test pilot, Hero of the Soviet Union P. M. Stefanovsky, who tested Polikarpov's machines, recalls:

> Polikarpov was always the first to open a new road, receiving at times the very palpable blows of fate. Although many of his designs were unsuccessful because of mistakes in planning or a poor choice of engines or armaments—as a whole the creative work of N. N. Polikarpov was of great benefit to Soviet aviation. All his craft were light, maneuverable, fast, with powerful weapons and originality of design. True, in attempting to design light aircraft, he could not always guarantee their reliability But other designers, although to a lesser extent, at times were guilty of the same sin.

The majority of aircraft that brought glory to Polikarpov were first flown by Chkalov.

Each new craft hides within itself uncertainties; no engineer or designer can foretell exactly how his aircraft will act aloft. Therefore, the first flight in any new craft is accompanied by a risk. This uncertainty was greater in Polikarpov's aircraft and that meant that there was a greater risk in testing them.

To think of the design as a whole, not being held back by details, to complete everything based on the recommendations of the test pilot, only after the first flights—these were the peculiarities of Polikarpov, the designer. For Polikarpov's aircraft, it was precisely Chkalov who was needed, and only Chkalov with his sensitivity, his ability to understand the potential of the machine, and his unusual flying talent. There were many excellent fliers, but there was only one Chkalov. The creative life of designer Polikarpov without test pilot Chkalov was changed drastically.

These are the facts. The best pilot in the Air Force Research Institute, Stepan Pavlovich Suprun, began to test the first new I-180. He valued this machine highly and the Air Force ordered a series of one hundred fighters. But in one of the final flights, Suprun flipped the plane while landing and this made the purchasers suspicious.

A remarkable fighter pilot of the Air Force Research Institute, A. F. Proshakov, flew the second model. He could not bring the I-180 out of an inverted spin and at the very last moment was forced to use a parachute.

The fearless experimental pilot Tomas Suzi flew the third model and also went into a spin. Seeing that the matter was leading to disaster, he jumped out of the aircraft near the ground, but his parachute did not open.

The I-180 was rejected and its mass production halted.[67]

Without diminishing the achievements of the great test pilots Suprun, Proshakov, and Suzi, I am convinced that Chkalov would have been able to bring the I-180 into final shape if he had not fallen into a snare, which turned out not to be his fault.

After Chkalov's successful flights, the VIT-1 craft was put into mass production. Hero of the Soviet Union Pavel Golovin was assigned to complete the testing of this machine: Golovin soon afterwards perished in this plane. The Air Force canceled its order and the work in Polikarpov's design bureau on the VIT-1 was stopped.

A more advanced plane, the VIT-2, with large-caliber armaments, had also been flown by Valery Pavlovich. But several concluding flights still had to be flown. First, a factory test pilot died in the experimental model, then a flier in the Research Institute of the Air Force suffered an accident in the second model. After this, work on the VIT-2 by Polikarpov was also terminated.

The same fate was shared by the experimental scout plane the Ivanov. It was Chkalov who had given life to this plane and made the first successful flights in it. The person continuing Valery Pavlovich's work suffered a catastrophe. Aviation industry also terminated this work of Polikarpov's.

The well-known aircraft designer A. S. Yakovlev and test pilot P. M. Stefanovsky discussed the fate of these planes in their books.

Knowing the conditions of the VIT-1 and the VIT-2 and the Ivanov, including their test pilots, I again maintain that Chkalov could have brought these designs of Polikarpov's into complete working order.

But the chief designer was persistent and stubborn in attempting to provide the Soviet Army with better armaments. Despite all the misfortunes and accidents, he reworked his design and produced in a short period of time a remarkable fighter under the title I-185. The work was carried out at a hectic pace and, as a result, in 1940, the factory produced five models of the experimental plane. The first flight was flown by test pilot Evgeniy Uliakhin and he landed almost in darkness. Again he was rushing, hurrying when it was important to be composed and careful. However, the M-71 engine, which the I-185 was designed for, did not exist and still had not been produced. At this time, World War II first rumbled and then exploded. The war consumed Uliakhin. He died on the front in aerial combat.

In November 1942, the long-awaited M-71 engine was placed in the I-185. Stefanovsky, who had been in many dangerous accidents, continued the work of Uliakhin. He attained a speed of 708 kilometers per hour, a speed that no fighter in Hitler's army at that time was able to match! But the M-71 engine flew into pieces and Stefanovsky made a forced landing at the field. The engine was changed and on December 26, 1942, Stefanovsky again reached a speed of 708 kilometers per hour! But again, the engine broke down and Peter Mikhailovich made a forced landing at a neighboring field. However, during this landing, while trying to keep from hitting another plane parked on the ground, he was forced to level out the I-185 at a high altitude, as a result of which the plane, upon landing, hit with such force that the wings broke up and flew over the head of the surprised pilot. The pilot was barely able to get out of the cockpit and, although he gave the plane a high evaluation, he was deeply disappointed by the complete unreliability of the M-71 motor.

While the next I-185 was being prepared with a newer engine, Stefanovsky was assigned to test another type of aircraft made by a different designer. He burned up the new plane in the air and once again ended up on the operating table of a hospital.

Polikarpov came to the test pilot. Stefanovsky advised him to ask the Air Force to let the Research Institute pilot V. A. Stepanchenok continue the testing of the I-185.

The remarkable fighter test pilot and gifted designer Vasilli Andreevich understood very well how necessary the I-185 was to our Air Force. Stepanchenok liked Polikarpov's craft very much, but in March 1943, in one of his flights, the fate of Valery Pavlovich also befell this test pilot—the merciless M-71 failed while approaching

Central Field. He was no more than one hundred meters short of the landing strip when the aircraft crashed into the hangar of an aviation factory.

Polikarpov lived amost six years after the death of Chkalov and during all these years the chief designer was besieged by failures, which in the end destroyed the diligent, stubborn, and very talented individual. He became ill. When Nikolai Nikolaevich was ailing, the government ordered that all the specialists connected with the I-185 be transferred to the design bureau of Semen Alekseevich Lavochkin. This helped Lavochkin create the well-known La-5 fighter, in which the thrice-named Hero of the Soviet Union, I. N. Kozhedub, attacked the fascists during World War II. This fighter was a threat to Hitler's air force and helped to bring about the victory against the pernicious fascists.

Polikarpov himself died on August 19, 1944.

But the contributions of Polikarpov and Chkalov, as well as of the test pilots who died after them, were enormous in defending our nation, regardless of the many tragic mistakes and failures. Therefore, their service is preserved in the memory of the Soviet people and the history of the world's first socialist government.

Notes

1. Vasilevo (renamed Chkalovsk) is located near Gorky, a major city on the Volga River. This ancient urban center, known also as Nizhny Novgorod, has occupied an important place in Russian history.

2. Region.

3. All dates are new style, following the Western or Gregorian calendar. Prior to February 1, 1918, Russia followed the old or Julian calendar, which in the twentieth century was thirteen days behind the Western calendar.

4. The season of the Christian calendar that falls on the eve of Lent, the preparatory time of forty days before Easter. It is a time for parties, visits to familiy and friends, and general celebration before the rigors of fasting during Lent.

5. The term *Old Believer* refers to Russian Orthodox Christians, who refused to accept the church reforms under Patriarch Nikon in the seventeenth century.

6. Bogatyry refers to individuals of great strength and courage, who were associated with the warriors or knights of Russian folk legend.

7. This is a reference to the Russian Civil War (1918–1921), which included many battles along and near the Volga River.

8. Chkalov soloed in an Avro trainer. The Soviets had obtained a number of Avro 504 series trainers, and these durable two-seat planes were used extensively in the early 1920s.

9. During World War I the Russians employed several types of Farman aircraft built under license. During the Soviet period many of these now-obsolete aircraft found extended service as trainers.

10. Refers to a rectangular flight path around the airfield, typically flown at 1,200–1,500 feet.

11. By 1923, the Soviets had obtained a number of advanced aircraft from the West, mostly from Weimar Germany. This exchange of technology was a consequence of the Rapallo Treaty of 1922. The Germans and Soviets agreed to a clandestine arrangement whereby the Germans built and tested aircraft on Soviet soil, allowing the Germans to circumvent the restrictions of the Versailles Treaty and the Soviets to acquire modern aircraft. This covert arrangement endured to 1933, when Adolf Hitler assumed power in Germany.

12. Pilots performed several aerobatic maneuvers: a barrel roll, the technique of revolving the aircraft around a linear axis; an Immelmann, a maneuver in which the aircraft makes a sharp climb until the moment its wheels are up, and then, with the

application of the rudder (controlling yaw), revolves around a linear axis, moving into a horizontal position in the opposite direction; and a spin, the movement of an aircraft with the nose pointed steeply downward, revolving rapidly around a vertical axis. Valery Chakalov executed these maneuvers with considerable boldness and skill.

13. Alexander V. Kolchak (1874–1920), a former admiral in the Imperial Russian Navy and Arctic explorer, led an unsuccessful campaign against the Bolsheviks in Western Siberia during the Russian Civil War. He was ultimately captured and executed by the Bolsheviks.

14. Mikhail M. Gromov (1899–1985) was a famous, record-breaking Soviet pilot, who completed a transpolar flight in July 1937, one month after Chkalov's historic flight. Later Gromov was an Army air commander during World War II and a postwar leader in the Soviet Air Force.

15. Peter Nesterov (1887–1914) was a pioneer Russian aviator who executed the world's first successful loop in 1913. Nesterov was killed in the first month of World War I (August 1914), when he rammed an Austro-Hungarian airplane over the Eastern Front.

16. The Fokker D-7 was an effective fighter used by the Germans in World War I.

17. The Gatchina Aerodrome, located outside St. Petersburg (Leningrad), became the center for pilot training in the old Imperial Russian Air Force. See Alexander Riaboff, *Gatchina Days: Reminiscences of a Russian Pilot*, Washington, D.C.: Smithsonian Institution Press, 1985, edited with an introduction by Von Hardesty.

18. This battleship, named after the French revolutionary Marat, was sunk by the German Air Force in the opening hours of World War II.

19. Kliment Ye. Voroshilov (1881–1969), a former metal worker and organizer of the Red Army, became a close associate and favorite of Stalin. Between 1925 and 1934 Voroshilov served as Peoples' Commissar of Military and Naval Affairs, an assignment that led to his subsequent appointment as Commissar of Defense (1934–1940). During and after World War II Voroshilov held various high military and political posts, including Deputy Prime Minister. Named a Marshall of the Soviet Union in 1935, he played a key role in the promotion of aviation.

20. Yakov I. Alksnis (1897–1938) commanded the Red Army Air Force during the years 1931–1937. Stalin purged the popular Latvian-born air commander in 1938, along with many other high-ranking military officers. Peter I. Baranov (1892-1933), another prominent aviator, joined the Bolsheviks as early as 1912 and served in the Civil War. Baranov died in an air crash in 1933.

21. Mikhail I. Kalinin (1875–1946) played a prominent political role during the Stalin period. A peasant turned factory worker, Kalinin participated in the revolutions of 1905 and 1917. Kalinin held a number of ceremonial positions, including Chairman of the All-Russian Central Executive Committee of the Soviets. In 1937 he became Chairman of the Presidium of the Supreme Soviet of the USSR. His patronage of Chkalov is noted by Baidukov as a pivotal factor in shaping Chkalov's career.

22. The Junkers J-13 was a German-made, all-metal transport aircraft of the interwar years.

23. Dmitry P. Grigorovich (1883–1938) was an early Russian designer of flying boats. His M-5 and M-9 types were used extensively in World War I and during the Russian Civil War. Following the Bolshevik Revolution he worked with Nikolai N. Polikarpov (1892–1944) on the design of the first generation of Soviet fighters, the I-2 and I-5 models. Polikarpov played a major role in Soviet fighter development in the 1930s. His designs of the I-15, I-16, and I-153 types were noteworthy and, for a time, represented the state of the art. It would be in Polikarpov's experimental I-180 that Chkalov would die in 1938. The prewar classification *I* derives from *Istrebitel'*, which designates a fighter or pursuit-type combat airplane.

24. Nicholas Ye. Zhukovsky (1847–1921), the "Father of Soviet Aviation," founded the Central Aero-Hydrodynamic Institute—Tsentralnyy Aerogidrodinamicheskii Institut (TsAGI)—in 1918. Zhukovsky was a world-renowned theorist of aerodynamics who accepted the Bolshevik Revolution and enjoyed the patronage of Lenin and the Soviet government. Andrei N. Tupolev (1888–1972) designed over one hundred different types of Soviet aircraft, including the ANT-25 that Chkalov flew to the United States in 1937. Arrested during the era of the Great Purges, Tupolev spent much of World War II as a prisoner, designing aircraft from his design bureau in prison, under the supervision of the secret police. This unusual form of prison internment was imaginatively reconstructed by Alexander Solzhenitsyn in his novel *The First Circle.*

25. The two-engine TB-1 (ANT-4) entered series production in 1929. During the 1930s the TB-1, and its four-engine variant the TB-3, gave expression to the Soviet Union's brief flirtation with strategic bombers. Both aircraft were slow and cumbersome, but nevertheless represented important technical breakthroughs for Soviet aviation in the field of large multiengine aircraft. The classification *TB*, or *Tyazhelyy bombardirovshchik*, designates a heavy bomber. The Soviets also developed commercial designs such as the five-engine ANT-14, which could accommodate thirty-six passengers.

26. Lieutenant Peter P. Shmidt (1867–1906) was a revolutionary leader and martyr during the 1905 Revolution. Shmidt was executed in 1906 for his revolutionary activities.

27. The R-3 (ANT-3) was a two-seater Soviet reconnaissance aircraft that underwent several modifications, largely with powerplant changes. The R-5, developed by the Soviets between 1928 and 1933, became the standard prewar reconnaissance aircraft for the Red Army Air Force.

28. Today a complex of apartment houses in Moscow.

29. Sergei A. Chaplygin (1869–1942) was a famed Russian aerodynamicist and one-time director of TsAGI, the Soviet aeronautical research center.

30. Soviet experiments with so-called "parasite" fighters were pioneered by Vakhmistrov.The use of parasite aircraft, always a difficult and dangerous maneuver, aimed to expand the range of military aircraft and to provide bomber escort. The dramatic character of these high-risk maneuvers also served obvious propaganda purposes at Soviet air shows in the 1930s. Two I-4 fighters were used with the TB-1. Later three I-5 fighters were flown with the larger, four-engine TB-3.

31. The MiG-3 (Mikoyan i Gurevich Design Bureau), designed as a high-altitude fighter, proved ineffectual in World War II.

32. Alexander I. Pokryshkin (1913–1985) and Ivan N. Kozhedub (1920–) emerged from World War II as the top-ranking Soviet aces, with fifty-nine and sixty-two air victories respectively. Baidukov gives Chkalov credit for anticipating the air tactics developed largely by Pokryshkin and others during World War II.

33. The Five Year Plans, beginning in 1928, gave priority to building a highly centralized economy and heavy industry. Stalin demonstated a keen interest in aviation, seeing in the airplane a useful tool to dramatize technical progress and to provide for national defense.

34. Igor I. Sikorsky (1889–1972) became an influential aircraft designer in pre-revolutionary Russia. His "S" series of aircraft included a sequence of monoplane and biplane designs. The S-16 was an advanced fighter produced at the Russo-Baltic Factory in St. Petersburg (Leningrad) during World War I. Sikorsky's *Il'ya muromets*, based on his pioneering 1913 four-engine *Grand*, made a historic round-trip flight from St. Petersburg to Kiev in 1914, just on the eve of World War I. During the war the "Murometsy," as these four-engine behemoths were called, played an active role as reconnaissance/bomber aircraft, operating as a special squadron on the Eastern Front

from 1914 to 1917. See K. N. Finne, *Igor Sikorsky, The Russian Years*, edited by Carl Bobrow and Von Hardesty, Washington, D.C.: Smithsonian Institution Press, 1987.

35. Soviet historiography has displayed a set of contradictory impulses toward Sikorsky, on the one hand admiring his achievements but on the other hand finding his rejection of communism a source of embarrassment. For many years under Stalin, the name of Igor Sikorsky disappeared from official histories and aviation reference books. Baidukov's essentially negative comment here was no doubt obligatory and reflects the still hostile official posture toward Sikorsky in the 1970s. In 1988, the Soviets published a highly favorable biography of Sikorsky, on the occasion of the centennial of his birth; see G. I. Katyshev and Vadim R. Mikhayev, *Aviakonstruktor Igor Ivanovich Sikorsky*, Moscow: Nauka, 1989. This publication marked the enthusiastic rehabilitation of Sikorsky under Mikhail Gorbachev.

36. Another popular mass organization supporting aviation during the interwar years was OSOAVIAKIM (Obshchestvo sodeistviya oborone, aviatsionnomu i khimicheskomu stroitel'stvu). Such volunteer organizations stressed mass mobilization and technical education.

37. The Soviets faced enormous problems in the development of their own aircraft engines. For many years they purchased foreign engines or built them under license. The M-22 was a Soviet copy of the Bristol engine, manufactured in Great Britain. It was named after A. A. Mikulin, a noted Soviet engineer. Other Western engines were built under license in the 1930s, including the M-25 and M-62, which were based on Wright engines developed in the United States.

38. The I-16 saw considerable service during the Spanish Civil War (1936–1939), and for a brief time the I-16 gave the Spanish Republican air force command of the air. However, the introduction of the German Messerschmitt Bf-109E quickly altered the situation in favor of the Nationalists under Francisco Franco.

39. The ANT-20 *Maxim Gorky*, named after the famed Russian novelist, made a powerful impression on the international aviation community in the 1930s. It mirrored the Soviet emphasis on large aircraft with its eight engines, outsized dimensions, and impressive load capacity. It was used extensively for air shows and propaganda campaigns until its destruction in a midair crash in 1935.

40. In the 1930s a new generation of Soviet aircraft designers emerged. They would play an important role in World War II. Chief among them were Alexander S. Yakovlev (1906–1989), Sergei V. Ilyushin (1894–1977), Artem I. Mikoyan (1905–1970), M. I. Gurevich (1893–1976), and S. A. Lavochkin (1900–1960).

41. The kilometric or measuring base consists of a straight line at the end of which are located instruments that determine the precise moment the aircraft passes.

42. Vilhjalmur Stefansson was a prominent explorer who welcomed Chkalov and his crew to New York City. Later Stefansson urged the U.S. Army Air Corps to deploy its aircraft in the vain quest to find Levanevsky.

43. Walter Duranty served as the *New York Times* correspondent in Moscow for over a decade. His highly favorable accounts of Soviet life and politics, concealing the famine in the Ukraine and other events, prompted criticism, then and now, concerning the accuracy of his reports on Soviet affairs. Duranty's *USSR, The Story of Soviet Russia*, New York: J. B. Lippincott , 1944, mirrored the wartime optimism in America regarding the Soviet Union.

44. Vladimir K. Kokkinaki (1904–1985) was a well-known Soviet flier in the interwar years. He established a series of speed records in the 1930s, but his ill-fated attempt to fly from Moscow to New York in 1939 brought an end to the Soviet campaign for long-distance records in the 1930s.

45. Vasily K. Blyukher (1890–1938), a Marshal of the Soviet Union, was the Soviet military commander in the Far East. He was executed during the purge of the Red Army in 1938.

46. The ANT-35 was a low-wing all-metal two-engine aircraft designed by A. A. Arkhangelsky (1892–1978).

47. Robert L. Bartini (1897–1974) joined the Communist Party in Italy in 1921. He moved to the Soviet Union in 1923, where he designed over ten experimental aircraft.

48. The Soviet miner Aleksei Stakhanov, in an extraordinary display of zeal, mined 102 tons of coal in a single shift (the quota was seven tons!). His achievement became a convenient vehicle for Soviet propaganda to mobilize workers to increase their work quotas and gave birth to a Stakhanovite movement.

49. The VIT-2 was a sleek two-engine aircraft, the first high-speed dive bomber developed in the Soviet Union. It was not put into serial production.

50. Mikhail Vasil'yevich Vodopyanov (1899–1980) was one of the first Soviet pilots to receive the gold star, "Hero of the Soviet Union," for his participation in the rescue of the crew of the ice-bound *Chelyushkin* in 1934. Vodopyanov was also the first flier to land at the North Pole.

51. Theodore Dreiser, the American novelist, made a trip in the 1920s to the Soviet Union at the invitation of the Soviet government. Following this visit he published *Dreiser Looks at Russia*, London: Constable and Company, 1928. Dreiser's novels (e.g., *An American Tragedy, Sister Carrie*) were popular in the Soviet Union.

52. Ivan D. Papanin (1894–1986) led a team to establish a Soviet scientific station on an ice floe in the Arctic in 1937. He received extensive press coverage in the West. Papanin served in the Soviet navy in World War I and, following the war, headed the Institute of Oceanography of the USSR Academy of Sciences.

53. Alexander Belyakov served with the Bolshevik 25th Chapaev Division during the Russian Civil War. The veterans of this division were called "chapaevites."

54. Belyakov used an astrocompass.

55. AMTORG was a special agency created by the Soviet government to promote trade with the West.

56. Vancouver, a small city north of Portland on the Columbia River, is the site of the historic Vancouver Barracks. At the time of Chkalov's landing, Brigadier General George Marshall was the post commander. Marshall went on to serve in a number of major military and civilian positions in the 1940s, including Secretary of State under President Harry Truman.

57. "Miss Marshall" refers to Molly Brown Winn, the stepdaughter of George Marshall and the daughter of Katharine Tupper Marshall.

58. General Oscar Westover was the Chief of the U.S. Army Air Corps at the time of Chkalov's transpolar flight.

59. Jimmie Mattern was a prominent American flier who, in 1933, crashed in Siberia near the Chukotsky peninsula on a long-distance flight. He was rescued by the Soviet flier S. A. Levanevsky, who perished in an unsuccessful attempt to fly to America over the North Pole in August 1937.

60. Levanevsky and his crew were never found, although a spirited effort was made to locate the aircraft in August 1937. See Von Hardesty, "Soviets Blaze Sky Trail over Top of the World," *Air & Space/Smithsonian*, Vol. 2, No. 5 (December 1987/January 1988), pp. 48–54.

61. Grigory K. (Sergo) Ordzhonikidze (1886–1937) played a prominent role in Soviet political life in the interwar years. During the First Five Year Plan he served as People's Commissar for Heavy Industry.

62. Valentina S. Grizodubova (1910–   ) and Polina D. Osipenko (1907–1939) were Soviet women pilots. In 1938, together with Marina M. Raskova, they completed a nonstop flight from Moscow to the Far East, establishing a new long-distance record for women.

63. Cosmonaut Yuri Gagarin followed this same script two decades later. He stated that when he peered out into space he did not see God. Such ritualistic expressions of atheism by fliers and cosmonauts mirrored official Soviet propaganda, which aggressively exploited Soviet technical achievements as a repudiation of religion.

64. Kuzma Minin (d. 1616) was a Russian patriot who resisted the Polish intervention during Russia's "Time of Troubles." He remained a national hero during the Soviet period, at a time when Stalin warned of "capitalist encirclement" and the threat of foreign invasion.

65. The author wrote again about Chkalov's death in December 1988 ("Esli govorit' vsyu pravdu," *Vozdushnyy transport*, December 10–17). This four-part article, written in the more liberal atmosphere under Mikhail Gorbachev, openly blamed the design bureau, in particular Polikarpov, for the tragedy.

66. Josef Pilsudsky was the anti-Soviet political leader of Poland during the interwar years. Pilsudsky earned national recognition for his military leadership in the Polish struggle against the Bolsheviks in 1920.

67. Work on the I-180 began in 1937 under the leadership of Polikarpov. The I-180 was a single-seat monoplane equipped with an 850-horsepower Mikulin M-87A engine. Chkalov was killed in the first prototype on December 15, 1938. The second prototype, the I-180-2, met a similar fate in February 1939, when test pilot T. P. Suzi inexplicably flew it into the ground from a high altitude. Subsequent variants were plagued by mechanical failures and the project was abandoned.

Bibliography

Baidukov, G. F., *Cherez polyus v Ameriku* [Over the pole to America], Moscow-Leningrad, 1938.

———, "Moskva-Severnyy polyus-SShA, God 1937" [Moscow-North Pole-USA in 1937], *Novaya i noveishaya istoriya*, 1987, No. 2, pp. 96–124.

———, "Nash polet v Ameriku cherez Severnyy polyus," *Nauka v SSSR*, 1987, No. 3, pp. 116–127.

———, *O Chkalove* [About Chkalov], Moscow: Molodaya gvardiya, 1975.

———, "Pervyy bespodsadochnyy perelet SSSR-SShA" [First non-stop flight from the Soviet Union to the United States], *Economika, politika, ideologiya*, 1973, No. 12, pp. 71–82; 1974, No. 1, pp. 74–91.

———, *Pervyye perelety cherez ledovityy okean. Iz vospominanii letchika* [First flight across the icebound ocean. Recollections of a flier], Moscow, 1983.

Baranov, N., and Bobrov, N., *Nashi letchiki i nashi samolety* [Our fliers and our airplanes], Moscow: Gosvoyenizdat, 1931.

Belopol'skiy, N. P., *Cherez polyus v Ameriku* [Over the North Pole to America], Leningrad, 1939.

Belyakov, A. V., *Dva pereleta* [Two flights], Moscow, 1939.

———, *Valery Chkalov*, Moscow: DOSAAF, 1977.

Bobrov, Nikolai, *Chkalov*, translated by Cynthia Rosenberger, Moscow: Raduza, 1987.

Boyd, Alexander, *The Soviet Air Force Since 1918*, London: Macdonald and Jane's, 1977.

Chkalova, O. Ye., *Valery Pavlovich Chkalov*, Moscow: Sovetskaya Rossiya, 1982.

Chkalova, O. Ye., Editor, *Valery Chkalov: Fotoal'bom* [Valery Chkalov: Photograph album], Moscow: Planeta, 1980.

Dubravin, A. K., *Samolety v arkticheskikh usloviyakh* [Aircraft into the Arctic], Moscow-Leningrad, 1936.

329

Glines, C. G., *Polar Aviation*, New York: Franklin Watts, 1964.

Gromov, M. M., *Cherez vsyu zhizn'* [Through life], Moscow: Molodaya gvardiya, 1986.

Hardesty, Von, *Red Phoenix: The Rise of Soviet Air Power, 1941–1945*, Washington, D.C.: Smithsonian Institution Press, 1982.

———, "Soviets Blaze Sky Trail over Top of the World," *Air & Space/Smithsonian*, Vol. 2, No. 5 (December 1987/January 1988), pp. 48–56.

Jackson, Robert, *Red Falcons: The Soviet Air Force in Action, 1919–1969*, New York: International Publications Service, 1970.

Karpov, I., *Aviatsiya strany sotsializma* [Aviation of the land of socialism], Leningrad, 1939.

Kilmarx, Robert A., *A History of Soviet Air Power*, New York: Frederick Praeger, 1962.

Kuzovkin, A., and Makarov, A., *Pod nami polyus* [The North Pole beneath us], Moscow: Politizdat, 1977.

Lee, Asher, *The Soviet Air Force*, New York: John Day, 1962.

Lee, Asher, Editor, *The Soviet Air and Rocket Forces*, New York: Frederick Praeger, 1959.

Lukin, V. P., *Krylatoye imya—Chkalov* [A winged name—Chkalov], Gorky, 1987.

Ordin, A., *Velikiy letchik nashego vremeni Valeriy Pavlovich Chkalov* [Valery Chkalov, a great flier of our age], Moscow, 1949.

Sal'nikov, Yuri P., *Zhizn', Otdannaya Artike: O geroye Sov. Soyuza S. A. Levanevskom* [Hero of the Soviet Union S. A. Levanevsky: A life dedicated to the Arctic], Moscow: Politizdat, 1984.

Shavrov, V.B., *Istoriya konstruktsii samoletov v SSSR do 1938 g.* [The history of Soviet aircraft designs up to 1938], Third edition, Moscow, 1985.

Vodopyanov, M. V., *Letchik Chkalov* [The flier Chkalov], Moscow: DOSAAF, 1963.

———, *Outstanding Flights of Soviet Airmen*, Moscow: Foreign Language Publishing House, 1939.